THE POLITICS OF CULTURAL RETREAT

The Politics of Cultural Retreat

Imperial Bureaucracy in Austrian Galicia, 1772–1867

IRYNA VUSHKO

Yale
UNIVERSITY PRESS
NEW HAVEN AND LONDON

Published with assistance from the Kingsley Trust Association Publication Fund established by the Scroll and Key Society of Yale College.

Copyright © 2015 by Yale University.
All rights reserved.
This book may not be reproduced, in whole or in part, including illustrations, in any form (beyond that copying permitted by Sections 107 and 108 of the U.S. Copyright Law and except by reviewers for the public press), without written permission from the publishers.

Yale University Press books may be purchased in quantity for educational, business, or promotional use. For information, please e-mail sales.press@yale.edu (U.S. office) or sales@yaleup.co.uk (U.K. office).

Set in Electra type by IDS Infotech Ltd. Chandigarh, India.
Printed in the United States of America.

Library of Congress Cataloging-in-Publication Data

Vushko, Iryna.
The politics of cultural retreat : imperial bureaucracy in Austrian Galicia, 1772-1867 / Iryna Vushko.
  pages cm
Includes bibliographical references and index.
ISBN 978-0-300-20727-9 (cloth : alk. paper) 1. Galicia (Poland and Ukraine)—Politics and government—19th century. 2. Galicia (Poland and Ukraine)—Politics and government—18th century. 3. Bureaucracy—Galicia (Poland and Ukraine)—History. 4. Austria—Politics and government—1740-1848. 5. Austria—Politics and government—1848–1918. I. Title.
DK4600.G347V87 2015
947.7'907—dc23
2014041591

Catalogue records for this book are available from the Library of Congress and the British Library.

This paper meets the requirements of ANSI/NISO Z39.48–1992 (Permanence of Paper).

10 9 8 7 6 5 4 3 2 1

To those who lost fear

CONTENTS

Acknowledgments ix
List of Abbreviations xii

Introduction 1

ONE
Bureaucratic Enlightenment and Galicia 18

TWO
Civilizers at Work, 1772–1794 46

THREE
The Napoleonic Test, 1792–1815 83

FOUR
Between Vienna, St. Petersburg, and Warsaw, 1826–1832 105

FIVE
Austrian Bureaucracy and Polish Aristocracy 127

SIX
Literature, Politics, and Galician Ruthenians 157

CONTENTS

SEVEN
Administering the Jews 182

EIGHT
Bureaucracy and Revolutions, 1846–1848 206

Conclusion: 1848, 1867, and Beyond 231

Notes 253
Index 301

ACKNOWLEDGMENTS

This book would have been impossible without the long-standing support of Timothy Snyder. He influenced my thinking about history more than anyone else, believed in my project, and read numerous drafts with great diligences: for all of this I am very grateful. Ostap Sereda introduced me to history some twenty years ago and has remained a friend ever since. I became a historian because of him. Paul Bushkovitch provided invaluable feedback on my dissertation and helped keep things in perspective at Yale. Larry Wolff shared my interests in Galicia, agreed to serve as an outside reader, and read my text with great care. Serhii Plokhii read and commented on the manuscript and helped with logistical advice while I was preparing it for publication. Ute Frevert brought in her expertise in German history. Yaroslav Hrytsak taught me history in L'viv and Budapest, helping me to make the transition from Ukrainian to American academia over ten years ago. Ingo Trauschweitzer, in Florence and later Ohio, read and commented on the entire manuscript.

Börris Kuzmany in Vienna, at the time working on his dissertation on Galicia, kept company and shared some of his sources with me. I spent many days in the archives with Ke-Chin Hsia and even more evenings in the Viennese opera. Giving in to his addiction, I learnt to appreciate opera through his eyes and his ears. Isabelle Chauche arranged my research trip to Paris in the summer of 2007. Louic Blanc opened his doors for me there, making that trip special. In 2010, back in Vienna, Anne Dwyer helped keep my spirits up and maintain my confidence in academia. Joachim Tepperberg

ACKNOWLEDGMENTS

helped navigate the somewhat complicated archival collections in Vienna, digging up documents that had no catalogue records. Helga Wasicki, also in Vienna, shared with me with some of the key documents upon which this book is based. Joshua Dermann and Susan Karr read and commented on my work under the Tuscan sun, during our year spent in Florence. Over the years, Petro Bilyan, Roman Dubasevych, Ihor Kosyk, and Bohdan Kundys hosted me in various places in Austria, France, and Ukraine.

This book became possible due to the financial support that I received over the years from numerous institutions. At Yale, I was funded by the Center for European Studies, the John Enders Grant, and the International Security Studies Program. The Central European Conference Group provided funds for archival research in the summer of 2009. Between 2008 and 2009, my research was supported by the Max Weber Program at the European University Institute in Florence, Italy. I rewrote the manuscript almost entirely during my fellowship at the Harvard Ukrainian Institute between 2009 and 2010. The Ukrainian Studies Fund and the Hunter College Presidential Award covered part of the expenses of editing a preliminary draft of the manuscript. A preliminary version of Chapter 4 was published as an article in *Central Europe* 9, no. 2 (November 2011), available online at www.maneyonline.com/ceu. Parts of Chapter 2 appeared in *East European Politics and Societies* 25, no. 4 (November 2011), available online at http://online.sagepub.com. I am grateful to Maney Publishing and Sage Publications for permission to republish this material here.

Avram Brown read the very last draft of my manuscript with painstaking attention, performing magic on the style and presentation. Christian Werkmeister generously agreed to go over my German footnotes. Christina Tucker from Yale University Press took this project under her wing and guided the manuscript though the initial stages of editing and production. Gavin Lewis did a superb job of editing the monograph. For all of their support and help I am very grateful.

What I offer here is a distant history of the place that I still call home. All of my grandparents were born as subjects of the Habsburg Monarchy in the Austrian province of Galicia. None of them—as far as I know—received any

ACKNOWLEDGMENTS

education. My maternal grandmother—the only one of the four who was alive by the time I was born—spoke Ukrainian with a strange admixture of Polish, which I as a child attributed to her peasant background and lack of education. The Polish tinge, as it turned out, was the result of her growing up in a mixed Polish-Ukrainian village. There were no Poles by the time I came to visit as a child.

Both of my parents were born in interwar Poland. In September 1939, my father's family, residing near Przemyśl in southeastern Poland, fell under German occupation. He was one year old, the youngest of three children. The same month, my mother's family, residing in the vicinity of L'viv, was "liberated" by the Soviet army that marched on Poland from the east. She was just over a month old. By 1945, the two families lived in two different countries—the Soviet Union and Poland. In July 1947, my paternal grandparents were forced to move east as part of the resettlement operation between the Soviet Union and Poland, and more specifically, the Polish Communist government's effort to uproot Ukrainian nationalist opposition. My parents went to the same school in Soviet Ukraine, just across the border from Poland. They met again, years later, as students attending the May 1 demonstration in L'viv—not necessarily of their own accord—and have spent the following forty-six years together. Had it not been for Stalin, the war, the resettlement, involuntary attendance at various Soviet celebrations, and pure accident, my parents would have never met—a fact of life that helps me keep things in perspective.

I grew up in a family where education was valued above all—another fact that made it possible for me to get the best postgraduate education in the world after finishing a mediocre Soviet—and later post-Soviet—school. My parents gave me a very happy Soviet childhood and have supported me unconditionally through my capitalist adulthood. I will never be able to repay them enough.

As I am completing final revisions of my text in the summer of 2014, a full-fledged war is going on in Ukraine. The recent events and all the people who participated in them—fighting for the right cause—taught me more about the meaning of history and human courage than all the books combined that I had read up to the present. This book is dedicated to all those who lost fear.

ABBREVIATIONS

Abt.	Abteilung
AMAE	Archive du Ministère des affaires étrangères, Paris
AS	Acta Secreta (in HHStA)
AVA	Allgemeines Verwaltungsarchiv (in ÖStA)
BCK	Biblioteka Czartoryskich, Krakow
BPP	Biblioteka Polska, Paris
CP	Correspondance Politique (in AMAE)
f.	Fond ("collection"): TsDIAUL archive designation
FA	Familienarchiv (in HHStA)
HHStA	Haus- Hof- und Staatsarchiv, Vienna
HK	Hofkanzlei (in AVA)
HR	Hofreißen (in HHStA)
IB	Informationsbüro (in HHStA)
KA	Kabinettsarchiv (in HHStA)
KFA	Kaiser Franz Akten (in HHStA)
MKA	Minister Kollowrat Akten (in HHStA)
ÖStA	Österreichisches Staatsarchiv, Vienna
op.	opys ("inventory") (in TsDIAUL cites): division of archive holdings below *fond*
PÖM	*Die Protokolle des Österreichischen Ministerrates 1848–1867*
spr.	*Sprava* (file) (in TsDIAUL cites)
StK	Staatskanzlei (in ÖStA)
TsDIAUL	Tsentralnyi Derzhavnyi Arkhiv Ukrainy, L'viv

INTRODUCTION

This book offers a history of state-building, nationalism, and bureaucracy in the Habsburg Monarchy, focusing on the province of Galicia and how it was administered between 1772 and 1867. It traces the creation of the professional bureaucracy in the eighteenth century and the changes this institution underwent in the decades that followed. It describes how bureaucrats endorsed or rejected the ideas of the Enlightenment, and how they both slowed and stimulated the rise of nationalism. By analyzing the mechanisms of administration, I explain the bureaucracy's dual role in both maintaining the integrity of the monarchy and, on the other hand, contributing to its demise in 1918.

This is an untypical history of bureaucracy in that it focuses on people rather than institutions. I explore the political and personal choices of the many men (and some women) who found themselves on opposite sides of the administrative process: on the one hand, state functionaries in various offices, who participated in decision making and decision execution; on the other, those on the receiving end of such decisions, subject to regulations over which they had little control. I address the bureaucracy as at once an instrument and an object of reforms, stressing the contingency of divergent processes, namely, the making of the bureaucracy and its role in the creation of a new society.

As for the wider context of the Habsburg polity, this book explains how constant interaction between administrators and those they administered influenced the bureaucracy, and how this reformed bureaucracy affected the empire and its society. It will be shown that conflicts within the bureaucracy were sometimes more severe than tensions between the administrators and the administered, that local bureaucrats all too often defied the expectations of their higher-ups in Vienna, questioning the logic of central legislation and reforms.

Galicia exemplified Austria's difficult passage to modernity. Annexed from Poland-Lithuania in 1772, it remained part of the Habsburg Monarchy till the end of the First World War. Between 1793 and 1918, Galicia formed an important frontier in Europe, separating the Germanophone Habsburg Monarchy from the Russian Empire. Despite no longer appearing on maps of Europe, Galicia remains alive in the political imagination of people on either side of the Polish-Ukrainian border, still serving as a common term to describe the lands of western Ukraine around modern L'viv and eastern Poland around Kraków. In the twenty-first century, it once again separates West (as incarnate in the European Union) from East.

Habsburg Galicia was a quintessential imperial borderland. The partitions of Poland for the first time in history created a direct border between the Russian and the Habsburg monarchies. After 1772, Vienna and St. Petersburg were dealing with some similar issues: masses of new subjects—Polish, Ruthenian, and Jewish; an untypical social structure of the newly annexed population, most notably, a remarkably high percentage of nobles. Similar intentions generated similar reforms, which were oftentimes carried out concurrently in the Russian and Austrian parts of the partitioned territories. The results were often contradictory, as neither of the two monarchies managed to carry their plans to completion. Each stumbled along the way, making numerous adjustments that sometimes defied the very intentions behind the reforms. All the difficulties notwithstanding, Austrian rulers proved to be more efficient in generating loyalties favorable to Vienna. Between 1772 and 1918, two Polish revolutions took place in the Russian Empire and none in its Austrian counterpart, an important achievement that should not be underestimated.

This book covers the period from the annexation of Galicia through 1867, the year of the Austro-Hungarian Compromise, after which Galicia received autonomy. I stress continuities between the eighteenth and nineteenth centuries that have been somewhat neglected in scholarship. Within my general focus on state-building, I explain how the German-speaking bureaucracy contributed to the emergence of modern nationalism in the empire, and how national politics affected imperial bureaucracy and administration before 1848 and thereafter.

The Habsburg province of Galicia was created by Austria's Enlightenment-minded rulers in the eighteenth century and shaped by Austrian bureaucrats arriving there from throughout the monarchy and beyond after 1772. These men traced their roots to Bohemia, Habsburg Italy and the Netherlands, the Kingdom of Hungary, and the Germanophone regions in and around what is now Austria, as well as several German states outside the Habsburg Monarchy. These bureaucrats used the German language in their offices, but often switched to Czech, French, Italian, Dutch, or combinations thereof in private. In their day-to-day activities, they interacted with people who spoke Polish, Ruthenian (Ukrainian), and Yiddish.

German-speaking Austrian bureaucrats were expected to impose supranational uniformity via Germanophone culture, administration, and education. In Galicia, they replaced officials from Poland-Lithuania and enforced a new administrative hierarchy hitherto unseen in this part of the world. They had come to erase ethnic differences and remnants of traditional estate-based society, and combat what Vienna viewed as backwardness. The new Galicia was to be the model province of a reformed monarchy.

The end result of these efforts was oftentimes the exact opposite of the initial expectation. Traditional institutions and their representatives were never fully erased; and Germanization was hardly as effective as originally thought. Over time, some Austrian bureaucrats, defying their senior colleagues in Vienna, increasingly identified with the region and society they had come to administer. While Austrian bureaucrats failed to impose German culture, Galician society to some extent infiltrated the imperial administration. Few Poles or Ruthenians turned German; but it was not too long before a number of Austrian bureaucrats chose to become Poles or Ruthenians.

The inability to impose ethnic uniformity was contingent upon other reforms or failures thereof. Galicia's failing economy became a symbol of unrealized expectations. At the time of the annexation, Austrian statesmen declared their intention to transform Galicia into a model province by reforming the backward region and imposing civilization from above. Civilization, in Austrian understanding, implied not only a different political culture but, ultimately, economic improvements. By 1918, however, Galicia remained a largely agricultural land: the living standards of the average Galician—a peasant or even one of the poorer nobles—was lower than in most regions of the monarchy. The traditional landowning elites retained their status and many of their privileges. Compounded by Austrian inability to properly provide for the masses of its bureaucrats, these economic failures created a certain co-dependence between administrators and those they administered, which few in Vienna envisioned at the time of the annexation. Galicia never became a model province of the empire, a symbol of progress—it remained a byword for backwardness.

In this vein, the concept of unintended consequences serves as the central organizing principle for my inquiry. This book shows how the ideas of supranational uniformity and human perfectibility, inspired by the Enlightenment, backfired in the long term, and how measures meant to achieve these ideals brought about results starkly contradicting their intentions.

The politics of the Enlightenment is one of the overarching themes of this book. With most other scholars, I share an understanding of the Enlightenment as a major turning point in European history; in this study, however, I shift focus from ideology to praxis, and address the Enlightenment as a specific mode of politics and a reform movement with practical consequences. In 1971, Franco Venturi explained the need "to rethink the European Enlightenment from the origins of the Enlightenment as a system to how the ideas of Enlightenment worked in practice."[1] In a 1994 study, Franz Szabo stresses the positive, reform-oriented tendencies of the Austrian Enlightenment;[2] and Derek Beales and R. J. W. Evans have argued that the Austrian and German Enlightenments should be viewed as having focused on practical reforms as opposed to their more ideology-driven French counterpart.[3]

In this book, I examine how ideas germinated in the Habsburg Monarchy of the eighteenth century, how bureaucrats tried to put these ideas into practice, and what became of these efforts in the long run. Through an analysis

INTRODUCTION

of the day-to-day actions of individual bureaucrats responsible for the implementation of reforms—such as the creation of schools, the enforcement of new language policies, and the nationalization and redistribution of Church property—I also explain how the bureaucrats endorsed or refuted the principles of the Enlightenment, and what the Enlightenment meant for them and for the society they hoped to create.

Galicia offers fruitful ground for the analysis of imperial policies and modern nationalism. The Austrians in a very real sense invented their new province, creating it out of a territory that had never had clear boundaries in the past, and reviving the name "Galicia" to justify the annexation. In the thirteenth century, the medieval Galician principality had briefly belonged to Hungary, but was later taken over by Poland. No administrative or political unit under the name of Galicia existed in Poland-Lithuania. In 1772, Vienna annexed parts of regions historically known as Rus', Czerwona (Ruthenia) and Małopolska. This territory eventually became known as Eastern Galicia, in contrast to Western Galicia, annexed by Vienna in 1793. Eastern Galicia included parts of several separate administrative units from the Polish-Lithuanian Commonwealth: part of the Kraków palatinate (without the city of Kraków) together with Principalities of Oświęcim and Zator as well as the palatinates of Sandomierz, Ruś, Bel'sk, Podollia and Volhynia.[4] Some 2.8 million individuals, including Poles, Ruthenians (present-day Ukrainians), Jews, and a small community of Armenians, became Habsburg subjects in 1772. The Ruthenians were a majority in Eastern Galicia, about 64 percent of its entire population. The annexation of Western Galicia in 1795 added more subjects to the monarchy, and more administrative complications. After 1795, the proportion of Poles and Ruthenians in united Galicia became virtually even, each group making up about 45 percent of the province's population, with Jews accounting for the remaining 10 percent.[5] In this book, I focus upon Eastern Galicia—the territory that Vienna annexed in the first partition of Poland in 1772, and which remained part of the monarchy until 1918.

Having divided East from West, or Europe from "the rest," Galicia also offers analytically fertile ground on which to trace the making of political borders in modern European history, exemplifying the general rule that European divisions are products of politics and economics rather than strictly of geography. Following Larry Wolff's influential study, *Inventing Eastern Europe*,⁶ I show that during the Enlightenment, Austrian rulers viewed their new province through the prism of East-Europeanism. I also explain how stereotypes and prejudices formed the basis for Austrian policies, and what consequences these produced.

One Enlightenment product that was more successful, surviving to this day, was the Austrian professional bureaucracy. Before 1740, the Habsburg Monarchy had been governed by local elites on a provincial basis; after, under the leadership of Empress Maria Theresa and her counselors, a new professional bureaucracy and a centralized administration began to take shape. New institutions were created in Vienna and the provinces, all linked in a sophisticated hierarchical scheme leading from periphery to center. Bureaucrats were recruited and selected centrally, and typically assigned to regions other than their places of origin. Officials in Vienna secured unprecedented control over the provinces as part of an effort to unite them all under a single central authority.

The annexation of Galicia opened a new era in the history of the Habsburg Monarchy and its administration. In their efforts to forge a new and perfect province out of a former part of Poland, Austria's Enlightenment-minded rulers hoped to build an exclusively Austrian administration by excluding locals and rejecting Polish tradition and precedent. Galicia became a land of experimentation, the only territory in the Habsburg Monarchy where Austrian rulers planned to build institutions and bureaucracy from scratch.

The year 1772 marked a never before seen encounter, as shocking for German-speaking officials as for the people they came to oversee. Many of these newly arrived bureaucrats had come farther east than they ever had before, to a place that Austrian Chancellor Klemens von Metternich would describe as a meeting point of Europe and the Orient.⁷ Provincial governors, for instance, would be of quite cosmopolitan (albeit decidedly Western) origin: Johann Anton Baptist von Pergen arrived from what is today Austria, Joseph Karl von Brigido from Italy, August von Lobkowitz from Bohemia, and Peter von Goëss originally from Portugal; Franz Stadion Count von Warthausen was a native of Vienna, though he came to Galicia from Italian Trieste; and Alexander von Mensdorff-Pouilly moved to the new province from Lorraine via Italy and Austria. All these men had different backgrounds and career expectations, and spoke different languages. All were bound by their loyalty to the Habsburg dynasty. Accepting their new assignments to Galicia, they relocated their families and households across hundreds of miles of roads that grew ever more ramshackle the nearer they came to their destination. Given the distances covered, and the fact that the only means of locomotion available at the time was the horse, these individuals' travel alone strikes the modern observer as a Herculean feat.

Bureaucratic carousels, the frequent rotations of officials between the most diverse regions, played an important role in the functioning and modernization of the European continental empires — the Austrian, Russian, and Ottoman ones, as well as the Prussian monarchy — but remain little known to historians. This book explains some nuances of these carousels: the mechanisms of appointments, transfers, and relocations. I argue that these rotations were part of an official policy, and show how they helped impose a certain sense of unity and maintain imperial integrity.

This bureaucratic merry-go-round, however, could have ill effects on the specific regions under respective jurisdictions. Studying their arrangements, one gets the impression that ministers in Vienna (just like their peers in St. Petersburg, Istanbul, or Berlin) had little knowledge of various provinces, and no specific vision of who should be appointed where, and why. Appointments, especially to key offices, were never absolutely random; career records, recommendations, and command of languages played a certain role in selection, promotion, and rotation. But practically no official, not even a governor, was expected to have prior expertise in any specific region. It was not uncommon for administrators to switch positions between the most diverse regions within months of their original appointments. The results of such policies could be devastating: while some bureaucrats developed a judicious outlook during their work in a given place, many others were concerned solely with their own careers and, viewing their service as nothing more than the temporary assignment it was, showed little to no interest in the local matters that constituted, in fact, their duties.

When dispatching officials from Italy, Bohemia, the Netherlands, and beyond to Galicia, Austrian rulers expected unquestioning compliance, loyalty, and professionalism. Far from the civilizational attractions of the monarchy's core regions, Austrian bureaucrats—who had no personal interest in Galicia—were expected to put all their efforts toward the benefit of the monarchy. Few lived up to the lofty expectations placed upon them by their superiors in Vienna. Some were patently unqualified for their duties, while others succumbed to corruption. Most did not conceal their frustration with Galicia, viewing their assignments to it as, more or less, an exile. Some expected a quick relocation, but others sought strategies of adjustment instead; thus officials often questioned central legislation, proceeding with measures that directly contradicted Vienna's policies. Austria's reform efforts stumbled over its own bureaucrats, who either did not know how to execute their duties, or else refused to do so.

In time, Vienna incorporated aspects of administration and political tradition from Poland-Lithuania. Though initially excluded from the Austrian bureaucracy, Polish nobles became an integral part thereof in Galicia as early as the 1780s. The original intention to reform Jewish society in Galicia by way of exclusively Germanophone administration also proved a failure; over the years, Vienna incorporated structures of Jewish self-administration that survived from the Polish period, with rabbis and community leaders as their core. Galician Ruthenians, meanwhile, received access to Austrian educational institutions, and later to the administration.

While opening itself to adjustments from outside, the Austrian bureaucracy was changing from within. Reciprocal assimilation between German-speaking bureaucrats and Polish aristocrats became increasingly common in the late eighteenth and early nineteenth centuries, but the general trend favored Polishness over Austrianness. Mixed Austrian-Polish families became known for producing generations of cherishers of Polish culture—especially Polish sons raised by German-speaking fathers; most in this category remained loyal to their Habsburg sovereigns, but many switched allegiances along with language, eventually coming to rank their Polish identity higher than their Austrian one.

These unconventional choices among Austrian bureaucrats shed new light on our understanding of absolutism, centralism, and nationalism in Eastern Europe and the Habsburg Monarchy. In his recent biography of the

Austrian Enlightenment ruler par excellence, Emperor Joseph II, Derek Beales alludes to an overall consensus that Josephinian reforms of the 1780s were effective.[8] A closer analysis of the relationships between Vienna and the provinces reveals, instead, a great deal of friction and a widespread sense of failure. The limits of absolutism were clearer and more significant in the provinces than at the center. The gradual erosion of central policies—more precisely, these policies' undermining by local bureaucrats—and the unforeseen assimilation of Austrian personnel into a non-German culture both reflected and further strengthened the appeal of traditional elites and their influence upon the imperial administration.

Vienna's original intention to exclude local cadres entirely from the Austrian administration reflected the spirit of the Enlightenment, with its belief in the power of persons and institutions to effect radical change, sweeping away remnants of the past. But this initial tabula rasa notion that Austrian bureaucrats would build Galicia entirely from scratch gave way to a gradual and highly significant shift toward inclusion and accommodation. As early as the 1780s, Austrian officials, in Vienna and in the new provincial capital of Lemberg (Lwów in Polish and L'viv in Ukrainian), adjusted their expectations and modified policies, marking an important retreat from the ideals of perfection and uniformity that had been projected onto Galicia in 1772.

The Austrian bureaucracy took root in Galicia, eventually flourishing with a life of its own. Within a few decades, it comprised a highly diverse group, including German-speaking Austrian bureaucrats who decided to become Polish nobles; Polish nobles who decided to become Austrian bureaucrats; and Ruthenians who, until 1848, were unsure of exactly who to become, but whose options in this department were definitely expanding. Even Jewish community leaders became integrated into Austrian institutions. Reciprocal assimilations between Austrians and Poles were especially common. The empire's largest province, situated on the strategically crucial border with Russia, Galicia became a model of ethnic heterogeneity and socio-political complexity unseen anywhere else in the Habsburg Monarchy.

In the 1830s, Lemberg featured only two hotels, the Hôtel de l'Europe and the Hôtel de Russie,[9] the rather charged symbolism of this pair of names suggesting the poles of identification of nineteenth-century Galicia. While Austrian policymakers sought to tether Galicia securely to Europe, the province's inhabitants were inevitably always conscious of Russia, just across Galicia's border. Cross-frontier ties between Poles, Ruthenians, and Jews in Galicia and in other territories of partitioned Poland were no minor concern in Vienna through 1918. A Polish revolution anywhere in the former Polish lands would invariably have repercussions in Galicia. The transborder connections between Ruthenians in Austrian Galicia and Russian Poland at times posed an even greater political threat. While Austrian rulers sought to impose Austrian imperial identity upon their new Ruthenian subjects in Galicia, Russian statesmen and intellectuals strived to convert Ruthenians to Russian culture instead.

Ties between partitioned Polish territories and the Austro-Russian borderland influenced Austrian policies in Galicia, but the exclusive focus on the Polish and Russian aspects of the Galician frontier that has dominated historical scholarship on Galicia can conceal the complexity of the province's borders. Indeed, the Habsburg Monarchy itself could best be described as an assemblage of borderlands, of which Galicia was one. Ties between Galicia and other Habsburg frontier regions, such as northeastern Italy and the Banat of Temesvár, were as important as the more immediate connection between Galicia and other Polish territories across the imperial border. Galicia, to be sure, never became another Italy; but the political establishment of borderland Lemberg resembled that of borderland Trieste more than that of other parts of the former Poland-Lithuania, or even that of neighboring—and ostensibly Galicia-like—Bohemia.[10] The Italian connection played a peculiar role in Galician history and historiography. Beginning in the 1860s, Polish and Ukrainian patriots spoke of Galicia as a "Piedmont," a border province with national separatist potential.

The very notion that a "Piedmont" could be fashioned from Galicia, meanwhile, became a symbol of Austrian efforts run amok. Austrian bureaucrats fell under the charms of traditional society and its increasingly national appeal. Some sons of German-speaking Austrian officials helped promote a "Polish Piedmont" in Galicia, while others became involved in the Ruthenian national project. In the struggle for cultural hegemony, the balance tipped this way and that, with influence remaining ever reciprocal. Poles and Ruthenians alike would build upon institutions Austrian bureaucrats had established (and eventually left behind). Habsburg administrators thus did not only not suppress ethnic difference, but in some ways helped promote nationalism; they made, moreover, a modern national administration possible.

When Galicia became its own version of a Piedmont, the bureaucratic carousel acquired new forms. From 1772 to 1848, leadership transfers most often occurred en masse between one province and another. Bureaucrats could often travel for hundreds of miles to and from Vienna on their way between Italian territories, Bohemia, Galicia, and beyond. This pattern of appointments underwent changes after 1848. On the one hand, local elites, mostly ethnic Poles, came to play an increasingly important role in the administration of Galicia; their appointment to the central administration and government in Vienna itself was a concession in the wake of the 1848 Revolution. At the same time, the status of German-speaking bureaucrats, who had made up the administration before 1848, became jeopardized: some were forced to resign, and many moved away to other regions.

The Revolution of 1848 did not create modern nationalism; neither did Galicia's post-1867 autonomy bring about a national administration. But between 1848 and 1867, the imperial administration succumbed increasingly to national impulses. The dismissal of German-speaking Austrian officials, oftentimes against their will, revealed a new political reality on the eastern borderland and across the empire. It would be mistaken, however, to assume that the Polish administration in the age of autonomy was built from scratch to replace Galicia's previous Germanophone administration; the modern administration in the province, as in the empire generally, remained a product of reforms conceived by Vienna in the 1770s to 1780s. Its institutions survived all upheavals, as did the principle of a centralized administration and a professional bureaucracy, imposed upon these terrains by the Habsburg rulers and their bureaucrats.

Though the history of administration is a burgeoning field in the historiography of East-Central Europe, most existing works focus on particular

INTRODUCTION

institutions, prominent statesmen, or the central bureaucracy in Vienna. Institutional histories often present administration as an accumulation of abstract structures that functioned by their own rules, independently of the men who ran them.[11] At the other extreme, research on Austria's political establishment often tends toward the strictly biographical. Several studies have explored the central bureaucracy in Vienna.[12] In the 1990s, Franz Szabo and P. G. M. Dickson stressed the essential role of local midlevel bureaucrats in the Austrian Empire's day-to-day functioning, its Enlightenment, and its reform movements during the eighteenth and nineteenth centuries. Both also noted the sheer absence of research on the local bureaucracy in the Habsburg Monarchy.[13]

The dearth of knowledge on provincial bureaucracies has engendered certain interpretive problems. Historians tend to describe the Austrian bureaucracy as an abstract institution comprising Germanophone officials who imposed the will of the central government on non-German elites in the provinces.[14] In their a priori acceptance of the bureaucracy as uniform, scholars make the concomitant error of analyzing the impact of the modernizing empire upon its provinces and provincial elites as unidirectional. The reverse side of the story, namely the influence these elites exerted in their turn upon the bureaucracy, on both institutional and individual levels, is practically unknown.

Two major works on the pre-1848 administration of Galicia have come from the pens of Horst Glassl and Stanisław Grodziski, prominent German and Polish historians respectively. Each offers very detailed information, but approaches Galicia from a different angle. The former focuses on the Austrian side, exploring Vienna's reform intentions for the new province; the latter evinces, by contrast, a Polish bias, describing the damage the Austrian administration inflicted upon the Polish civilization of Galicia. Glassl and Grodziski thus reflect a typical dichotomy in the scholarship of the empire and its provinces, with one school of thought generally definable as "imperial" and focusing on Austrian reform efforts as part of a "civilizing" project,[15] and the other as "national," emphasizing the reaction of traditional elites to imperial reforms.[16] These two schools labor under a crucial shortcoming: the former often overlooks the fact that even the best-intentioned measures can, when imposed by an outside authority, elicit opposition, which may well be justified. The latter goes to the opposite extreme, underestimating the good intentions of the imperial government, or overemphasizing evidence of its nefariousness. Their differences notwithstanding, adherents of these schools tend to view the Austrian bureaucracy too holistically: for Horst Glassl, it is a uniform instrument of (failed) modernization; for some of his Polish colleagues, a uniform means of cultural destruction.

Another set of problems stems from chronological imbalance: most of the works, recent or otherwise, on the Habsburg Monarchy and its provinces focus on the late nineteenth and early twentieth centuries, a tendency notable in research on Eastern Europe in general; that is, the *national* period in the history of Eastern Europe has long been dominant in scholarship.[17] As R. J. W. Evans has noted, while Western, especially Anglo-American historians have paid a great deal of attention to East European nationalism, most studies have focused on the "post-1848 brand."[18]

I have sought to build upon several recent works that present the history of Galicia, and the empire of which it was a part, in a new light. One is Larry Wolff's *The Idea of Galicia*—an intellectual history of the Galicia *concept*, a "study of a place as an idea."[19] I follow the conceptualization of Galicia as an invention by analyzing the practical measures Austrian officials undertook in the hopes of transforming their idea into reality. Another recent groundbreaking work, Isabelle Röskau-Rydel's 2011 study, analyzes the history of German-Polish coexistence in Galicia by focusing on ten families from among German-speaking Austrian officialdom who adopted Polish identity.[20] I take this approach a step further by exploring reciprocal influences among Austrian bureaucrats, Poles, Ruthenians, and Jews.

With this study I aim to overcome several conventional shortcomings in the scholarship: the conceptual or abstract nature of administrative history, the overemphasis on biography in discussions of political elites, and the excessive concentration on Vienna in research on the Austrian bureaucracy. Detailed analysis of the interaction among individual bureaucrats reveals numerous underexplored aspects of imperial administration as practiced on the periphery. It shows how political decisions were driven by local conditions and personal choices, and how these choices often led to the most unpredictable consequences.

A closer analysis of provincial bureaucracies should help yield a new history of imperial administration, a more nuanced picture of the interaction between the administrators and those they administered. Austrian bureaucrats, Polish landowners, Jewish merchants, and Ruthenian peasants all too often shared common interests.[21] An emotionally detached, politically neutral, and uniformly Germanophone bureaucracy was indeed the ideal that Enlightenment-minded Habsburg rulers set for themselves in the late eighteenth century. But such a thing never materialized.

In the 1980s, Piotr Wandycz explored the impact that Polish elites had upon the Austrian Empire, explaining that many German-Austrian officials fell under the spell of Polish culture and became Polonized while in Galicia.[22] Stories of Austrian bureaucrats deciding to become Poles or in some cases Ruthenians have survived in popular memory and the historical imagination, but they do not receive their due coverage in scholarship; we have remained underinformed as to how common this trend was, why German-speaking bureaucrats decided to become Poles, and what consequences their choices had for Galicia, the empire, and Europe as a whole.

Each chapter of this book focuses on a paradox of Austrian policy—a contrast between intentions and final results—and addresses a gap in the historiography. The opening chapter, "Bureaucratic Enlightenment and Galicia," introduces two intellectual constructs—the new Austrian bureaucracy, and Galicia as a laboratory for Habsburg reforms. "Civilizers at Work" discusses the formation of the Austrian bureaucracy in Galicia between 1772 and 1794 with a focus on two Austrian governors, Johann Anton von Pergen (1772–74) and Joseph Karl von Brigido (1780–94); the chapter explains how and why provincial officials came to play an ever more significant role in regional reforms. "The Napoleonic Test" discusses Galicia within the context of the French Revolutionary Wars and the postwar administrative reorganization of the monarchy. Senior Austrian officials were at times oblivious of the radical socio-political upheavals occurring in their provinces; but local bureaucrats would find these changes impossible to ignore, and in some cases hard to resist. "Between Vienna, St. Petersburg, and

INTRODUCTION

Warsaw" deals with early interrogations of national identity as incarnate in the figure of August von Lobkowitz, who served as Galicia's governor from 1826 to 1832. Originally from Bohemia, and a scion of one of the most illustrious aristocratic families in the monarchy, Lobkowitz claimed to be a Pole and supported the reestablishment of an independent Poland. Lobkowitz and his policies, as carried out between Vienna, Lemberg, Warsaw, and St. Petersburg, are the focus of this chapter.

Subsequent chapters analyze Austrian attempts to administer different groups in Galicia—the Poles, Ruthenians, and Jews—foregrounding the contradictory consequences of Austrian modernization. Local society infiltrated imperial administration; and mixed marriages became one of the most visible signs of ongoing transformations. "Austrian Bureaucracy and Polish Aristocracy" explores the relations between the imperial administration and Polish aristocratic elites, focusing on imperial bureaucrats' adoption of Polishness. "Literature, Politics, and Galician Ruthenians" explores the interactions between Austrian bureaucrats and Ruthenians, the reciprocal assimilations and fluid identities of these national representatives, and the ambivalent effects of Austrian reforms upon the Ruthenian minority. "Administering the Jews" is a case study illustrating reciprocal relations among Austrians, Poles, Ruthenians, and Jews, especially highlighting the impact Galician Jews had upon the modernizing empire. The last chapter, "Bureaucracy and Revolutions," examines the revolutions in Galicia in 1846 and 1848, which marked the end of an era in the history of Austrian Galicia. The conclusion expands the field of view to 1867, analyzing the transition from a German- to a Polish-dominated period in the life of the province.

None of the chapters offers comprehensive biographies of the individuals described, but their lives and careers form a prism through which to analyze the functioning of administration. The focus is on specific aspects of governance—what Austrian officials themselves described as political administration, and what is today known as civil administration. Judicial and military administration are considered only to a limited degree, mainly as pertains to the civil arena. Both the judiciary and the army formed distinct domains that differed significantly from the civil administration, and as such they fall outside the scope of this study.

INTRODUCTION

Most of the voices heard here come from bureaucrats themselves as recorded in their reports or correspondence. The organizing approach of this study and its focus upon the bureaucracy defined the choice of materials presented; I am most interested in the mechanisms of administration as executed by individual bureaucrats. Other Galicians are represented only insofar as warranted by their contacts with Austrian officialdom, whether via personal connections as members of bureaucratic families or through dealings with officials.

This book places Galicia within the broader context of European state-building during the modern period, albeit relegating discussion of various historical contexts to the narrative background. Prussia thus appears as a model of the reforms undertaken in the eighteenth-century Habsburg Monarchy; France serves as one instantiation of the Enlightenment, of which the Habsburg Monarchy was decidedly another. Parallels between the different partitioning powers—Russia, Prussia, and Austria—are more direct, due to the strong reciprocal influences among these polities.

The discussion is based on several groups of sources from archives in Vienna, L'viv, Kraków, Paris, and Trieste. Most materials concerning the administration are located in the Austrian Administrative Archive in Vienna and the Central National Archive in L'viv.[23] Correspondence among Austrian rulers and some Austrian bureaucrats is stored in the Habsburg Court Archive in Vienna. The chapter on the Napoleonic Wars draws on materials housed in the Diplomatic Archive in Paris. For information on individual bureaucrats, I also made use of select collections located in Kraków and Trieste.

Geographical definitions are always a challenge in regions such as Galicia. Formally titled the Kingdom of Galicia and Lodomeria, the region was known in the monarchy simply as Galicia, and I use this term consistently throughout the text. The provincial capital is designated as Lwów in references to the pre-1772 and post-1848 periods (except for occasional use of L'viv in the context of the present day); the city was called Lemberg in official documents between 1772 and 1848, and I follow this usage for these years. Broader geographical and political definitions—for instance, Eastern Europe, East-Central Europe, and Central Europe—are even more problematic; my provisional solution is to use the term East-Central Europe for the period between 1772 and 1848, when Galicia was part of the German-speaking territory of Habsburg Europe; and Eastern Europe for the period following 1867, when Galicia became Polish and Ruthenian.

When Poles took over Austrian offices around 1867, they imitated earlier Austrian policies and used Austrian institutions toward their own political ends. While the Austrians had hoped to create a uniformly Germanophone administration, the Poles attempted to create one that would be monolithically Polish. Each endeavor involved the attempt to silence criticism, and each failed; it was specifically the multiethnic heritage of the Habsburg polity that lived on. Until 1939, Galicia upheld its reputation as a land of diversity and coexistence. These ancient patterns were only broken during the Second World War, when Galicia became a battlefield for the clash of two radical ideologies, Nazism and Stalinism. After 1945, two divided Galicias represented models of unprecedented ethnic homogeneity: Western Galicia, centering on Kraków, became part of Poland, with Poles forming an absolute majority there. Eastern Galicia, on the other hand, was integrated into Soviet Ukraine, ethnic Ukrainians gradually coming to form an absolute majority of its population.

But the Habsburg legacy has not been entirely erased. It manifests itself through the architectural and cultural landscape that the former Habsburg territories share to the present day. The similarities between L'viv and Kraków are hard to miss. Their Habsburg heritage sets them apart from Kyiv and Warsaw, each of which at different times belonged to the Russian Empire, and which also resemble one another in certain ways. Parts of today's Poland and Ukraine, then, cannot be fully understood outside their common Austrian heritage.

ONE

Bureaucratic Enlightenment and Galicia

The year 1918 marked a turning point in the history of Europe. The same year brought an end to the "unfathomable and incomprehensible land" of Kakania, as Austrian writer Robert Musil dubbed his fictionalized Habsburg domain. Kakania, writes Musil, was "imperial-royal," though none could say when it was royal and when imperial. It was administered in an enlightened manner by Europe's finest bureaucracy, which featured a single flaw: in Kakania, a genius was often mistaken for a boor, though a boor was never mistaken for a genius.[1] Perhaps Kakania was a land of genius, and this is why it did not survive.

Set in the year 1913 and published in the 1930s, Robert Musil's *The Man Without Qualities* depicts the growing uncertainty pervading Viennese life shortly before the outbreak of the First World War.[2] Descriptions of the chaos that reigned in the late empire were not uncommon after 1918, and were often marked by unconcealed longing for what Stefan Zweig called the "world of yesterday."[3] Along with Zweig, Joseph Roth, and other contemporaries, Musil shared nostalgia for the world irrevocably destroyed in 1918. *The Man Without Qualities* is a story of people no longer having a place in an empire on the verge of collapse. Many are distinguished by titles and lofty ranks, but otherwise indistinguishable; they lose their identities, and thus emerges a world of men without qualities. The world of qualities never returned, but the myth of Kakania lived on.[4]

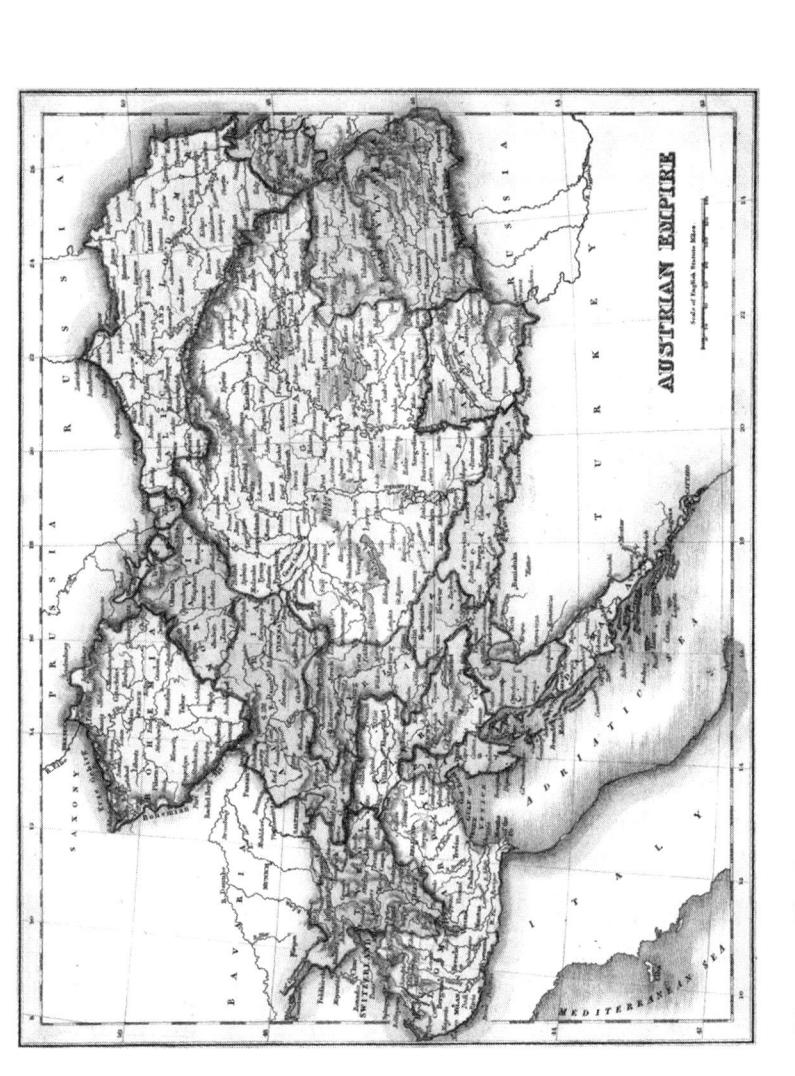

Map 1.1: The Austrian Empire, 1832. Contemporary atlas map by John Dower and W. M. Higgins, Edinburgh. David Rumsey Historical Map Collection.

Chaos manifested itself also in imperial administration, both a cause and result of the world without qualities. Musil's Kakania is a product of its bureaucracy. Created in the eighteenth century by Austria's Enlightenment-minded rulers as an instrument of progress, the Habsburg bureaucracy was designed to transform the heterogeneous monarchy into a uniform state. In the center of Europe, where the axes of the world meet, Kakania should have been a perfect state governed by an ideal bureaucracy.[5] But men, of course, proved imperfect. Even during the glory years of the monarchy, its bureaucracy was more pitiful than rational, mired in hierarchical disorganization and unfathomable in its complexity. Theoretically composed of the best and most talented citizens, in reality it was often the opposite.

What became of this bureaucracy of genius and the almost a-historic monarchy that, it seemed to many contemporaries, could never end? The questions that preoccupied Austrian writers after 1918 have since made their way into scholarship of the Habsburg Monarchy and Central Europe. While Austrian writers immersed themselves in nostalgia for a lost "world of yesterday," their German contemporaries showed increasing scholarly interest in the issues of bureaucracy and administration. Max Weber's research on German imperial administration laid the foundations of modern sociology and institutional history. Weber described the ideal model of a perfect bureaucracy, which, he indicated, could never be fully implemented in practice.

Some regions, however, were even less amenable to realizing the bureaucratic ideal than others. On the monarchy's eastern periphery, the province of Galicia, formerly part of Poland, was paradigmatically disordered and confused. Envisioned as the model province of a reformed Habsburg Monarchy, it became an emblem of chaos instead. Its economy barely improved after the partitions. Comparisons between Galicia and other Habsburg territories became progressively more unfavorable with time. However, the idea of Galicia never disappeared from the political imagination, even as the reality of the place only remotely resembled initial expectations.

Galicia and the Austrian bureaucracy had somewhat similar fates. Both were products of the eighteenth century; both reflected the high aspirations of Austria's Enlightenment-minded rulers. Both caused much disillusionment: the Austrian imperial bureaucracy—always inefficient, sometimes corrupt—fell short of the hopes of its founding fathers. Galicia, too, proved a land of failed promises, economically poor and politically unstable. These failures, however, should not conceal certain important successes: the professional bureaucracy created in the eighteenth century has survived to the present day as the major basis of a modern state. Galicia, too, has withstood the centuries. This study is a story of how ideals become transformed into reality; how they may fail in the short term, but succeed in the long run.

Imperial Organization

The lands of Musil's Kakania were known at various times as the Habsburg Monarchy, the Austrian Empire, or Austria-Hungary. A dynasty of German princes, the Habsburgs had historically possessed the territories encompassing modern-day Switzerland and Austria. In the late fifteenth century, they added Spain to their family domains. Between 1521 and 1526, Ferdinand I acquired Bohemia and Hungary, thus creating an essentially tripartite territorial configuration: the Habsburg (family) hereditary territories; the kingdoms of Hungary and Bohemia, each with its own distinct status; and the Kingdom of Spain together with its possessions in the Netherlands and Italy and its New World empire, which formed a separate realm under a second, "Spanish" branch of the dynasty.[6] In the west, the "Austrian" Habsburgs shared borders with the German states; in the southeast, they faced the Ottoman Empire. The Habsburg Italian possessions, such as Venetia, Lombardy, and Tuscany, most of which were annexed in the early eighteenth century, formed the southwest bastion of the expanding monarchy. Galicia became Austria's northeastern frontier in 1772.

Between the thirteenth century and 1806, Habsburg monarchs commonly ruled as Holy Roman Emperors.[7] The Holy Roman Empire formed a loose confederation of territories rather than an empire in the typical sense of the word; it featured no central government, common system of taxation, or common army. The empire included Habsburg German domains, Bohemia, and a great number of various German states, Prussia among them. It excluded other Habsburg possessions, for instance Hungary, the Netherlands, and Galician and Italian territories. It was dissolved in 1806, and its Habsburg component acquired a new title—the Austrian Empire.

The Holy Roman Empire had been a complicated political unit, its existence exerting crucial influences upon such territories as at one time or another found themselves under its jurisdiction. All regions of the empire, for instance, were subject to a certain philosophical tradition that, in the eighteenth century, laid the groundwork for reform. Intellectual transfers between different sections of German-speaking Europe were more significant than similar exchanges between other, unrelated, parts of the continent. Before 1806, the Habsburg Monarchy and Prussia, by virtue of belonging to the Holy Roman Empire, existed in the same intellectual and political space of Germanophone Central Europe.

During the 1750s and 1760s, Prussia served as a model for reforms in the Habsburg Monarchy. Several leading Austrian statesmen, including Chancellor Wenzel Anton von Kaunitz, were educated in German universities. Most of them returned to their Habsburg homeland with a clear realization of the monarchy's economic and political backwardness when compared to the leading German state, Prussia. The Prussian educational system became a model to be imitated for some Austrian officials concerned with the decline of the Habsburgs' international reputation and the economic backwardness of their lands in comparison with some of their German neighbors; the empire should be brought up to date, it was thought, and its standing among nations improved, by borrowing tactics already successfully tested in Prussia. Educational reform was designed to create a basis for subsequent changes, most notably preparing the cadres for a new administration.

Having ascended to the throne in 1740, Empress Maria Theresa launched a series of reforms in an effort to restore the international status of the Habsburg Monarchy and ensure domestic stability. Her son Joseph II, who became co-regent in 1765 and succeeded to the throne upon Maria Theresa's death in 1780, continued the reforms, but proceeded in a more radical manner. Their different tactics notwithstanding, both Maria Theresa and Joseph II shared a commitment to the creation of a uniform state out of a conglomerate of heterogeneous provinces.

In the spirit of the Enlightenment, Maria Theresa transformed relations between ruler and subjects, as well as between elites and the lower classes. The Catholic Church lost its dominant status, and in 1781–82, Eastern Catholicism, Protestantism, Orthodoxy, and Judaism were officially recognized as legal. Maria Theresa imposed limits upon landlords' authority over peasants, and Joseph II granted the latter their personal freedom. Taxes on land were increased. German was made the official language of administrative and educational institutions, and the latter were newly purposed to modernize the monarchy and prepare cadres for its management.

Administration became both the main target and the instrument of reforms. After 1740, new imperial and regional institutions imposed in the various Habsburg territories a governance of hitherto unseen uniformity and centralization. In 1762, the United Austrian-Bohemian Court Chancellery became the primary administrator of the Habsburg family's "hereditary lands"—the Austrian territories and Bohemia. Most other territories acquired or reacquired by war and diplomacy between the sixteenth and eighteenth centuries (among them, Lombardy, Belgium, Hungary, Transylvania, Croatia, and Slovenia) were then placed under the authority of the State Chancellery, created in 1742 and reformed in 1754, and originally responsible for foreign relations. Some regions enjoyed autonomous status within the central administration; for example, the Kingdom of Hungary was governed by the Hungarian Court Chancellery.

Between the 1750s and 1770s, central institutions were supplemented by the new regional offices, the Gubernia. Each Gubernium was divided into smaller administrative units—circles and districts (beneath circles).[8] The Gubernium became the major link between each of the provinces and its respective institution in Vienna—either the State Chancellery or the Court Chancellery. First introduced in the monarchy's hereditary lands in 1753, Gubernia were eventually established in other regions as well, including Galicia.

After the 1740s, administrative offices across the monarchy were staffed by professional bureaucrats dispatched from Vienna. Typically, officials were assigned to regions where they were not native; thus, officials from Trieste traveled to Prague, Tyroleans moved to Bohemia, Galicians found themselves in Austrian-held Italy. They all shared a common background of professional training, and all performed their work in German, the mandatory language of education and administration. Most had no control over assignments, and could anticipate multiple rotations and changes of venue during their careers. These new bureaucrats infiltrated the various branches of the provinces' administration so that, to a large extent, political and economic control of Habsburg holdings no longer required the consensus of local elites; the managerial centralization they provided was, for the empire, unprecedented.

Centralization did not, however, begin with Maria Theresa. The first common institutions were founded shortly after 1526. Similarly, well before the 1740s Habsburg rulers had had in their disposition cohorts of officials who were regularly dispatched from Vienna to provinces on various missions. Tax collection was one of them, and the men responsible for it represented an early equivalent of the modern bureaucrat. Efforts toward administrative centralization were at times halted by external factors, such as, for example, wars (against the Turks in the east and the French in the west). The idea of centralization was not new, but mechanisms toward achieving it changed with Maria Theresa's accession as empress. Her intended reforms were more comprehensive than perhaps at any previous time, as she targeted different domains of politics, economy, and social organization all at once.

Similarly, the social composition of state functionaries did not change dramatically in the eighteenth century. Maria Theresa and Joseph II created new institutions, hierarchies, and requirements, but not new men. The vast majority of Austrian bureaucrats in the late eighteenth and early nineteenth centuries held noble titles, just as they did centuries earlier. Members of several most prominent aristocratic families—Kolowrat, Lobkowitz, Auersperg, and several others—occupied key offices, many of them starting their careers in the provinces before landing positions in Vienna. Family background and connections played an important role in professional careers, before and after the eighteenth century. Positions were sometimes distributed in conversations over coffee or wine. Intermarriages between members of the same class facilitated social and professional networking, which was as important in the eighteenth century as it is in the twenty-first. At the same time, the reforms of the eighteenth century created new opportunities for those who, because of their social status or background, could not have qualified for administrative positions before. Many of these new men came to administer Galicia after 1772.

Cameralism, the Police, and the Enlightenment

These new institutions emerged within a specific intellectual and political climate in the Holy Roman Empire, particularly within the Habsburg Monarchy. The ideas of a modern state and professional bureaucracy were first introduced by intellectuals, then applied to the practice of institutional change. Most reforms were products of the Enlightenment, but their roots can be traced to intellectual and political traditions of earlier epochs. The core aims of the orderly state and the perfect society were the centerpiece of cameralist and police sciences—two interrelated schools of thought in German-speaking Europe between the late seventeenth century and the 1760s.

Cameralism was a theory of state management that foregrounded the production of wealth. Unlike the Enlightenment, a pan-European or even world movement, cameralism had its stronghold in Germanophone Europe. Its major representatives published their works before or during the 1760s; and thus aspects of the cameralist sciences influenced the Enlightenment as conceptualized in the Habsburg Monarchy and Prussia. Insofar as it traced its roots to German states outside the Habsburg Monarchy, most notably Prussia, cameralism was a *German* doctrine; but owing at least in part to their common membership in the Holy Roman Empire, intellectual affinities between these two sections of German-speaking Europe were perhaps stronger in the eighteenth century than at any time thereafter. The prominent cameralist theoretician Johann Heinrich von Justi, for example, by origin a German rather than an Austrian, dedicated one of his major works, *State Economy, or a Systematic Treatise of All Economic and Cameral Sciences*, to Maria Theresa.[9]

The implied endorsement of Maria Theresa's reign was not accidental: cameralists supported strong absolutist rule, and they justified their views by economic reasoning. Justi and other such cameralist thinkers as Christian

Wolff reasoned that only a strong state, headed by an all-powerful ruler, could secure the prosperity of its subjects; they thus defended the monarch's right, for instance, to unilaterally impose taxes and dues.

While cameralism was an economic doctrine, explaining how wealth is achieved, "police science" or *Polizeiwissenschaft* taught how to keep this prosperity once created.[10] The main task of the police, Justi wrote in 1759, was to "secure the retention and increase of wealth through an efficient inner administration."[11] In the eighteenth century, functions of the police varied greatly—this institution handled everything from the prosecution of criminals to street-cleaning—but its main aim was to ensure a stable domestic order through a functional administration. As understood by Justi, the police resembled the modern conception of civil administration.

The interconnection of cameralism, the police, and the Enlightenment in the Habsburg Monarchy was effected by certain intellectuals and statesmen who started in the tradition of cameralism, contributed to the police sciences, and matured during the Enlightenment. One of these was Joseph von Sonnenfels. A major representative of the Austrian Enlightenment, he was, at the same time, a product of reforms and changing mentalities in the Habsburg Monarchy, being as he was the son of a converted Jew, and the first person of Jewish descent to make a career at the Habsburg court, where he served as adviser to the emperor.[12] Sonnenfels left a twofold legacy. He is most remembered for his efforts in political reform and the relaxation of the censorship;[13] but he also produced some of the most influential programmatic texts of the Austrian Enlightenment.

Sonnenfels' *Basics of Police, Trade, and Finance*, published in 1786–87, revealed important shifts in the conceptualization of the police and the state since the 1750s. Effective control, argued Sonnenfels, is best achieved through a balanced combination of reward and punishment.[14] Sonnenfels did not invent the police as we know this institution today, but his views on the subject revealed a gradual separation of civil administration and law enforcement, whose functions further diverged in the nineteenth century, eventually forming two separate domains. This separation itself, the story of which is beyond the scope of this study, constitutes a very important—and somewhat underresearched—chapter in the history of state-building in modern Europe.[15]

Links between cameralism, police science, and Enlightenment marked a key distinction between German-speaking Europe and France. In France, the Enlightenment was an intellectual movement in defense of individual rights, of the people's sovereignty and representative institutions against absolutist rule. The Enlightenment in Germanophone Europe followed a different path: its major representatives endorsed absolutism as an instrument of prosperity and national well-being.

As Derek Beales has noted, Enlightenment was not a homogeneous concept. "What was acceptable in the way of monarchical rule to the great majority of German representatives of the *Aufklärung* went far beyond what was acceptable to Montesquieu, Rousseau and Diderot, and to English and American thinkers in general."[16] Temperamentally hostile to philosophical theorizing, Empress Maria Theresa denounced certain philosophes, while her son Joseph II banned their writings; yet the Habsburgs endorsed some of the premises of the European Enlightenment.[17] Radical, liberal, theoretical, and philosophical in France, in the Habsburg Empire the Enlightenment could best be characterized as utilitarian or pragmatic—a project of state-sponsored reforms imposed from above.[18] Centering as it did on policy rather than ideological debate, the Austrian Enlightenment's amenability to French influences was rather limited.

On Bureaucracy

Aside from his work in the sphere of police and the state, Joseph von Sonnenfels was also a prominent voice in debates on the new type of citizen at the center of the reformed polity. In 1765–66, he edited a periodical called *The Man Without Prejudice*, containing his own programmatic statement under the same title.[19] A state can prosper and its subjects flourish, Sonnenfels argues herein, via the creation of a new man, "the man without prejudice" (*Der Mann ohne Vorurtheil*)—an active citizen choosing his own allegiances and occupations; a free man who, unlike a slave, voluntarily places himself in the service of the state. Such an individual recognizes that his personal freedom can only be secured in a harmonious society, whose members peacefully coexist. Sonnenfels thus proposes a utilitarian concept of patriotism: all citizens should share in the common happiness and help create this state of perpetual well-being, which goals require certain sacrifices of individual liberties and privileges. Like other theoreticians in German-speaking Europe, and even in France, Sonnenfels valorized the common good attainable via individual sacrifice, prioritizing, as did cameralists generally, the collective interests of the state over the personal rights of its citizens. Thus Sonnenfels not only endorsed his rulers, he indeed contributed to the crystallization of absolutism in the Habsburg Monarchy; and his models would find new life during the major phase of the Austrian Enlightenment.

While Sonnenfels was a symbol of this Enlightenment, Emperor Joseph II was its driving force, transforming ideas into practice. Co-regent with Maria Theresa after his father's death in 1765, the relatively young Joseph II observed his mother's reform efforts throughout the 1770s and 1780s, and her attempts to impose unity upon an extremely diverse monarchy. Traveling widely both before and after his accession to co-rule, in 1773 Joseph was among the first to report to Vienna regarding the situation in the province the Habsburgs had annexed from Poland only months earlier. Even when physically in Galicia, his mind apparently ranged well beyond the Habsburg Monarchy: like his mother, he was hardly oblivious to the reforms taking place in Prussia, to intellectual currents roiling at an even greater distance, in France. Upon the death of his mother in 1780, Joseph II became sole ruler, and launched a new phase of reforms.

Unlike Maria Theresa, Joseph II involved himself in debates surrounding the intellectual basis of such reforms. In 1783, the emperor published a short text that eventually became known as his "pastoral letter."[20] Originally written in French, the pamphlet was translated into several languages, with German editions the most widely disseminated. In twenty-four pages, Joseph explains the intentions behind his reforms, focusing particularly on the bureaucrats responsible for the implementation of the changes envisioned. To the same extent it treats ideas, the pamphlet deals with practical complications of their application, with problems of a nascent bureaucracy.[21] Committed to reform, the emperor expected unquestioning compliance from his officials. The reality of average bureaucrats was, of course, quite different from that of their emperor-manager, their far more humble station creating the possibility of certain problems. For instance, these bureaucrats, being underpaid, willingly accepted gifts, which were typically seen by them as not only harmless, but indeed necessary for their financial survival. But professional administrators, in Joseph's view, must be prohibited from receiving any kind of external compensation. The separation of public office and private domain, which would be an operating principle of Weberian rational bureaucracy, already formed a theoretical cornerstone of the new system: "Self-interest of different kinds is harmful to work and an inexcusable burden of every state official. Under self-interest we understand not only material rewards but also all kinds of secondary motives and objectives, which harm the general good, and obscure the clarity and precision of reports."[22]

Nowhere does Joseph II refer to Sonnenfels, but parallels between the emperor's ideal bureaucrat and Sonnenfels' man without prejudice are striking. Both conceptions foreground a kind of personal self-purification, and the notion that persons thus reformed could serve as the basis of a new state under the Habsburg Monarchy. Such confluences, moreover, reveal another important aspect of the Austrian Enlightenment, namely that boundaries between intellectual and statesman in the Habsburg Monarchy were more fluid than elsewhere in eighteenth-century Europe, specifically France. In Vienna, the emperor composed philosophical treatises, and philosophers numbered among his administrators. Such links between ruler and theoretician present a sharp contrast to our conventional conception of the Enlightenment, which relies heavily on the French model. In Paris, *philosophes* opposed absolutist government, paving the way for its overthrow; but Austrian intellectuals designed reform strategies that helped preserve absolutist rule over a would-be uniform empire.[23]

The Man Without Qualities

Sonnenfels' man without prejudice was of course an ideal; in practice he became a man without qualities. It did not take long to notice the obvious tendency of models to misfire when applied to reality. New officials were full of old prejudices and shortcomings; bureaucratic mechanisms showed signs of failure as early as the 1780s. Part of the problem, as Joseph II himself realized, stemmed from the design of the bureaucracy itself, the fundamental mismatch between its anticipated benefits and reality that would persist right up to 1918. Expectations placed on bureaucrats were high, but rewards remained minimal. All high-ranking officials were to have a law degree; and as an anticorruption measure, incoming personnel were required to present proof of their financial resources upon entering state service.[24] At the same time, new bureaucrats were expected to undergo lengthy training periods, for which they were compensated meagerly if at all; nor did such required internships guarantee any permanent position upon their completion. Underpaid or unpaid, Austrian bureaucrats were prohibited from taking other part-time jobs.[25] Professional insecurity and financial hardship thus plagued junior and senior officials alike, and became a major hindrance of successful administration.

Against the backdrop of such difficulties, Joseph II was willing to face criticism, ordering in 1781, as one of his first decrees as independent ruler, the liberalization of censorship throughout the monarchy. As historians have noted, such openness to debate marked one of the most important distinctions between the new emperor and his mother Maria Theresa.[26] In 1789, Joseph II would reverse his 1781 censorship liberalization; but during the 1780s, relieved of previous censorship restrictions, the public sphere flourished, with new publications often targeting the administrative reforms and the emperor behind them.[27]

One of the decade's most prolific public commentators was Joseph Richter, who became the emperor's most outspoken critic. Richter's anonymously published pamphlets—*The Reign of the Tomfool: A Comedy from the Previous Century*; *The Letter of the Tomfool: An Appendix to the Reign of the Tomfool*; *The Death of the Tomfool: The last Appendix to the Reign of the Tomfool*—stood as trenchant exposes of the newly introduced structures and bureaucrats, each bitingly satirizing the people who had recently settled into various offices across the monarchy.[28]

> It is quite a nice thing to be a ruler;
> One has some money in his hands

But suffers no accountability;
In the meantime, he leads a gregarious life,
With eating and drinking and all else that goes along with it,
And indulging his every whim and desire.[29]

One could hardly expect administrative effectiveness, insisted Richter, from such bon vivants. Some, meanwhile, were illiterate; but few of even those who had learned to read held out, in this view, much promise. Such was the estimation of Richter, who in 1787 went so far as to publish a pamphlet titled *Why the People Do Not Like Their Emperor*.[30] But it was the bureaucrats who suffered most under his pen, rather than their sovereign manager; whatever the emperor's intentions, the reforms seemed likely to produce discontent.

For his part, Joseph II was willing to address some of these problems. In his writings he had opened his heart to bureaucrats; and in the implementation of his ideas, he said, "I opened the doors [of my chambers] for them every day and every hour . . . to listen to their ideas and allay their doubts."[31] In his capacity as enlightened despot, the emperor saw himself as the primary critic of his own creation. To him, the sine qua non of administrative routine was hierarchical compliance, ideally voluntary rather than enforced; in any case, those who did not fulfill their designated task did not deserve the status of new bureaucrat.

But Joseph II enjoyed no actual monopoly on political critique, and in the 1770s and 1780s, satirical descriptions of imperial bureaucrats constituted a literary genre of seemingly broad appeal. "How can one become a court councillor? And what should this councillor do in his daily activity?" asked "Sangilla von Freundsperg" at the opening of *Court Councillors in *****, another political pamphlet of the 1780s. The answer to the first question, the author states, should of course be to prove the qualifications of "love of one's profession, and patriotism"; but "you should not expect," he warns his readers, that such categories apply to "our" court councillors, who acquire their positions in two ways: by the privilege of birth, or by marrying well. Once having secured his post, a councillor concerns himself with "exploiting the interns, and being seen by his department head on a regular basis. He is often seen at various receptions."[32]

But even the most critical observers had to admit that some bureaucrats, at least, showed dedication and patriotism, even if their efforts should ultimately prove futile. One anonymously published pamphlet, *Fragment of a Conversation about the Relationships between the State and Its Bureaucrats*, presented two protagonists engaged in a Socratic dialogue. One, Count Wellenberg, emphasizes the competence of the imperial civil service, while his opponent, Count Berger, focuses on its flaws. "We do have some hard-working, talented, and devoted men," notes the former. "We do, indeed," answers the latter, "but we need so many more of them." Without denying the goodwill of particular officials, Berger explains that good intentions can only take one so far: "Some bureaucrats are too intelligent, others are too kind, and yet others are neither intelligent nor kind."[33] When the latter outnumbered the former—as was often the case in various offices—administrative efforts were doomed to failure.

This text, not incidentally, is marked by the rhetoric of cameralism and the Austrian Enlightenment. The well-being of the state far outweighs the personal comfort of particular bureaucrats; but at the same time, individual commitment is crucial to the envisioned shared prosperity. "It is common for despots to rely on slave labor, to force them to work through fear. [Our] monarchs need patriots, bound by their love for the fatherland."[34] Patriots, of course, existed, but as polemical literature of the 1780s emphasized, there was only so much they could do in the face of the bureaucracy's systemic shortcomings— especially the poverty and professional insecurity in which it kept so many of its personnel mired. With so many officials forced to work for "salaries too low for their dignity,"[35] literature of the time gained another important subgenre: the tale of the destitute bureaucrat. *The Fate of an Intern of Fifty-Five Years*, for instance, tells the story of a man beginning a civil service internship in his mid-twenties with the hope of securing a permanent position; this aspiration never materializing, he winds up spending most of his life as an underpaid intern. The story was written as a warning to young men completing their studies and considering careers in the imperial bureaucracy. "I have spent so many years doing office work that I have no other qualifications or knowledge of any other profession."[36] The poor fellow's dedication and talent could not spare him the humiliation of a thirty-year apprenticeship.

The Fate of an Intern is, at the same time, a story of corruption, of the failure of meritocracy, themes treated in numerous publications of the 1780s. While the hapless protagonist of that tale remained rooted to his lowly spot, many of his colleagues secured promotion, reaching the upper echelons of power. But those who succeeded were not always the most qualified candidates: "It was intolerable: we were required to demonstrate thousands of talents, for which we received meager salaries. Those who could barely read or write received promotions instead, and became court councillors."[37]

Joseph II would not give up on the idea of reforms, despite the voluminous criticism of their implementation. In his optimism, the emperor put his faith in the self-purification of bureaucrats; but in his pessimism, he resorted to measures of command and control. Thus came about experiments with combining military and civil administration, a conventional instrument of rule in other empires now finding its way into the Habsburg domain as well. In the 1930s, Musil explored Joseph II's dilemma: "It remained to be decided where the real spirit of Kakania—*der Geist*—lay: in the army or in its civilians."[38] In the 1780s, Joseph II arranged for new means of control and disciplinary action toward achieving his ideals.[39] The so-called *Conduitlisten* ("conduct lists")—ranking procedures ensuring the order of subordination and hierarchy in the military—were adopted in the civil administration, signaling a new military-style control thereof.[40] First introduced in 1781, the lists recorded the career tracks and professional reviews of every single bureaucrat below the rank of minister. The entire enterprise became marked by secrecy and hierarchical rigidity. In 1783, dissatisfied with the ostensible neutrality of the lists as originally constituted, Joseph II ordered the introduction of new ones that eventually came to be known as the Black Lists. These registers listed only those officials whose professional performance had come under scrutiny resulting in negative reviews at any point in their careers. Blacklisted Austrian bureaucrats in effect lost any chance of promotion.[41]

The qualification tables and the Black Lists marked a new turn in Joseph II's policy of bureaucracy. Their meaning has since been debated by historians, who see them as everything from normative instruments of control to a means of reducing bureaucrats to the status of slaves.[42] Easily overlooked with regard to the qualification tables, perhaps, is that they laid bare the sheer inefficiency of a modernizing state. In any case, a powerful state, as envisioned by Joseph in his earlier writings, was one that was voluntarily embraced by its subjects/model citizens, not ruled by coercion.

During the 1780s, and in general right up to its demise in 1918, the Habsburg Monarchy applied military methods judiciously; unlike in the Russian Empire, civil and military administrations were almost always demarcated as separate domains. The stereotype of a rather lenient (or tolerant) Habsburg Monarchy in comparison to autocratic Russia is not entirely devoid of reality. Different models of administration marked one important point of distinction between the two polities.

Problems with bureaucracy and control were never fully resolved. Yet all the opprobrium heaped upon individual bureaucrats and the civil service as a whole should not conceal one crucial success of the entire enterprise: the bureaucracy became a reality seemingly impossible to erase. Even its most vituperative opponents did not question the need for such an institution per se. Joseph II, willing to negotiate certain aspects of it, never altered his commitment to a new form of administration. This innovation, and the new bureaucracy it engendered, remained the basis, however imperfect, of state organization till 1918.

Annexing Galicia

These administrative forms were put to the test numerous times in the eighteenth and nineteenth centuries. One of the first trials came as early as the 1770s, with the monarchy's eastward expansion proving a major challenge and turning point in the history of the imperial bureaucracy. Geopolitical growth also created new grounds for comparison between the Habsburg Monarchy and its European neighbors. In the three consecutive partitions of 1772, 1793, and 1795, the Habsburg Monarchy, the Russian Empire, and Prussia divided Polish territories, thereby bringing an end to one of the largest states in eighteenth-century Europe.[43] All three annexed large populations of Poles, Ruthenians, and Jews, each of these becoming a diaspora people with cross-border ties to other polities.

In 1772, Vienna participated in the First Partition of Poland, and annexed a large section of Polish territory. A new province emerged in the monarchy's eastern periphery. The Habsburgs had initially expressed no interest in the partitions, being primarily interested, rather, in Silesia, lost to Prussia some twenty years earlier. But as keen as Austria was to repossess that region, Prussia was equally determined to retain its recent gain. New Polish territories could compensate for recent Habsburg failures. The southern Polish lands provided direct access to Silesia and, with faded hopes of reclaiming that region suddenly revived, perhaps in the future the two neighboring regions could be exchanged.

When the partitions were first proposed, Empress Maria Theresa allegedly wept,[44] overcome with concern for the fate of the Poles, which, however, did not prevent her from moving ahead with gusto. "She cried, but the more she cried, the more she took," Prussian King Frederick mocked his Habsburg counterpart.[45] Austrian Chancellor Wenzel Anton Kaunitz, an advocate of aggressive foreign policies, endeavored to secure the best possible gains,[46] and in 1772, the Habsburg Monarchy annexed the largest of the three parts of Polish territory, including the city of Lemberg, eventually the new Habsburg province's capital. Though Kraków remained part of the Polish-Lithuanian Commonwealth, the monarchy annexed the strategically crucial salt mines in Bochnia and Wieliczka, situated in Kraków's immediate proximity. The Habsburg Monarchy also acquired Kraków's neighboring suburban region of Kazimierz, where most of the Jews of western Galicia resided.

Geopolitics was further complicated by religion. The fate of Polish Catholic souls was no minor concern in the Vatican. If divided, Polish territories and the Catholics therein subject to Russian and Prussian rule would fall to the perceived schisms of Orthodoxy and Protestantism. Well into the twentieth century, Polish intellectuals and historians have presented Poland as a major bastion of Catholicism in Europe, a buffer against the expansion of Orthodoxy; in the eighteenth century, it was perceived much the same way, and also as a bulwark against Prussian Protestantism. Despite opposing the partition, the Vatican supported Austria's involvement.[47] Pope Clement IV allegedly "wept bitter tears" over the fate of Poland and sought to the last

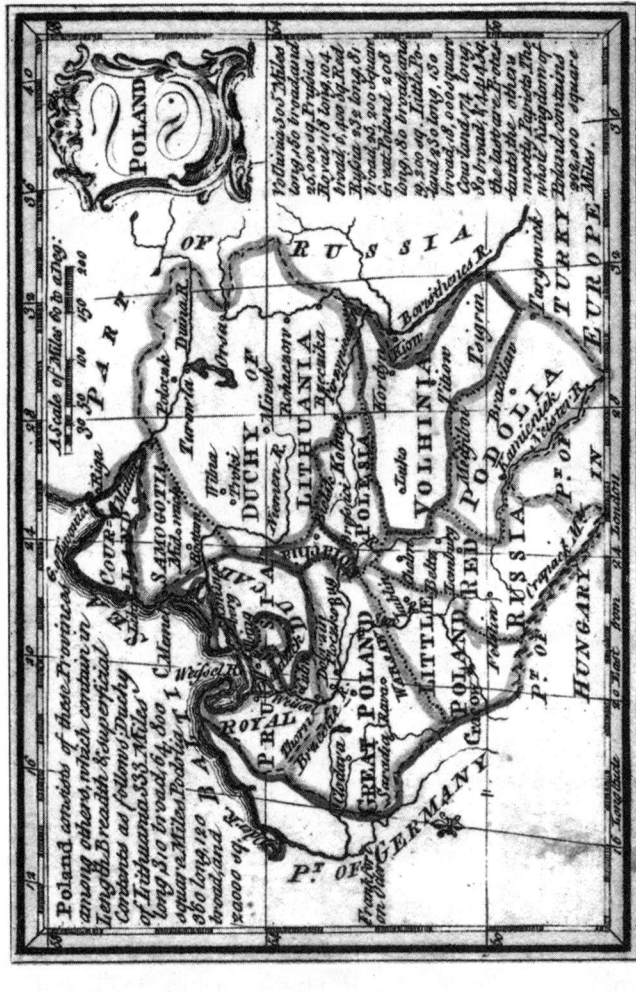

Map 1.2: Poland, 1758. Contemporary atlas map by Emanuel Bowen and John Gibson, London, showing the Polish-Lithuanian Commonwealth on the eve of the partitions. David Rumsey Historical Map Collection.

minute to prevent its partition.[48] He relied on the help of Maria Theresa, the only Catholic ruler among those interested in the Polish territories.

The integration of the new region promised to be problematic. Unlike their Prussian neighbors, Austrian statesmen had done nothing by way of preparation for the new annexation.[49] No precise maps of Poland were available in Vienna. Confusing geography generated confused policy choices. For instance, two small Galician towns, Jarosław and Przemyśl, were initial candidates for the provincial capital,[50] until it was realized that only Lemberg had the capacity and infrastructure (however limited) to meet Austria's political and administrative purposes.

The Habsburgs based their claims to the annexed territories on the historical links between this formerly Polish region and the medieval Kingdom of Hungary. In the twelfth century, the king of Hungary bore the additional title of *Rex Galatiae et Lodomeriae*.[51] The Austrian rulers rediscovered this historical heritage, reviving the long-forgotten name and establishing thereunder a new kingdom—the Kingdom of Galicia and Lodomeria.[52] In 1772 Austria annexed only the Galician part of the medieval kingdom, with Lodomeria, or Volhynia as it was actually known, becoming part of the Russian Empire. Citing the Hungarian connection to justify this annexation, Austrian officials initially intended to incorporate Galicia into Hungary, which seemed to make sense administratively and due to certain shared characteristics. Both Hungary and Galicia claimed high percentages of nobles within their general populations, and both had considerable Jewish minorities as well. But the option of annexing Galicia to Hungary was discarded precisely because of these similarities: a united Hungary and Galicia could represent an even stronger political challenge to the Habsburg dynasty than that already posed by the Hungary, the only region in the monarchy which, before 1772, had retained the status of kingdom.[53]

The administrative organization of the province was further complicated by conflicting jurisdictional notions. Joseph II favored the model of the Habsburg hereditary territories—the Austrian lands and Bohemia—which in the 1770s were governed uniformly by the Austrian-Bohemian Court Chancellery.[54] Kaunitz, however, opposed the accumulation of disparate territories—in this case, old Bohemia and new Galicia—under the auspices

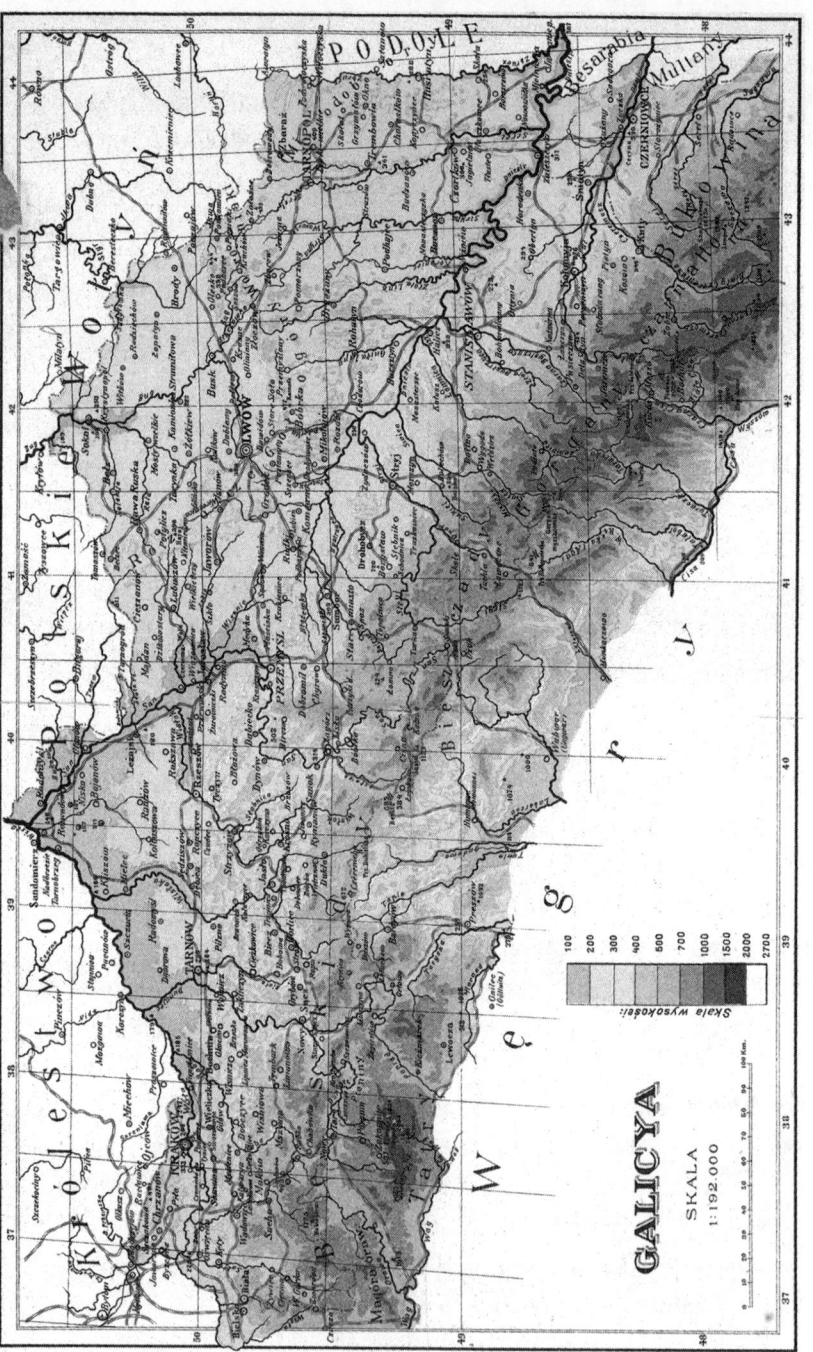

Map 1.3: Galicia under the Habsburgs. Map from 1918 by Stanisław Majerski, Lwów, showing Galicia as an Austrian province between Russian-ruled Poland to the north and Habsburg-ruled Hungary to the south. Polish National

of that institution; from 1772 to 1774, the new province remained under the jurisdiction of the State Chancellery. This jurisdictional placement revealed the particular status of the new province, signaling that its annexation was viewed with uncertainty even by key administrators at the Habsburg court, who had, moreover, concerns regarding differences between Galicia and the rest of the monarchy. Until this new eastern province could be integrated into Austria's institutional structures, and its contrast with the Habsburg realm as a whole made less striking, Galicia would bear a somewhat nebulous status—something between foreign territory on the one hand, and nonhereditary region on the other.

As head of the State Chancellery, Kaunitz played a key role in creating new structures of governance in Galicia from 1772 to 1774. The first major revision of the province's administration came in 1774 when, as an improvement measure, Joseph II ordered the establishment of a separate Galician Court Chancellery in Vienna. In 1776, however, the Galician Court Chancellery was liquidated, and the province was placed under the jurisdiction of the Austrian-Bohemian Court Chancellery. The administrative reform reflected a change in the status of Galicia from a temporary annexation to a permanent province.[55] The Galician Court Chancellery was re-created in 1797 and liquidated once more in 1802, its foundation and subsequent dissolution motivated by considerations similar to those from the 1770s. A separate chancellery was a concession to the province, as it implied its autonomous status within the central administration, resembling that of Hungary. Its creation was driven solely by administrative considerations, as part of Vienna's efforts to improve the government of the largest province. Within years, it became clear that this new administrative configuration was not only no more efficient than the previous one but that it also produced additional chaos. In 1802, therefore, the province was reintegrated into the centralized administration of the Austrian-Bohemian Court Chancellery.[56]

These institutional experiments vis-à-vis Galicia underscore the Habsburg Monarchy's uncertainty regarding administration as a whole. In eighteenth-century Europe, the concept of civil or political administration as we know it today was still in the making. Galicia gave rise to broad organizational questions: Should political administration, the judiciary, and trade be handled by the same institutions, or should they be separate domains? Where is the line between domestic and foreign policy? Should different regions be governed by separate institutions, or combined under the jurisdiction of one authority? These were questions facing the monarchy in general; but with regard to Galicia, they were particularly complicated by Vienna's lack of knowledge of the province, and by differences between this territory and the rest of the empire.

Local administration, too, underwent numerous changes over the years. Only one principle remained unchanged: Galicia always formed a separate province, governed by the Gubernium in Lemberg. The Galician Gubernium was first created in 1772. In 1795, with the annexation of more Polish lands, a new West Galician Gubernium was founded, with its center in Kraków. In 1803, the two Gubernia were united, with the seat in Lemberg. The distribution of districts and their centers was another problem to resolve. When first annexed, Galicia was divided into fifty-nine districts, all under the jurisdiction of six larger administrative units. In 1776, the number of districts was cut to nineteen, and in 1782, to eighteen.[57] Each of these administrative reforms—the foundation and liquidation of the Galician Court Chancellery, changes in the number of districts, and the corresponding shuffling of officials between Vienna, Lemberg, and Kraków—were contingent upon each other. Most of the changes confused contemporaries as much as they now do historians. Crucial for our purposes, however, is not administrative tinkering per se (which was hardly limited to this province), but the uniqueness of this experimentation in light of the specific attitudes some Austrian officials and intellectuals harbored toward Galicia during the 1770s and 1780s.

Polish Civilization

After its annexation, Galicia became a laboratory of Habsburg reforms. Rulers sought, as Larry Wolff has shown, to shape a piece of geography into a particular administrative and political unit; they discovered in Galicia their tabula rasa, and meant to mold the region into the empire's master province, transforming premodern alleged barbarism into an enlightened ideal.[58] Galicia provided a unique case where any reform could be tested from scratch. Maria Theresa best revealed the political mood at court when she declared her wish "to organize Galicia on an entirely new basis, and not to imitate the mistakes that Austrian officials had committed in other regions of the monarchy."[59]

It was, of course, one thing to imagine fresh opportunities for reform from Vienna, and quite another to encounter an ancient Polish province face to face. Galicia could no more be a tabula rasa than any other place of human habitation. Poland-Lithuania represented a different political culture, one based on republican governance—the only state in continental Europe at the time that retained a parliamentary political model and did not endorse absolutist rule.[60] Prevailing Polish political thought of the period considered monarchy, or central government, as something to be limited and controlled.

The Polish parliament—the Sejm—was a key political institution from the Middle Ages onward. It had been in decline for centuries before 1764, as sessions had become irregular, and intervals between them sometimes reached decades. Yet the year 1764 opened a new era in the history of Polish parliamentarism. The Coronation Sejm of that year launched a period of reforms in the Polish-Lithuanian Commonwealth by voting some key legislation. Historians estimated that as many as 180 decrees and laws were approved by the Sejm in 1764 alone.[61] One of the most important of them concerned the limitations on the *liberum veto*, a procedural device that required each decision to be passed by unanimous vote. The *liberum veto* was not abolished entirely, but after 1764 some of decisions could be passed by a majority vote.

The Polish nobility had played a key role in this political system, as that estate alone exercised the right of political participation. Nobles furthermore held authority over Poland's administration, which was organized on the regional principle. The concept of a professional bureaucracy, which became a core of Austrian reforms in the period under discussion, was both foreign and novel to Polish administrators. The anomalous nature of the Polish system extended to the nobility itself; for instance, nobles were proportionally more numerous in Poland than elsewhere in Europe. They enjoyed unprecedented political privileges, public service and office being their exclusive preserve.[62] In intra-estate terms, they rejected hierarchies, espousing the complete equality of all nobles, differences in individual, social, and financial status notwithstanding. This equality was a myth, but the myth itself revealed differences between nobles in Poland and elsewhere in Europe.[63] Nowhere else did nobles play as important a role as they did in Poland.

For centuries, Poles, Ruthenians, Jews, and Armenians had shared space in Galicia, despite occupying different social and political statuses. Most nobles regarded themselves as Poles. Peasants, by contrast, were mixed: Ruthenians, for example, formed a majority in southeast Poland, annexed to Austria in 1772. Not only did Ruthenians and Poles speak different languages, they also belonged to different churches: Poles were predominantly Roman Catholic, while Ruthenians were Uniates, adherents of the church that had emerged as a result of the Union of Brest, whereby part of the Ruthenian (formerly Orthodox) clergy concluded a pact with Rome. Formally subordinate to the Vatican, the Uniate Church retained many of the Orthodox traditions, and in Galicia, membership in it almost invariably identified one as Ruthenian, an association as close as that between Roman Catholicism and Polishness. Jews constituted about 10 percent of the population, which matched the historical development of Poland as a whole; indeed, as Gershon David Hundert notes, "the ancestors of about 80 percent of [modern] world Jewry lived in the Commonwealth of Poland-Lithuania in the eighteenth century."[64] Poland's Jews had become part of the local economy, playing an indispensible role as mediators between peasants and noble landowners. Often described as a Jewish paradise, Poland-Lithuania allowed for unprecedented freedom, granting rights prohibited to Jews in other parts of Europe. Another important minority in Galicia was its Armenian community, prominent in the region since the Middle Ages. Each of these different groups occupied distinct quarters in the center of Polish Lwów, and continued to do so in Austrian Lemberg.

When Joseph II first journeyed to Galicia in 1773, his carriage allegedly became stuck in the local mud.[65] He reported his first impressions back to Vienna: "I can already tell that we will have to perform an immense quantity of work here. Everything is confusing, and the spirit of the country is really horrible."⁶⁶ For his part, the Swiss-born traveler Franz Kratter characterized the region as "a remote and hidden corner of the Earth."⁶⁷ Bearing a law degree from Vienna, Kratter had sought a position at Lemberg's newly reopened university, but without success;⁶⁸ bitterly disappointed, he produced one of the eighteenth century's most detailed, and at the same time most fault-finding, descriptions of the region and its people. Another contemporary wrote off Galicia as a "horrible and poor land."⁶⁹ In general, its dwellers rather than its geography came in for particular critique: "Galicia could be a paradise were it not inhabited by its people, its poor peasants, rude nobles, and uneducated priests."⁷⁰

These early perceptions were of course largely shaped by prejudice. Travelers from Western Europe assessed Poland-Lithuania via preconceived ideas of culture and civilization, especially those foregrounding urban space. Boundaries between town and countryside, for example, had never been as sharply defined in Poland as in Western Europe. Towns in old Poland were often reserved for commoners, burghers, and Jews, while Polish aristocrats resided in the countryside.⁷¹ Polish towns were in decline partly because nobles looked down on commoners, and thus hindered the prosperity of cities, as Karin Friedrich has demonstrated through the example of Prussian Poland.⁷² In any event, the grim descriptions cited above notwithstanding, Joseph II had a rather optimistic view of the new acquisition, hopeful that Galicia could become a model province for the reforming monarchy, an inspiration for other imperial regions.⁷³

The Polish-Lithuanian Commonwealth, meanwhile, existed for another twenty-three years after its first partition; and while Austrians were busy with designs for a perfect province, Polish statesmen and intellectuals worked feverishly in the hopes of regaining their country's integrity. The eighteenth century proved a highly paradoxical period in Poland's history. This was a time, on the one hand, of devastating political catastrophes, resulting ultimately in national demise; but it was also a period of intellectual revival, of some of the most progressive reforms in Polish history, and in the history of Europe as a whole. In 1768, Polish nobles had approved the country's first budget.⁷⁴ The mandatory taxation of manorial estates was introduced, an innovation that might have radically altered Poland's finances had the country survived. Meanwhile, a new political system in the spirit of centralization and, in some measure, popular rather than noble-based republicanism, would more closely resemble contemporary European models of government. Reforms in the still extant Poland-Lithuania were more far-reaching than efforts concurrently under way across the border in Austrian Galicia. The basic fact that Galicia missed what was perhaps the most progressive, albeit tragic, period in Poland's history has remained engraved in the Polish historical imagination ever since.

Poland-Lithuania, moreover, experienced its own Enlightenment, though this intellectual tradition remains largely unknown to the rest of Europe.[75] One key fruit thereof was the country's educational reform,[76] whereby Latin was replaced by Polish, and new institutions were linked in a strict hierarchy, from primary schools up to universities and such professional institutions as military academies. Headed by the leading Polish intellectual of the era, Hugo Kołłątai, the Educational Commission in 1773 became the first ministry of education in Europe.[77]

The Austrian and the Polish Enlightenments evolved concurrently with one another, each occupying a rather marginal position with respect to the Europe-wide Enlightenment. Despite the preponderance of French models in the general conception of this phenomenon, however, Gallic influences upon the Austrian Enlightenment were rather limited, and even weaker in the intellectual tradition of the Polish Enlightenment. Catholicism was an essential aspect of Poland's political culture, uncontested even as the Enlightenment manifested itself in radical or anticlerical fashion elsewhere. Unlike in France, few in Poland questioned the role of religion and the Church and, as in the Habsburg Monarchy, major debates of the Polish Enlightenment took place within, rather than outside of, the sphere of religion.[78]

Yet another Enlightenment, the Jewish Haskalah, arrived in Galicia from Germany via Austrian lands. Jewish Enlighteners—the maskilim—came to Galicia from Vienna, Berlin, Trieste, and beyond, bringing with them a modern understanding of Jewish culture and civilization, and espousing Jewish integration into Gentile society. Largely educated in various German-speaking institutions in Central Europe, the maskilim also brought the

German language as an instrument of progress and modernity. Austrian and Jewish Enlighteners shared a common language, as well as certain common goals, among them the integration of traditional Polish Jewry into German-speaking society.

Galicia, then, albeit modernized by Austrian Enlighteners, in fact lived through several different Enlightenments. Polish influences were always important, but the Jewish Enlightenment arrived in Galicia not from Poland but Germanophone Europe. After 1772, Austrian bureaucrats added their German language and diverse backgrounds to Galicia's socio-cultural complexity. Officials dispatched by Vienna would have to make sense of their lives and careers in an entirely new and unfamiliar region, and this encounter between Austrianness and Polishness would be complicated, often traumatically so, for Austrians and Galicians alike.

TWO

Civilizers at Work

1772–1794

From 1772 on, hundreds and thousands of Austrian bureaucrats from across the Habsburg Monarchy moved to Galicia. Some came from neighboring Bohemia, but many others traveled great distances from Italian regions, Hungary, and Illyria (modern Croatia). Educated in German, most conversed privately in a variety of other languages—French, Italian, Czech, or Dutch. They all arrived in Galicia aiming to bring a new political culture to the formerly Polish region, thereby integrating it into a reforming monarchy.

In September 1772, Johann Baptist Anton Count von Pergen moved from Vienna to Lemberg, having been recently appointed first Austrian governor of Galicia. Following some worrisome signs of political and administrative shortcomings, and his own pleas for transfer, he was relieved of his duties and recalled in early 1774. In 1777, Joseph Karl von Brigido arrived from Capua via Trieste, Graz, Laibach, and the Banat. He became governor in 1780, serving a good fourteen years until his dismissal (on corruption charges) in 1794. Brigido's native culture was Italian; his first language was German; part of his family was Czech; his residence was (at one time) Polish. His politics, of course, was Austrian; for all his different identities, above all Brigido was defined by his loyalty to the Habsburg dynasty.

Pergen and Brigido had different backgrounds and working patterns, and they demonstrated different attitudes toward Galicia. Pergen had one of the shortest tenures as governor, supervising in the brief period of 1772–74 the establishment of the province's new Austrian administration and bureaucracy. Brigido held one of the longest governorships, and headed Vienna's efforts in perfecting the new administration. While Pergen had been assigned to enforce Austrian practices and institutions, Brigido, due to the force of circumstances, spent much of his energy revising earlier policies and adjusting the institutions installed by his predecessor. Pergen and Brigido were both expected merely to carry out central decisions handed down from Vienna; but each, it turned out, had his own ideas of government and administration. They developed their own social and political networks, and intervened in policymaking with initiatives that sometimes undermined the very core of central legislation.

The two governors left different legacies with respect to Galicia. Pergen found the region ungovernable, soon begging for a transfer that was eventually granted. Pergen moved back to Vienna and was replaced in Galicia by Andreas Hadik von Futak. Brigido in the meantime worked in other provinces and arrived in Galicia three years after Pergen's departure. There he was left to deal with political and economic chaos stemming partly from the Polish-Lithuanian period, but also from Austrian administrative failures. When he departed to Vienna seventeen years after his first arrival, he left behind a different Galicia—no longer a Polish tabula rasa, but rather a province with an Austrian political and architectural façade. Galicia acquired a distinct territorial identity within the monarchy; the Austrian bureaucracy there, meanwhile, took on a life of its own, as a new institution only remotely resembling Vienna's original intentions.

Pergen and Brigido each approached Galicia with certain prejudices to some extent engendered by the Enlightenment. The history of their governance is also a story of Vienna's attempt to combat purported backwardness and enforce civilization in an Austrian image. The integration of Galicia, if successful, would imply its inclusion into German-speaking Central Europe. This project was executed only in part, but all of the processes involved—Enlightenment-inspired reforms, the integration of the new province, and the remaking of European boundaries—were contingent upon each other.

Between 1772 and 1794, these bureaucrats established a connection between Galicia and Europe that was different from what existed anytime before or after. Pergen was bound to Vienna not only by his professional functions but also by personal ties. Vienna was where he learned politics, and he transported both the knowledge and the models thereof to Lemberg. Brigido's school of politics, by contrast, had been the Habsburg Italian borderlands and the Austrian Littoral; personal and professional ties to Trieste remained essential to him during his entire stay in Galicia. Both Pergen and Brigido were well aware of broader imperial currents beyond Galicia. Their decisions concerning the province were shaped by various personal motives—not least by career considerations—but also by the monarchy-wide political situation, and by the career tracks of their many colleagues between Trieste and Lemberg.

The years under Pergen and Brigido also exemplified key patterns of Austrian rule in Galicia in the eighteenth and nineteenth centuries: the stereotypes informing policy decisions; the tensions between Vienna and Lemberg manifesting themselves already in 1772 and worsening thereafter; the expectations failing to materialize. Failures, however, are often more conspicuous than successes, and we should not lose sight of the fact that the early years of Austrian rule produced certain important achievements. Despite numerous and almost desperate reports of administrative dysfunction, Austrians did succeed in building new institutions and enforcing a new bureaucracy, however imperfect both proved to be. The most important success, defying the perception of widespread ineptitude, was that Galicia remained part of the monarchy from the 1770s through 1918, which was in itself a major achievement of the same ostensibly dysfunctional bureaucracy.

First Governor

The years 1772–73 were crucial for the history of Austrian Galicia. Over the course of a few months, Polish offices were abolished, new Austrian institutions were created, and German-speaking officials replaced most Polish cadres. In this period, Galicia was at the center of Austrian policymakers' attention. Some of the decisions reached in these early years of imperial rule would shape the region through 1918.

One such decision concerned the composition of the Austrian bureaucracy in the new province. Between 1772 and 1773, Maria Theresa, Joseph II, and Kaunitz agreed upon one fundamental principle in the development of the new bureaucracy, namely, they proposed to exclude Polish nobles from Austrian institutions almost entirely, with officials recruited from outside Galicia instead.[1] The decision to restrict the employment of Poles was concealed by elaborate rhetoric conceptualizing the new bureaucracy as essentially Austrian and German-speaking, marked by a definitional loyalty to the Habsburg dynasty. Only a few low-ranking positions remained accessible to Poles.[2]

Personnel policy reflected Vienna's broader plans. Shaping Galicia into a model province of a reforming monarchy required a large number of qualified Austrian officials, persons having achieved, in particular, some successes in other regions. Chancellor Kaunitz foregrounded these expectations, pledging to furnish the new province with the highest-caliber exemplars Austrian officialdom had to offer. Career records and qualifications thus became key criteria; all candidates for top positions were selected from a cohort of prominent officials who had evinced administrative and political talent in other parts of the monarchy. Lower-level administration, however, was problematic, defying Joseph II's expectations of perfection. In any event, certain patterns inaugurated by Austria's Enlightenment-minded rulers in 1772 remained unchanged through 1867, and with some revisions, until 1918: all governors of Galicia were selected from a pool of highly qualified candidates who (prior to 1867) had had their first career successes elsewhere in the monarchy;[3] and bureaucrats from Bohemia formed a visible presence in the lower administration of the Galician districts.

The first governor, Pergen, was one of the most prominent imperial officials ever employed in Galicia.[4] Born in Vienna in 1725, he was the son of a president of the Lower Austrian administration. At age twenty-two, he began serving in the diplomatic corps, first of all in the Austrian mission in Mainz. In 1748, he moved to London as a principal aide to the head of the Austrian chargé d'affaires there—an impressive success for a young diplomat. In 1753, at age twenty-seven, he was appointed Austrian minister to the Holy Roman Empire, responsible for the relationships between the Habsburg

Monarchy and a variety of German states. Between 1757 and 1763, during the Seven Years War, he administered the territories that the Monarchy conquered from Prussia. In 1766, he moved back to Vienna, where he joined the State Council (the emperor's advisory body) and concurrently served as vice president of the Austrian State Chancellery. Shortly thereafter, he was appointed head of the Austrian and Dutch departments in the chancellery. Pergen seems to have enjoyed Kaunitz's support, and in the late 1760s, Joseph II also valued Pergen's opinion on Austria's role within the Holy Roman Empire.[5]

In 1769, Pergen was appointed head of the Oriental Academy in Vienna, a diplomatic institution that prepared Austrian ambassadors for service in the east. He received instructions to improve the academy's financial standing and revise its curriculum to better match the needs of a modernizing state. Pergen's involvement in education was perhaps a sign of the ongoing special favor he enjoyed in comparison to his colleagues at court. His assignment to the academy indirectly paved the way for his subsequent appointment to Galicia.

Pergen used his new position in the academy as a launch pad to intervene in broader reform efforts, specifically education.[6] He had long become convinced of Prussian organizational superiority, one of a cohort of Austrian statesmen espousing the replication of Prussian models in the Habsburg lands. In 1770, Pergen presented for the consideration of the empress a comprehensive program of educational reform, proposing the foundation of a tri-level system that would, for political and economic reasons, target only the upper classes and exclude the poor. All instruction excepting in medicine would be conducted exclusively in German. Most importantly, he proposed a radical change in the status of the Catholic Church. Before the 1760s, Catholic priests had formed a majority of school teachers; Pergen insisted on firing all of them, clearing vacancies for lay teachers instead.[7]

Debates about the role of the Catholic Church in education, and in the political system generally, had commenced before Pergen; but his demand that all Catholic priests be removed from schools went beyond the suggestions of most of his contemporaries. Additionally, he proposed replacing the dismissed personnel with teachers recruited from Prussia.

Such schemes, of course, implied a highly unfavorable view of Austrian Catholics as compared with Prussian Protestants, which led to an embarrassing setback. In November 1771, the empress issued a formal invitation to Friedrich Justus Riedel from Erfurt, the first German to arrive in Vienna as part of the education reform project.[8] Three German colleagues followed shortly thereafter. The news of the arrival of German professionals caused discontent among those members of the State Council reluctant to jeopardize the status of the Catholic Church in the monarchy. Later the same year, Maria Theresa reversed her decision and advised Pergen to send all four invitees back to the German states. Pergen's reform plans were buried for good; he was dismissed from the State Council, receiving a relatively minor and nominal position in the Lower Austrian administration—quite a comedown from his earlier status as member of the State Chancellery. In 1772, Kaunitz weighed candidates for the appointment of Galicia's first governor, and his choice eventually fell on his one-time protégé from the State Chancellery; on 29 September 1772, Pergen arrived in Lemberg.[9] Whether his appointment was in any way connected with his previous involvement in education remains an open question; in any event, the new position carried some political importance. Historian Franz Szabo has argued that Pergen's assignment to Galicia should be seen as a sign of Kaunitz's favor.[10] His German colleague Horst Glassl, by contrast, deemed Pergen's appointment a career setback.[11] Long before such scholarly assessments were made, Pergen himself seemed to have considered his new assignment as something of an exile.

By appointing Pergen as head of the Galician administration, Kaunitz, Maria Theresa and Joseph II affirmed their intention of abiding to the principles of civil administration. In designing such an administration, they had no recent models to rely upon. Before Galicia, the Habsburgs had annexed territories from the Ottoman Empire—southern Hungary and Transylvania, during the 1680s, and the Banat in 1718—all conquered as a result of Austro-Turkish wars, so that the Austrian army was stationed in these regions for years after the annexation. More importantly, the military component became dominant in the new administration: practically all officials in the new administration of the Banat were recruited from Habsburg German-speaking territories. Most had previously served as army officers and had no experience of civil administration before their appointment.[12]

Galicia on the Russian-Austrian frontier never posed dangers similar to those of the Austrian-Ottoman borderland. The Austrian army was stationed in Galician territory for some months during 1772 and 1773, but the building of an efficient civil administration remained a priority. Galicia was the first new annexation in centuries whose administration did not involve the army.

In Lemberg

The new governor came to Lemberg alone, leaving his family behind. Many in Vienna considered Galicia backward and uncivilized, and Pergen shared this belief; Lemberg was, in this view, not a proper place for his family. Meanwhile, he received a generous allocation that covered his moving expenses and his two households—that in Vienna, and the new one in the exilic provincial capital.

After Pergen's arrival in Lemberg, Vienna took the opportunity to celebrate the official establishment of Austrian rule. A grand ceremony was organized on 4 October featuring the participation of Galician Polish aristocrats. The pomp and circumstance, however, concealed the broader mistrust simmering between the Austrians and the new province's local population. Polish troops had evacuated the city of Lwów only weeks before Pergen's arrival, and at least some Poles looked upon the founding of the new Austrian administration in disbelief.[13]

It was perhaps not until his arrival in Lemberg that the governor realized all the difficulties that loomed before him and his colleagues, and that would do so for years to come. Pergen's early reports (1772–73) gave voice to many of the stereotypes of Galicia in force well into the twentieth century. In his first report to the Court Chancellery, Pergen described the overall situation in the new province in two words: "very bad."

> The current situation of the land is very bad, and efforts to build a good government will run into various difficulties. The people have been corrupted by the Russians and the Confederates.[14] The

clergy and the nobles enjoy unlimited freedom. Here no one knows of the *Rusticalis* [a land tax], and no contributions have ever been enforced here as well. . . . [I]n some [cities], Jews outnumber everyone else.¹⁵

In Lemberg, Pergen arranged for meetings with local elites, starting with the major ecclesiastical dignitaries representing the Roman Catholic, Uniate, and Armenian churches. He also received prominent Galician Polish aristocrats. Weeks after assuming his new duties, Pergen conveyed his impressions to Vienna:

> I have tried to meet the most important members of the clergy and win them for Austria. I must admit that I particularly appreciate the Armenian Bishop Augustynowicz, who is such an honest and highly respected man that he serves as a model for imitation for many others. . . . The Archbishop Sierakowsky, who is also a senator, did not come to see me, and only after many others pointed out his behavior as unacceptable did he finally appear for a meeting. The local Greek bishop is a bon vivant and . . . an intriguer. The bishop of Przemyśl, Kiersky, is familiar to you and I could not add much more.¹⁶

The attitudes of the Galician elites to their new rulers varied greatly. In 1772, Austrian officials and Polish nobles regarded the annexation as only temporary, anticipating further developments: the former hoping to enter into negotiations with Prussia over a potential exchange of Galicia for Silesia; the latter anticipating the restoration of Poland-Lithuania in its former boundaries. None of these schemes materialized, but right after the annexation the Austrians and the Galicians alike existed in a state of suspension. Borders between different parts of Polish territories remained open for years after the initial partitions, allowing some members of the Polish nobility to observe the developments in Austrian Galicia from outside. At least some of them rented out their estates, and collected incomes while residing someplace else, for example, in Warsaw (which before 1793 remained the capital of the Polish-Lithuanian Commonwealth). Some in

Galicia tried to exploit the confusion that ensued after the partitions for their own benefit. Several prominent Polish aristocrats, for example Tadeusz Dzieduszycki, expressed their willingness to cooperate with the Austrian authorities.[17]

A least some of these aristocrats had long expressed their frustration over Poles' inability to produce a viable political system even at a time when the survival of their state was at stake. None seemed to have rejoiced at the partition of Poland-Lithuania, yet sentiments stressing the gradual decline of the Polish state prior to 1772 and Polish responsibility for the collapse ran strong among sections of the Polish elite.

This is not to deny the trauma that many of these nobles experienced as a result of the partitions. Yet cooperation was an integral aspect of transition from one system to another in a situation when a violent confrontation would offer few or no benefits. Antagonism, when it ensued, oftentimes focused not on Austrian rule but rather on mechanisms of its implementation. In their complaints, Polish nobles targeted specific decisions of the administration, or very often office holders who carried out concrete actions, such as statistical surveys, military conscription, land measurement, and tax collection. Loyalty and opposition coexisted with one another as people constantly adjusted their allegiances to specific political situations.

The Ruthenian elites were small and politically marginal at the time of the annexation. It was often hard to distinguish a Ruthenian from a Pole, and belonging to a church became a key identification. Within a few years, practical Habsburg measures, such as support of the Uniate Church (renamed as the Greek Catholic Church), changes in the relationships between the noble landowners and the peasants cemented Ruthenian loyalty, making them eventually into one of the most loyal groups in the monarchy.

In a similar vein, Galician Jews based their perception mostly upon calculations of practical benefits and drawbacks. On the one hand, the Polish-Lithuanian Commonwealth was known for its tolerance toward the Jewish minority. On the other hand, annexation to the Habsburg Monarchy opened new economic markets to Jewish businessmen and industrialists.

Representatives of Jewish communities participated in the official welcoming of the first Austrian governor of Galicia. Many became disillusioned with Austrian policies designed to radically transform the status of the Jewish minority in this important borderland.

The reactions of the first Austrian bureaucrats to different groups in Galicia were equally fluid. Pergen's early reports reveal his contempt for Polish elites.[18] His attitude toward Jews was even more problematic, if not outright antagonistic. He immediately noted with dismay the visible Jewish presence in the provincial capital and other Galician towns.[19] Jews had long played a very important role in Poland's economy, and residency restrictions had been more lax in Poland than anywhere else in Europe. Despite often living among Christians, Poland's Jews stood out because of their distinct clothing and customs. The presence of "ever-wandering" Jews made a strong impression upon the first Austrian officials.

Pergen arrived in Galicia with a certain "civilizing" mission. The introduction of a new regime meant that Polish rebels were required to submit to the Austrian authorities; Ruthenians gained access to Austrian schools, and would subsequently take back to their countrymen the Austrian aims imbibed therein, assisting the enforcement of Austrian reforms. Jews faced a series of measures aimed at containing their demographic growth, residency, and movements; some Jews would be welcome to integrate into Austrian imperial culture, while others lived under the fear of expulsion.

Austrian plans required not only a sufficient number of qualified officials, but an efficient infrastructure as well—a category particularly lacking in the province. Roads were notoriously poor in Galicia, and most houses were made of wood with thatched roofs.[20] With construction regulations more or less unheard of, fires were not uncommon. Reporting to Vienna on substandard living conditions in Galicia, including Lemberg, Pergen highlighted several major issues requiring immediate attention, namely, where should Austrian bureaucrats be housed and Austrian documents stored, and how should correspondence be delivered between Vienna and Lemberg? How long would deliveries take? Postal stations were rare, and according to Pergen, not even Galicia's horses were up to par.[21]

Neither the governor's reports nor his attitudes, however, were entirely unreflective. Though critical of the Polish nobility as an institution, Pergen expressed some solicitousness toward individual nobles facing new hardships under Austrian rule. When nobles from other Polish territories were forced to return to their estates in Galicia in 1773, Pergen took a moderate stance in their defense. He claimed that requiring Poles to accept new citizenship before they had had the opportunity to renounce their fealty to the Polish king would amount to a judicial transgression: "By making those not yet relieved of obligations to their previous Sovereign submit to a new pledge, we force them to commit perjury."[22] Pergen granted general amnesty to all Polish nobles who had fled the region during the advance of the Austrian army.[23]

His reasoning concerned the particular geopolitical situation of the Polish territories, conditions that would remain until 1795. Following the First Partition, most Polish nobles enjoyed freedom of movement, a right they exercised, naturally, to their own benefit. With Austrian troops and civil officials moving into Galicia, at least some Polish landowners moved out, choosing to resettle in regions either remaining in Poland-Lithuania or annexed by a different state. In leaving Galicia, they were also removing therefrom money that could have been spent locally: "In this land of poverty," Pergen wrote in one of his reports, "in order to prevent the further outflow of money, we recommend the creation of favorable financial conditions for small and large landowners."[24]

During his first months in Galicia, Pergen fulfilled the expectations placed upon him by Kaunitz. He engaged with local elites and made efforts to improve governance, and generally confirmed the reputation of diligent administrator he had earned in his previous positions. This pattern, however, was soon broken. It took only a few months for Pergen's attitude to undergo a dramatic shift; precipitously, it seems, he came to the viewpoint that Galicia was generally ungovernable, that no effort he was capable of making would render the place more livable or orderly. Some answers to the question of how and why Galicia became such a hard case for Pergen reveal important nuances of the nature of Austrian administration in the new province.

Recruiting Candidates

A large number of men were required to carry out the tasks Vienna had set for itself in Galicia. How many bureaucrats were assigned to the new province? How many arrived? These questions are exceedingly difficult to answer with any precision. While we know little about the composition of the central bureaucracy (the most prominent personalities excepted), we know even less about the makeup and functioning of this institution at the provincial level.[25] Austria's eighteenth-century modernization was designed to be carried out by an "applied bureaucracy," and the reforms produced a "mounting number of clerks."[26] Yet contemporaries were, and historians remain, unclear as to just how fast that number in fact grew, and how many people were employed in the reorganized Austrian civil service. Imprecise definitions of bureaucracy complicated attempts to produce reliable statistics. The word "official" (*Beamter*) existed in the German language before the eighteenth century, but the idea of professional state services, as the Austrian historian Karl Megner has aptly noted, is a product of eighteenth-century reforms.[27]

Between late 1772 and early 1773, Pergen had few officials at his disposal.[28] Two of his colleagues, the advisers Törrock and Koczian, had come to Lemberg previously to make arrangements and prepare for the inaugural governor's arrival;[29] each would eventually play an important role in Pergen's career in Galicia. Two more secretaries, Franz Scheiner and Joseph Ignaz Knopp, arrived from Bohemia and Silesia respectively. In November 1772, Pergen requested two accountants and three *Kanzlisten*—the lowest-ranking, often unpaid functionaries within the administration.[30] In April 1773, the governor complained to Kaunitz of the meagerness of the Galician Gubernium's administration: a governor, vice governor, and three *Kanzlisten*; and in June, the Gubernium listed twenty-six staff members.[31] Personnel shortages in the Galician administration were not unknown to Vienna, in fact Joseph II acknowledged that Pergen had virtually no staff to assist him in his work.[32] In the earliest stages of Austrian rule, local offices across Galicia remained unformed, and a few dozen bureaucrats bore full responsibility for the entire province.[33] By late 1772, officials probably numbered some fifteen hundred governing a territory of approximately 81,900 to 89,669 square kilometers and some 2.48 million subjects.[34] Eventually, personnel numbers grew, but one thing remains certain: initially the administration of Austrian Galicia was severely understaffed.

Cadre shortages stemmed in part from Vienna's recruitment policies. Kaunitz personally reviewed and selected bureaucrats for Galicia. Standards were high, and the chancellor had specific qualities in mind: age, education, skills, and such languages as were required in the new province.[35] Command of languages, especially, became an important criterion for appointment to the subaltern administration; Kaunitz preferred bilingual or even trilingual individuals, fluent in German but also capable of communicating in one of the Slavic languages, preferably Czech, which would likely ease adjustment to life in Galicia.[36]

Such selectivity, however, rendered recruitment a long and grueling process. Well-qualified candidates were often unwilling to transfer to a land considered, from a Vienna-centric standpoint, remote. Those amenable to coming to Galicia, by contrast, often had questionable qualifications. Kaunitz finally concluded his selection process in September 1773, his 572-page report listing some sixty officials to head regional administrations under the Gubernium.[37] After months of work, the chancellor found it appropriate to explain the delay and express his frustration. He had reviewed the files of hundreds of candidates, yet was still unable to come up with an adequate number of bureaucrats suitable for employment in Galicia. Faced with this dearth, Kaunitz was bound to resort to candidates admittedly falling short of his expectations of perfection; not all those who matched his criteria accepted offers to take up posts in Galicia.[38]

There were, moreover, specifically financial complications. Kaunitz had hoped to supply a large number of bureaucrats at relatively low cost by skimping on salaries. But the chancellor's wager, in effect, on quantity over quality militated against his opposite aspiration for bureaucratic competence; minimal pay made it nearly impossible to attract to Galicia qualified candidates who had made their careers, and earned decent salaries, in Austrian state service before 1772. Few veteran officials would agree to the terms proposed. Those who accepted were usually younger bureaucrats with little or no experience in the administration, or if more experienced, those whose prospects for better posts elsewhere were dim. This is not to suggest that officials who ended up in Galicia were all inexperienced, unqualified, or corrupt. But statistically speaking, because of specific recruitment policies, the large number of new staff members required, and the widespread perception of the new province as a backwater, the proportion of problematic candidates was perhaps higher for Galicia than for other, more established regions.

All these initial problems notwithstanding, Kaunitz's endeavor to launch a model bureaucracy should not be underestimated. Even amid difficulties recruiting the most suitable candidates for Galicia, he never faced a shortage of applicants. His final list of candidates reveals the sheer extent of the effort to create an entirely new bureaucracy. The chancellor drew his applicants from the entire Habsburg Monarchy and beyond. Several Silesians—Joseph von Lippa, Ignacy von Bujakowski, Karl Thanhauser, and Karl Baron von Bess, among others—were appointed heads of Galician districts (fifty-nine altogether) in 1773.[39] Several other Silesians, namely Anton von Beck, Franz Fitek, Anton Singer, and Johan Theiner, filled in lower-ranking offices across Galicia.[40] Franz Böll, a lawyer and native of Strasbourg, knew no local languages, but was employed in the administration nevertheless. New appointee Johann König hailed from Saxony, while Ignazius Gruet was a native of Warsaw.[41] One Ruthenian, Leo (or Lev) Bratkowski, secured a position within this highly diverse group, becoming head of one of the district administrations.[42] Six officials from Habsburg Austrian territories, Bohemia, and Italy were put in charge of the six circles—administrative units above districts;[43] among these was Pompeius von Brigido of Trieste, a brother of Joseph von Brigido.

In their polyglotism and their mobility, Austria's first bureaucrats were more modern, in a cosmopolitan-professional sense, than most who succeeded them in the nineteenth century. They reflected the political complexity of the Habsburg Monarchy. Quite a few hailed from regions that did not belong to the Habsburgs. Pergen's earlier attempt to recruit Prussians into the service of the empire almost cost him his career, but in many less sensitive areas, non-Habsburg administrators were routinely employed in various Austrian provinces.

Austrian initiatives in the nascent Galician bureaucracy also revealed the first cracks between Vienna and Lemberg. While Kaunitz was in Vienna poring over lists of ideal candidates, in Lemberg Pergen was moving ahead with real-world solutions to the staffing problem. Given the difficulty of recruiting suitable officials from other provinces, and the general sparseness of Austrian bureaucrats in Galicia, the governor advised opening offices' doors to local Polish cadres.[44] He had originally regarded Polish nobles as unqualified for state service; yet as early as November 1772 he was arguing that Austrian administration in the province would be better off staffed with local Polish nobles than with German-speakers from other regions.[45] Without the court's direct authorization, he proceeded to hire a number of Polish officials. Empress Maria Theresa approved his choices, but insisted that Poles should be employed only at the bottom of the administrative hierarchy.[46] It is not entirely clear whether hiring a limited number of Poles as a concession to staffing exigencies was an element of official policy, or rather just a temporary adjustment to be subsequently reversed when possible.

Even when Pergen's strategies met with the general approval of his superiors, the overall situation in Galicia caused much concern in Vienna. Proper statistics regarding the province remained nonexistent; taxes could not be collected; borders were open, virtually uncontrolled. Administration seemed dysfunctional.[47]

In the summer of 1773, a commission headed by Count Pagnis arrived in Galicia from Vienna to assess the situation in the province, and specifically to evaluate the work of the Galician governor. In his report, the inspector noted that Pergen had completely withdrawn from his duties, and that "a young man, who currently serves at Pergen's house as his personal secretary, also carries out most of the work of the governor."[48] But the governor was not the only problem that Pagnis identified: the composition of the bureaucracy itself left much to be desired. Insofar as Kaunitz, rather than Pergen, played the decisive role in recruiting bureaucrats for Galicia, the chancellor, too, came in for blame for the disastrous state of Galician administration: instead of providing reliable candidates, he had "picked up people off the street."[49] Thus, while Pagnis's conclusions do not exonerate Pergen, they highlight a complex picture of which the frazzled provincial head formed only a part.

An efficient bureaucracy might have made up for the shortcomings of an individual governor; and a diligent governor might have been more efficient in creating a functional bureaucracy. In 1772 and 1773, Galicia was possessed of neither.

In any event, it was the governor's organizational failings that seemed the most glaring obstacle to modernizing the region. One of the reports described the cumbersome processing of papers, and Pergen's reluctance to engage in the process: "Count von Wratislaw had long before designed a plan for the administrative division of Galicia. The document was sent to Vienna and arrived back in Galicia on 22 June [1773]. Here it was reviewed by Hofrat Koczian, who on August 2 transferred it to Councillor Urbino and Count von Wratislaw, on the suggestion of the governor who never personally reviewed this plan."[50] This was a matter that required approval of the governor, who appeared particularly slow to react to major political and administrative decisions. Failure to reach agreement on the number and geographic configuration of districts in Galicia came to symbolize overall confusion.

Even if we take into consideration the sweeping or self-serving nature of such accusations, problems of early governance indeed seem ascribable, at least in part, to Pergen himself. His correspondence reveals an ever-growing frustration.[51] Pergen complained of being separated from his family and feeling overworked. Later, he seems to have favored leisure over matters of state, seeing to his allegedly ailing health by taking long holidays.[52] By late 1773, Pergen was openly begging for transfer back to the imperial capital. "I anticipate permission to depart to Vienna and to place myself at the feet of Your Majesty. I request a transfer and permission to return to Vienna; my honor and my conscience force me to such actions."[53] The situation in the region, he continued, rendered it impossible to maintain his peace of mind, and weighed heavily upon his family life.

Pergen's incompetence, moreover, became the subject of rumors in Galicia. During his 1773 trip to the new province, Joseph II noted the catastrophic state of affairs there, and described the governor as lazy and inept, blaming him for Austria's failure in the region thus far.[54] In 1774, Pergen was dismissed; he made no attempt, for that matter, to cling to his post, requesting release from service in Galicia both in petitions of his own and in responses to accusations of professional misconduct.

Pergen's appointment to, career in, and dismissal from Galicia highlight the peculiarities and paradoxes of Austrian administration in the province. He was the first in a cohort of highly respected officials to be transferred from various Habsburg regions to Galicia, which seems to have been, not a tabula rasa for him to inscribe on, but rather a magician's cabinet that transformed him. Once in Galicia, Pergen defied all expectations, and behaved as never before. Once flawless, his record was tainted by his professional conduct here; Galicia became a challenge he could not—or did not want to—overcome.

Joseph von Brigido: A Career in the Making

Pergen's early departure marked a turn in Austrian political strategies. Between 1772 and 1774, Kaunitz coordinated, in his capacity as head of the State Chancellery, the administration of the Galician Gubernium. But cooperation between Kaunitz and Pergen seemed anything but productive. In 1774, Galicia was removed from the jurisdiction of the State Chancellery. A new institution, the Galician Court Chancellery, was created in Vienna; between 1774 and 1777, Galicia would be administered separately from other provinces.[55] Unlike any other imperial territory, Galicia was placed under military administration, with Austrian General Andreas Hadik von Futak appointed governor. This episode of military rule, however, proved brief; Vienna remained committed to the model of civil administration. Since practically all structures were new, administrative practices across the monarchy appeared to be somewhat experimental. Institutions sometimes changed from year to year, as did the people who filled them.

In 1774, months after Pergen's dismissal, a new governor arrived in Galicia from the Austrian Adriatic.[56] Heinrich von Auersperg had worked in Graz, Trieste, and the Banat before coming to Lemberg. His pedigree was even more illustrious than his predecessor's. The Auerspergs, originally from Carniola (in modern Slovenia), supplied a great number of Austrian officials, including, in the nineteenth century, several ministers. But Auersperg's tenure in Galicia (1774–80) proved rather disappointing. He seemed to be more interested in culture than politics or administration. He authorized the opening of a theater in Lemberg, an event of great significance for the province; but while culture prospered under Auersperg, the economy stagnated, and the administration remained provisional.[57]

His rather limited achievements notwithstanding, Auersperg set an important precedent in the history of Galician administration. His appointment marked the first collective transfer of officials between the Italian Adriatic and Galicia. In moving from Trieste to Lemberg, Auersperg brought along several officials who would subsequently serve as his subordinates in the provincial capital. After 1774, such collective transfers became increasingly common. While the reason for such group rotations is not entirely clear, economic factors and the borderland status of the regions involved must have played an important role. Like Galicia, Habsburg Italy was a heterogeneous territory, featuring a mix of Slavs, Germans, Italians, and Jews who had lived together for centuries. Like Italy, Galicia would become one of the most important transfer points of the monarchy's international trade. The port of Trieste opened access to the Adriatic, an important avenue of eastward commerce; the Galician town of Brody on Austria's eastern border offered land access to the east and convenient connections to the Russian Empire. Another shared characteristic was that both in Galicia and in Habsburg Italy, the Austrian government planned to institute reform unilaterally, without the involvement of local elites.[58]

Joseph Karl von Brigido was one of a cohort of officials who moved along with Auersperg. He arrived in Lemberg in 1777 as vice governor of the Galician Gubernium and the same year received the title of Count. In 1780, he was appointed governor, retaining his post for fourteen long years. Brigido became one of the most important, and at the same time controversial, administrators in the pre-1867 history of Austrian Galicia.[59] He came to Lemberg during the reign of Maria Theresa and was appointed governor by Joseph II, at the height of the Austrian Enlightenment, of Austrian centralism and absolutism. He remained active during the reigns of Leopold II (1790–92) and Francis II, who became emperor in 1792. Brigido left Galicia in 1794, two years after the commencement of the French Revolutionary Wars.[60]

Unlike Pergen, who, during the early months of Austrian rule had run up against the problem of the sparseness of Austrian administration in Galicia, Brigido was part of a larger cohort of officials who, by 1777, had taken up offices of imperial governance across the province.[61] Among his colleagues in the Galician Gubernium were Count Heinrich von Auersperg, Franz von Hraubenthal Kuczera, and Jan Václav Margelik, all originally from Bohemia; Count Aloys von Ugarto and Count Anton von Apponyi from Hungary;[62] Johann Georg Urbino, another Italian; and Vinzent Guinigi, who traced his roots to the Habsburg Netherlands.[63] Within this international group of officials, Brigido was both typical and an anomaly. Like most of his colleagues, he had been subject to numerous rotations; but while most of his peers left Galicia at a certain stage of their careers, Brigido spent seventeen years in the province, departing it for good only upon retirement.

Like many of his colleagues, Brigido took a long and circuitous path to Galicia. He was born in 1732 in Capua, but his family moved to Trieste in 1754.[64] Brigido's father, Hieronim von Brigido, bore only the modest title of Freiherr, he and his five sons initially numbering among the lowest ranks in the monarchy's hierarchy of nobility; but the eighteenth century proved a time of remarkable achievements for the Brigido family, and of titles to match. Each of the five Brigido brothers—Joseph Karl (or Joseph Carlos), Johann Wenzel, Karl Ludwig, Michael Leopold, and Pompeius (or Pompeo)—received an excellent education and enjoyed successful careers.[65] Two—Joseph Karl and Pompeius—had careers in the Austrian civil service, both holding offices in Galicia. In 1773, Pompeius von Brigido worked in one of the Galician district administrations. He later served as governor of Trieste.

In 1752, Joseph von Brigido received a law degree from the University of Salzburg.[66] During the 1760s, he worked as both a councillor of the Inner Austrian Gubernium in Graz and a member of the Commercial Council of Carniola in Laibach.[67] He moved in 1775 to the Austrian military frontier, on the border with the Ottoman Empire, where he served as vice governor of the Habsburg province of the Banat of Temesvár.[68] In 1777, the Banat Gubernium was dissolved and its officials reassigned,[69] whereupon Brigido was appointed to Galicia.

In some respects, Brigido represented precisely the type of Austrian bureaucrat Kaunitz had envisioned as ideally suited for service in Galicia. He was a native speaker of German, but because of his Italian background he was personally familiar with the characteristics of a heterogeneous border region.[70] By the late 1770s, both Maria Theresa and Joseph II preferred Brigido over Auersperg as governor of Galicia.[71] In 1780, Joseph II personally supported Brigido's nomination for the governorship, pinning great hopes on this rising administrative star.[72]

As governor of Galicia, Brigido divided his time between Lemberg, Vienna, and Trieste, this last city constituting for him a second home, where most other members of his family still resided. This key seaport and its social networks also played an important role in Brigido's professional development. Upon coming to Trieste in the mid-eighteenth century, the Brigido family had quickly joined its social and political establishment. Joseph and several of his brothers maintained long-standing good relations with Count Karl von Zinzendorf, governor of Trieste in the same period as Brigido headed Galicia. Zinzendorf was particularly impressed, and infatuated, with the wife of one of the Brigido brothers, though it remains unclear which one. ("I met today with Madame Brigido, mother of everything that I know," Zinzendorf noted in his diary on 22 June 1776.)[73] When in Trieste, Brigido was a frequent guest at Karl von Zinzendorf's residence, where the two governors discussed politics and exchanged rumors. In the 1780s, Zinzendorf moved to Vienna, serving until 1788 as head the Taxation Commission responsible for land and tax reform in the monarchy.

The Auersperg family, and Count Heinrich von Auersperg in particular, also played a very important role in Brigido's career. As was the case with the Zinzendorfs, the Brigidos moved in the same Trieste social circles as the Auerspergs. "Madame Brigido," notes Zinzendorf, "became quite close with Madame Auersperg."[74] While these women developed social ties in Trieste, their husbands and brothers forged equally important professional connections in different offices across the monarchy. In all of his important appointments—in Trieste, Graz, the Banat, and Lemberg—Brigido worked as Auersperg's colleague and subordinate until he eventually replaced him as governor.

Social networks, and the discussions these officials and their associates held among themselves, shed light on professional appointments and the distribution of offices in the empire. Joseph II maintained that his new bureaucracy would embody pure meritocracy.[75] In reality, the administration of the monarchy remained, as it long had been, both meritocratic and at the same time highly personalized. In the 1770s, administrative positions were often distributed in the most personal of manners, with the criterion of "who you know" standing as potentially crucial. For instance, when Joseph II ordered the reorganization of the monarchy's administration in July 1777, Judas Reischach was appointed chancellor of Transylvania, at which point, in switching regions, he switched also his previous position as second chancellor of the Austrian-Bohemian Court Chancellery. "I will give it to Brigido, if Auersperg does not want it for himself," declared Reischach in a conversation with a friend.[76] Such horse-trading of positions was not uncommon.

In the years following 1772, the situation in Galician administration improved in some respects, but deteriorated in others. One essential problem—the shortage of bureaucrats—was addressed and, in a way, resolved. During his second trip to Galicia in 1780, his first as independent ruler, Joseph II encountered a situation entirely different from what he had observed in 1773: the bureaucracy in Galicia, so far from being meager, had now expanded to the point of excess. Now, the emperor believed, the province was populated with too many officeholders, and the overemployment was resulting in chaos.[77] Administration had become increasingly cumbersome; documents wended their way around offices, and decisions on them took an inordinate amount of time to reach. This state of affairs, Joseph II wrote, reflected broader problems with the bureaucracy in the monarchy at large.[78] But in Galicia the excess officialdom seems to have reached its nadir. Particularly frustrating was that personnel often lacked the skills requisite for administration, with governance correspondingly hindered. That year, Joseph II suggested reducing the number of non-Galician cadres occupying local positions, and employing in administration a larger number of Polish nobles instead.[79]

In a rare confluence, the will of the emperor happened to coincide with the popular mood in Galicia. The number of complaints against newly appointed officials increased in proportion to their growing number.[80] "Vienna became a much better place after all its bandits were sent to Galicia to work as Austrian bureaucrats there," Katarzyna Kossakowska, née Potocka, allegedly commented to Empress Maria Theresa.[81] Few in Galicia enjoyed access to the Habsburg court, let alone so lofty a status as would allow the making of such remarks to the sovereign's face; but many shared Kossakowska's view of Austrian bureaucrats in Galicia.

The disastrous quality of subordinate Austrian officials became something of a byword in Lemberg and Vienna. For example, the Gubernium official Guinigi, from the Habsburg Netherlands, had the dubious distinction of knowing all manner of languages—except German, Polish, and Latin, namely those used in Galicia's administration. Similarly, the head of the administrative district in Myslynice by the name of Messarosch arrived from Hungary bringing with him fluency in neither Polish nor German.[82] Meanwhile, Count Rudolf von Strassoldo, head of the district administration of Lemberg, made headlines by his addiction to gambling. He eventually absconded from Galicia with a large sum of money he had won at a Lemberg casino.[83] "German" bureaucrats had "nothing to gain, nothing to lose, and nothing to fear" in Galicia.[84]

Brigido was of course well aware of the problems plaguing Galician administration. As vice governor under Auersperg, he had witnessed no end of complaints, mostly filed by Polish nobles, against Austrian bureaucrats.[85] Like Joseph II, Brigido attributed some of the difficulties to the legacy of his administrative predecessors in Galicia; emperor and new governor alike had been particularly frustrated with Auersperg. Brigido held Heinrich von Auersperg responsible for the province's glaring lack of progress. In his six years as governor, Auersperg had done remarkably little; "he introduced the alcohol tax but accomplished nothing else," commented Count Sigismund von Gallenberg, a councillor of the Galician Gubernium.[86] Forced to revise the administrative division of the province, Auersperg had reduced the number of districts in Galicia, but decided to keep the number of officials unchanged. Crowded offices caused much administrative confusion, to say the least, as Joseph II noted in his 1780 report;[87] superfluous officials, maintained Gallenberg, were moreover depleting Austrian finances. Brigido could not have agreed more with such assessments. Even before becoming governor in 1780, he privately expressed contempt for all Austrian officials in the province, including Auersperg, who, Brigido claimed, had done Galicia more harm than good.[88]

Brigido no longer preoccupied himself with issues connected to the Polish-Lithuanian socio-economic legacy, at least not to the same extent as his two predecessors. He instead revised Austrian policies and decisions that had backfired between 1772 and 1780. In September 1780, Brigido reported to Vienna on the situation in Galicia. He asked and answered a question which by now had become an administrative commonplace: Does the current situation of the province correspond to initial expectations, and if not, why not?[89] He described the parlous state of Austrian administration in Galicia. Like Pagnis before him, Brigido saw trouble as stemming in large part not from Lemberg, but rather from Vienna. Austria's policies in the province, he argued, had numerous flaws; the initial decision to exclude Polish cadres, for instance, had caused more harm than good.[90] By its alien character, the German-speaking bureaucracy of officials from other Habsburg provinces created inevitable tension in relations between Austrian authorities and the local population; many of these bureaucrats, moreover, received low salaries, or none at all, and were hence especially prone to corruption.

The meager pay of Austrian bureaucrats had by now become a notorious problem throughout the monarchy. Financial difficulties were particularly grave in Galicia, where salaries were lower than elsewhere.[91] Because of the province's reputed backwardness, Brigido's colleagues in Vienna had assumed it must be cheaper to live there than in other regions.[92] But their calculations were incorrect; rents and the overall cost of living in Lemberg were comparable to those in Vienna.[93] In 1786, a family of three in the provincial capital was said to require an annual income of 1,098 gulden; typical families in the eighteenth century were often larger, and the average salary of a regional official was around 500 gulden.[94] Low salaries made it exceedingly difficult to attract well-qualified candidates for positions in Galicia.[95]

Top-ranking administrators, on the other hand, were rewarded generously for their services. In 1776, Governor Auersperg received an annual salary of twenty-four thousand gulden, plus a housing allowance.[96] But the amount of remuneration dropped precipitously with each step down the administrative hierarchy; for instance, the first councillor of the Gubernium, still a prestigious position at the time, earned the significantly lower sum of two thousand gulden. Such huge disparities in income could easily incite further discontent within the bureaucracy.

Brigido insisted that including local cadres, at least on a limited basis, could improve the overall political and economic situation in Galicia. Employing such personnel would help forge a better image of the Habsburg Monarchy among the local population;[97] it could, moreover, save money. Brigido was especially interested in Polish youth from relatively prosperous noble families. More or less financially self-sufficient, these Poles, the governor hoped, would have no need to maintain themselves through bribery and corruption, or at least, would be less inclined toward these vices than the Germanophone newcomers manning the bureaucracy over the previous decade.[98] Brigido personally reviewed the qualifications of bureaucrats employed at the district level. He also assumed exclusive responsibility for the appointment of officials in the province generally; no one could be hired except with his authorization.[99] He particularly stressed reconsidering the composition of the lowest rungs of governance. "Brigido believes that at this time it would not be advisable to employ foreign bureaucrats in place of local officials for the administration of Galician landowners' estates."[100]

Beginning in 1781, young and preferably prosperous Polish nobles were encouraged to apply for positions in the Austrian state service. In 1783, a commission investigating complaints about Austrian bureaucrats in Galicia proposed replacing low-qualified German-speaking bureaucrats with Polish nobles from the region.[101] The following year, Vienna eased its otherwise strict educational requirements for incoming bureaucrats, a concession targeting the recruitment of Galician Poles: those willing to enter the Austrian civil service were allowed a chance to pass specific exams without completing the usual preparatory curriculum.[102] Relatively few Galicians received degrees from Austrian institutions during the late eighteenth century, and by lifting strict accreditation requirements for candidates from the province, Austrian officials were removing a crucial obstacle to entry into the bureaucracy.

During the 1780s, Poles from Galicia received preferential treatment over German-speaking candidates from other regions in consideration for low-ranking positions in Galicia's administration.[103] In 1783, Jan Václaw Margelik, a former governor of Bohemia, was recruited by Vienna to conduct a comprehensive review of the administration of Galicia; his report (1784) focused especially on regional branches. A lengthy questionnaire, distributed among the regional offices, was designed to supply detailed information on the province. In his assessment of this data, Margelik's reviews of administrative employees were rather mixed. Some highly qualified officials, Margelik noted, shared their offices with complete illiterates. In his report, Margelik paid specific attention to the so-called *Nationalisten*, Polish nobles employed in the Austrian administration. In 1783, of sixty-three chairs and vice-chairs of district administrations, ten were Poles.[104] His assessment of these officials was no worse, and in some cases better, than of bureaucrats of any other ethnic background employed in Galicia. He commented favorably on such Polish officials as Wyszynski, Sierkowski, and Zulakowski, all serving in the administration of Galicia's Turka district.[105] Margelik also supported the gradual inclusion of local cadres into the province's administration.[106]

This is of course not to suggest that Brigido or Margelik harbored some specific ethnic preference for Polish candidates; the latter, in fact, later acquired a rather negative reputation in Galicia for his alleged hatred of Polish nobles and for forceful imposition of German culture and administrative methods.[107] But during the 1780s, both Brigido and Margelik seemed to value capable officials regardless of background; they especially appreciated command of local languages.[108] Each saw the benefits of including Poles as outweighing potential drawbacks.

Bureaucracy and Reforms

Brigido not only advocated forging a new personnel composition for the state service; he also hoped to achieve a more autonomous status for local bureaucracy with respect to Vienna. The governor had his own ideas of provincial governance, foregrounding especially autonomy, and as Derek Beales has argued, "strongly backed the local administration against the bureaucracy in Vienna."[109] As a result, relations between the imperial capital and Lemberg could become strained. In helping to secure a more independent role for provincial vis-à-vis central administration, and evincing thereupon a reluctance to comply with expectations and simply follow orders, Brigido also exemplified the tensions of the period of radical reform during the reign of Joseph II.

In 1780, Brigido was called to Vienna for a personal appointment with the emperor.[110] The subject of their conference was Joseph II's reform plans for Galicia. Here the emperor disclosed his intention to introduce a major land reform in the province, as part of a broader modernization of policy throughout the empire. Those who worked the land would be granted their personal freedom. (Most of Galicia's peasant population had been enserfed for centuries.) Still obliged to labor for landlords, peasants would be free to move and marry without permission. Joseph II also would impose new regulations governing peasant labor and compensation. Polish landlords, meanwhile, would be required to pay taxes on their land, initially set at 12 percent—a rate that would likely strike its payers as especially steep, considering they had never before been required to pay anything—and Joseph II planned to engage in further discussion concerning the mechanism of tax calculations and collection.[111]

Joseph II's project of peasant liberation was hardly altruistic; the plan, and agricultural reform generally, was like most of his innovations inspired by the financial considerations of the state.[112] Ensuring better control over especially his aristocratic subjects, he would at the same time create new sources of revenue for the monarchy's finances. Designed for the entire monarchy, the land reform would have more radical implications for Galicia than for any other Habsburg region. The proposed 12 percent land tax, for example, was in sharp contrast to the traditional Polish practice of landlords paying voluntary contributions.

Joseph II's land reform quickly came under attack from various members of the central bureaucracy. Composed mostly of aristocrats with close ties to their milieu across the monarchy, Austria's high officialdom opposed this radical assault on the traditional privileges of their class. Prince Ludwig von Kolowrat, head of the Austrian-Bohemian Court Chancellery, and Count

Fig. 2.1: View of Lemberg, 1772. Polish National Library, Digital Collection Polona.

Karl von Zinzendorf, head of the Taxation Commission (the same Zinzendorf who had earlier worked as governor of Trieste), both opposed the reforms, claiming that chaos and huge economic losses might result. Only one member of the Austrian-Bohemian Court Chancellery, Hofrat Eger, supported Joseph II's project of land taxation.[113] These political debates in the central offices, however, revolved around the old territories of the monarchy, and did not touch Galicia. Both Zinzendorf and Kolowrat focused their attention upon the core Habsburg territories, including Austria's German regions and Bohemia. They voiced no opposition to the proposed reforms in Galicia, a new province where Vienna, they believed, could proceed unilaterally, without considering the interests of local elites. The region that would be most affected by the reforms, thus, had no advocates in Vienna.

Even if the question of how the emperor's agricultural reform would go over in Galicia was to some extent ignored by the central bureaucracy, the plan drew the attention of bureaucrats in that province. Joseph Koranda, head of the Galician taxation office, became closely involved in the implementation of the planned reform. Before proceeding with Joseph II's measures, he described the potential complications as he saw them. Koranda insisted that liberating the peasants would lead to their further deprivation, as they could only survive within the existing social framework on land owned by nobles.[114] For his part, Brigido declared that any radical social changes required a functional and permanent administration, which—as Joseph II was all too aware—had not yet been established in Galicia.[115]

Opposition from the Galician Gubernium prevented the implementation of the reform as originally drawn up. Each piece of proposed legislation was promulgated in Galicia with significant modifications. None was fully implemented during Joseph II's reign, and all were reversed during its last year, in early 1790, or afterward by his successors. In 1782, peasants in Galicia were granted personal freedom, but most would see little change in the short run. On Brigido's insistence, Vienna agreed to make a very significant amendment to the Galician legislation: peasants would be allowed to leave their landlords only after finding other peasants willing to take their place.

Finding such replacements would be virtually impossible in those locations where most peasants were similarly bound to their land.

The tax reform proved equally difficult to carry out. The proposed regulation left many questions unanswered. It never became clear what exactly the 12 percent tax would entail: was it to be 12 percent of the estimated value of the land, or of the annual income the land could generate? Either way, the provisions remained vague. And in the meantime, they drew growing criticism from the bureaucrats responsible for their implementation and the noble landowners subject to them. The new tax regulation was scheduled to take effect in 1789, but it was never fully implemented.[116]

Disagreements between senior officials in Vienna and their subordinates in the provinces did not of course end with Joseph II's death. Defiance, insubordination, or simply lack of coordination among different branches of the administration remained endemic right up to 1918. After 1790, Viennese inspectors and Gubernium officials alike noted again and again in their reports the transgressions of provincial bureaucrats and their reluctance to comply with central decisions. In one report (1792), Galician Gubernium councillor Lezzeny reflected on the defiance of lower officials: "In today's Galicia, we get the impression that local bureaucrats represent the interests of the landowners and not their sovereign."[117]

Vienna's inability to carry out tax and agricultural reforms had long-term political consequences. Polish landlords retained their property, and their status remained largely unchanged amid Austria's would-be innovations. Because their economic domination was never fully broken, they found it that much easier to avoid the direct impact of other Austrian reforms. Relatively prosperous, noble landowners often enjoyed a superior status vis-à-vis Austrian bureaucrats. They retained their traditional social networks and some of their privileges; their children received education in Polish, French, Latin, and—less frequently—in German.

While Polish children went to study abroad, the project of introducing Austrian-German educational institutions suffered major setbacks. In 1774, Maria Theresa ordered the establishment of German-language schools in Galicia.[118] Each regional center in the province was required to have at least one Germanophone middle school as a preparation for the high schools.

Each of the provincial capitals, Lemberg included, would have a number of such high schools that led to the university. In 1781, Joseph II introduced mandatory primary education for children aged six to twelve.[119] German became the compulsory language of education in all subject areas except Latin and math.[120]

Mandatory primary education required a corresponding educational infrastructure. New schools also needed a large number of German-speaking teachers, who, like other Austrian bureaucrats, were to be recruited from other provinces. But school construction was a challenge, as was in many cases attracting Germanophone instructors to relocate to Galicia. Mandatory education for children created certain difficulties, moreover, on the land, where youngsters often constituted a vital part of the work force; time that could be spent working in the fields was often too valuable to a family to be "wasted" in the classroom. Polish elites were also reluctant to accept new schools, but from a different standpoint, viewing the forcible imposition of German education as a cultural-political assault.

During his inspection of Galicia in 1784, Margelik assessed the school situation in the province. His findings were rather bleak. "Why do high schools [*die Normalschulen*] not function properly in Galicia?" he inquired.[121] German-language schools were few and far between, and such as existed often remained empty for months. Attendance was a major issue; new schools were built in Przemyśl and Jarosław but their classrooms for a long time had no pupils.[122] Parents refused to send their children to the new institutions; in towns, where elites were accustomed to education in Polish or Latin, German schools were disparaged as an infringement upon personal liberties or ethnic pride, while on the land, where the populace was less in a position to value such education, children were needed for manual work. Thus, even where they succeeded in building schools, the Austrian authorities faced the task of forcing children to attend them. The situation in Przemyśl and Jarosław was difficult, but still worse in many other locations across Galicia; in 1783, for example, a single middle school in the town of Tarnów served the entire Tarnów region—and not a new German school at that, but an old Latin school that had survived from the Polish period.[123]

Despite initial difficulties with grade schools, the imperial authorities proceeded with the establishment of a German-language university. In 1784, Brigido participated in the opening ceremony and gave a speech in Latin before a large audience. The university was developed on the basis of an equivalent Polish institution that had first opened its doors in Lwów in 1661. Unlike its Polish predecessor, the new Austrian university was designed to prepare professional cadres for the monarchy's administration and disseminate German culture throughout the province. In his speech, Brigido described Austrian achievements in Galicia, stressing the successful building of German-language schools as a basis for the new university.[124] His laudatory remarks presented a sharp contrast to the picture of desolation and failure Margelik painted in his report the same year. The historical meaning of the shortage of German-language schools across Galicia can hardly be overstated; it meant the survival of Polish culture, tradition, and language. Even when German was declared the sole official language of administration and education, Polish and Latin continued to play important roles in other domains. Polish never disappeared from Galicia, and despite Vienna's plans from 1772 on, German never became the dominant language.

A number of the schools established with such difficulty in Galicia occupied buildings that had previously belonged to the Catholic Church and had functioned as churches or monasteries. During the 1780s, Joseph II launched a radical assault on the Church as an institution. Some religious orders, including the Jesuits, had been dissolved as early as the 1770s. In the 1780s, Joseph II ordered the nationalization of a large part of church-owned properties, including buildings and land. Before 1772, Polish Lwów had been home to fifty-seven churches and a number of monasteries adjacent to them;[125] afterward, at least some of this property was seen by Austrian officials as potential administrative infrastructure. In 1784, the former Jesuit college in Lemberg became home to the Gubernium administration. The Galician Diet held its meetings in the former Jesuit residence. Not all Church facilities were immediately available for use.[126] Brigido explained the delays as technical in nature, and insisted that the problems were temporary. While expropriating and renovating some buildings, the governor made an effort to preserve other churches and monasteries according to their original designations; thus Brigido saved the Bernardine Cathedral in the center of Lemberg, which was never converted, as some places of worship were, into a school or a warehouse. Without directly reversing central decisions, local bureaucrats intervened with important modifications.

In part due to complications in the field of education, German never became the uniform language of Galicia. The province operated in a number of languages—German, Polish, Latin, French, and Ruthenian—the status of which varied not only from year to year, but from situation to situation. This linguistic multifariousness affected the functioning of Austrian administration as well. Each imperial decree was initially issued in Vienna in German, and subsequently delivered to local bureaucrats in the Gubernia. Here the documents were numbered and passed along to personnel responsible for the matters concerned. Each document was also translated by members of the Gubernium's professional staff, a process that inevitably involved not only rendering, but also reworking meanings, so that decrees acquired significances other than those original intended.[127] Thus, a number of important provisions of each piece of legislation were introduced in Lemberg, not Vienna. For that matter, Austrian bureaucrats also routinely leaked news of upcoming legislation before it was officially promulgated.[128] Information could be powerful, forearming opposition to specific measures still in draft form. Given all this, certain major decrees wound up radically altered in transit from Vienna to Lemberg.

Local governance always involved a combination of central decisions and regional initiatives; compromise between imperial officials and their subjects in Galicia appears to have been a frequent phenomenon. The limits of absolutism, indeed, are best revealed not in the center but on the peripheries, where local Austrian officials often questioned the logic of central legislation and hindered its implementation. I would stress that the effectiveness of Josephinian reforms should be tested especially in the provinces; that is, the impression of overwhelming efficiency of Josephinian legislation described by Derek Beales in his biography of Joseph II[129] may have been characteristic of Vienna, but certainly not of Galicia.

Enlightenment Instrumentalized

In 1789, Joseph II was nearing the end of his life, terminally ill with tuberculosis. During his last months, he reversed many of the decrees and orders he had tried so hard to implement in previous years. In early 1790, he rescinded his land and tax regulations for Galicia. A call for action on this issue had come from Lemberg, initially involving neither Brigido nor his Gubernium colleagues, but rather an anonymous report reaching the gravely ill emperor on 15 December 1789. It described the catastrophic situation in Galicia, ascribing it to Josephinian legislation; heavy taxation and restrictions on peasant labor, the author claimed, had ruined the local economy and had a devastating effect on individual landowners. On 16 January, Joseph II wrote to Brigido requesting his opinion on the matter.

Brigido responded without delay, and his report arrived in Vienna on 26 January. He agreed with most of the allegations and confirmed the dire economic state of the province. According to the governor, Galicia's problems had their roots precisely in the ambivalent legacy of the Austrian Enlightenment and concomitant imperial reforms. In one of his last reports from Lemberg, in 1793, Brigido wrote: "The so-called Enlightenment spread over many peoples and classes, and it has strongly affected Galicia, too. Yet, in my view, there remains one problematic question: whether the all too hastily and forcefully imposed Enlightenment is beneficial or rather dangerous to the state."[130]

Perhaps for the first time in his career, Brigido had a chance to express his dissent in a letter addressed directly to the emperor. He made no secret of his views, explaining the dangers of Joseph II's policies for the monarchy. Both emperor and governor regarded the Enlightenment as a reform movement with immediate practical implications; but the two disagreed on the meanings of the reforms. For years prior, Brigido had opposed measures proposed by Joseph II, and had partially succeeded in preventing their implementation. Thus, though many monasteries had been nationalized and transformed into schools or warehouses, some remained open, serving their original purpose. The equality of citizens, another principle of the Enlightenment, also had different meanings for the emperor and the governor. When Joseph II attempted the radical reform of taxation and landownership, claiming to treat landlords and peasants as equals, Brigido protested with the counterargument that such radical change would do more harm than good.

This is not to imply that Brigido was a champion of the anti-Enlightenment. Intellectual debates over the Enlightenment were never as intense in the Habsburg Monarchy as in France. Brigido had a very practical vision of the Enlightenment, viewing reform especially through the prism of his personal position in Galicia as one of many Austrian bureaucrats forced to coexist with Polish aristocrats, Jewish merchants, and somewhat more remotely, Ruthenian peasants.

In January 1789, Joseph II ordered the establishment of a commission to assess the situation in Galicia. On 2 February, the commission confirmed Brigido's assessments. Count Ludwig von Kolowrat, then serving as head of the Austrian-Bohemian Court Chancellery, and Court Councillor Baron Kressel advised cutting the land tax by a quarter to 9 percent and restoring traditional estate privileges. The tax reform was still new, and a system of collection had not yet been implemented. Later that same year, the tax and agricultural reform was abolished outright.[131] The province and its elites—their various ethnic and political allegiances notwithstanding—had shown remarkable resistance to an ostensibly powerful center.

It would be a mistake, however, to assume that it was solely domestic opposition or local administrators' antipathy to Joseph II's policies that had induced the emperor to rethink his course and rescind some of the most radical reforms. The monarchy was willing to make concessions to domestic opposition because of threats looming in the international arena. In 1789, a revolt broke out in the Habsburg Netherlands, territories Vienna had annexed in 1714 as a result of the War of the Spanish Succession. The same year saw revolution in Paris. Domestic discontent, combined with revolutionary rumblings emanating from France and hardly contained there, increased the chances of uprisings in the monarchy. Calling off unpopular legislative projects was one way to placate opposition and pacify the social groups affected by recent reforms and standing at the vanguard of resistance to Joseph II.

Joseph died in February 1790 a disillusioned man; some reforms as outlived him were largely reversed by the two emperors who followed, Leopold II (1790–92) and Francis II (1792–1835). Yet the overall effects of the reforms were significant enough to transform Habsburg politics and society through the generations to come. The peasants remained free. The landlords would never again have complete freedom of action toward the laborers working their land. The clergy was now better educated. The new bureaucracy persisted, as did the principle of administrative centralization. The same bureaucrats formerly responsible for the implementation of Joseph's reforms were then charged with their undoing, a phenomenon that the prominent Austrian historian Roger Bauer has dubbed the "Josephinian trauma."[132] It is true that many of them had resisted the reforms during the 1780s, and at least some would have reason to welcome a new course. Brigido was likely to endorse at least some revisions brought about by the change of rulers, for instance the return to old patterns of landlord-peasant relations that had existed before 1780, and the giving back of Church property expropriated during Joseph II's reign.

Meanwhile, Brigido faced new professional crises. In 1793, during investigations into malfeasance in the Galician Gubernium, the governor fell victim to the political plotting of his subordinates. Gubernium councillors D'Ellex, Bujakowski, Kohlmanhuber, and Trautmansdorf made a case against Brigido, denouncing him for corruption. Most of the accusers had come to Galicia between 1772 and 1774 among the cohort appointed by Kaunitz.[133] All had survived the changes of political regimes, and now several joined forces in an effort to remove the governor. Although the exact details of the case remain unclear, Brigido seems to have been the victim of factional politics. He had, to be sure, his own lobby in the Gubernium; but before 1790, his main basis of support had been located not in Lemberg, but Vienna. Despite their numerous disagreements, Joseph II had been determined to keep the governor in office; this backing having vanished with the emperor's death, Brigido's position became particularly precarious, and the corruption scandal in the Gubernium administration in 1794 was enough to bring an end to his career.[134]

Similarly to Pergen, Brigido fell victim to internal opposition within the bureaucracy. Yet the two of them took two different paths after leaving Galicia. Pergen left Galicia in disgrace. Still relatively young in 1774, he hoped to continue his career in Vienna, but received no warm welcome in the capital. He was appointed the Landmarschall of Lower Austria and Vienna—a rather marginal position compared to his previous appointments and a professional setback resulting from his failures in Galicia. Yet it was in Vienna that his career took a new dimension: as Landmarschall, Pergen started paying increased attention to mechanisms of law enforcement and policing, a domain that had received little attention from his predecessor. In 1782, he was rewarded by being promoted to the position of head of the Lower Austrian administration. Now endowed with new authority, Pergen put efforts into creating a network of police institutions, each linked together in a strict hierarchy. By 1789 he secured the jurisdiction over all police institutions in the Habsburg Monarchy. By then, the Galician episode had been forgotten. Pergen came into the annals of history primarily as the founding father of the professional police in the Habsburg Monarchy.[135]

Brigido instead retired, and spent the last years of his life in Salzburg. His case illustrates two important paradoxes in the functioning of the Austrian bureaucracy that remained relevant well beyond the 1780s. The first had to do with the contradictory nature of the ostensible meritocracy informing this institution. Brigido spent years in Galicia, but some of his subordinates served much longer, in some cases occupying offices in the same agency for decades. Most of those appointed to Galicia by Kaunitz in the 1770s had expected timely promotions or transfers; but many remained in the same or similar positions much longer than they had originally imagined. During the 1780s and early 1790s, Galicia was governed by much the same cohort of officials as had arrived beginning in 1772.[136] For example, Joseph Lippa made his career in Galicia during the 1770s; the province was home to the full careers, moreover, of Ignacy Bujakowski, D'Ellex, and Bratkowski. Designed to be only temporary, Kaunitz's selection of personnel affected Austrian bureaucracy in Galicia for many decades. Over the years, these bureaucrats would have acquired some knowledge of the region and its people, which most had lacked at the time of their appointment; organizing an informed officialdom was, of course, an important achievement for Vienna. But at the same time, the lengthy Galician stays of these men also signaled the failure of meritocracy, evincing promises unfulfilled and personal aspirations dashed. While their senior colleagues rotated from one top position to another, many low-ranking bureaucrats failed to secure any promotion at all. On the other hand, Brigido's case meant that meritocracy had made some progress. The governor had been patronized by an emperor who did not always share his political views, but respected him; he met his downfall under a new regime whose convictions were apparently in accord with his own.

Brigido's career also revealed the paradoxes of the Austrian Enlightenment, of the combination of absolutism and reform. He arrived in Galicia as an instrument of the central government, at the climax of the Austrian Enlightenment. In the Habsburg Monarchy of the late eighteenth century, provincial governorships were designated as institutions of execution, and such governance left little room for local initiative.[137] But in Lemberg, Brigido reinterpreted his mission and his status, in relation to both his superiors in Vienna and his subjects in Galicia. The bureaucracy was one product of the many reforms and adjustments introduced in the 1780s. But this same bureaucracy, for its part, introduced numerous revisions of its own to central policies and reform plans, in some cases challenging the very logic of policy intent. These bureaucrats created new links between Vienna and its provinces, on the one hand, and among the provinces on the other, imposing a new kind of uniformity upon Habsburg territories that had not existed before.

THREE

The Napoleonic Test

1792–1815

When Joseph von Brigido departed from Lemberg in 1794, he left behind a Galicia firmly integrated into imperial structures; on the surface, it resembled other Austrian provinces more than it did Polish regions over the border. But even given this relative stability, Governor Brigido voiced growing concerns over impending catastrophe. His fears were linked to military conflicts and revolutionary upheavals taking place far from Galicia. In 1789, the Austrians had begun a war with the Netherlands; Vienna's relations with Prussia were meanwhile reaching a crisis point, and a new outbreak of hostilities seemed probable. Most portentous of all, the same year saw revolution in Paris. In 1792, the Habsburg Monarchy became the first of the European states to enter into war against the French revolutionary armies.

Mere months after the beginning of hostilities with France, Brigido sounded the alarm as to the potential effects this new military confrontation might have on Galicia; in 1793, he warned Vienna that Galician Poles would likely take up arms against Austria and attempt to rebuild an independent Poland with their own region very much included.[1] Also that year, the governor requested funds for the establishment of a secret police force in the province. Chancellor Kaunitz rejected Brigido's proposal.[2] Galicia, on the far eastern periphery of the Habsburg Monarchy, did not seem to present any serious threat. It was the western and central territories of the realm, specifically Italy and Hungary, that constituted major centers of pro-French, anti-Austrian propaganda.[3]

Brigido's dismissal in 1794 signaled the end of an era in the history of Austrian Galicia; none of his successors would spend nearly as much time in the province as he had, nor would any seem as involved in Galician life and politics as he had been. Most of the post-Brigido governors looked upon Galicia as the merest career stopover, moving in and out of Lemberg in the span of a few years, if not months. The Hungarian Mailath Szekely served as governor briefly in 1794–95, and Jan Gaizruck from 1795 to 1801; then Joseph Kermenyi headed the Galician administration until 1806.[4] The next governor, Christian von Wurmser, would face the task of leading during the Austro-Polish War of 1809.

For many years, Galicia remained relatively unaffected by the wars. Only in 1809 did Austria's eastern province become drawn into the pan-European conflict. That year, the Polish general Józef Poniatowski, based in Warsaw in the Russian part of Poland, took matters into his own hands. Inspired and supported by Napoleon, Poniatowski built an army, marched into Galicia, which at the time had no large Austrian military garrison, and occupied the province. Within weeks, Poniatowski ordered the establishment of a new administration in the hope of creating a new Polish state. In 1809, the Habsburg Monarchy came closer to losing Galicia than at any time before or since.

The Polish conquest of Galicia in 1809 comes under the rubric of the French Revolutionary Wars; but Galicia's experience during this period was remarkably different from that of many other Habsburg provinces. This was the story of a borderland region torn between two competing empires, the Austrian and the Russian. Unlike other Habsburg territories, Galicia never fell under French occupation, nor was it ever administered by French-appointed officials. The army that entered Galicia in May 1809 was composed mainly of Polish soldiers. That same month, several Russian divisions arrived in Galicia as Napoleon's ally, obliged by the tsar's armistice with the emperor to assist the pro-French Polish forces of General Poniatowski. The Polish contingent expanded further once it crossed the border, as some local Poles, too, welcomed the idea of a restored Poland with Galicia included.

Fig. 3.1: Józef Poniatowski. Portrait by Marcello Bacciarelli, 1816. Polish National Library, Digital Collection Polona.

The Austrian defeat in 1809 raised many questions in Vienna. How could a stateless army, only theoretically supported by Napoleon, occupy an Austrian province? How did Austrian subjects—Poles, Ruthenians, and Jews—respond to Polish occupation, and how did the bureaucracy handle the crisis? All these factors were aggravated by the fear of Russian expansion, a threat that suddenly loomed large in 1809, and would go on to last as long as the Habsburg Monarchy itself. War over Galicia was a fight for the integrity of the empire, and proved to be a major test for imperial administration and bureaucracy.

The Wars

With the outbreak of the French Revolution in 1789, and the beginning of the French Revolutionary Wars in 1792, the Habsburg Monarchy found itself in a particularly precarious situation. Austrian politicians initially expressed little concern about the revolution, considering it a matter of French domestic politics that would have little impact upon Austrian territories; but such notions proved false.

The Galician war was also a result of Austria's expansion to the east. The annexation of new territories meant a new border and all its concomitant risks. Even in 1772, not everyone in Vienna supported Austria's involvement in the Polish partitions; but when the first partition was followed by a second and third, Vienna found it increasingly difficult to remain neutral. The Habsburgs had anxiously observed the territorial expansion of neighboring Prussia and Russia that resulted from the Second Partition of Poland in 1793; realizing in 1795 that Poland would be wiped from the political map of Europe with or without their participation, the Habsburgs opted for "with."

In 1795, Vienna annexed a new portion of the formerly Polish territories in the third and final partition of the Polish Republic. Western Galicia, with its center in Kraków, neighbored the "old" (Eastern) Galicia, and was organized on a similar administrative model. Between 1795 and 1803, Western Galicia constituted a separate Austrian province, but adding it to the empire itself engendered numerous difficulties in the 1790s. This latest annexation of another section of Poland revived the memory of the first, and of the carving up of that country generally. Bureaucrats willing to move to the new province, meanwhile, were few, and the mass relocation of officials from Eastern to Western Galicia caused chaos in Lemberg.[5]

Domestic policies were complicated by the international situation. The Second Partition of Poland in 1793 created a direct border between the Russian Empire and the Habsburg Monarchy—a destabilizing frontier, which Vienna had previously sought hard to avoid.[6] The partition and the new annexation also affected the relative percentage of Poles and Ruthenians in this borderland. Ruthenians formed a majority in Eastern Galicia and, by and large loyal to Vienna, they formed a bulwark of Austrian power there. On the other hand, Western Galicia was predominantly Polish. When the two regions were amalgamated in 1803, the percentage of Poles and Ruthenians in the united province was almost even, 45 percent each; but in Vienna the sheer volume of new Polish subjects was seen as an imbalance, a potentially destabilizing factor. The war confirmed Austria's concerns: the direct border would indeed facilitate Russian involvement in Austrian domestic affairs. In 1809, cross-border ties between Galicia and the neighboring former Polish territories now under Russian rule became decisive.

The new border and the shift of balance in the ethnic composition of Galicia gained especial significance as the Habsburg Monarchy found itself drawn into a Europe-wide war. The French Revolution, and the Napoleonic Wars that followed, opened a new chapter in the history of the partitioned Polish territories. In 1799, Napoleon Bonaparte became first consul, and in 1804 he was crowned emperor. Over the years of his reign, he toyed with the idea of an independent Poland as a buffer against his major rivals, Prussia, Austria, and Russia; and even if his maneuvers were geopolitical games, Poles living under these rival powers' rule took them seriously. Many came to believe that the reestablishment of an independent Poland was imminent;[7] in any case, France certainly possessed the power necessary to make the Polish dream come true.

In the War of the Fourth Coalition (1806–7), Prussia, Russia, Saxony, Sweden, and Great Britain allied their forces against Napoleon. Attempting to recover from its previous setbacks, Vienna took no part in this coalition;

but the war had an important impact on the monarchy's eastern territories. Both Prussia and Russia suffered major defeats, and were left at the mercy of the French emperor. Napoleon concluded alliances and redrew maps so as to secure his flanks both east and west. Prussia would be allowed to continue existing, but would have to surrender parts of its Polish territories; while Tsar Alexander I was forced to ally Russia with France and provide support to Napoleon's other partners. The 1809 Galician war would be, in a way, a direct continuation of the 1806 conflict.

In 1807, the Polish territories Napoleon had seized from Prussia were formed into the Duchy of Warsaw, a semi-independent Polish state under French protection, formally governed by the king of Saxony. For the French emperor, the duchy was primarily a *place d'armes* to prepare his military actions against Austria from the east;[8] but many Poles saw it as the first step toward a reconstituted Poland, and after 1807, Napoleon became an iconic figure of the Polish independence movement. The duchy developed institutions of semiautonomous governance, including a constitution, administration, and army.

While Poles celebrated, Austrian officials feared the worst. The creation of the duchy opened Austria to Napoleon's potential attack from the east. Galicia was just across the border from the duchy, with Poles on either side hoping the province might soon be added to it. True, that would require a war, but the Poles seemed better positioned for military confrontation than the Austrians; if assisted by Russia, the Poles could pose a real threat to the Habsburg Monarchy.

Intrigues and Espionage in the Borderlands

At the crossroads of the Russian and Austrian Empires, administered by French officials on behalf of the king of Saxony, the Duchy of Warsaw became a major intelligence hub in Europe's east. Warsaw hosted a number of French officials, the so-called *résidents*, a corps of diplomatic personnel who oversaw the administration of the duchy. The Austrians had reason to believe that the *résidents* were also collecting information on the Habsburg Monarchy, and particularly on Galicia.[9]

The small border town of Brody became a hotbed of Austrian, Polish, French, and Russian intelligence activity. Brody was one of the most important centers of commerce and transit between the Austrian Empire and the east, especially, just over the border, Russia. This meeting place of empires meant there was a great deal of cross-border population movement that created economic hurdles and security challenges for both Vienna and St. Petersburg. Not least important was the fact that Brody was one of Europe's major Jewish centers, a town where Jews made up as much as 70 percent of the population. The Jews of Brody made perfect spies: they knew local languages, and they played a key role in cross-border trade, easily traversing borders bearing goods and, potentially, information of great use to the Austrians and French alike.[10] After 1809, Jewish Brodyites increasingly attracted the attention of French functionaries, who strived to recruit them into French intelligence operations.

One of these functionaries—the French *résident* Aubernon—traveled across Galicia between July and September 1813 on a twofold mission. Outwardly, in his diplomatic capacity, he was to confer with and assess major representatives of the Austrian administration, individuals with whom the French were bound to deal, whether as allies or enemies, in the future. Aubernon managed to arrange several unofficial meetings with such key Gubernium officials as Governor Peter von Goëss and one of his counselors, Baron Baum.[11]

Covertly, meanwhile, Aubernon had an interest in freelance reconnaissance. Paris instructed that "M. Aubernon should do everything in his power not to jeopardize the aim of this [diplomatic] mission."[12] But the Austrians, who organized a friendly reception for Aubernon in Lemberg, rightly suspected that their guest was keen to gather intelligence information for the French. As a result, they issued an official travel route he would be obliged to follow on his way through Galicia. While Aubernon had no outright anti-Austrian task to accomplish on his route, he did intend a secret operation in his final destination—Brody, where he hoped to recruit local Jews for the French intelligence services.

Aubernon's scheme was exposed not by Austrian security agents but rather by local residents of Brody who anticipated his arrival. The French were known to pay well for information, and their efforts to recruit agents often turned into public events with large gatherings, a state of affairs naturally detrimental to secrecy. Even after Aubernon had changed his route to give the Austrian police the slip, he ran into difficulties after arriving in Brody.[13]

Aubernon's trip to Galicia had been authorized by the French Foreign Ministry. But it remains unclear whether senior officials in Paris ever approved, or were even aware, of Aubernon's forays into anti-Habsburg espionage. Just as Austrian bureaucrats in the provinces at times defied orders of the central government in Vienna, so did French *résidents* not always comply with the instructions of their higher-ups in Paris. Many of them maintained a distance from the Foreign Ministry, and even pursued their own personal ambitions.[14]

Beginning in 1807, Austrian police agents reported on "French machinations" and intrigues taking place in Galicia via the Duchy of Warsaw.[15] As early as 1805 — even before the duchy had been established, that is — there were approximately 120 French spies in Galicia.[16] Numerous reports came in to Vienna implicating the French in instigating anti-Austrian activities among Galician Poles; especially alarming was the fact that Poles responded well to what were, in Austria's view, French provocations.[17] While the French dispatched their agents to Galicia, the Austrians sent their own spies to the duchy, where they gathered evidence on French and Polish activities and transmitted their findings back to Vienna.[18] These reports painted a picture of a serious crisis in Austria's eastern borderland; even without direct French military intervention, Polish territories were a ticking time bomb that could explode at any moment.

The Austro-Polish War

In March 1809, the Austrian government decided it was ready to take military action. The Duchy of Warsaw made up one of three fronts on which warfare was under way that year, the others being Spain (where Austrian forces were not involved) and Germany,[19] where Archduke Charles commanded Austrian armies that directly confronted the French revolutionary armies of Emperor

Napoleon. The forces earmarked for the Duchy of Warsaw were commanded by Archduke Ferdinand, whose task it would be to remove a base for potential French attack on the Habsburg Monarchy from the east, and at the same time to stifle the national hopes this Franco-Polish polity had engendered in Austrian Galicia.[20] The Austrian campaign on the eastern front was regarded as only secondary, a preparation for the far more serious operation in the west. The Duchy of Warsaw seemed to be an easy target, and foreign minister Count Philip Stadion did not expect serious complications.

In April 1809, Archduke Ferdinand announced the beginning of operations on the eastern front.[21] At the same time, the Austrians launched a broad propaganda campaign, hoping to secure the neutrality of the Galician Poles. They issued appeals in the name of the "Austrian imperial nation," of which the Poles of Galicia were said to constitute an integral part.[22] That month, the Austrian army marched into the Duchy of Warsaw, crossing the border on the fourteenth and meeting little in the way of resistance.[23] Six days later, the Austrians took Warsaw, and two days after that, General Poniatowski's army signed an armistice and quit the city.

Once in Warsaw, the Austrians sought to maintain order and improve the general quality of life in this crucial Polish city. Count Stadion and Archduke Ferdinand, keenly aware of Austria's international isolation, felt obliged to put forward an image of benevolent Austrian administration, which would, it was hoped, mobilize the duchy Poles for the Habsburg cause. In one instance of order-restoring, on 23 April the Austrians reopened a theater.[24] Civil administration functioned as usual. Both Stadion and Archduke Ferdinand had reason to be satisfied: their eastern campaign seemed to have gone as quickly and smoothly as predicted.

But neither Napoleon nor Poniatowski accepted this Austrian victory as final; in April and May 1809, the two corresponded to discuss the subsequent military strategy of the Polish army. Busy on the western front, Napoleon informed his ally that he would be unable to grant any assistance; on the other hand, Poniatowski could still count on help from a most unlikely source, given his independence aims—Russia. According to the armistice signed by Tsar Alexander I at Tilsit in 1807, St. Petersburg was obliged to grant military support to Napoleon or any of France's allies. Both

Napoleon and Poniatowski expected that the Russian Empire would join the war against Austria.

Advised by Napoleon, Poniatowski regrouped his forces and prepared a Polish counteroffensive on Galicia, to be staged from the duchy. The plan involved encouraging a Polish uprising against Austria in both the duchy and Galicia; such a revolt would lay the ground for Poniatowski's counterstrike against the Austrian army. In the meantime, Poniatowski launched a new series of negotiations with St. Petersburg, hoping to secure Russian assistance for these maneuvers.

The Polish counteroffensive proved successful. On 11 May, Archduke Ferdinand reported to Emperor Francis II on the catastrophic military situation in Galicia, where local Poles were organizing an anti-Austrian uprising.[25] Within days, Polish troops were marching into Galicia. On 18 May, one of the French *résidents* in Warsaw, Serra, informed Paris of the very enthusiastic welcome given in the province to the Polish soldiers.[26] On 27 May, an army division headed by General Rozhnetsky entered Lemberg.[27] Following the Polish army's lead, Russian troops also moved into Galicia; a division headed by General Sergei Golitsyn reached Lemberg on 3 June.[28] This Russian involvement was crucial: when conjoined, the Polish and Russian armies made a formidable military force, one capable of facing that commanded by Archduke Ferdinand.

These two consecutive occupations—the Austrian takeover of the Duchy of Warsaw and the Polish conquest of Galicia—yield much ground for comparison. Warsaw seemed to fare better under Austrian control than Lemberg under Polish occupation, even if this latter city was of course the traditional Lwów; the collapse of its Austrian civil administration caused disarray. City residents experienced all manner of privations; many were pressed by financial needs,[29] and some even lost their homes. While Warsovians looked to Lemberg as the Polish Piedmont, Lembergers, who had initially welcomed the Polish victory, were willing to see the Austrians return as guarantors of the order and stability their city was sorely lacking.[30]

The chaos of Lemberg notwithstanding, Polish forces moved to swiftly organize a new Galician administration. On 2 June, Poniatowski announced the establishment of a new temporary government under the protectorate of Napoleon, to be headed by Count Zamoyski. All officials were required to swear an oath of allegiance to the French emperor.[31] On 7 June, Zamoyski announced the cessation of Austrian rule in the province.[32] On 9 June, Count von Komblinski, the former prefect of Płock, was nominated the General Intendant of Galicia.[33] Within weeks, Poles took control of the administration, removing Austrian officials unwilling to cooperate with the new authorities and retaining those who were amenable. Crucial in overseeing the establishment of a new Polish administration in this until recently Austrian province were Russian army officers.

Vienna anxiously looked on as Habsburg subjects cooperated with the Polish and Russian authorities in Galicia. Count Dietrichstein, an Austrian official tasked with observing troop movements and political attitudes in the province, spent the spring and summer months there, relaying significant information back to the imperial capital. In May 1809, Dietrichstein described what he defined as the Russian intention to build a new administration in Galicia. Given the dearth of administrative personnel, the new authorities retained both Austrian administrative structures and Austrian-German officials who wished to keep their positions.[34] Particularly appalling to Dietrichstein was that so many officials accepted the Russian offer to remain. "No loyal and trustworthy official would be willing to retain a post in these circumstances," asserted Dietrichstein, who saw this collaboration between Russian and Polish military authorities and the officials formerly employed in the Austrian state service as an unconscionable treachery.[35]

The Russian presence in Lemberg caused a great deal of confusion. Poles and Austrians alike considered St. Petersburg a potential ally, and both appealed to Russia for support. The Russians, it is worth emphasizing, had been forced into an alliance with France; Stadion hoped that Alexander I could switch sides in the course of the war.[36] The foreign minister's feeling was echoed in Galicia, where the Russians openly favored the Austrians over the French, as Polish bureaucrats recently assuming formerly Austrian posts in the province attested.[37] Meanwhile, both Austrians and Poles feared that St. Petersburg might have its own plans for Galicia, regardless of the wishes of Paris, Vienna, or Warsaw.

In late April, Polish operatives intercepted a communication between the Russian general Gorchakov and Archduke Ferdinand in which the former pledged future support to Vienna, even as, at present, the Russians were officially acting as Poniatowski's allies.[38] The same month, Henryk Wołodkowicz, a Polish general in the French army, reported rumors of Russian plans to seize Galicia.[39] On 26 May, a French spy in Galicia by the name of Bellefrois registered his concerns about the ambivalent status of the Russians in the Galician war; he had reason to believe they had entered the province in the hope of eventually annexing it to the Russian Empire.[40] Austrian prisoners in Polish captivity reported that the Russians had no intention of militarily supporting the Poles' political struggle against the Habsburgs.[41]

On 15 June 1809, the Russian general Nikolai Meller-Zakomel'skii reaffirmed St. Petersburg's commitments to its Polish allies.[42] On 19 June, the French *résident* Serra reported to Paris on his visit to Galicia; the Russians had as yet fired only a few shots against Austrian forces, explaining this passivity by reference to logistical problems.[43] On 21 June, Poniatowski, determined to find the truth about Russia's plans, met with the Russian general Ulanov, who reiterated that St. Petersburg would adhere to its armistice with Napoleon, and denied any rumors of betrayal.[44] On 15 June 1809, General Meller-Zakomel'skii again made reassurances of Russo-Polish military cooperation.[45] But Polish suspicions were not unfounded; St. Petersburg had indeed been carrying on secret negotiations with Vienna.

In hindsight, it is clear that Vienna's success in these clandestine dealings with St. Petersburg determined the outcome of the war. On 18 April, Russia and Austria reached an accord by which the tsar pledged to refrain from active campaigning against the Austrians, and most importantly, to help suppress any Polish uprising in Galicia.[46] On 15 May, the Russians and Austrians secretly settled upon another point, according to which St. Petersburg committed to avoiding war with Austria in general.[47] In mid-June 1809, the Russians, Poles, and Austrians launched a new round of talks; whether the Austrians were better negotiators or simply luckier than Poniatowski's side, the result was that the Russians switched, now allying themselves with Vienna.

On 19 June, an Austrian division headed by Engerman entered Lemberg, facing no Russian resistance.[48] Within days, the Austrians had retaken a large area of Eastern Galicia. On 28 June 1809, Count Christian von Wurmser, the recently appointed military governor of the city of Lemberg, was ready to take over the administration of the province.[49] A new series of negotiations followed, this time concerning the status of the Russian army in the recaptured Austrian territory.

Russia's involvement proved almost as problematic for Vienna as it was for Warsaw. Through the summer of 1809, Austrian officials had to coordinate their actions with Russian generals. Indeed, the reinstatement of the Austrian administration was overseen by a Russian, General Meller-Zakomel'skii, who underscored his control by, for instance, forbidding the official announcement of the Austrian administration's return to Galicia.[50] Beginning in July, all taxes collected in Galicia were funneled to St. Petersburg.[51] The ongoing Russian military presence in Galicia naturally raised much concern in Vienna. Austro-Russian negotiations concluded with a peace settlement at Schönbrunn (October 1809), by which the Habsburg Monarchy retained Eastern Galicia, the territory it had annexed in 1772, while Western Galicia was added to the Duchy of Warsaw.

Under Polish Occupation

For the Habsburg Monarchy, the crisis of 1809 served as a test not only of the loyalty of its subjects, but also the effectiveness of its military and bureaucracy. The fact that some Poles remained loyal to Vienna reflected the extent of positive changes made in the province over the previous decades; many others' enthusiastic welcome or even joining of the anti-Habsburg army, on the other hand, revealed the failure of efforts to integrate the province into the empire. The fact that at least some Poles, Jews, and Ruthenians debated which side to join—the Austrian or the Polish—proved most interesting of all; the war had opened old rifts in Galician society, but Vienna could put the ethnic, religious, and social diversity of the province to good use.

Count von Dietrichstein explained how different Galicians reacted to the conflict and occupation. He drew a stark distinction between the loyal

Ruthenians (mostly peasants) of Eastern Galicia and the treacherous Roman Catholics, most of whom were Poles (and many noble) of both Eastern and Western Galicia.[52] Among Jews, allegiances were divided, but there seemed to be a preference for the pro-French Poles over the Austrians.[53] The disparate reception of Austrian rule in Galicia is not difficult to explain. For the Ruthenians, Austria represented a tolerant government and defender against oppressive Polish neighbors. For the Poles, Napoleon symbolized a potentially independent Poland, and the end of years of unwanted Austrian rule. The economy may have played an important role in shaping Jewish allegiances: decades after the dissolution of Poland, Jewish trade was still east-oriented, concentrating on cross-border Polish territories. In 1807, the Austrian government imposed restrictions on trade with the Duchy of Warsaw, a decision that had caused much discontent among Galician Jews.[54]

Dietrichstein made several important points. First, even though some of the Polish elite fell under the spell of Poniatowski's separatist agenda, others remained loyal to the Habsburgs. Moreover, the vast majority of non-Poles in Galicia continued to support Vienna—the fact that no Galician started an uprising during one of the most vulnerable periods in Austrian history is highly symbolic. By 1809, few in Galicia nurtured the aspiration for independence. Even after Poniatowski marched into Galicia promising an independent Poland, many Poles remained split in their allegiances. Vienna's major task was thus to prevent the spread of separatist and nationalist propaganda from outside and, at the same time, maintain loyalty inside the monarchy.

After 1809, Dietrichstein played a key role in constructing an Austrian interpretation of the Galician war. His approach could best be described as the politics of forgetting. Dietrichstein defined the events occurring between April and July as the "foreign invasion" of Galicia; such would be the meaning of Russian and Polish forces having marched together into the province. While stressing the crucial part Russia had played in the conquest of Galicia, Dietrichstein minimized the role of the duchy's Polish army, and of those Polish Habsburg subjects who had taken up arms against their sovereign.[55]

Three different forces occupied Galicia in the spring of 1809: the Polish army of General Poniatowski, mobilized in the Duchy of Warsaw; the

Austrian army of Archduke Ferdinand; and the Russian army of Golitsyn. Each could be regarded as "foreign," but this foreignness would have to be precisely defined. Poniatowski's army expanded immensely by recruiting local Galician Poles, relying heavily on their participation. Galician Poles also made up part of the Austrian forces commanded by Archduke Ferdinand. General Golitsyn's Russian army was the only full-fledged "outsider" military force in Galicia, but—contrary to Dietrichstein's politically forgetful view, which stressed the foreignness of the non-Habsburg forces over all—it had played a rather marginal role in the temporary Polish conquest of the province.

Dietrichstein's interpretation of the war, however, is useful in revealing the broader course Vienna would take toward Galicia after 1809; in his report, he expressed the need to show leniency toward Austria's subjects in the province, blaming the Habsburg setback primarily on "foreign occupiers." Leniency indeed became a key aspect of Vienna's subsequent Galicia policy. Before persecuting the disloyal, the Austrians resolved to reward those who had remained loyal. The approach, as such, was innovative; for the first time in the history of Austro-Polish relations, Austrians, foregrounding coexistence, expressed gratitude to a number of Galician Poles for their support of the dynasty in a time of crisis. A "Description of every Galician landowner and inhabitant who distinguished himself by his involvement in state affairs and by his support for the Russo-[Austrian] forces . . ." listed Galician Polish landowners who had assisted in fighting the enemy.[56] Adam Czartoryski, Adam Szydlowski, Peter Komorowski, and Ignaz Niemczewicz all came in for recognition and awards.[57] The Gubernium councillor Count Ugarto expressed his gratitude to those who had remained loyal to the Habsburg dynasty, and also proposed a general amnesty for those who had fought on the enemy side.[58]

Tolerance and leniency had their limits, however. In November 1809, Christian von Wurmser, who had recently become governor, drew up a list of Austrian officials who had committed various transgressions during the occupation: Szumlanski, head of the district police in Brzezany; Blekynski, commandant of Lemberg; Weglinski, a lawyer; and many others.[59] Most of those whose names appeared on Wurmser's list were of Polish descent, and occupied rather low positions within the administration. A number of them had sworn the oath of allegiance to Napoleon Bonaparte. The Galician Gubernium compiled a list of officials who had remained in service during the occupation or who showed up for work after the Polish and Russian armies had left the province.[60] Each would undergo a thorough review concerning wartime whereabouts and professional performance. Local bureaucrats protested against such treatment, insisting that they had been loyal. A number of police officials fell under political scrutiny, but they received support from some prominent Galician Poles; in the fall of 1809, for instance, Henryk Lubomirski defended the police chief of Kraków, accused of having collaborated with the Poniatowski occupiers.[61]

The events of 1809 revealed numerous fissures within Austrian structures. Officials in central institutions in Vienna accused their Galician subordinates of treason. These bureaucrats in turn accused Vienna of breaking its governmental and defense commitments; in May 1809, the Austrian governor had been among the first to quit the province, while many lower-level officials remained, receiving no salaries or support from their own state. Vienna's announcement of the return of Austrian administration to Galicia raised the issue of unmet Austrian financial commitments during the war; officials requested regular payments starting from September and back pay for all preceding months.[62]

While Austrian officials fought to secure their positions, Galician Poles hoped to use the dire lessons of the war to make a push for political concessions. In 1809, "The System of the Organization of the Kingdom of Galicia"—one of many Polish petitions of this period—addressed some of the problems of Austro-Polish coexistence in Galicia and suggested improvements. The pamphlet outlined a program of extensive autonomy modeled on the political system Napoleon had introduced in the Duchy of Warsaw.[63] It envisioned the expanded use of the Polish language in administration and education; the establishment of such institutions for Polish nobles as would allow them to influence political decisions concerning Galicia; and the inclusion of Poles in the Austrian administration.

Any political changes would be contingent upon decisions of the local bureaucrats employed in Galicia. In 1809, Governor Wurmser opposed further concessions to the Poles under his jurisdiction. He admitted that the recent war had revealed the many failings of Austrian policy in the province; but from his standpoint, these problems stemmed not from Vienna's overbearing rule over Galician Poles, but from its excessive leniency.[64] The governor now became a major proponent of absolutist control as opposed to representative institutions.

Wurmser, however, found little support for his stance, not only (naturally enough) among Galician Poles, but also among his fellow Austrian officials, many of whom advocated concessions instead. The year 1809 marked an ambiguous watershed in the history of Austrian Galicia: the war had not restored the independent Poland so many Poles had hoped for, but the Austrians, their position in Galicia gravely weakened by the conflict, were willing to negotiate concessions, and local officials became increasingly proactive in their defense of the province's interests vis-à-vis the wishes of Vienna.

In late 1809, the intransigent Wurmser was replaced with a new governor, Peter von Goëss. One of a cohort of Austrian officials transferred to Galicia from the Austrian Adriatic, Goëss had served as governor of Dalmatia, Carinthia, Styria, and Trieste.[65] A Habsburg official of Portuguese descent, Goëss left his mark on the administration of Galicia by advocating cooperation with Polish nobles.[66] During Goëss's governorship in Lemberg, Napoleon's troops marched through Galicia on their way to invade Russia, followed by French agents engaged in intelligence work in the province. The French official Aubernon remained busy during 1811–12; even before the launching of Napoleon's Russian campaign, Aubernon had been assessing the Poles' attitudes toward the French and the economic situation in Galicia. The Napoleonic armies relied heavily on provisions from the local population, whose support could alleviate the situation for Napoleon's soldiers. The Poles, Aubernon believed, would readily welcome Napoleon; the Austrians, on the other hand, would pose certain problems for French military operations.

During his years in Galicia, Aubernon had familiarized himself with the nuances of local politics and made the acquaintance of some of the key figures of Galician administration. In the summer of 1812, he met with

Governor Goëss; reporting his impressions back to Paris, he noted that unlike many of his predecessors, Goëss had few enemies in Galicia, but even fewer friends.[67] Goëss's rather neutral status, in Aubernon's assessment, was the result of a specific policy of nonintervention. Goëss proved rather open to Polish demands and had quickly gained the reputation of a supporter of Polish national aspirations. On the other hand, he granted concessions only insofar as these would not conflict with policies imposed by Vienna; and it was this stance of limited accommodation that produced the mixed Polish reception of Austrian officials. Though sympathetic toward Goëss, Polish elites, claimed Aubernon, nevertheless looked upon the imperial administration as their enemy. The Austrians had become captives of their own policies: treating their Polish subjects as rebels, they inevitably incited these subjects' resentment.

Even with the Galician war receding into the past, the year 1812 proved another decisive moment in the history of Austrian rule of this province, whose political fate, according to Larry Wolff, hung at this time in the balance.[68] The plan of an independent Poland hinged upon a war waged east of Galicia, in Russia; if that empire, or the Austrian, or Prussia—or indeed, any one of the three—had been defeated by Napoleon, Poland would have acquired a new chance for revival. 1812 was also a major turning point in the course of the Napoleonic Wars; his armies having suffered a devastating defeat in Russia, Napoleon never marched back across Galicia. After 1812, it became clear that Galicia would remain part of the Habsburg Monarchy.

In September 1814, all members of the anti-Napoleonic coalition arrived in Vienna to discuss postwar settlements. With some intervals, the allies' negotiations continued through June 1815. The Congress of Vienna redrew the political map of Europe, returning France to its 1790 boundaries, creating new states in the western and central parts of the continent, and theoretically if not in reality, restoring stability. The Austrian Empire survived; albeit damaged territorially and exhausted financially, the Habsburgs managed to preserve a semblance of Old Regime dynastic order in Central Europe. The monarchy retained Eastern Galicia in its entirety, but lost large parts of Western Galicia, whose center, Kraków, was granted the status of a free city. The Tarnopol district, also in Western Galicia, became part of the Russian Empire.

The end of war also signaled a new phase in the political reconstruction of Galicia. Gone were the French *résidents,* and Russian generals no longer intervened in the politics of the province. At the same time, these former non-Habsburg "interlopers" left their mark on the postwar administration of Galicia. It is not entirely clear whether Austrian officials, including Goëss, ever had access to secret French reports; but the governor's postwar suggestions resembled, sometimes in the minutest detail, the earlier French assessments of Austrian policies, especially policy failures, in the eastern borderland. Both before and after 1812, Goëss criticized the harsh administrative purges Vienna had been carrying out in Galicia.[69] The 1809 war, Goëss insisted, was a turning point in the history of the partitioned Polish territories. Vienna having regained the province, Poles could no longer hope for an independent homeland; the governor therefore felt that, accommodating their aspirations to this state of affairs, Poles would likely be most favorably disposed toward whichever partitioning power offered the best conditions for their political and cultural life. Goëss insisted that Vienna should seize this moment by offering concessions to the Poles; improving the political climate in Galicia would secure the support of the empire's Polish subjects.

In 1815, Goëss advocated new parliamentary representations, to include Polish participation. He also proposed a new vision of citizenship. For decades, Vienna had hoped to impose, along with Germanophone administration, German culture and education upon Galicia's Poles. These efforts had initially caused much political tension in Galicia, and failed in the long run. If Poles refused to become Germans, they should be allowed to become Galicians instead. Goëss thus espoused a new vision of political loyalty based on regional affiliation rather than ethnic or linguistic allegiance. The concept of the *echte Galizianer*—the true Galician—rested not only on national indifference; it was also contingent upon serious political concessions, which, Goëss claimed, would strengthen the Poles' allegiance to Vienna.[70]

Goëss's proposals had immediate results. The years 1812–17 witnessed something of a Polish renaissance in the province. In 1817, the Ossolińeum, a private cultural institution funded by a Polish magnate with the support of the Austrian authorities, opened in Lemberg; it would go on to be a mainstay of Polish public life in Galicia throughout the nineteenth and part of the twentieth centuries.[71] Meanwhile, a Galician diet met in 1817, thirty-five years after the last session of such a body in 1782. None of these institutions matched the Poles' earlier expectations; the new diet was particularly disappointing, as it secured no legislative functions. But the postwar years nevertheless proved a period of remarkable political achievements that would have been impossible had it not been for the war.

Even if the governor had hardly fulfilled Polish dreams, he may have become too "pro-Polish" for Vienna's taste. Goëss's initiatives seem to have cost him his career. In August 1810, a police inquiry investigated his personal ties with the French and his involvement with Poles.[72] The governor had offered an unusually high number of positions to Poles, precisely at a time when elites from among this population were eager to overhaul the Austrian administration in Galicia.[73] Some of these Polish appointees were known to be Goëss's personal friends, and their political loyalties were considered questionable. Placed under police supervision, the governor was allowed to retain his position. But rumors of his ties to the French persisted, and in 1816, Goëss was removed from Galicia.

That same year, Franz von Hauer became the new governor. But the change of regime did not disrupt the continuity of policy; like Goëss, Hauer supported cooperation with the Poles. He defended the opening of a new diet in the province and the expansion of the use of Polish in the administration. His views were based upon his personal assessment of the recent war and the political stance of Galician Poles in the conflict; while not denying that some had sided with the enemy, Hauer noted that many other Poles had rendered financial and military assistance to the Austrians.

As much as the 1809 conflict made up part of the Napoleonic Wars in Europe, so did the subsequent reconstruction of Galicia embody part of a broader project of postwar reorganization in the monarchy. Within this broader initiative, Galicia was both similar to and different from other regions. Still considered a relatively new and economically backward province, it was treated differently than, for example, Lombardy and Venice, which politically and economically belonged to the monarchy's most important territories. But in at least one respect, the administrative models of the postwar reorganization of Lombardy and Galicia resembled each other: after 1815, an ever more important role in the administration of the monarchy was played by local officials.

Galicia and the Wars

One way to understand Galicia's experience in 1809 is to situate the conflict within the general framework of the Revolutionary Wars (1792–1815). The Revolution of 1789 had little direct impact on developments in the Austrian Empire; but the Revolutionary Wars that followed had profound implications for the monarchy and each of its provinces.

Critical failures of Vienna's policies toward its Polish subjects became most glaring during the war. Foremost was the question of who was responsible for the empire's having temporarily lost one of its possessions. When Galician Poles rallied to the pro-French or, as they understood it, pro-Polish cause, the Habsburg dynasty found itself at war with its own subjects. Even more worrisome was the behavior of the province's Austrian bureaucrats in this period, some of whom took the oath of allegiance to Napoleon. Austro-Russian tensions also exploded with new urgency in 1809, with the ambiguous nature of Russia's involvement looming large for its imperial rival. The fact that Vienna could regain its position in this eastern borderland only with the assistance of St. Petersburg was an alarming signal, impossible to ignore.

The year 1815 marked the beginning of a new era in the history of the Austrian Empire. Galicia is but one example of the influence of war on the design of new policies. As the hope of remaking Poles into "perfect Austrians" vanished, Vienna was forced to contend with the new socio-political realities of the province. Some Austrian officials responded by advocating a degree of local self-administration and greater participation of Poles in Austrian administrative structures.

The war created a paradox. Polish hopes for the rebirth of Poland were dashed with the final defeat of the French Revolutionary Armies in 1814; but the war enabled the Poles of Galicia to gain the kind of concessions from Vienna that would have been impossible in peacetime. In 1817, the Galician estates convened for the first time in decades; Polish nobles gained access to Austrian administrative services. Perhaps most importantly, Poles secured the right to remain Polish rather than Austrian, as two consecutive Austrian governors espoused a new concept of citizenship that revised the previous, unrealistic intention to fashion the monarchy's Galician subjects into "perfect Austrians."

FOUR

Between Vienna, St. Petersburg, and Warsaw

1826–1832

The 1820s were a relatively calm period in the history of the Habsburg Monarchy. After 1815, Austrian territories were included in an international security system, the first of its kind in European history. Chancellor Klemens von Metternich, attuned to the potential of international political conspiracies to threaten the Habsburg crown, sought especially to create new mechanisms of control and cross-border supervision with the involvement of major European powers. His efforts initially seemed to bear fruit; political opposition in the monarchy appeared to be under control. The period was, of course, not entirely devoid of tensions, but Vienna waged no major wars and faced no domestic revolutions in the first post-Napoleonic decade and a half.

By 1815, Galicia had become an integral part of the monarchy, no longer defined as a new acquisition. Vienna's priorities in the meantime shifted as well: no longer concerned about creating a perfect administration, Austrian rulers designed new mechanisms of political control, combining civil administration and the police. As early as 1815, Metternich promoted the creation of a new international security system and intelligence cooperation across the borders. He based his policy on the assessment that a revolution anywhere in Europe could easily extend beyond the boundaries of one state, posing dangers to the neighboring countries as well. Within the Habsburg Monarchy, Metternich focused his efforts upon the imperial borderlands that were most susceptible to revolutionary propaganda stemming from outside.

The Austrian administration and its security mechanisms were put to the test again in 1830. In November of that year, revolution broke out in Warsaw, which now belonged to the Russian Empire. Due to the cross-border ties among the various Polish territories, the uprising in Warsaw caused a great deal of concern in Vienna and Berlin. Senior Austrian officials long pondered how to formulate their official position on the Polish revolt. In the meantime, their junior and oftentimes younger colleagues in Lemberg proceeded with decisions of their own, choices that could jeopardize Vienna's stated policy.

In 1830–31, Prince August von Lobkowitz, the young Austrian governor of Galicia, found himself at the center of a political scandal. Since 1829 or earlier, he had advocated the idea of an independent Poland as a buffer state between the Habsburg Monarchy and the Russian Empire. If, as Lobkowitz planned, Galicia would remain part of the Austrian Empire, and Russia's Polish holdings would be formed into an independent state, then presumably everyone (except St. Petersburg) would be satisfied. Such was the governor's answer to Austria's geopolitical and domestic problems; and in 1830, he corresponded with Poles in the Russian Empire and gave assurances that, in the event of a Polish revolution therein, Vienna would extend its support to independence-seekers against the tsar.

Lobkowitz is the most prominent example of an imperial official who "went local," switched allegiances, and, while remaining an Austrian patriot, decided to become a Pole. His Polish schemes caused confusion all around: revolutionaries in Warsaw believed that Lobkowitz's support of their plans reflected official Habsburg policy. The governor's higher-ups in Vienna, meanwhile, were appalled: when Russia, Prussia, and Austria had agreed to the partitions of Poland, they had all recognized each other's territorial integrity. Each expressed interest in preserving the political status quo, by which the territories the partitioning powers had taken possession of in the late eighteenth century would be governed by these same polities indefinitely. Before 1830, no senior official within the Austrian or Russian political establishments had openly contemplated revising the political order established by the final partition of Poland in 1795. Metternich and Austrian police chief Count Joseph von Sedlnitzky did their best to safeguard the political and military stability of Austria's eastern borderland. Each considered the Polish revolution to be a Russian domestic matter; but both faced a serious dilemma in 1830, when their subordinates—Austrian officials in Galicia—conspired with Polish revolutionaries in a scheme that could have redrawn the political map of Europe.

The Making of a Career

Lobkowitz's connections to Poland were by no means obvious. He was born in Vienna in 1797, from a family that traced its roots to Bohemia. Long part of the empire's political and intellectual elite, the Lobkowitzes were an old aristocratic dynasty that rose to prominence in the early seventeenth century, benefiting from the religious uprising in Bohemia and the Habsburgs' suppression thereof. After the Catholic victory in the Battle of White Mountain in 1620, German-speaking families came to replace formerly rebellious Bohemian elites, and would subsequently form a cornerstone of Austrian power in that kingdom; but even before 1620, not all Bohemians had opposed the Habsburgs. Those aristocrats who remained loyal to their imperial sovereigns during the religious wars benefited most from the postwar overhaul, being rewarded with titles, positions, and estates. The Lobkowitz family was one such beneficiary.[1]

For centuries, select members of the Lobkowitz family had held important offices in Prague and Vienna, a tradition August Lobkowitz would continue.[2] Also like many of his ancestors, he secured a propitious marriage; his wife, Anna Berta Princess von Schwarzenberg, came from an originally Bohemian family as well, and one no less important than his own.[3] Through his sister's marriage, moreover, August was related to the Kolowrat family, as prominent as the Lobkowitzes in the political establishment of the monarchy.

Thus Lobkowitz enjoyed inherited privileges; his family milieu could hardly have been any more illustrious. His personal contacts, meanwhile, secured important professional patronage. A product of the Enlightenment, the Austrian bureaucracy was designed to operate solely on the basis of meritocracy; but in reality, personal networks remained at least as important

Fig. 4.1: Prince August Lobkowitz. Portrait by Jan Haar, 1840. Polish National Library, Digital Collection Polona.

as individual professional achievement. Starting his career young, Lobkowitz quickly progressed through the ranks with an ease that would be the envy of many of his colleagues.

Hailing from a far more prominent family than the typical official, he furthermore evinced a remarkable degree of confidence, which would aid his career, but also harm it. Following in his forebears' footsteps, Lobkowitz entered the Austrian civil service at the youthful age of twenty in 1819, for four years serving as a low-ranking official in Bohemian districts. In 1823, Lobkowitz became head of the Budweis district administration, an impressive career achievement for so young a bureaucrat.[4] That same year, he was appointed to Galicia. By 1825, Lobkowitz was appointed vice president of the Galician Gubernium, and the following year he became governor.[5] Emperor Francis II personally supported the consecutive promotions of his young protégé.[6]

Like Governor Brigido, as well as many other officials employed in key offices across the monarchy, Lobkowitz was a product of the Josephinian bureaucracy, with its particular valuation of both merit and the privileges of birth. Lobkowitz's monarchy-wide personal networks created certain advantages for other members of his family interested in careers in the administration. Even when underpaid and mired in job insecurity, bureaucratic posts carried a definite social prestige; they were often distributed among members of the imperial elites, in some cases passed from fathers to sons in a manner belying Joseph's original meritocratic vision.

As had most of his colleagues, Lobkowitz initially expected his tenure in Galicia to be brief, a temporary layover in his career, if nevertheless a very important one. Lobkowitz seems to have preferred diplomacy to civil administration, and in this period there was no better place for an administrator to show his diplomatic skills than Galicia;[7] because of the province's crossborder ties to Russia, civil governance there was inextricably linked with diplomacy, and diplomacy became an aspect of domestic politics.

Between St. Petersburg and Vienna

The political situation in the lands of the former Poland-Lithuania, meanwhile, was a result of the Napoleonic Wars. After the Congress of Vienna in 1815, portions of the Polish territories under Russian rule came to form the Kingdom of Poland, with Tsar Alexander I crowned king that same year; his brother Prince Constantine officially headed the Polish army, unofficially governing the kingdom on behalf of his sibling.[8] Part of an absolutist political order, the Kingdom of Poland was the only territory in the Russian

Empire to enjoy its own constitution, educational system, and administration, and in the immediate post-Napoleonic period it offered, among the partitioned territories, the most favorable conditions for Polish political and cultural life.[9]

But Alexander I died in 1825, marking the end of an era of constitutional experimentation in the Russian Empire. The tsar's death caused great uncertainty, not only in St. Petersburg—Foreign Minister Vasilii Tatishchev, who would normally offer a mass in honor of the new emperor, was unsure "for whom to pray," and ordered a liturgy for Russian subjects instead[10]—but also in Vienna and Lemberg, where Austrian officials wondered what political impact the new regime in Russia might have on Austria's own Polish territories.

In 1825, Lobkowitz, vice governor of the Galician Gubernium, closely observed the political situation in neighboring Russia. He spent some time in the town of Brody, which was just across from Russia, and as full of cross-border news as it was of spies. In a report to Vienna dated 17 December, Lobkowitz cited sources naming Alexander's brother Nicholas as a potential successor to the Russian throne.[11] When the accession of Nicholas I became common knowledge, Metternich shared his anxiety in a letter to Lobkowitz; the new tsar's coronation, he feared, could provoke an uprising in Russia's western guberniias (provinces), and the turmoil could then extend to Galicia.[12]

Metternich had reason to be concerned. The new tsar believed that the creation of the Kingdom of Poland had been one of Alexander I's biggest mistakes.[13] He showed no enthusiasm for his predecessor's constitutional experiments; on the other hand, he sought to maintain political stability by not entirely antagonizing Polish elites. His policies at times seemed contradictory. During the late 1820s, Nicholas allegedly considered expelling impoverished Polish nobles from the Russian Empire, though this particular plan was never carried out.[14] But in 1828, with Russia entangled in war with the Ottoman Empire and domestic tensions potentially affecting its international standing, Nicholas even demonstrated some support for Polish elites, simplifying the procedure of ascending to the aristocracy and granting an increasing number of titles and awards to Polish troops.[15]

Vienna and St. Petersburg alike toyed with the Polish nobles under their rule in the hopes of securing their loyalty and preventing open revolt. During the reign of Alexander I, Russia enjoyed certain advantages in this regard; because of the tsar's constitutional promises, his Polish subjects had little incentive to take any radical action against their sovereign. But all that changed after 1825, and Vienna was ready to exploit this shift in an effort to gain Polish support. The political climate in the Austrian monarchy during the 1820s, meanwhile, was rather favorable toward the Poles; during this decade, as Piotr Wandycz has noted, Vienna "courted" Galician Poles through a number of pro-Polish gestures.[16] Even as Vienna and St. Petersburg played their own political games to gain Polish favor, then, Poles indirectly benefited from the geopolitical struggle between the two.

Lobkowitz supported the general liberalization of Austrian policies toward Galicia. In October 1823, months after his arrival in Lemberg, he reported to Vienna on the oppressiveness of Austrian political and economic measures in the province. "The Gubernium," he wrote, "receives many complaints from landlords about the heavy taxation of their domains. I would prefer that the Gubernium and district administration publicize these complaints."[17] In another report to Vienna, he described the perilous state of the province's economy and the strained ties between the Austrian authorities and their subjects here: "In the best interests of this land, I would like to draw attention to the much damaged relationships [with the landlords], and the economic oppression that results from heavy taxation." To alleviate this situation, he proposed that taxes in Galicia be cut.[18] In 1826, Lobkowitz successfully lobbied for the creation of a chair in Polish language and literature at Lemberg University.[19] The following year, he financially supported the construction of the Ossoliński Library, which eventually became a major center of Polish cultural and political life in Galicia.[20] The improved image of Habsburg rule in the province, meanwhile, contrasted sharply with the increasing disaffection of Poles under the Romanovs; Austrian reports of 1825–26 noted a gradual improvement in Poles' perception of the Austrians and a concurrent deterioration of their attitudes toward Russia.[21] Austrian travelers to Lithuania, Volhynia, and Podolia also recorded Vienna's improving image among Poles, especially as compared to that of Russia.[22]

In 1826, an Austrian official and diplomat named Lorenz traveled through Galicia into Russia, to St. Petersburg and back. One of a cohort of Austrian bureaucrats serving in two capacities, as civil servants and diplomats, Lorenz in 1826 was tasked with surveying the political situation in the Austro-Russian borderlands and, in particular, the attitudes of Austrian and Russian Polish subjects toward their sovereigns. In his final report to Vienna (14 December 1826), Lorenz contrasts politics as practiced in the Austrian and Russian Empires. "It is my task," he wrote, "to draw a comparison between the orderly and humane procedures we can witness there [in the Austrian Empire], and the arbitrary and sometimes more than arbitrary procedures of the Inquiry Commission here [in the Russian Empire]." But Lorenz did not just mean to praise Austrian law and order as against Russian arbitrariness; he further explained that this Habsburg-favoring imbalance in Polish perception resulted also from specific political decisions, claiming in particular that Governor Lobkowitz had personally contributed to the favorable image enjoyed by the Austrian Empire as against the Russian.[23] It is impossible to tell whether Lorenz truly believed in Lobkowitz's role as a guarantor of stability in the Austro-Russian borderland, or whether with this report he aimed to flatter his superior and improve his chances of promotion. It is, however, an undeniable fact that such comparisons were not uncommon; reports about Lobkowitz's rather cordial relations with his subjects in Galicia became routine in the years after 1826.

Lobkowitz indeed became Galicia's main advocate in Vienna. His popularity among the Poles, however, was based not on his policies alone, but on his personal choices as well. His pro-Polishness was not limited to administrative decisions, but was also a matter of national identification. By the late 1820s, the governor was boasting of his Polish roots, even claiming to be a descendant of the Piast family that had ruled medieval Poland, and that his ancestors had moved to Bohemia only in the fifteenth century.[24] Lobkowitz seemed to have forgotten his Bohemian ties—his only actual verifiable aristocratic pedigree—and decided to become a Pole.

This was not the first time that a key official in the Galician administration had appealed to his superiors in Vienna to revise policies toward the province. Just like his predecessor Governor Brigido, for example, Lobkowitz reasoned that political and economic concessions would improve the economic situation and positively influence the attitudes of Galicians toward their Habsburg sovereigns. However, no one had hitherto used such trenchant terminology; Lobkowitz's reports carry signs of colonial rhetoric, except that here the sides were muddled or reversed: himself part of an imperial administrative elite, Lobkowitz eschewed solidarity therewith, defending instead the interests of "oppressed" (in his own definition) subjects against his senior colleagues in Vienna.

The governor's Polish self-identification and pro-Polish politics were related aspects of a causal process, though it is not entirely clear what was the cause and what the effect: did Lobkowitz's decision to declare himself a Pole stem from his increasing affiliations with Polish nobles, or did his pro-Polish policies lead to his choice to become a Pole? By 1828, he had become known for his provocative actions, and was characterized as immature by some contemporaries, even among the provincial aristocrats with whom he had especially associated himself; in March 1829, Ludwik Jabłonowski, a Polish landowner, described him in a report to Vienna thus: "Prince Lobkowitz is certainly a decent man. He is, however, young, only six years a governor, and still lacks experience. He often acts childishly and relies too much upon the judgments of Galician nobles."[25]

Between 1828 and 1830, Lobkowitz hoped to exploit the international situation for the benefit of the Polish cause. In 1828, a new conflict in the Balkans threatened to turn into a Russo-Ottoman war. Chancellor Metternich tried to negotiate a peaceful solution to the looming confrontation. A potential Russian victory in the Balkans could pose new threats to the Habsburg Monarchy; but offering support to the Ottomans against the Russians, on the other hand, could lead to a Russo-Austrian conflict, which Vienna was trying to avoid. When war did ultimately break out, the Habsburg Monarchy declared its neutrality.

In 1828, for the first but not the last time in his career, Lobkowitz openly defied Vienna's stated policy. Anticipating Russia's defeat, he saw the war in the Balkans as a chance to revise the political map of Europe and reconstruct an independent Poland.[26] That year, he opened a session of the Galician Diet in Lemberg wearing traditional Polish apparel and giving a speech in Polish. His pro-Polish appearance provoked protests from Vasilii Tatishchev, at the time the Russian ambassador to Vienna. Austrian Police Chief Count Joseph Sedlnitzky was similarly alarmed by the Galician governor's behavior, and reproached him for his politically provocative moves.[27]

In the late 1820s, hoping to induce Vienna to undertake a political or even military campaign against St. Petersburg, Lobkowitz drew his superiors' attention to political changes taking place in the Kingdom of Poland. Early in 1829, St. Petersburg transferred six districts from the Kyiv guberniia to other Russian territories, thus depriving these Kyivan regions of the distinct status the former Polish territories had maintained within the Russian Empire since 1815. In March 1829, Lobkowitz argued that St. Petersburg had violated its own international commitments toward its Polish holdings.[28] Political and administrative changes in Russian Poland were, of course, no secret to senior Austrian officials. Metternich insisted that the administration of Russian Poland was a matter of Russia's domestic policy: Vienna would not intervene.[29]

As early as 1830, Lobkowitz became involved in schemes that might have led to the creation of an independent Polish state. In early 1830, revolutionary activist Ludwik Byobzanski traveled from Warsaw to Lemberg to meet with Lobkowitz. In the provincial capital, the two discussed the status of the "Polish nation" divided among three empires, and touched on the possibility of restoring Poland as a country just over Austria's eastern border.[30]

Lobkowitz's encounter with Byobzanski was not an isolated case, but part of broader moves by Polish revolutionaries. By 1830, Polish independence-seekers in Russia had been preparing an uprising against Russian rule. Any such rebellion, as the Poles well realized, would require outside assistance. Recommending Austria in this regard was the fact that the Habsburg Monarchy seemed rather favorably inclined toward Poles, while relations between St. Petersburg and Vienna were not entirely friendly. Most important of all was Lobkowitz's open support for an independent Polish buffer state between Russia and Austria. In him the Poles had discovered their main ally. They had reason thus to anticipate Austrian support; as is clear from later Austrian reports, starting at least in early 1830, Lobkowitz promised Austrian assistance in the case of outright hostilities between Polish rebels and the Russian army.[31]

Lobkowitz's reports to Metternich in this period reveal either a lack of political experience, overconfidence, or perhaps both. He made no secret of his meeting with Byobzanski, immediately reporting on it to the chancellor. The governor insisted that a Polish state would play a significant role in defending Austria's Polish territories and supporting the Austrian government generally.[32] But no one in Vienna seems to have seriously considered any dramatic revision of the existing political order, nor was anyone eager to risk interfering in Russian affairs. On 28 February 1830, Metternich expressed grave concerns regarding the issues about which the Galician governor was so enthusiastic. Polish conspiracies in Galicia, Metternich explained, were dangerous not only for that province, but the entire monarchy as well.[33]

Revolution

In November 1830, a Polish uprising indeed broke out in Warsaw. In January of the following year, Polish statesmen gathered in a diet session to vote on one of the most important decisions since the demise of the Polish state in the eighteenth century. They stripped Tsar Nicholas I of the Polish crown, thus denying his authority over Poland. St. Petersburg mobilized its army in February, and Polish revolutionaries found themselves at war with Russia. The Russian army outnumbered Polish forces tenfold, and if left to themselves, the latter would stand no chance.

The outbreak of the Polish revolt caught Austrian officials unawares; they were especially concerned, and in the dark, as to how Galicia's Polish subjects would react to the uprising. The Poles of Galicia, it seems, knew even less about how the Austrian government might respond.[34] Vienna did not sever relations with the Kingdom of Poland and maintained two official Austrian embassies, one in St. Petersburg and one in Warsaw. Austrian officials continued to receive regular delegations from the Kingdom of Poland. A genuine turn in Vienna's relations with the Polish revolutionaries came only when the defeat of the latter became imminent.[35]

Beginning in November 1830, Lobkowitz became a major conduit of communication between Vienna and the rebel Poles, conferring especially with Adam Czartoryski, one of the leaders of the revolution. Lobkowitz and Czartoryski knew each other personally, probably through the governor's earlier involvement in Polish issues. Early on, Czartoryski wrote to Lobkowitz pleading for Austrian aid in support of the Polish uprising.

> With your permission, my Prince, under grave circumstances, I appeal to your good sense and ask you to deliver two letters to His Majesty the Emperor that the Polish government addresses to him. In the first, we rely on the intelligence of His Imperial Royal and Apostolic Majesty and request the recognition of our independence; in the second, we appeal to his human and religious sentiments and request his intervention with a force that would provide indispensable means for defense.[36]

Czartoryski had reason to believe that Lobkowitz would be willing to intercede on the Poles' behalf in Vienna. Lobkowitz did not disappoint his Polish friend; between November 1830 and January 1831, the governor feverishly sought Austrian assistance for the rebels. The Polish revolution, according to Lobkowitz's assurances to Vienna, would have no adverse effects upon the Polish territories in the Habsburg Monarchy; his Polish friends pledged to respect Austria's borders as presently constituted. In December 1830, Lobkowitz reported: "From my knowledge I can guarantee that no revolutionary disturbances will have any impact upon the province."[37] The Poles, meanwhile, established a hierarchical system of civil and military administration, with General Józef Chłopicki appointed dictator. This highly centralized government could offer some advantages for the Poles and their potential allies: most important decisions went through Chłopicki, who transmitted them internationally. Neither he nor any other Poles seem to have broken their international commitments. In his correspondence with Vienna, Lobkowitz referred to Chłopicki's promise to keep the revolt confined to Russian-ruled territory, without any interference in neighboring states.[38] During the early months of the revolution, Polish subjects in Galicia remained loyal to the Habsburg dynasty, and evinced no political animus toward the monarchy.[39]

But even if most Poles remained faithful to Vienna, a number of Austrian Polish subjects moved to Russian-ruled Poland to join its army of independence.[40] Members of the Sanguszko, Lubomirski, Potocki, and Dzieduszycki families supported the revolution in various ways,[41] providing financial support and hosting Polish refugees after the uprising collapsed in the spring of 1831. Polish students from Lemberg University took part in the struggle as well.[42] In December 1830 and early January 1831, Lobkowitz personally reviewed reports from Galician districts; he was thus aware that many Poles were moving from the province to the Kingdom of Poland to fight against the Russian authorities there.[43]

In 1830–31, meanwhile, controversy emerged over the involvement of Austrian bureaucrats or members of their families in the Polish revolution. Since the 1820s, Johann Georg von Ostermann had served as head of the Austrian district administration in Sanok. His two sons, Georg Benjamin and Moritz Hugo, studied at the university in Lemberg, where some of their close Polish associates made no secret of their involvement in Polish political conspiracies. In late 1830, the elder Ostermann officially condemned the Polish revolution; but on 28 February 1831, the Lemberg newspaper *Gazeta Lwowska* published reports that one of Ostermann's sons, Georg Benjamin, had traveled to the Russian Empire and tried to join the Polish revolutionary army. The article provoked a sensation and official bewilderment: how could sons of Austrian dignitaries fight in the Polish national revolution?[44]

The report caused a major scandal. Governor Lobkowitz personally interviewed the elder Ostermann, inquiring about his and his family's involvement in the revolution. Ostermann hastened to assure his senior colleagues that both sons had stayed at home. Indeed, none of the Ostermanns had ever crossed the border. But allegations about their involvement in Polish conspiracies were not entirely unfounded. The Polish revolution had become the subject of feverish debate in the Ostermann household. The father, who would have almost certainly lost his position for any engagement in the Polish cause, officially condemned the revolt. His elder son, Georg Benjamin, took a pro-Polish stance, and some personal risks as well; he indeed tried to join Polish revolutionaries in the Russian Empire. The article in the *Gazeta Lwowska* may have been based on information about his attempt to cross the frontier, which was ultimately unsuccessful: stopped by border guards, he was forcibly returned to his father's home.[45]

Lobkowitz did not approve of such actions, nor did he encourage any involvement of Galicians in the revolution. As with his colleagues in Vienna, the governor's priority was to maintain political stability in the province, and he must have realized that great enthusiasm for the Polish uprising might have profound implications for the Austrian Empire. But even as they shared a consensus on the need to preserve the status quo in Galicia, Lobkowitz and his colleagues in the imperial capital disagreed on the mechanisms of securing this domestic order. The governor believed that Vienna's intercession on behalf of the Polish cause in Russia would ensure the long-term loyalty of Galician Poles. By contrast, Metternich and Sedlnitzky feared that any Austrian involvement would damage relations with Russia and stir revolutionary impulses among Poles without regard for borders, including in Galicia. Vienna would take no such risks.

Lobkowitz's pro-Polish choices, however, caused much cross-border confusion. In 1830 and 1831, he became an object of Polish hope, Austrian frustration, and Russian suspicion. He was also the center of multifarious attention: Austrian statesmen, Russian diplomats, and Polish revolutionaries all closely watched the governor. By January 1831, the disagreement between Lobkowitz and Metternich had come to a head: the former insisted that an independent Poland would serve Austria as a key security buffer against Russia, while Metternich feared, with reason, that any independent Polish state could lay claim to Austrian Galicia, and thus endanger the integrity of the Habsburg Monarchy.[46] When Metternich considered deploying Austrian troops from other provinces to Galicia to head off any potential pro-Polish unrest, Lobkowitz advised against it. He recognized Austria's weak military presence in Galicia, but saw no cause for concern, believing, moreover, that a heavier Habsburg hand in the province would only negatively impact the political loyalty of its inhabitants.[47]

Metternich's writings from the early months of 1831 reveal his growing frustration with the Galician governor. Their correspondence has not been entirely preserved, but what remains leaves no doubt about the serious disagreements between them. In early January 1831, the chancellor commented on Lobkowitz's Polish policies, which found no support in Vienna: "Prince Adam Czartoryski will have to pardon Governor Lobkowitz for his hasty and unreflective actions. We do not acknowledge any changes of the current political order in Poland."[48] The "hasty and unreflective actions" might have been Lobkowitz's individual commitment to the Polish cause, his promise of Austrian support to the Polish revolutionaries, or both.

In his report of April 1831, Lobkowitz informed Czartoryski of Vienna's final decision regarding the Polish issue: "Dear Prince: I have the honor to inform you that I delivered your message to His Majesty the Emperor without delay. The circumstances of the great conflict between Russia and Poland are not well known here. . . . The Emperor wishes an end to the struggle that desecrates a happy and flourishing country, torn by an inconceivable misfortune for an entire generation, and inflicts great suffering on many innocent families." By April 1831, the "circumstances" of the Russo-Polish conflict, of course, were exceedingly clear; but Emperor Francis II, Chancellor Metternich, and Police Chief Sedlnitzky had made their final choice. As Lobkowitz continued in his letter to Czartoryski: "The Emperor does not wish to authorize intervention into this [Polish] cause, as it would produce tensions with his ally, the Emperor of Russia." Reluctant to intervene, the Austrian emperor advised the Poles to "turn to the Russian Emperor with their own hearts and confidence."[49] Lobkowitz was left with nothing to offer.

Both Lobkowitz and Czartoryski could easily see at this point how the Polish revolution would turn out. The rebels had become increasingly isolated in the international arena, with no military or political assistance in sight. The experienced elder statesman Czartoryski had been correct, upon reluctantly joining the revolutionary project once it was under way, to believe that any such uprising against St. Petersburg was likely doomed to fail. Young Lobkowitz, by contrast, had seriously miscalculated Austrian policies and Vienna's responses; by encouraging his Polish friends, he may have indirectly helped incite the Polish revolution. When the uprising did break out, he could not keep his early promises.

From January on, Austria enforced new restrictions on contact between Galicia and Russian Poland. With the outbreak that month of cholera among Polish troops in Russia, Vienna tightened control of the border with its imperial neighbor. These cordoning measures, only to some extent induced by health considerations, would also serve to prevent the numerous Polish independence forces, infected or otherwise, from entering Galicia. The two major local newspapers, the *Lemberger Zeitung* and the *Gazeta Lwowska*, published daily travel restrictions; Galicia's Polish subjects were likewise prohibited from visiting Russian Poland. Due to the spread of cholera, Lobkowitz supported cross-border restrictions as well.[50] The Austrian ambassador to the Kingdom of Poland, Baron Oechner, was no longer permitted to issue the authorizations required for Russia's Polish subjects to come to Galicia, where, for their part, Polish nobles were strongly discouraged from going abroad. Violations of travel restrictions were severely punished by the Austrian authorities.[51] Only in July 1831 did Vienna lift its cordon sanitaire, much to the joy of the people of Galicia.[52]

Having lost all hope of securing Vienna's military assistance, Lobkowitz sought to ensure the safe transfer of the Polish army—or at least part of it—from Russian Poland to Austrian Galicia. As defeat of the independence cause became patently inevitable, Czartoryski continued to write to the governor, requesting assistance. Austrian Galicia, Czartoryski hoped, would open its doors to Polish soldiers who would otherwise fall victim to the tsar's reprisals. A transfer to Galicia seemed to be the lone escape route, but one that would be available to the Poles only as a concession from Vienna. On 5 May 1831, Czartoryski once more turned to Lobkowitz for support: "We again confirm that General Dwernicki, trapped on different sides by superior forces, is forced to seek refuge in the territory of Galicia. In this moment of trouble, the Poles find their consolation in the generosity of the Sovereign of Austria."[53]

Czartoryski pleaded for help, appealing to the various human and moral sentiments that might help save Polish lives. "How could the Austrian court, out of respect for justice and law, not offer asylum to those who need it?"

Referring to the events of the war, Czartoryski insisted that the Poles had kept their promises, refraining from crossing into Austria even in the face of impending doom on their side of the border: "You may not forget, my prince, that the Poles, out of respect for Austria and at the risk of their own lives, honored Austrian neutrality and took no actions against the crimes which the Russians inflicted upon them."[54] Early on, it will be recalled, Lobkowitz had negotiated with Vienna on the assurance that the Polish revolutionaries would keep the conflict contained within the borders of the Russian Empire.

The Russians, Czartoryski argued, had been the first to cross into Austrian territory, while in Galicia Poles were only seeking refuge. "It is impossible, my prince, that your August Sovereign would not recognize the differences in the conduct of the two parties."[55] Why, he wondered, should Vienna consider Poles its enemies? Such an attitude had practical consequences for the Poles; the Austrians' cordoning off of Polish territories had severed lines of communication with the rest of Europe, effecting a commercial and informational blockade that only exacerbated the independence-seekers' plight. "I do not understand," Czartoryski complained to Lobkowitz, "why Poles deserve such treatment."[56]

In his efforts to rescue the Poles, Lobkowitz found support among colleagues in the Austrian diplomatic mission in Warsaw. The Habsburg ambassador in that city, Baron Oechner, cooperated with Lobkowitz and assisted in securing the transfer of Poles into Galicia.[57] Lobkowitz's and Oechner's combined efforts helped save the lives of many Polish officers and civilians. Often these Polish asylum seekers were received upon their arrival in Lemberg by the governor personally, who even hosted some Polish officers in his own residence.[58] Lobkowitz's rescue plan would have a significant long-term impact on Polish political life across borders. Some of the Polish refugees remained in Galicia after 1831, while many others traveled farther west, to Paris, which during the 1830s became a center of Polish emigration and political conspiracies.[59] Refugees in the French capital would prepare a new uprising that would bear even more directly on Galicia.

Amid aiding the transfer of Polish troops to Galicia, Lobkowitz advised Czartoryski to launch diplomatic negotiations with Russia, and offered

Austrian mediation therein. The governor advised the Poles to lay themselves at the feet of the Russian emperor and plead for an armistice.[60] This of course would imply Poland's ultimate defeat: the Poles' war aim had been to separate themselves from Russia, and now Lobkowitz was proposing that his Polish friends should accept peace on the tsar's condition that Polish territories remain part of the Russian Empire.[61] Czartoryski seems to have found it difficult to accept such a proposition.

By offering safe passage to Polish troops, meanwhile, Lobkowitz had once more jeopardized relations between Vienna and St. Petersburg. When the first Polish refugees crossed the Russo-Austrian border in January 1831, Tatishchev lodged official protests, insisting that his government's Polish subjects must be tried by Russian military tribunals.[62] While Polish officers enjoyed the hospitality of the Galician governor, Russian diplomats complained to Vienna about Lobkowitz's provocative actions. When the defeat of the Polish uprising sealed Poland's fate for the time being, it derailed Lobkowitz's individual career plans as well. Reconciling himself to the Polish defeat, the governor altered his expectations and his strategies; he even credited Russia with halting the spread of the Polish uprising, and thus securing the stability of the Austrian monarchy.

The defeat induced in Lobkowitz a new rhetoric in his correspondence with Vienna. In July 1831, the governor wrote to higher-ups in the capital with a proposal completely contradicting most of his earlier initiatives vis-à-vis Polish political aspirations. He advised that Russian officers be rewarded for helping to prevent the spread of revolution to Galicia. He singled out several individuals in the tsar's military, described their contributions toward defeating the uprising, and provided suggestions for awards. He explained his motives thus: a number of Austrian officers had been rewarded for their role in the Russo-Turkish War. Such a reciprocal exchange of awards, Lobkowitz noted, would resonate well with public opinion in Russia.[63] The governor's new attitude, however, came too late, and had little if any impact on Vienna's decisions with regard either to the province or to Lobkowitz's position within the Austrian administration.

Lobkowitz's dismissal was imminent, as he himself was likely aware. For years, he had sought to use the international situation for the benefit of

Poland, a country that, as Lobkowitz saw it, could only be revived with (or rather outside of) a defeated Russia. While Lobkowitz interfered with Russian politics over the years, tsarist officials in turn kept an eye on the Galician governor. He eventually fell victim to Russian disfavor; Nicholas I personally insisted on Lobkowitz's removal from Galicia.[64] By then, Lobkowitz had also antagonized Metternich. For security and other reasons, he would no longer be allowed to stay in the province.

The escalation of the political crisis in Galicia was probably a result of miscalculations on the part of senior Austrian officials, most notably Metternich himself. Information about Polish conspiracies across the Russian-Austrian borders was abundant, and so were the Austrian spies and police officers stationed in the borderland province. Yet months after the explosion of the revolution and despite the openly defiant stance of the Galician governor, the Austrian authorities in Vienna showed little concern. Part of it perhaps had to do with the general and largely correct assessment that the majority of Galicians—Poles, Ruthenians, and Jews—remained loyal to the monarchy. The Napoleonic episode, which triggered separatism among Habsburg Polish subjects, was in itself an exception, and Polish loyalties and allegiances had by 1830 shifted in Vienna's favor.

The political situation in Galicia became critical only after the defeat of the Polish revolution in Warsaw. The influx of Polish officers into the Austrian province, facilitated by Lobkowitz, could no longer be ignored as it posed a direct security threat to the monarchy. Only then did Metternich take radical action by imposing travel restrictions, issuing police ordinances, and, finally, dismissing the governor.

Lobkowitz's removal was a major setback for the Poles. Even when unable to keep his promises, the governor had ever seemed their staunch ally and advocate. A few prominent Poles remained in Russian captivity. In the summer of 1831, Czartoryski hoped to secure Lobkowitz's support for the release of these individuals, including Roman Sanguszko, an acquaintance of Czartoryski's and Lobkowitz's who had earlier that year been captured by Russian forces in the Volyn' region. Czartoryski personally intervened on Sanguszko's behalf, inquiring as to his whereabouts and well-being. He was, however, unable to rescue Sanguszko, at which point he turned to Lobkowitz for help.[65]

Even when he lost his post in Galicia, Lobkowitz remained in a position of power. His personal network, which had been instrumental in launching his career in the first place, proved a great help during his professional crisis. Emperor Francis II had no choice but to move Lobkowitz to another position, even consulting with him about his personal preferences regarding his next appointment. As Mélanie Princess Metternich noted in her diary: "Klemens talked to me about Lobkowitz. The emperor already declared that he would no longer remain the governor of Galicia and that this post would go to Archduke Ferdinand. In the meantime, the emperor, who did not mean to offend anyone, arranged for a post in the Chamber of Commerce, which Lobkowitz accepted."[66]

Lobkowitz's story bears remarkable similarities to that of at least one of his predecessors. Johann Anton von Pergen, decades before Lobkowitz, was forced to resign as governor of Galicia. He had moved back to Vienna in the hope of recovering his reputation and his career. His return was less that triumphant as he was only able to secure a relatively marginal position within the administration of Lower Austria. Yet Pergen found his new passion in a domain that had received little attention from his predecessors. It took only a few years for him to resurface on the political and administrative scene with in full force, eventually making a name for himself as the founding father of the professional police in the monarchy.

Lobkowitz followed a similar path. His first appointment in Vienna in 1832—that of a minor official in the Chamber of Commerce—did not match his expectations. Police agents followed him in Vienna. Yet within months after his arrival, he was promoted to a more prestigious post at the Austrian-Bohemian Court Chancellery, most likely as a result of his personal and professional connections. Two years after his return to Vienna, he was promoted yet again, this time becoming head of the imperial Chamber of Commerce and Mining. His Galician Polish episode seemed to have remained in the remote past, and Lobkowitz engaged himself fully in financial matters. In the 1830s, he became a leading force behind a currency reform in the Habsburg Monarchy.[67] No longer able to influence Austrian Polish policies, Lobkowitz discovered a new passion in finance.

The collapse of the revolution caused greater harm to the Poles in Russia, of course, than it did to Lobkowitz. New restrictions followed, and the Kingdom of Poland, and Russian Poland in general, would never again offer such favorable conditions for Polish cultural and political life as had existed under Alexander I. Concomitant with the turn in tsarist policy was a geographical shift in Polish political life, with Paris now a key center of Polish emigration and conspiracy. The contracting of Polish political life in the Russian Empire also meant a corresponding increase in its significance in the Habsburg Monarchy.

The Austrians did not delay in adopting preventive measures against Polish revolutionary plots. The year 1832 saw the establishment of the Galician Information Bureau, a semisecret international institution complementary to the Austrian state police.[68] Its agents collected information on Galician politics and filed regular reports to Vienna. During the 1830s, the bureau came to play a major role in the province, where its agents remained busy, albeit with little of note to report: within months of the revolt's downfall, life in Galicia returned to normal. Austrian police agents attended numerous theaters, dance parties, and celebrations, but could not find anything particularly suspicious. The political upheavals of the previous several months were almost forgotten.[69]

Lobkowitz did not cause the Polish revolution, nor did he prevent its defeat. His political role in 1830–31, however, should not be underestimated. As governor of Galicia, Lobkowitz was authorized only to follow the instructions of his superiors in Vienna. He overstepped his authority on several occasions, coming up with initiatives not only never sanctioned in the capital, but also fraught with risk to domestic stability in the monarchy and to its relations with the Russian Empire.

By declaring himself a Pole, Lobkowitz broke political conventions and defied the expectations placed upon him as governor of a Habsburg province. But his choices were, in a way, products of Austrian policies and the specific political situation in the Austro-Russian borderland. Austria's relations with Russia were never entirely friendly, and Vienna's policies toward its Polish subjects in Galicia were never exclusively hostile. In some ways,

Lobkowitz reflected ongoing changes within the Austrian bureaucracy in Galicia, as an increasing number of individuals in his milieu integrated into local Polish society. Such bureaucrats, who defied Vienna's central policies and supported the Polish cause, could pose a more serious danger to the integrity of the Austrian Empire than native elites in Galicia or elsewhere in the monarchy.

The case of August Lobkowitz reveals many nuances of imperial administration, including stark disagreements between the central government in Vienna and Austrian officials in the provinces. Such splits within the administration, and the often related phenomenon of bureaucrats making unconventional choices regarding their cultural-national identity, are essential for our understanding of the history of the region during the nineteenth century and beyond. The central government in Vienna viewed the intervention of Polish nobles in Austrian policies with great wariness, but the situation on the ground in Galicia looked quite different. Even when not directly involved in the administration, Polish elites came to exert a strong influence upon particular local bureaucrats, influencing decisions that bore not only on Galicia, but on the entire monarchy.

FIVE

Austrian Bureaucracy and Polish Aristocracy

August Lobkowitz was one of a large cohort of Austrian officials who succumbed to the charms of the Polish aristocracy. In 1809, one Austrian official remarked upon the impact Polish society had on German-speaking bureaucrats in Galicia: "The luxury of Polish women impressed the Germans, and these women's influence on the business of court councillors is often quite obvious. Their style, furniture, and all the little things [*Kleinigkeiten*] proved to have an irresistible impact on Austrian bureaucrats."[1]

Some of these newcomers brought their families to Galicia, but many came unmarried. Outside their offices, German-speaking officials could easily discover a world of culture and politics defying the many stereotypes of backwardness and poverty attached to the province. Literary salons in eighteenth-century Galicia were organized on the French model, and accordingly conducted in French. Theater life was particularly rich during summer seasons, and performances were staged in a variety of languages. Yearly fairs oftentimes became events of great political and cultural significance. While men settled their business behind closed doors in offices, the outside world offered numerous attractions—one of which proved to be local women.

The women who made the strongest impression upon Austrian bureaucrats belonged to the local Galician elite—the Polish aristocracy having traditionally dominated Polish life. Often prosperous, refined in taste, and conversant in French, some of these women presided over salons across Galicia. Others, though not as well off, attended these gatherings, as well as the many coffeehouses and theaters that opened their doors throughout the province beginning in the 1770s, and whose style and glamour proved irresistible.

Ongoing social and political changes in Austrian administration are particularly revealed in mixed marriages between Poles and Austrian Germans. By the early nineteenth century, an increasing number of German-speaking Austrian bureaucrats in Galicia were wed to Polish women. These bureaucrats, one must remember, had arrived in the province tasked with bringing German culture, politics, and civilization into formerly Polish terrains. By marrying Polish women, hence involving themselves in Polish cultural and political life, these officials accomplished, in effect, the opposite of their purported mission.

Writing at the turn of the twentieth century, the Polish historian Władysław Łoziński revealed his impression of Austrian rule: "Galicia was designed to become a German school for the Poles. It became a Polish school for the Germans instead."[2] Long after Łoziński, in the 1980s, Piotr Wandycz discussed the remarkable civilizational appeal Polish nobles exerted upon Austrian bureaucrats.[3] Tales of Germanophone Austrian bureaucrats having culturally transformed themselves into Poles (and Ruthenians as well) survive to the present day. How and why Austrian bureaucrats and Polish aristocrats came to draw so close to one another during Austrian rule is the subject of this chapter.

Polish Nobility

Poland-Lithuania had boasted the largest per capita percentage of nobles in early modern Europe. According to various estimates, on average, nobles constituted 7–8 percent of the population, with up to 750,000 Polish subjects claiming titular nobility.[4] The proportion of Galicia's population that was noble (around 3 percent) was lower than the average for Poland at large, but several times greater than that of other Habsburg provinces.[5] The sheer number of nobles in Galicia was one problem; their density in certain of the province's localities was another. In some East Galician districts, for example Sambor, nobles numbered up to 25 percent of the population.[6]

Like any other part of Poland-Lithuania, Galicia was a land of great social contrasts. On the one hand, it was home to prosperous aristocratic families who in wealth and political influence could compete with Polish kings. At the same time, the vast majority of nobles in this region were rather poor, with 75 percent owning no land of their own. Some villages were populated solely by landless nobles, who in their financial situation and lifestyles resembled peasants.[7]

The Polish-Lithuanian nobility espoused principles of political and social equality that rendered the version of their estate quite different from its counterparts in the rest of continental Europe. Even the poorest of the poor had access to education, reserved for this class alone. Nobles exercised their political rights in parliaments. Even those who worked the land in principle formed part of Poland's political elite. But, as distinct from any other territory in Europe, no proper registers of nobles and their property were ever produced in Poland.[8]

Self-proclaimedly egalitarian, this nobility in reality constituted an elitist, strictly hierarchical society with rather limited access for outsiders. Only a minute portion of Polish nobles enjoyed their privileges to the fullest, and only the most prominent aristocrats held the top offices in Poland-Lithuania, the prestige of which was considerable. Given the venal nature of such positions, only prosperous nobles could afford such posts.[9] Landownership and administrative titles thus marked important social and political distinctions between Polish aristocrats and relatively prosperous nobles, on the one hand, and the remaining masses of poor nobles on the other. Poland never had an official hierarchy of titles. The prefixes of prince and count were commonly used in informal communication, but had no official legitimacy.[10]

The nobility in the Habsburg Monarchy contrasted sharply with its ostensibly democratic counterpart in Poland; nobles in the Habsburg lands had traditionally been identified with specific provinces, with the concept of an "Austrian aristocracy" emerging only after the dissolution of the Holy Roman Empire in 1806. A strict hierarchy divided the nobility into various categories—the upper, middle, and lower aristocracy, all of which had distinctly different social statuses.[11] Only aristocrats of the highest ranks—princes and counts—were allowed to own land and hold major administrative offices.[12] Unlike in Poland, noble hierarchies and titles were inscribed in registries. Only Hungary resembled Galicia in its social structure, with a full 4 percent of the kingdom's population claiming noble status; for Austria's German territories, the average percentage was 1 percent or less.[13]

Vienna's attempt to reform the nobility in Galicia thus implied a twofold change. The number of Polish nobles was to be reduced to the monarchy's average; and poorer nobles, possessed of neither land nor great financial resources, could expect to lose their political privileges—formerly in any case in practice a function of status, but now to become openly so. With their numbers reduced, all nobles would be divided into different categories in accordance with the existing Austrian system, which included the ranks of prince, count, baron, and simply "noble."[14] This hierarchy of titles having no previous official existence in Poland-Lithuania was to be introduced in Galicia. Each member of the Polish nobility, of whatever rank, was subjected to the process of nobilitation, with his or her status required to be confirmed by the Austrian authorities. The procedure itself created problems; its implementation, rather than the motivation behind it, eventually caused much discontent among high-ranking Polish aristocrats and nobles, forced thus to present themselves in person and negotiate their status with Austrian officials, whose ranks and status were often lower than their own.

Austrian rulers were quite generous to prosperous and politically important Polish aristocrats. Two hundred and twenty-five aristocrats owned 70 percent of the estates in Galicia.[15] These individuals represented twelve families having borne (informal) princely titles in Poland-Lithuania.[16] Administrative office became the most important criterion for award of titles. Members of the Polish Senate and holders of ministerial offices in Poland-Lithuania could expect to have their princely titles confirmed after 1772.[17] Polish princes were rewarded additional titles as princes in the Holy Roman Empire. Only a few had their titles confirmed during the 1770s and 1780s, but many others passed this muster over the course of the nineteenth century.[18]

Lesser titles were distributed accordingly. Holders of regional offices in Poland-Lithuania were granted the title of count in the Habsburg Monarchy. Twenty-seven individuals were awarded the title of baron, a common Austrian rank very often awarded to members of the business elite. In Galicia, the "baron" title marked a certain compromise: it was extended to persons who could trace their nobility back at least two generations. In all, some thirteen hundred Polish subjects received aristocratic titles, granted by the Habsburg monarch as Holy Roman Emperor.[19]

The very idea of noble registers was a radical innovation for those aspiring to maintain their status. Titles were recorded in noble charters granted by the king of Poland, starting from the Middle Ages. By the eighteenth century, an individual status was oftentimes recorded in oral lore rather than on paper. Considering the possibility that documentation of titles might have been indeed lost over the years, Austrian officials included a financial regulation as a criteria of inclusion or exclusion into the ranks of nobility: landownership became a sufficient proof of belonging to the elite.

After 1772, the Austrians also introduced the practice of merit-based nobilitation. Some Poles serving in the Austrian administration or military became eligible to receive noble titles as a reward for their services. Most of these new titles were venal, but this Austrian initiative could hardly be explained by financial motives alone; the process had significant political ramifications as well. By offering such titles, Vienna expected to mobilize the elite's support for the Austrian regime. The number of titles granted by the Habsburg monarch was comparable to the number of titles recognized in Poland-Lithuania.[20] The transition to the Austrian period thus did not mark a radical decline for the Polish nobility as an institution.

The year 1772 was of course a political shock for many Poles. But the most prosperous aristocrats experienced little in the way of adverse effects from the partitions; their social status remained as before, or even improved, while their financial situation did not necessarily worsen. Through the Habsburg Monarchy they gained access to new markets, and were afforded economic opportunities unavailable in the Polish-Lithuanian polity. Their lives changed, but this change was not necessarily to their detriment.

Poor nobles, on the other hand, faced quite a different reality. Those who had no proof of their status, nor the requisite financial resources to compensate for this lack, could expect to lose their privileges. By excluding poor and landless families from the noble hierarchy, Vienna could reduce the Polish nobility to the monarchy's average without losing the support of prosperous aristocrats. Only one in four nobles in Galicia owned land. That one could expect to retain his title, while the other three, Austrian officials hoped, would lose their status.

The reform of the Polish nobility was not an Austrian innovation. The so-called declassification of poor nobles was an ongoing process, begun in Poland-Lithuania and continuing in different Polish territories after the partitions.[21] Debates regarding the status of the poor landless nobility had gotten under way in Poland-Lithuania as early as 1764. Initiatives for social reforms were partly driven by economic contingencies. For centuries, nobles had enjoyed exemption from taxation, but their outsized percentage in the population, combined with their economic privileges, presented political and economic problems; a land tax, it was proposed, could serve as an important source of revenue for Poland at a time of crisis. Debates concerning the status of poor nobles continued in Poland-Lithuania after the First Partition, creating interesting parallels: Warsaw and Vienna concurrently engaged in similar reform movements. But neither carried the reforms to completion.

The reforms in Poland-Lithuania were brought to an abrupt end by the Third Partition in 1795.[22] In the Habsburg Monarchy, the reform of the nobility continued through 1817, through the reigns of four consecutive rulers: Maria Theresa, Joseph II, Leopold II, and Francis II. In 1775, nobles in Galicia were required to confirm their status by presenting proof of their respective titles in the form of their families' genealogies, or, alternatively, proof of their having owned land in the region under Polish-Lithuanian rule.[23] In 1782, Joseph II adjusted the reforms via new strategies. Insofar as genealogical proof could have been lost over time, as some nobles claimed, evidence of sufficient financial means was accepted by the Austrian authorities as an appropriate alternative. Those able to provide proof of adequate financial resources would be allowed to retain noble titles in the Habsburg

Monarchy. This financial provision was an important concession. Other formal requirements were gradually relaxed as well, and beginning in 1782, the testimony of four witnesses would suffice to certify an individual's noble status.

Joseph II had envisioned completing the registries of the nobility within the first six months of their introduction. This deadline was extended several times, with six months eventually turning into six years; but even by 1788, no end was in sight. The number of nobles who voluntarily registered with the Austrian authorities was rather small. Those failing to comply suffered no consequences; the differences in status between Polish nobles who had their titles confirmed and those who did not were miniscule.[24] The review of noble titles and noble estates was officially concluded in 1817, when, partly as a result of the Napoleonic Wars, Vienna opened a new Galician Diet. But neither in 1775 nor in 1817 did Austrian officials know the exact number of nobles in Galicia, nor their political and economic statuses.

In their encounter with the Polish nobility, the Habsburgs were dealing with a typical imperial dilemma: how to incorporate a new territory and subordinate its population to a new center without entirely antagonizing the local elites. The proximity of other Polish territories—most specifically, the Russian portion across the border from Galicia—had a defining impact upon Austrian policies. Both Kaunitz and his counterpart in St. Petersburg were acutely aware of the fact that Polish loyalty could be a guarantor of stability on the borderlands. Disloyalty, in turn, could be a major destabilizing factor affecting the situation not only in one region but in the empire as a whole.

Major reform of the Polish nobility started in the Russian Empire during the 1780s under Catherine the Great. Similarly to their Austrian counterparts, the Russians declared their intention to proceed in a radical manner by completing new registers of Polish nobles, reducing their overall number, integrating the most prominent aristocrats into the Russian imperial elite, and relegating poor nobles to the status of the peasants. The intention was not just a political but above all an economic one. St. Petersburg, unlike Vienna, planned to monopolize control over the land by nationalizing the property of the declassified Polish nobles.[25]

Russian and Austrian statements sometimes expressed similar attitudes toward their new subjects. Equally important was their inability to carry some of their reforms through to completion. Just like their Austrian neighbors, Russian officials found it exceedingly hard to carry out proper statistics that would form a basis for the reform of the nobility. In the meantime, Polish nobles exposed remarkable solidarity at the face of forceful Russian modernization. They resold the land among themselves so as to help the poor nobles maintain their status.

Austria's failure to complete the registries of nobles, in turn, could be partly attributed to the extensive collaboration between Habsburg officials and Polish nobles. Austrian bureaucrats and Polish aristocrats constantly complained about one another, but each group, albeit in different ways, depended on the other. Austrian officials could provide access to social status and positions in education, the military, and administration for the sons of impoverished nobles. Favors were reciprocated by various gifts, which, as we have seen from his "pastoral letter," Joseph II would have regarded as bribes. Some Austrian bureaucrats hindered the enforcement of new rules and restrictions, while others issued false certificates, thus further complicating the efforts of Vienna.

Polish responses were as complex as the multifarious Austrian policies. Some Poles supported Austrian rule, taking full advantage of the new economic and social opportunities it afforded. Others endorsed it conditionally, hoping to retain their property and status. As a result, some contemporaries in the eighteenth century, and Polish historians in the nineteenth and twentieth centuries, blamed Polish nobles for acquiescing to the foreign regime, in effect facilitating the Germanization of Galicia.[26] These charges reflect a national bias and misinterpret the reality: opposition against Germanization—specifically German-language schools—was quite prevalent among the Polish nobles, both the prosperous and the poor. Many others opposed the regime as such, despite never staging open revolt or provoking confrontation.

The variety of Polish responses to the Austrian regime can only be understood within the specific political context of the Polish territories in the late eighteenth century, namely the ongoing political crisis in Poland-Lithuania, when it still existed; the division of Polish lands among three monarchies; and the ensuing competition among these states for the loyalty of their new Polish subjects.

At the same time, conditional endorsement of the Austrian regime opened new avenues for political participation, as well as opportunities for organized opposition. The most effective resistance could be mobilized within the framework of parliamentary institutions of the kind that had long existed in Poland. But what recourse remained to those underprivileged (both politically and economically) Poles, possessed of influence over neither their own individual fates nor over the question of what would become of this province formerly part of Poland?

Parliament or Representation

Even if the social status of individual Polish aristocrats was not significantly altered after 1772, the institutional structures of the Polish nobility underwent radical changes. The center of political decision making was transferred from Lwów/Lemberg to Vienna, and for some time, the nobility was excluded from administration. Most importantly, Vienna abolished the traditional Polish Diet formerly at the center of political authority in Poland.

Before 1772, diets functioned as full-fledged parliaments, wielding a broad range of political and economic authority. They voted to go to war, monitored Poland's foreign relations, and controlled taxation. Their status in Poland-Lithuania had changed little over the centuries, and they were the cornerstone of a "republican" political system that rejected absolutism and strong central government. Poland's historic parliamentary structures were abolished once Galicia became part of the Habsburg Monarchy, with Austrian central institutions, Gubernia, and districts replacing the diet in the region.

The first diet following the partition met in Lemberg in 1775. That year, Maria Theresa authorized the holding of an assembly of the Galician noble estate under the jurisdiction of the Austrian authorities; Governor Heinrich von Auersperg opened the assembly that had once represented the Polish ruling class. The convocation of this diet was a symbolic move, a concession to Polish nobles: even denied access to the administration, they would be allowed some measure of participation in official political discourse. But the body meeting in Lemberg in 1775 was only a pale reflection of the traditional diets many of its members remembered from the Polish period. In the 1770s, Polish nobles were stripped of decision-making authority, and they could only offer policy suggestions to their Austrian sovereigns. None of these suggestions was legally binding.[27]

Still, the holding of this diet was an important moment in the political history of Galicia. The Galician diet resembled similar estate assemblies that existed throughout the Habsburg Monarchy. These parliamentary bodies, which met in Lemberg, Prague, Brünn, Vienna, Trieste, and other provincial capitals, created a façade of uniformity across the realm. Within this uniformity, Galicia still presented an exception of sorts. If other provinces had become accustomed to Vienna's intervention over the decades, everything was still quite new in Galicia.

One of the most vociferous advocates of Galician self-government and the privileges of its nobility was Count Józef Dzieduszycki. In 1775, Dzieduszycki appealed to Vienna, requesting a different type of noble representation in Galicia, one that would have full-fledged political authority.[28] Dzieduszycki considered the radical introduction of new institutions in Galicia as a sign of Austrian unwillingness to cooperate with local elites, a form of oppression.[29] He appealed to the logic of imperial aims, explaining that central reluctance to accommodate local realities jeopardized Austrian political and economic efforts in Galicia. The province's politics and economy raised serious concerns in Vienna, but Dzieduszycki's petitions produced no change. The Galician Diet met again in 1776 and reconvened under Joseph II in 1782, with its status remaining unchanged throughout its existence.[30]

Joseph II's death marked the end of a political era in the history of the monarchy, and brought new hope for autonomy-minded Poles in Galicia. The new ruler, Emperor Leopold II, the Grand Duke of Tuscany, arrived in Vienna from the Habsburg Italian territories, where he had supported local institutions counter to the increasing centralization advocated by Joseph II. Unlike his predecessor, Leopold II favored government by regional consensus.³¹ He set out to reverse the reforms of the 1780s that had remained in force after 1790. The new emperor even encouraged provincial elites to register their grievances directly with Vienna; he claimed to take their complaints seriously, and used them as justification for new policies.³²

Leopold II's political initiatives bore fruit across the monarchy. The diet in Bohemia regained the right to impose and control taxes, of which Joseph II had deprived it in the 1780s.³³ Encouraged by the recent changes, Polish nobles in Galicia hoped to secure a similar status for themselves within such newly created institutions as would monitor Austrian policies in Galicia. A new round of petitions from Galician nobles, however, produced no tangible results. Galician nobles were allowed to hold the diet, but in contrast to Polish parliamentary tradition, this body retained only nominal functions.³⁴ Other requests, such as the replacement of Austrian German officials by Polish nobles, were dismissed out of hand.³⁵

In 1792, a delegation of Polish nobles led by Józef Ossoliński, a member of a prominent Polish magnate family, brought their grievances directly to Leopold II. They presented an elaborate program of reforms for Galicia, informally titled the "Magna Charta."³⁶ The plan focused on institutional aspects of Austrian politics. Within the new state structure, noted Ossoliński and his colleagues, Poles had no control over decisions concerning their province. The Polish statesmen registered their objection to the exclusively German administration, requested greater access to Austrian institutions, and, most importantly, anticipated the establishment of a system of representation of estates with political, not merely symbolic, functions. Leopold II died shortly after this petition was submitted, in effect never having a chance to respond.

The document did, however, catch the attention of several Austrian officials in Galicia, and provoked debate. Responding to the Poles' requests, and generally tolerant toward Polish nobles, Governor Brigido encouraged their integration into the Austrian state service. But even he opposed what he considered to be radical Polish propositions. An assembly of and for the nobles would impinge, he argued, on the interests of the majority, that is, the peasants. Brigido compared the state to a pyramid: the stability of the vertex depends on that of the foundation. This foundation was essential to the survival of the whole construction; but an estate assembly composed of nobles alone would defy the interests of the majority of Galicia's population.[37]

A new diet was convened in 1817, thirty-five years after its initial suppression by Vienna. Brigido's successors, Governors Peter von Goëss and Franz von Hauer, advocated political concessions to accommodate Polish elites in Galicia after a difficult war. Allowed thus to engage in political debate, Polish nobles were nonetheless virtually powerless. Real change in the history of Polish parliamentarianism in Galicia) came only with the Revolution of 1848.

Polish Nobles into Austrian Bureaucrats

Austrian policies were thus full of paradoxes. Determined to draw wealthy and politically important Polish aristocrats into the imperial fold, Vienna confirmed their titles and did little to affect their financial position. Austrian rulers were more aggressive toward poor landless nobles, but such intentions notwithstanding, the status and lifestyle of most in this category changed little after 1772. Institutional representation hardly changed between the 1770s and the 1790s, but nobles came to influence Austrian politics nevertheless. Vienna partly facilitated Poles' entrée into Austrian politics. Beginning in the 1780s, Austrian officials, Governor Brigido in particular, welcomed their increasing involvement in Austrian administration. Austrian educational institutions, designed to create administrative cadres, opened their doors to Polish nobles as well.

Vienna never endorsed rule by force in Galicia. After 1772, Austrian officials took measures to mobilize Polish support, and encouraged cooperation with prominent Polish elites. These efforts on the part of the center initially encountered local opposition. When Vienna drew up initial plans for the administration of its new province, at least some Galician Poles still hoped that Habsburg rule would only be temporary. Until 1795, the Polish Commonwealth, still extant beyond the border with its capital in Warsaw, was the primary focus of the harborers of such ideas. Warsaw and Kraków were common places to visit.[38] Those with the requisite financial resources seemed to prefer having their children educated in Poland-Lithuania rather than in the Habsburg Monarchy. Prior to 1795, few Poles managed to establish careers in imperial administration.[39]

The year 1795 marked an important turning point. After the Third Partition, Warsaw became part of Prussia, an international transformation affecting domestic Habsburg politics as well. In the mid- and late 1790s, Vienna increased its efforts to engage Polish nobles in its government structure.[40] The period 1791–1810 saw increased Polish involvement in Austrian offices and institutions, with nobles attending universities in Lemberg, Kraków, and Vienna, and many taking up permanent residence in Vienna.[41] By the early years of the nineteenth century, Polish nobles constituted approximately one-third of the entire bureaucratic corpus employed in Galicia.[42] At the turn of the 1830s, Józef Bobowski, Antoni Bielawski, Karol Mierzwinski, and Tadeusz Chochlik Wasilewski, among others, occupied top positions as councillors in the Galician Gubernium.[43] While Austrian bureaucrats accommodated themselves to this province on the periphery, the Poles of Galicia accommodated themselves to the centralizing empire.

The new configuration of Polish territories under the partitions limited the socio-political options available to Poles. After 1772, the three partitioning polities were rather tentative in their treatment of their new Polish subjects, and Poles retained the right of free movement throughout all the divided territories.[44] Open borders, however, created economic problems for the partitioning states, rendering customs regulation difficult and giving rise to black markets. Shortly after 1795, St. Petersburg and Vienna simultaneously tightened their borders, thus imposing restrictions on Polish migration.[45] Frontiers became more permanent, the control of movement more strict. In 1797, Austria and Prussia abolished the institution of multiple citizenship and prohibited Polish nobles from retaining property in several partitions simultaneously.[46] Józef Dzieduszycki sold his property in the Russian part of Poland, and settled permanently in Galicia.[47]

Even before the partitions, Vienna had not been entirely unknown to Poles; in that period, for instance, Andrzej Poniatowski, the younger brother of Poland's last king Stanisław Poniatowski, had lived in the Austrian capital, and it was here that he married Maria Theresia Countess Kinsky, scion of a prominent family from Bohemia. The couple's son Józef would go on to lead Polish troops from the Duchy of Warsaw into Austrian Galicia in 1809.[48] Walerian Dzieduszycki, son of Tadeusz Dzieduszycki and Salomea Dzieduszycka, née Trembicka, was the first Polish *chamberlain* (a prestigious honorary title) at the Habsburg court before the Polish partitions.[49] Adam Kazimierz Czartoryski and Isabella Lubomirska (of the Czartoryski family) maintained close ties with the Habsburg court. Such Polish poets and intellectuals as Julian Niemcewicz (1758–1841), Franciszek Karpinski (1770–1825), and Hugo Kołłątai (1758–1812) spent parts of their lives in Vienna. Of all the Viennese Poles, Józef Maksymilian Ossoliński was the most important. Scion of an old and prominent aristocratic family, a famous patron of culture, and founder of a private trust supporting Polish cultural institutions in Galicia, Ossoliński spent a substantial period of his life in Vienna.[50] Adam Czartoryski relocated to Vienna together with his family after 1795. Elżbieta Lubomirska resided in Vienna as well, and two of her grandsons, Alfred Potocki and Artur Potocki, grew up there.[51] After 1772, Dzieduszycki, Potocki, and Ossoliński became familiar names in Vienna.

Vienna long encouraged Polish involvement in various Austrian institutions. In 1781, Emperor Joseph II ordered the establishment of the Galician Personal Guard in Vienna, a military unit consisting of Galician noble youth.[52] Some of its members would later serve as Austrian officials in Galicia.[53] The Galician guards were disbanded in 1789. However, that same year also witnessed the establishment of a charity foundation in Vienna in support of impoverished Galician nobles.[54] The last Polish partition and the demise of Poland-Lithuania in 1795 opened a new phase in the history of Polish emigration to Vienna.

Austrian Bureaucrats into Polish Nobles

By the 1830s, Poles had come to form a visible presence in the Austrian administration. Meanwhile, even as Poles were becoming Austrian bureaucrats, some Austrian bureaucrats were becoming Poles. The inclusion of Poles in governance was a matter of Austrian policy; the integration of German-speaking bureaucrats into Polish society was, by contrast, an unforeseen side effect. This assimilation starkly revealed the complexities of Austrian efforts in Galicia. Beginning in 1772, bureaucrats arrived in the province from the center, tasked with producing citizens in their own image—loyal Germanophone subjects of their Habsburg sovereigns. Those Austrians who decided to become Poles accomplished, instead, the exact opposite, and laid bare an important national element in imperial politics.

Austrian officials harbored a long-standing interest in the Polish aristocracy. Governor Pergen criticized the Polish nobility as an institution, but often evinced a considerable amenability in his dealings with individual Polish aristocrats he encountered during his stay in Lemberg—Trembliński, Hordyński, Skarbek, Krajcy, Potocki, Katarzyna Kossakowska, and Princess Kantakuzena.[55] These rather sympathetic attitudes were reciprocal. Upon his departure from the provincial capital, Pergen received a generous sum of six thousand ducats, a personal gift from Galician aristocrats, and a huge sum especially in light of the region's reputation for poverty.[56] Even more favorably inclined toward Polish aristocrats, Governor Brigido was a regular guest at Kossakowska's house. The widow of a prominent official during the Polish-Lithuanian period, Kossakowska expressed dissatisfaction with the masses of Austrian bureaucrats Vienna had unleashed upon Galicia, but was more tolerant of high-ranking officials. Kossakowska routinely held receptions and parties at her house, which Governor Brigido frequently attended.[57] This count's social networks in Lemberg, indeed, resembled similar networks in his native Trieste, where Ludwig von Zinzendorf, Brigido's contemporary and a close friend of the Brigido family, served as governor. Like the Brigidos, the Zinzendorfs were a family of the bureaucracy, its members holding various offices across the monarchy.

The elite's increasingly active social life was facilitated by the new architectural and administrative façade of the Galician capital. New buildings—coffeehouses, theaters, schools, and a university—emerged in the city after 1772. Polish aristocrats and Austrian bureaucrats shared loges together in two Lemberg theaters—one holding performances in Polish, the other in German—both founded during the 1780s with the authorization of Austrian officials. Poles and Austrians gambled together at the local casino, drank coffee side by side in the same cafés. Lemberg's coffeehouse culture was probably an Austrian innovation; but some of its most famous exemplars in the early nineteenth century were owned by Poles. Ethnic differences, however, played no important role. For instance, the Lewandowski coffeehouse, named for its Polish owner, became a regular destination for the many Austrian residents of the city, and German was more commonly heard at its tables than Polish.[58]

Theaters were also apt to reveal the nuances of imperial and national politics during the eighteenth and nineteenth centuries. The Germanophone Austrian theater in Lemberg was an imperial project. It featured Italian actors and architects; and its construction was supported by the Austrian authorities. The Polish-language theater was an alternative that long had no proper quarters, for some time offering only open-air productions during the summer season.

In 1774, Governor Auersperg supported the creation of an Austrian-German theater in Lemberg. The first German-language performance in the city took place in 1776, before the theater had its own home. Wandering theater troupes often made stops in Lemberg; their performances were popular and attracted large crowds.[59] When Austrian officials debated the establishment of a new theater, several Italians offered their services as entrepreneurs. Shortly after 1776, Italian theater entrepreneur Antonio Mezzodi of Trieste wrote the Lemberg Gubernium offering his services in the construction of a new theater.[60] His proposal was not approved, but a new German theater did open its doors as early as 1780.

The 1770s also ushered in debate regarding an alternative, Polish theater in Lemberg. While German productions could be staged by Austrian Germans or Austrian Italians, the alternative theater, it was envisioned, would accommodate the Poles regularly visiting Galicia from different territories during those years. The plan for a Polish theater took some time to materialize, but even during this delay, in the 1770s and 1780s, the Austrian authorities evinced no open opposition to such a Polish institution. A permanent Polish theater opened its doors in Lemberg only in 1809, but summer productions had already been introduced much earlier in the city's capacious gardens. In the 1780s, Governor Brigido mediated the creation of a Polish summer theater. An amphitheater was erected in the Jabłonowski

Garden, which featured theatrical productions until 1809.[61] Other venues hosted performances as well; the Voronovsky Palace, situated on a hill where later the Austrians would construct a citadel and prison, was a popular theater destination, and a winter theater was arranged in a former Franciscan monastery earlier dissolved by Joseph II.[62]

At least on the surface, Lemberg of the 1780s and 1790s seemed a model imperial capital, foregrounding the peaceful coexistence of Austrians and Poles. After performances, Polish and Austrian theatergoers might head for the same coffeehouses and eateries; Żorża Hoffman's restaurant "Under the Three Hooks" was a premier destination.[63] German and Polish performances sometimes ran in tandem, with the same plays presented in different theaters in the German and Polish languages.[64] Joseph Bulla performed the marquee roles in the German theater in Lemberg during the 1780s, while Wojciech Bogusławski became the most famous director of the Polish theater. In the 1790s, the boundaries between the two institutions increasingly blurred; Bogusławski, for example, often directed both German- and Polish-language plays on different stages.[65]

Austrian officials not only endorsed new institutions but also at times granted financial assistance. Between 1774 and 1780, Heinrich von Auersperg was closely involved, as noted above, in the construction of a German theater in Lemberg. Governor Lobkowitz rendered financial assistance to the Polish theater in 1830.[66] The Austrians also supported a variety of other institutions and entertainments in the provincial capital. A gallery of wax figures opened its doors in Lemberg. A new hippodrome, where equestrian lessons were offered, also enjoyed popularity among Poles and Austrians alike.[67]

Entertainment often crossed institutional boundaries and spilled out into the street. The months of January and February were the most hectic periods of social life. Despite severe temperatures, city residents spent much of their time outside their homes. The fourteenth of January opened the season of the so-called *Kontrakten*—a major trade fair held in Lemberg every four years as a continued tradition from the Polish period. While trade fairs were holdovers of the past, the gala ball season was a novelty, introduced after the annexation, with Lembergers dancing for weeks during an annual season peaking in February.⁶⁸ Venetian masks were common until masked carnivals were forbidden in 1797 for political reasons;⁶⁹ insofar as masks disguised faces and identities, such events had become a popular venue for Polish political conspirators.

At the turn of the century, Lemberg numbered some thirty thousand inhabitants,⁷⁰ but during certain weeks and months, it seemed to expand into a larger metropolis. Numerous visitors and an active social life transformed the urban setting, making the capital appear much larger and more populous than it actually was. Various buildings, institutions, and patterns of social life revealed the city's new status: no longer just a regional town in Poland, it was the capital of Austria's newest and largest province.

Neither wars nor revolutions seemed to hinder regular socializing. After the defeat of the Kosciuszko uprising in Poland-Lithuania, masses of refugees made their way to Galicia; in the early 1790s, Polish migration accelerated generally. Prince Maciej Jabłonowski, the Princes Radziwiłł, and Isabella Czartoryska moved to Galicia from still existing Poland.⁷¹ All were hosted by Governor Brigido as guests of honor. The Austrian authorities in Lemberg at the time did little to stem the massive Polish influx into the province, and Governor Brigido personally held biweekly dinners at his residence in honor of distinguished newcomers.

Another aristocratic luminary, the Countess Potocka, was also a regular guest in Lemberg. She had earlier opposed the last Polish king, Stanisław August Poniatowski, because he was from the "wrong" family (and was supported by the Russians). After 1772 she opposed Maria Theresa, because the empress had partitioned the Potocki estates right along with Poland in general. But Potocka's allegiances changed with time; she eventually sought to demonstrate her loyalty to the Habsburgs and, making frequent visits to Lemberg, managed to do so. Potocka was among the Polish refugees welcomed in the provincial capital by Governor Brigido.⁷² With so many notables in attendance, Lemberg eventually gained the reputation of a Polish resort. The social climate in Austrian Lemberg, one observer noted, was much more amicable than that of Warsaw, which, after 1795, became part of Prussia.⁷³

In 1813, Countess Ludowika (Lulu) Thürheim came to Lemberg to visit her sister Isabella, wife of the Galician Governor Peter von Goëss. During her stay, the countess attended various celebrations and met with local Austrian officials. She left unimpressed, and later mocked the provinciality of social life in Lemberg. The following year saw the visit of a personage of far greater prominence: Karolina Maria von Habsburg, Queen of Naples and one of the daughters of Empress Maria Theresa. Governor Goëss organized several balls in her honor, and such Polish aristocrats as Count Konarski, Count Jan Stadnicki, and Prince Paweł Sapieha attended the celebrations.[74]

Kossakowska, Potocka, and Czartoryska were no ordinary figures within the Polish social establishment. All belonged to old, very prominent aristocratic families. Against the backdrop of the persons populating Austrian officialdom, these Polish women stood out: their fashions were more sophisticated, their social status more secure. Police agents reported that Austrian officers eschewed romantic involvement with Polish women precisely because of the chasm between their statuses. Lemberg's Austrian police chief Leopold von Sacher-Masoch, who evinced no particular sympathy toward the Poles in Galicia, noted the exceptionally important status of Polish women as carriers of nationalism throughout the nineteenth century.[75]

Wars and revolutions, especially the 1831 uprising in Warsaw, caused certain setbacks in Austrian-Polish relations. In his reminiscences of 1830–31, police chief Leopold von Sacher-Masoch recounts the new tensions stemming from the Polish revolt: "A young district official arrested two Polish members of the Horse Guards with whom he had earlier frequented salons in Lemberg."[76] Such arrests, oftentimes authorized by senior personnel in the provincial capital or even in Vienna, were carried out by junior bureaucrats only reluctantly, especially since actions against friends or acquaintances could have personal repercussions for the arresting official: some aristocratic families might no longer welcome them among their guests; their daughters might no longer consider them appropriate suitors. It is not surprising that some bureaucrats involved in anti-Polish measures acted with heavy hearts not only out of personal disapproval of the political-legal mechanisms employed, but also from fear of jeopardizing their social status among the Austrian and Polish elites.

Fig. 5.1: View of Lemberg, 1840. Engraving by Teofil Czyszkowski. Polish National Library, Digital Collection Polona.

New social hierarchies in Lemberg increasingly came to favor Poles over German-speaking Austrians. Financially independent, versed in several languages and often well-traveled, the cream of Polish aristocracy formed a sharp contrast to most Austrian bureaucrats, even those of the highest rank, who could only dream of achieving an equivalent degree of affluence and social prestige. A Polish noble in Warsaw would not be allowed to sit at the same table with a Prussian officer; in Lemberg, however, Austrian bureaucrats deemed it an honor to dine with Polish aristocrats. Joseph Rohrer, who traveled through Galicia during the 1780s, noted the unconcealed fascination the wives of Austrian German bureaucrats felt for their Polish aristocratic neighbors. New patterns of social and family life arose: under the influence of this admiration, such women abandoned their native German language in favor of the French commonly employed by Polish aristocrats in Galicia.[77]

As almost everywhere else in Europe, salons in Lemberg were typically run by aristocratic hosts who spoke French, and French was common in Galicia among the upper classes generally: children of Polish aristocrats typically had French-speaking nannies. French was also the language of high culture; command of it emblematized good manners and education. But in Galicia, French also fulfilled far more mundane functions. Because Polish aristocrats rarely spoke German and Austrian bureaucrats had difficulties with Polish, French was often adopted as a common language for all manner of communication.[78]

Social hierarchies often hinge, of course, on financial resources, and the economic struggles of Austrian bureaucrats were proverbial. The arrival of the annual markets in the city meant entertainment for Polish visitors, but for Austrian bureaucrats, a chance to earn some extra income. The latter regularly rented rooms to Poles visiting Lemberg. Even top-ranking Austrian officials complained of how expensive life could be in the provincial capital.[79] In 1804, Christian von Wurmser, then vice president of the Galician Gubernium, insisted that the cost of living in Lemberg was comparable to that in Vienna, if not higher; timber was more expensive in Lemberg than in the imperial capital, he claimed, and rents were just as steep.[80]

Austrian complaints of economic privations should, of course, be taken with a grain of salt. Men such as Wurmser always received respectable salaries; and even if life in Lemberg was as expensive as Wurmser claimed, governors' salaries, set at about twenty thousand gulden per year, would have made them prosperous anywhere in the monarchy. Lower-ranking bureaucrats faced a different economic reality; even if relatively well off, Austrian bureaucrats constantly complained of being underpaid. Key for our purposes is that models of social interaction in Lemberg were governed by the perception of relative Austrian poverty versus Polish prosperity.

Mixed Austrian-Polish families became the most revealing symbol of long-term socialization and assimilation. The first generation of Austrian officials remained part of a closed group of German-speakers in Galicia, the boundaries of which, however, became increasingly porous with time. When Austrian bureaucrats married Polish women, their children usually grew up bilingual, and at least some identified as Polish as adults. These mixed Polish-German families produced generations of administrators and intellectuals who came to play a very important role in Polish society during the nineteenth century. Integration went both ways, but in the long term these ever-increasing contacts favored Polishness over Germanophone Austrianness.

Wincenty Pol, for example, was raised in a family of German-speaking Austrian bureaucrats. Growing up in a Germanophone household, he had the opportunity as a child to observe gatherings of local elites in the French-speaking salon held at his parents' residence. For him, Polish was only a second, perhaps a third language, after German and French, learned most likely under the influence of friends from Galician schools and university. As a young boy, he started writing poetry in Polish. At the time, few would have imagined that this enterprise would ever be successful: despite having apparently fallen in love with the language, young Wincenty had great difficulty with the grammar, and his early writings are full of basic errors.[81] But in time he mastered the grammar, remained true to his fascination with Polish language and culture, and went on to become one of the most prominent poets of Polish Romanticism; Pol has since secured his place in the annals of Polish national history and literature.

It is all too easy to forget that the choice of Polish language, culture, and identity was not an obvious one for a person of Pol's background, being only one of several options available in the consideration of career or life path. Pol became Polish not by birth, but by choice. Nothing in his family history could have predicted his decision for Polish over German or any other language at his disposal.

His family's name was recorded in various documents, as Poll or Pol. Wincenty's father, Franz Xaver Poll, was born in Warmia around 1751, but the family could trace its roots to Sweden. It was as a civil servant that Franz Poll came to Galicia, where he married Eleonora Longchamps from a French family living in Poland.[82] In this city's new incarnation of Lemberg, Franz changed his surname to Pol, became active in social, literary, and salon life, and raised several children, two of whom became writers. One of the sons, Franz, opted for German linguistic identity, publishing several novels in German newspapers in Galicia. Wincenty chose Polish instead. While Franz soon gave up writing, Wincenty remained true to his literary calling.

Yet he never fully abandoned his Germanness, bearing within himself a mixture of Polish and German culture, a combination that had important repercussions through the rest of his life. Writing in Polish for a Polonophone audience, Pol in effect created a barrier for potential German-speaking readers in Galicia; his commitment to Polishness was moreover a stumbling block to German-speakers beyond the province's borders. Torn between his Germanness and Polishness, he became, in a way, an outsider to all, and it is only with the passage of time, in hindsight, that Pol has taken his place in the pantheon of Polish Romanticism.

Albeit rather common at the time, this split allegiance became a major obstacle in Pol's career. In 1849, he finally secured an academic position, that of professor of geography at the Jagiellonian University in Kraków. Unlike the administrative center, Lemberg, Kraków was above all a cultural capital and a symbol of Poland's former grandeur. The latter was, moreover, never so altered by German language and culture as Lemberg, the difference remaining visible to this day, for instance, in the two cities' architectural façades. At a time when Lemberg was developing into a provincial capital of the Habsburg Monarchy, Polish culture was upheld, at least to some extent, by Kraków, and in securing a position at the university there, Pol could account his Polishness, as it were, endorsed.

This achievement, however, proved short-lived. In 1852, he was accused by one of his students of disloyalty to the monarchy. Concerns about Pol's political reliability had lingered since the 1840s; it was known to the police, for instance, that his personal secretary had maintained contacts with Polish political conspirators. The student's charges were never confirmed, but the allegations damaged Pol's standing with the imperial authorities. Already in 1841, Wincenty Pol had submitted a letter to the vice president of the Galicia Gubernium, Baron Franz Krieg, requesting the cessation of police surveillance of him, and also a passport that would allow him to travel abroad.[83] The student's denunciation now had a devastating effect on his career; he was dismissed and never again returned to academia.[84]

Józef Dietl, the first Pole to serve as mayor of Kraków under Austrian rule (1860s), is another example of a remarkable transition from Germanness to Polishness. Dietl was born in 1804 in Galicia into an Austrian (originally Germanophone) family that had been involved in the bureaucracy for several generations. His grandfather, Johann Georg Dietl, arrived in Galicia between 1772 and 1774 as an Austrian officer, and eventually married Anna Retschratner, daughter of German-speakers who had come to Galicia from Lower Austria. The couple's son, Franz Joachim, moved to Western Galicia and married Anna Kulczycka, a Pole from a prominent but impoverished noble family. Franz Joachim Dietl and Anna Kulczycka had six children, all of whom grew up bilingual in German and Polish and corresponded amongst themselves and with their parents in two languages.

The most famous member of the family, Joseph Dietl, left his mark upon the history specifically of Polish Galicia, but his choice of Polish over German was hardly foreordained. Like Wincenty Pol, Dietl combined within himself aspects of Polishness and Germanness, never completely abandoning one culture in favor of the other. Having imbibed Polish language and culture from his mother, he became immersed in German culture in his youth, not only through his father, but also through fellow students. Unlike the Pols, who received their education in Galicia, Joseph Dietl completed his studies at the University of Vienna. By that time, Vienna had become a hub for Polish writers and intellectuals, but young Dietl seems to have eschewed Polish circles, socializing with

German-speakers instead, and married a Germanophone native of Vienna who had no Polish ties.

Dietl's connection to Polish culture was upheld first and foremost through his mother, with whom as a young man he corresponded in Polish. His marriage proved unhappy; the couple had no children and became alienated from each other with time. We can only speculate whether this failed union in any way influenced Dietl's decision to move back to Galicia, where he would enter the world of its politics. Leaving a meager allowance for his wife, Dietl abandoned Vienna and, along with it Austrian-German social life, plunging actively into Polish politics instead, and eventually becoming, during the period of Polish autonomy in Galicia, the first Polish mayor of Austrian-ruled Kraków.[85]

We can note a similar trajectory in the life of Franz or Franciszek Smolka. During the 1860s and 1870s, Smolka was actively involved in Galician politics as one of the leaders of the Polish liberals. His father, Wincenty Smolka, traced his roots to Silesia, having come to Galicia as an officer in the Austrian military. Franz Smolka, born in Galicia in Kałusz (near Lemberg) in 1810, was raised and educated in German-speaking circles, but he too became quickly drawn to Polish life and even to Polish political conspiracies. Between 1841 and 1845, like Wincenty Pol, Smolka was placed under police surveillance. During the 1848 events in Galicia, Smolka played a leading role, and in 1849 he was called to Vienna as vice president of the first Austrian parliament.[86]

Ongoing changes are particularly stark against the background of revolutions and wars. When revolution broke out in Warsaw in late 1830, many Galicians could hardly conceal their enthusiasm—and not only Poles. For instance, Johann Georg Ostermann, an Austrian official and head of the Sanok district administration, had no Polish family ties; but he faced allegations of involvement in Polish conspiracies. Ostermann seems to have remained neutral during the uprising, but two of his sons openly endorsed the Polish cause, leading to suspicions that they had joined the Polish army in Warsaw.[87]

The Pols, the Dietls, the Smolkas, and the Ostermanns were part of a larger cohort of Austrian German-speakers that had come to Galicia and eventually involved themselves actively in Polish life. Other examples of mixed Polish-German families include the Mehoffers, the Seelings, and the Zolls. Most remained bilingual; some took part in Polish intellectual and political life; and some declared themselves as Poles. At least some descendants of these mixed families, for example Franz Smolka, Joseph Dietl, and Wincenty Pol, became significant figures in Polish politics and culture. In some respects, such assimilators resembled religious converts: those making a conscious decision to convert from one religion to another are often more adamant in their devotion than adherents of the same church by birth.

And indeed, nationality in the nineteenth century was often determined not by blood, but by individual choice. Such decisions were not always easy, at times engendering confusion for all involved. Having a Polish mother seems to have often determined a son's choice of Polishness over Germanness,[88] even if such sons never fully abandoned the latter. Before 1867, many would have had a hard time deciding in favor of one nationality over another.

The assimilation of Germanophone Austrian bureaucrats into Polish society is symbolic, not only because it reveals the contingent nature of national (self-)identification, but also because it reflects the contradictions of Austria's efforts in Galicia. The true extent of these reciprocal influences is very difficult to assess: no precise statistics are available, and different allegiances, Austrian, German, and Polish, remained vague, vacillating over time. But among Polish contemporaries and historians, assimilations became the subject of much talk, and matters of pride. Consider, for instance, the appraisal of Governor Lobkowitz's contemporary Zygmunt Kaczkowski, whose memoirs were published in the 1890s. Here Kaczkowski evinced the many stereotypes that had become inscribed in the Polish historical imagination, asserting, for example (and quite inaccurately), that most Austrian bureaucrats in Galicia became Polonized in the second generation; thus German-speaking officials arriving in Galicia in the late eighteenth century should have become Poles by the first half of the nineteenth century.[89]

Vienna's only way to break down the domination of Polish nobles was by radically reforming the Galician economy and transforming a backward agricultural province into one of the Habsburg heartlands. The state, specifically state investments, would have to play a decisive role in economic transformations. Galicia, however, not only remained a backward province, but its economy and living standards seem to have declined continuously during the Habsburg period. Some of the most dire assessments of the Galician economy came from the pens of Polish intellectuals and academics.[90] Yet Austrian imperial statistics confirm at least some of the Polish stereotypes. To be sure, the Galician capital was refashioned on the Austrian model, with its infrastructure and façades resembling ever more other provincial cities. Contemporary images from the 1830s prove that the urban landscape in the centers of Lemberg and Vienna looked quite similar. Yet the rest of Galicia remained a predominantly agricultural region relying mainly on the manorial estate system of production—similar to the one that had existed in the Polish-Lithuanian Commonwealth before 1772.[91]

The abundance of fertile land in Galicia became a major liability. The population growth at rates higher than anywhere else in the monarchy was a related issue. Exploiting the land seemed like a reasonable solution—to Austrian officials and local landowners alike.[92] Furthermore, Vienna was reluctant to invest in the industrial development of the region so heavily bound to the land. Bohemia became an industrial hub of the monarchy—a development that can be at least partly attributed to central policies; Trieste became a major economic and trading hub, also due to the planning and investments from Vienna.

Galicia, to be sure, did not lack resources that could stir industrialization. Before 1914, it had some of the largest oil reserves in Europe as well as deposits of coal and metals. Yet the Austrian government never monopolized control over these resources. Equally important—or detrimental—was the failure to integrate Galicia more efficiently into the Habsburg market, after it had been cut off from traditional trade routes formed before 1772. Galician industry never lived up to its full potential. Some previous centers of commerce, for example, small towns like Brody, never recovered from the assault of the partitions: once major trading posts, they became marginal socially and economically. Vienna's intervention in the Galician economy was limited at best. Yet even so, at least some Polish aristocrats would consistently find it as too meddlesome, complaining about the

Fig. 5.2: View of Lemberg, 1840. Engraving by Karol Auer, showing a western section of the city fortifications converted into a park and promenade. Polish National Library, Digital Collection Polona.

detrimental effects that the government's intrusion had upon the local economy. The economy thus became another victim of the clashes of imperial and local politics. Economic backwardness helped maintain the status of traditional elites, namely nobles.

During the 1830s, Austrian bureaucrats and Polish aristocrats mingled in various social contexts, with the same occasions often employed toward opposite goals; these Polish nobles sought to expand their conspiracy networks in Galicia and recruit new members; Austrian bureaucrats and police agents, to infiltrate and destroy such initiatives from within. However, conspiracies and politics scarcely impacted the entertainment milieu, where Poles and Austrians often socialized as a single group.[93]

Fig. 5.3: View of Vienna, 1835. Engraving by Augustin François Lemaître, showing a bridge over an arm of the Danube that by that time ran well inside the expanding Habsburg capital. Polish National Library, Digital Collection Polona.

Various historical accounts from the nineteenth and twentieth centuries, describe Galicia in terms of conflict and opposition, whether between Austrians and Poles or Poles and Ruthenians, or among Austrians, Poles, Ruthenians, and Jews. But this vision of conflict, while somewhat applicable to the second half of the nineteenth century, is less accurate with regard to earlier periods. Before 1848, social rank and status mattered more than national identity, and the public sphere in Galicia was more diverse and fluid, perhaps, than ever after. Austrian officials could become Polish nobles, and vice versa, without inciting much in the way of shock on the part of witnesses to such transitions. This quite fluid world only started to harden in 1848 and 1867.

When the Poles secured autonomy after 1867, Austrian German-speaking officials were forced to leave or resign. Galicia's public sphere became increasingly divided along ethnic lines, with little room for the sort of openness and diversity that characterized the region before 1848. Some German speakers forced to relinquish their positions to Poles moved away, whether back to their places of origin or to other provinces of the monarchy where their skills and qualifications were still required. But many others stayed in the region, bound to it by their new families, their Polish wives and children, and some of them had become Polish patriots.

In this context, children growing to adulthood built upon the experience of their Germanophone fathers—among other things, upon the models of government and the ideals of civilization that these role models had brought with them to Galicia. The same children were also raised on different ideals by their mothers, who bore the legacy of Polish independence and a type of government quite different from the kind exemplified by the Austrian Empire. Many such individuals did not definitively choose between their Germanness and their Polishness, but when an opportunity to combine these identities arose in 1867, they blended elements of both, building a new Polish administration and civilization even if within the Habsburg Monarchy.

SIX

Literature, Politics, and Galician Ruthenians

By the 1830s, it had become clear that Vienna's plan for an exclusively Germanophone bureaucracy would not be achieved in Galicia. This institution instead consisted of a highly mixed group of officials, including Polish nobles who had decided to become Austrian bureaucrats and Austrian bureaucrats who had become Polish nobles. Unlike Polish aristocrats, who divided their time between the town and the land, most Ruthenians resided in the countryside, leading a lifestyle of little or no appeal to Austrians. The number of Ruthenians in the Austrian administration was rather small before 1848. Apart from strictly administrative matters, interaction between high-ranking Austrian bureaucrats and Ruthenian peasants was rare, as was Austrian-Ruthenian assimilation. But one self-proclaimed Ruthenian became so famous as to make at least one exception memorable for generations to come: Leopold von Sacher-Masoch, one of history's best-known Galicians.

Born into an Austrian bureaucratic family in 1836 in Lemberg, Sacher-Masoch was raised in a somewhat cosmopolitan household. Outside Galicia, Sacher-Masoch's long-term reputation is linked to his most famous novel, *Venus in Furs*, published in Vienna in 1870, and describing in great detail a specific type of relationship between a man and a woman in which the former submits himself willingly to the domination of the latter. From the early twentieth century on, Leopold von Sacher-Masoch was best known as the history's first extoller of masochism.

Less widely remembered is that most of his texts, including *Venus in Furs*, reflect their author's preoccupation with Galicia, where he spent his childhood before his family moved to Prague in 1848. Sacher-Masoch's collection of stories on Galician Jews revealed a detailed knowledge of Jewish customs, leading to speculation that Sacher-Masoch himself was Jewish.[1] His preoccupation with the Polish and Ruthenian aspects of Galicia, meanwhile, raised the question of possible family roots among those groups. By the 1860s, having achieved considerable popularity as a writer, Sacher-Masoch became the object of public speculation as to his origins. "People have already taken me for almost everything," he noted regretfully, "for a Jew, a Hungarian, a Bohemian, and even for a woman."[2] On another occasion he remarked: "People call me a German, a Pole, a Czech, and finally a Slovene."[3] Sacher-Masoch seemed to combine features of the various nationalities of the Habsburg Monarchy, as he was so readily identifiable with any of them. When he decided to put an end to all these speculations, he declared himself a Ruthenian.

To such a stance could be contrasted that of Jan Lam, a writer and journalist who spent a lifetime working on subjects pertaining to Galicia. Born two years after Sacher-Masoch, in 1838, Lam too was raised in Galicia in a family of Austrian German-speaking bureaucrats. Despite sharing this background, and a commitment to literature, Sacher-Masoch and Lam trod different paths: the former wrote most of his works in German and eventually settled in Vienna, while the latter remained in Galicia and became Polonized. Lam's major novel, *Capowice High Society* (*Wielki świat Capowic*), was first published in 1869; a work that brought fame to its author as a great satirist, it tells the story of Wacław Precliczek, a German-speaking official from Bohemia working in Galicia's Austrian administration. Raised in a Germanophone family with ties to Bohemia, and fluent in Czech and German, Precliczek marries a Pole from Galicia. In various periods of his life, Precliczek describes himself as Czech, German, Slovene, Galician, and Ruthenian.

The battles Precliczek wages in *Capowice High Society* are remarkably similar to some of the dilemmas Leopold von Sacher-Masoch faced in real life. The persona behind Sacher-Masoch's activity and texts could have been German, Austrian, Slovenian, Galician, Ruthenian, or even a woman, in different periods of his life; by the same token, on different occasions, he could have been none of these. Wacław Precliczek, too, could be German or Czech in some situations, and Polish or Ruthenian in others.[4] Sacher-Masoch's loyalty to the Habsburg Monarchy remained more important than his numerous ethnicities, real or invented. It is not the real ethnic identity of these figures that deserves attention, but rather their unconventional national projections. How, that is, did descendants of Germanophone Austrians from Galicia come to consider themselves Ruthenian?

Sacher-Masoch, a scion of an Austrian bureaucratic family, and Precliczek, himself an Austrian official, symbolized a major achievement of Austrian policies: the new province had taken root, and by the 1830s its people had acquired a distinctively *Galician* identity.[5] Sacher-Masoch, who decided upon a Ruthenian identity, and Wacław Precliczek, who could not decide upon a particular ethnic affiliation, also reveal important contradictions of Austrian policies: few Poles or Ruthenians opted to become German-speaking Austrians, while at least some descendants of Austrian bureaucratic families opted to become Poles or Ruthenians.

These real-life and fictional stories also reveal the dilemmas of many bureaucrats that can sometimes remain concealed in traditional histories of administration: personal and professional insecurity, a multitude of choices, and unconventional life trajectories. At the same time, they demonstrate the effect of the Galician reforms upon the same bureaucrats responsible for their implementation. In the early decades of the nineteenth century, boundaries between administrators and those they administered became increasingly porous, creating a situation in which bureaucrats themselves acknowledged their dependence upon the people they ruled.

The Sachers and the Masochs

Even if some aspects of Sacher-Masoch's claims regarding his family origins remain uncertain, of his Galician roots there is no doubt. His ancestors arrived in the region in the late eighteenth century, between 1772 and 1793. Two of his grandfathers and his father held positions in various offices in

Galicia through 1848; the family spent many years in Austria's eastern province as part of its German-speaking professional establishment.

The deeper ethnic background of the family, however, remains unclear, precisely because in each successive generation, new details were added (not least by Leopold von Sacher-Masoch himself) that are virtually impossible to verify. Sacher-Masoch's paternal grandfather, Johann von Sacher, must have been born in Bohemia in 1759, but his family allegedly traced its roots to Spain. One Don Mathias Sacher allegedly served in the army of the Habsburg Emperor Charles V in the mid-sixteenth century, when a branch of the Habsburg family ruled over Spain.[6] Don Mathias is said to have been wounded in battle, brought to safety by a Bohemian nobleman, and taken care of by his daughter. He moved to Bohemia, found a wife, and settled there.[7] One of his descendants, Thomas Sacher, fought in the War of the Spanish Succession between 1701 and 1714, and against the Turks in the years that followed. By the early eighteenth century, the Habsburgs had lost their Spanish possessions, but in Sacher's family, memories of Spain lived on.

Don Mathias, having fought for Emperor Charles V in Spain, initiated the Bohemian (later Austrian) part of the history of the Sacher family; Thomas Sacher, having helped the Habsburgs in their efforts to retain their Spanish possessions, must have been rewarded with a noble title, which he passed on to his descendants.[8] Both secured a place in the annals of the Sacher family, a lineage made famous in the texts of Leopold von Sacher-Masoch in the late nineteenth century.

Johann Nepomuk von Sacher, Thomas Sacher's grandson, moved to Galicia as an Austrian official; born and raised in Bohemia, he bore the name of one of the major Czech saints, Jan Nepomuk. Like all Bohemian nobility, he spoke German and, like many Bohemian nobles, was also raised to be fluent in Czech. His knowledge of this latter was a distinct advantage in a cosmopolitan society, and also as a basis for learning other Slavic languages, such as the Polish spoken in Galicia. Yet Johann Nepomuk von Sacher was not Czech in the modern, national sense of the word; he belonged to Bohemia only insofar as Bohemia formed part of the Habsburg Monarchy. "My family is truly Austrian," his son proudly declared in a memoir, "in the particular sense that it does not belong to any nationality, but . . . like other families of imperial bureaucrats and military personnel, is a mix of different Austrian nationalities. Over the centuries, the family was infused with German, Italian, Czech, and Hungarian blood"—rendering it a typical example of cosmopolitanism in the Habsburg Monarchy.[9]

Johann von Sacher resembled many other bureaucrats who assumed Galician offices after 1772. Groomed to be a model of professionalism, he proved to symbolize human fallibility instead. Initially in charge of a financial branch of the Austrian administration in Kałusz, Sacher was promoted to the administration of the Wieliczka salt mines, and completed his career as a councillor of the Galician Gubernium, taking this post, a very important one in provincial administration, in 1800.[10] Around the same time, he was awarded the Leopold-Orden—one of the highest distinctions for administrative services.[11] But his career was not without blemish; subordinates accused him of corruption in 1803, and the same year, the Austrian authorities probed his professional performance. The investigators left behind reams of paperwork documenting Sacher's life and activities.[12] But it was a rather typical scenario of eighteenth-century bureaucracy—a superior denounced anonymously by his subordinates, with no serious adverse effects on his career. Sacher was promoted instead and moved to Lemberg.

The Masoch family was no less complex than the Sachers. Franz von Masoch, Leopold von Sacher-Masoch's maternal grandfather, was born in the Banat but moved to Vienna for his studies. Upon earning a doctorate in medicine, he was appointed to the medical faculty of the newly reopened University of Lemberg,[13] where he eventually became university rector. Austrian doctors were among various professionals often collectively brought in to Galicia from other Habsburg regions; a large such group, mostly surgeons and dentists, was sent to the province as early as 1772.[14] Franz von Masoch arrived directly from Vienna, and would be best known for his efforts in containing Lemberg's cholera outbreak in 1818.[15] He also made headlines as the first Christian doctor to enter the Jewish ghetto in Lemberg as part of the same attempt to halt the spread of the disease in the city.[16]

In the early nineteenth century the Sachers and Masochs resided in the same neighborhood in the city center, soon not only sharing common space, but also related by marriage; in 1829, Johann von Sacher's son, Leopold von Sacher, and Franz von Masoch's daughter, Charlotte von Masoch, made their vows in Lemberg. It was Franz von Masoch, the father of the fiancée, who insisted on adding the "Masoch" component to the Sacher name; after 1838, not only their children but Charlotte's husband as well would bear the double name Sacher-Masoch.[17] The couple spent the next nineteen years of their life in the Galician capital, for most of this period residing in the ostentatious building in the center of Lemberg that housed the Austrian police administration.

Between 1831 and 1848, Leopold von Sacher (and then Sacher-Masoch) served as Lemberg's chief of police, becoming most famous for his role in the suppression of Polish political conspiracies shortly after 1830. In 1836, the Austrian police chief celebrated the birth of his first son. Named after his father, Leopold became the youngest denizen of the Lemberg police headquarters. But he did not remain in the city long, and spent most of his childhood in the countryside outside Lemberg. Here he was nursed by a Ruthenian nanny, played with Polish and Ruthenian children who spoke no German, and learned Ruthenian before German.[18] The language of Goethe and Schiller became native for Sacher-Masoch only after 1848, when, as a result of his father's transfer, he found himself in Prague.

Not following in his father's footsteps, the young Sacher-Masoch initially chose the academic path, achieving some early success as a historian and holding a junior professorship for several years at Graz University.[19] In the 1850s alone, he published a number of works, beginning with his doctoral thesis on the history of an uprising in Ghent during the rule of Emperor Charles V, followed by a biography of Austrian Chancellor Kaunitz. In the 1860s, Sacher-Masoch planned to write a history of the Ruthenians in Habsburg Galicia, but this was never completed, much to the disappointment of his Ruthenian supporters.[20] He soon switched to literature, becoming one of the most prolific Austrian writers of his time.

His numerous publications seem almost consciously inspired by *épatage*. One of his first successes—the novella *Don Juan of Kolomea*—transposed the familiar lover to the rather unconventional setting of the Galician Carpathians. Love, lust, and betrayal became dominant themes in

Sacher-Masoch's writings; but unlike many of his contemporaries, Sacher-Masoch combined his interest in the erotic with explorations into ethnicity and a fascination with Galicia. To be sure, Sacher-Masoch was not the most sophisticated writer on the Austrian literary scene. His writings, most of them decidedly products of a particular epochal current, sold well in yellow-press venues, and eventually also came in for much criticism.

In 1865 and 1866, Sacher-Masoch would find his name on the pages of the Austrian government newspaper *Die Presse*. In 1865, decrying the allegedly lamentable state of current literature in the monarchy, a columnist for this publication, Hieronimus Lorm, ran a piece revealingly titled "Parasites and Renegades in Austria"—his term for representatives of the yellow-press literature proliferating throughout the Habsburg territories. The literary "parasites" who were, according to Lorm, legion, included Sacher-Masoch. Within months, Lorm aimed another article directly at Sacher-Masoch alone, titled "Japhet in Search of His Nationality," viewing the writer as a lost son questing this way and that after his own identity.

Lorm and Sacher-Masoch in 1866 disagreed on the fundamental principles of the Austrian Empire. Over the years, Sacher-Masoch became known especially for his interest in the Slavic aspects of the Habsburg Monarchy; he valorized heterogeneity and expressed his fascination with the variety of cultures in his native Galicia. His opponent, by contrast, was one of the espousers of Pan-Germanism, a movement that consolidated in the second half of the nineteenth century. The Pan-Germans based their politics upon the perception of German civilizational superiority over the Slavs, advocated the unification of all German-speaking lands, Habsburg and non-Habsburg, and viewed the Slavic presence in the Habsburg Monarchy as a threat.[21]

1866, the year of Austria's historic defeat by Prussia at Königgrätz, proved a turning point in modern European history, and also specifically for Sacher-Masoch and Lorm. As a result of this defeat, Vienna lost its once dominant status among German states. The war revealed the political ascendancy of Prussia in Central Europe, paving the way for Germany's unification in 1871. The new German state consolidated not, as many Austrians would have hoped, around Vienna, but around Berlin, in effect walling Austrians off from other Germans. The defeat at Königgrätz implied a civilizational crisis for those who considered German culture to be the core of the Austrian polity; Lorm read it as a sign of Austria's potential downfall.

Unlike Lorm, Sacher-Masoch saw some good coming out of Königgrätz. A Habsburg patriot to the core, he believed that, separated from the rest of Germany, the Habsburg Monarchy could follow its own particular path of unity with its Slavic subjects, whose culture he had come to cherish. For Sacher-Masoch, Austria presented a model of tolerance achievable only within the confines of a heterogeneous empire, outside of Germany; he hoped that the political shift of 1866 and after could open a door for a new type of culture combining German, Slavic, and Jewish elements, just as he did in his writings.

Lorm's publications from the 1860s seem to have had an eye-opening effect on Sacher-Masoch. He decided to bring an end to the considerable speculation surrounding his personality and nationality. The decision was not an easy one to make. For years, he had kept changing his mind, claiming to be now a German, now an Austrian, now a Slav. His fatherland was Polish, he once declared in reference to Galicia, but his identity was German. "I am German. I think, feel, and dream in German," he confessed in 1858.[22] In 1865, perhaps for the first time, he declared himself a Ruthenian. Even then, he could not precisely define what "Ruthenian" meant, and kept calling himself, alternatively, *ein Ruthene, ein Kleinrusse*, or just a *Russe*. All these notions seemed to be compatible for Sacher-Masoch: as becomes clear from his texts, they all referred to the same entity—the Ruthenians of Galicia.[23]

In December 1866, in an issue of *Gartenlaube für Oesterreich* (published in Graz), Sacher-Masoch decried the rampant speculation regarding his nationality; he was a Ruthenian, he declared, and thereafter he would never change his mind.[24] In this piece he traced the roots of his family to the sixteenth century, claiming that his mother's ancestors, the Masochs, had belonged to the Ruthenian nobility. Sacher-Masoch thus shone a Ruthenian light on his ancient family roots, cementing his new identity, and remained true to his Ruthenian claims ever after. It was not by accident that his Ruthenian revelations first appeared in this publication. *Gartenlaube für*

Oesterreich was a major venue for support of Austrianness as distinct from the rest of Germany; in this, it was the flip side of another journal called *Gartenlaube*, in this case published in Leipzig and long a forum for Pan-Germanism. As long as Ruthenians remained loyal to Vienna—as most did through much of the nineteenth century—Sacher-Masoch's Austrianness and his Ruthenianness were compatible; he could be at once both Austrian and Ruthenian.

Czechs, Germans, and Galicia

Jan Lam was born into a mixed German-Polish family in the Galician town of Stanisławów. His grandfather, Zenon Konrad Lamm, was an officer originally from the vicinity of Frankfurt who came to Galicia in the late eighteenth century. His grandmother, Joanna Ziołecka, belonged to the Polish nobility, and launched a Polish line in this family of German-speaking military personnel. While in Galicia, the Lamms shortened their surname by one letter. Two generations after his grandfather's arrival in the province, Jan Lam grew up to be a Pole—a Polish-language writer at that, eventually one of the most prominent journalists in the post-1867 Galician milieu.

Capowice High Society is a major example of social-political satire in nineteenth-century Polish literature, an artifact in large part rooted in the realities of Galicia. Partly autobiographical, the novel tells the story of an Austrian-Czech German-speaking official in Galicia from the 1840s to the 1860s. Like the Sachers, the Precliczeks of *Capowice High Society* trace their roots to Bohemia: "Wacław Precliczek, whose name can also be written as Wenzel Pretzlitscheck . . . [and who] belongs to the Czech language, prefers to use his family's original transliteration: Václav Precliček." Wenzel Pretzlitscheck was also German, because "the Czech of his kind is indeed an authentic German." His Polish wife, however, has little tolerance for her husband's mixed roots and confusing name; she calls him, a "Schwab" (a derogative name for a German), and raises their daughter to be a Pole. The young Milcia does not conceal her contempt for the German language, to her father's dismay: "How could it happen that his own blood, that his own daughter, *mein Milchen,* could not or did not want to learn German, and in her contempt for the dominant nationality, went as far as to call the language of Metternich and Krieg, the language of *Verordnungen* and protocols, she called it, ach . . . the language of cows."[25]

Finding a non-German husband for his beloved daughter presents certain difficulties for Wacław Precliczek. As a Czech, a German, or a "Schwab," Precliczek finds it hard to choose between different types of non-Germans in Galicia — Ruthenians and Poles. It does not escape Precliczek's attention, moreover, that some inhabitants of Galicia speak both Polish and Ruthenian, even if they use these languages for different purposes and on different occasions.

As a German-speaking Austrian official from Bohemia, Precliczek is forced to retire after 1867, when the Poles secured autonomy. He is beset with feelings of betrayal: many of the nation in favor of whom he is forced to resign are also involved in various political conspiracies. Ruthenians, by contrast, were long known for their unconditional loyalty to Vienna. Defiance and freethinking being decidedly not qualities Precliczek would wish for in a life's partner for his daughter, the choice of candidate pool falls upon the Ruthenians.

Johann von Safranowych, in particular, seems ideal. "The Safranowych family, which up until 1848 had belonged to the Polish nobility of the Uniate rite, had recently adopted the Austrian nationality." All are known for their loyalty to Vienna. Most important, the potential bridegroom also enjoys certain political connections; his uncle, Prince Nabutowych, is a well-known specialist in the Ruthenian language, *"a leader of the nation and defender of national rights in Lwów and in Vienna."* With access to many important personages, Nabutowych will surely extend his wings over a nephew and his family. To get into Safranowych's good graces, Precliczek yet again reinvents his own identity; if his daughter refuses to be a German, then he will proclaim himself a Ruthenian.[26]

The names of Lam's protagonists — Safranowych and Nabutowych — rhyme surprisingly well with the name of a prominent (and quite real, not invented) Ruthenian church dignitary: Bishop Angelowych, who, educated in Austrian institutions, became head of the Greek Catholic Church in Galicia. Safranowych and Nabutowych in Lam's novel, and Angelowych in real life, were, at any given moment, either Ruthenians of Polish background, or Poles of Ruthenian background: born into Ruthenian families, they were educated in German, but communicated with relatives and close associates most often in Polish. A radical shift from Polishness to Ruthenianness took place around 1848, which involved the political and cultural choice of choosing the Ruthenian language over Polish. The change also implied a new mode of politics, a recognition of the fact that Polish and Ruthenian political interests might conflict. This shift in self-identification was largely a result of Austrian efforts in Galicia.

The Ruthenians

The first large-scale contact between Austrians and Ruthenians occurred only in 1772, with Vienna's annexation of Galicia. Sacher-Masoch encountered Ruthenians during his childhood in Galicia. In the countryside surrounding Lemberg, peasant children spoke Ruthenian. Their parents, however, would define themselves in regional, rather than national, terms. Before 1848, even educated Ruthenians lacked distinct national and political commitments.

Ruthenians had lived in Poland for centuries, the majority being peasants without political representation. Most belonged to the Uniate Church, which had been formed at the Union of Brest (1596), when various members of the Ruthenian Orthodox clergy concluded a union with the Vatican, and which, as an institution, was socially and politically marginalized. Although in full communion with Rome, the Uniate Church retained Orthodox liturgical traditions. In an age when ethnic identities were less defined than they would be in the nationalism-minded nineteenth century, religion remained the most important distinction between Poles and Ruthenians: Roman Catholics were commonly considered Poles, and Uniates Ruthenians. Austrian Galicia, much like Polish-Lithuanian Rus' Czerwona or Red Rus', was home to representatives of some of the most prominent Ruthenian aristocrats—the Lubomirski, Radziwiłł, Fredro, Sanguszki, and Dzieduszycki families, among others;[27] but by the nineteenth century, few cared to remember their Ruthenian pedigree. By 1772, the traditionally

Ruthenian territories of Poland-Lithuania were more Polish than ever before.[28]

After 1772, the Austrian government reformed the status of each of the churches in Galicia. In September 1772, Governor Pergen was instructed to announce free exercise of religion for Ruthenian Uniates.[29] In 1774, on Kaunitz's personal insistence, the name of the Ruthenian church was changed from the rather provisional title "Uniate" to the more respectful and formal "Greek Catholic."[30] The following year, Maria Theresa opened the Barbareum in Vienna, a seminary with twelve places reserved for Ruthenian students. In 1782, Emperor Joseph II granted freedom of worship and expression to religious minorities, in principle equalizing the status of Greek Catholics and Roman Catholics, and 1783 saw the establishment of a Greek Catholic seminary in Lemberg.[31]

These institutions created unprecedented opportunities for Ruthenians, of which many were eager to take advantage. The reforms also helped halt conversions from the Uniate Church to Roman Catholicism. Austrian officials redrew the administrative boundaries of church dioceses in Galicia in such a way that parish boundaries better reflected different religious affiliations: regions with a predominantly Ruthenian population were assigned to Greek Catholics, and Poles fell under Roman Catholic jurisdiction.[32] In the 1780s, Joseph II decided to close a number of monasteries and consolidate churches in order to create an ethnic majority in specific areas. Ruthenians made up the vast majority of the countryside population; the number of Greek Catholic churches remaining open was thus greater than that of Roman Catholic churches, most of which were concentrated in towns.[33] Variations in the treatment of different churches led to speculation that the Austrian government favored Ruthenians over Poles.[34]

In 1808, in the midst of the Napoleonic Wars, a new Greek Catholic metropolitanate was created in Galicia's medieval capital, Halych[35] (with Angelowych its first metropolitan), in part as an Austrian reward for Ruthenian loyalty during the conflict. While Poles hoped to rebuild an independent state, and the allegiances of Jews remained unclear, most Ruthenians remained unconditionally loyal to their Habsburg sovereigns. In 1805, then Bishop Angelowych had published his first pro-Austrian pamphlet in Lemberg, and he issued several similar texts in the years that followed.[36] By their commitment to the Austrians, the Ruthenians further jeopardized their relations with the Poles. When Polish forces allied with Napoleon seized Galicia in the spring of 1809, Metropolitan Angelowych was declared an enemy of the state. He fled Lemberg before the arrival of Polish troops, but was captured, arrested, and interrogated in Stryj as a political prisoner, and released only after Austrian forces retook the province. Following the reestablishment of Austrian rule in Galicia, Angelowych became something of a living martyr, and Ruthenians in general were rewarded for their loyalty. It is rather symbolic that a new metropolitanate was founded during the war, in effect as part of Austria's effort to maintain possession of the province.

Having shown their fealty to the empire and benefited as a result, Ruthenians began to insist on taking part in its politics. In 1805, the Roman Catholic clergy had received access to the Austrian administration of Galicia, gaining the right to appoint one church dignitary who would be responsible for religious matters in the Gubernium.[37] This state of affairs elicited protests from the Greek Catholic prelacy (including Bishop Angelowych) against in effect an exclusively Roman Catholic religious supervision of Galicia's population; and inspired requests for separate representation in Austrian-Galician officialdom. The Gubernium took the proposal under consideration, but the debate on appointing a Ruthenian clergyman to the administration dragged on for years. "It is true," a Gubernium official noted, "that there are frequent conflicts between the Latin and Greek Catholic clergy." In 1810, the Gubernium revived the case: "The complaints of Metropolitan Angelowych against the *Gubernialreferent* now appear in a new light, and we declare our willingness to further investigate this matter."[38]

It is not clear whether, in considering the request for separate representation, the Gubernium took the interests of the Greek Catholic clergy sincerely to heart or was simply resorting to the ancient practice of pitting one group against another, in this case supporting Ruthenians against the more independence-minded Poles. Even if, in the end, it did not in fact establish the hoped-for separate representation, the Gubernium's consideration of the issue itself undermined the privileged status of the Roman Catholic clergy in the governance of Galicia.

The reform of the Greek Catholic Church and of Ruthenian education was by no means a smooth process, and opposition often cropped up in the unlikeliest places. By the early nineteenth century, it should be noted, a number of Ruthenians, especially clergymen, had graduated from various Austrian institutions. Even as they benefited from a German-language education, Ruthenian elites, whether secular or lay, were still deeply rooted in Polish culture. Many conversed in Polish at home.[39] For these elites, an education in the Ruthenian language would present certain difficulties.[40]

The first generation of lay literary intelligentsia to prefer Ruthenian over Polish emerged in Galicia in the 1830s, but Polish affinities remained strong among this social group as well. Johann von Safranowych, the prospective fiancée of Precliczek's daughter, was one of those who counted as "gente Poloni natione Rutheni"—"Poles by ancestry, Ruthenes by nationality," although it could also be the other way around, "gente Rutheni natione Poloni."[41] Ruthenian children educated in German-language schools tended to speak Ruthenian in the country, but switched to Polish when in town. Polish was the language of aristocratic elites, German that of administration, and Ruthenian—even in the perception of Ruthenian elites—was inferior to either.[42] But in time the language balance started to shift; by 1848, a Safranowych who had formerly conversed in Polish was more likely to use Ruthenian instead.

Vienna's role in promoting Ruthenian culture and politics did not go unnoticed by contemporary observers. Some Polish intellectuals between the eighteenth and twentieth centuries regarded such policies as imperial(ist) machinations. Jan Lewicki, for example, a Polish historian active in the second half of the nineteenth century, could not conceal his contempt for Vienna's moves in this regard: "The Austrian government," he wrote in 1879, "played games with the Ruthenians, and seduced them with empty promises. The Ruthenians fell into this trap, and always demonstrated their loyalty to Vienna."[43] Lewicki was one of a cohort of Polish intellectuals, statesmen, and historians who believed that Vienna's policies had a defining impact upon the Ruthenians, helping to establish among them a new political culture. Whether the Austrians intended to promote the Ruthenian cause or not, by creating new socio-political opportunities for them, they inevitably undermined the dominant status of Poles in the region.[44]

In retrospect, it must be said that the effects of Vienna's policies on Ruthenians were ambiguous. Many of the schools established by the Austrians became an instrument of Polish assimilation; just as the offspring of German-speaking officials were attracted to Polish culture through networks of school friends and colleagues, so too did educated Ruthenians, attending German-language schools, become easily attracted to the Polish language and culture as "superior" to or of higher status than their own. This consideration, however, should not diminish the value of the educational system per se. In particular, primary schooling became available to the Ruthenians of Galicia only upon the Austrian annexation. The policies of tolerance and the creation of new educational institutions, and an approach to language issues that at the very least did not discriminate against Ruthenian, all caused important changes in Galicia's socio-political mix, with the effects felt not only by Ruthenians, but by Poles as well.

Mixed Marriages

One symbol of Ruthenian social advancement was the increasing phenomenon of mixed Austrian-Ruthenian marriages. In Lam's novel, the alliance between the Precliczeks and the Safranowyches never comes to pass, but the fact that such a marriage was even contemplated reveals remarkable transformations in the status of Ruthenians in Austrian Galicia. In this domain, too, Poles were now facing competition from their Ruthenian neighbors.

The Ostermann family became emblematic of multidirectional assimilations. Georg Benjamin von Ostermann, the son of the Austrian bureaucrat and sympathizer with the Polish cause Johann Georg who was incorrectly rumored to have joined the Polish rebels against Russia in 1830, married another scion of an Austrian bureaucratic family from Galicia; his wife, Johanna Maria Fabricius, came from a mixed German-Ruthenian family. Her father, Johann Baptist Fabricius, was a German-speaking Austrian bureaucrat in the Galician city of Stanisławów. Her mother, Pelagia, was the daughter of a Ruthenian priest, Petro Lewyckyi, another example of those who were "gente Rutheni natione Poloni." Born in 1835, Johanna Maria was baptized on April 14 of the same year in the Greek Catholic rite.[45] Like other families of the Greek Catholic clergy, the Fabriciuses spoke Polish at home; Johanna Maria used Ruthenian only in her dealings with Ruthenian peasants.[46] In the tradition of her mother, she grew up to be a Greek Catholic.

Georg Benjamin von Ostermann and Johanna Maria Fabricius raised their children in an increasingly diverse setting. Their son, Georg Johann Wilhelm von Ostermann, was born in Stanisławów in 1856. His first and middle names were, like his last, German, as his father Georg Benjamin was keen on instilling Germanness in his children; but his culture and views were influenced in large part by his Ruthenian-identifying mother. Just as his father had before him, Georg Johann Wilhelm von Ostermann chose a Ruthenian fiancée, Iwanna (or Ioanna), daughter of the Ukrainian activist Ignat Tychowicz. After the wedding, she took her husband's surname, but remained true to the Ruthenian tradition instilled in her by her own family. Iwanna von Ostermann studied law at the University of Stanisławów and was active in the Ukrainian women's movement, in 1871 becoming the first woman to join the Ukrainian cultural organization "Prosvita" (Education).[47]

In the period of just over a century that had passed between the Ostermanns' first arrival in Galicia in the 1770s and the moment when Ostermanns became active in the Ukrainian political-cultural movement, the family had undergone remarkable transformations. Its members spoke German, Polish, and Ruthenian at different moments of their lives. The German and Polish of the earlier Ostermanns gradually gave way to the Ruthenian, and eventually Ukrainian, of their children and grandchildren in the late nineteenth century. They sought to maintain German culture in their family, and were split in their attitudes toward Polish uprisings. Some members of the family eventually chose a specifically Ruthenian path.

Cases of German-Ruthenian assimilation are more complicated than their German-Polish equivalents. In marrying Ruthenian women, Austrian German-speaking men were typically entering into clergy families: before 1848, priests formed the only representative group of Ruthenian elites in Galicia. In terms of social hierarchy, Ruthenian clergymen stood on a lower rung than Polish aristocrats, whose culture and lifestyle proved so attractive to Austrian bureaucrats. German-Ruthenian families were rare before 1848. It is hard to assess with any certainly whether the Ostermann-Fabricius example signals certain social trends, or rather constitutes an exception confirming the marginal status of Ruthenians in the Galician public sphere. In any case, such instances cannot be ignored: the fact that such marriages existed at all reveal the emergence of new national and social hierarchies in Galicia at least partly attributable to Austrian reforms in the province.

While German-Polish assimilation was facilitated by religious commonality, denominational division complicated German-Ruthenian assimilation. Most Germanophone Austrians (with some notable exceptions) and practically all Poles were Roman Catholics, wedding in Roman Catholic churches and raising their children in the Roman rite. The situation in German-Ruthenian families was more complicated; even as they tended to speak Polish among themselves, Ruthenians, especially members of the clergy, were likely to hold fast to their religion.

Descendants of mixed German-Ruthenian or Polish-Ruthenian families followed different paths. It became common to raise male and female children differently, baptizing boys in the religion of their fathers, and raising girls in their mothers' faith. It was not by accident that the Ostermann sons all became Roman Catholics despite being brought up by Ruthenian mothers. Women, by contrast, most often turned to the Greek Catholic faith. Johanna Fabricius, herself raised in a mixed Polish-Ruthenian family, grew up in the Greek Catholic tradition of her mother.

The Ostermanns present a revealing example of multiple assimilations: Polish-Ruthenian, German-Polish, German-Ruthenian. That the Ruthenian branch of the family eventually became dominant cannot be attributed to the Ostermanns or their mothers alone. The political mobilization of Ruthenians in the early nineteenth century stemmed from the combined efforts of Viennese administrators and numerically still rather limited Ruthenian elites. The political achievements of Ruthenians are remarkable not only because they would have been virtually impossible just decades earlier, but also because a large part of the stimulus behind this progress originated in Vienna rather than in Galicia itself. The Austrians helped break the Ruthenians' long-standing allegiance to Polish political culture, promoting the Ruthenian language at the expense of Polish, defending the distinct status of the Greek Catholic Church, and stanching the flow of conversions from it. Neither the Polish language, nor Greek-to-Roman-rite conversions disappeared in Galicia; but the effects of Austrian policy became increasingly visible in the years leading up to 1848 and during the revolution. After 1848, Ruthenians staked their claim to the province of Galicia, which Poles had long regarded as definitionally Polish.

Ruthenian Claims

It was one thing for Ruthenians to improve their social status, but it was something else entirely for a member of an old Austrian elite group to identify himself with the Ruthenians. Of course, Sacher-Masoch in real life and Wacław Precliczek in Jan Lam's novel played games with their identity toward different ends. Yet the moves they made, as well as the mechanisms of inventing Ruthenian claims, are important historical artifacts worthy of attention.

Sacher-Masoch's Ruthenian nanny, nicknamed Handscha, was one of the most important figures in his life. She nurtured him during his childhood and, as Sacher-Masoch later recalled, stood in his adult years as his ideal of womanhood.[48] This Ruthenian woman shaped Sacher-Masoch's first encounters with the sublime and, as Sacher-Masoch confessed, had more of an impact on his young personality than his heroic ancestors or his immediate family. Handscha played a crucial role in Sacher-Masoch's development because she was with him when his parents were not. His father also had a particularly strong influence on young Leopold, but their relationship remained rather distant, if not tense. In their mature conceptualization of Galicia, both Sacher-Masochs, father and son, seemed to favor Ruthenians over Poles, foregrounding the purported greater loyalty of the former.[49] Police Chief Sacher-Masoch espoused the conventional imperial view, emphasizing the numerous benefits Austrian rule afforded the province. The younger Sacher-Masoch was more nuanced in his assessment; in his Ruthenian revelations, he explored an idea of nationality contrasting with his father's imperial outlook.

Between 1874 and 1882, Sacher-Masoch published a number of autobiographical texts in various periodicals in Germany and France, each corroborating his Ruthenian claims. The earliest work in this category, "Eine Autobiographie," appeared in the *Hamburger Zeitschrift Omnibus* in December 1874; a new and revised version of the same piece was published in 1879 in another German periodical, *Deutsche Monatsblätter*. Between August and October 1877, the Parisian newspaper *Le Gaulois* ran a French-language version of Sacher-Masoch's memoirs, his "Souvenirs," and between February and May 1879, Paris's *Revue Bleue* ran his "Choses vécues."[50] In 1882, in Leipzig, Sacher-Masoch published (in the periodical *Auf der Höhe*, which he edited) one of the most controversial texts in this autobiographical series: the memoirs of his police chief father.[51]

In these various texts, Sacher-Masoch sketched a history of his family as an amalgam of various traditions and ethnicities, the specifics of which remain difficult to verify. His paternal grandfather, he claimed, originated from Habsburg Spain, and his maternal grandfather traced his roots to the Ruthenian nobility.[52] Painting such a picture of diversity constituted, from the standpoint of late nineteenth-century Vienna, something of a moral-political stance; and in order to endorse this view, the author may have totally fabricated some portions of the history. While the Spanish chapter was at least somewhat plausible, the Ruthenian account was more likely the product of Sacher-Masoch's imagination.[53]

Some contemporaries took Sacher-Masoch's fantasies seriously, and so a myth became ever closer to reality. At least one author describes one of the grandfathers, Johann Nepomuk von Sacher, as a "Ruthenian noble"; others believed that the other grandfather, Masoch, was Ruthenian as well.[54] In the early twentieth century, the great Ukrainian historian Mykhailo Hrushevs'kyi took Sacher-Masoch's Ruthenianness seriously, lamenting that a famous Austrian writer had abandoned his native language and opted for German.[55]

As Hrushevs'kyi may well have known, the Ruthenian choice was not an easy one to make during the 1860s and 1870s. Still politically marginal within the monarchy and relatively small within Galicia, the Ruthenian political establishment was deeply divided among several political orientations. Only in the late nineteenth century did Ruthenians in Galicia, or at least a large part of them, come to view themselves as belonging to a greater Ukrainian nation, at the time comprising approximately ten million people in the Russian Empire and Austrian Galicia.

Four political orientations, and at least three different national options, coexisted among Ruthenian elites during the nineteenth century, often concurrently and in conflict with one another: pro-Austrian, pro-Polish, pro-Russian, and Ruthenian (later Ukrainian). The first two were dominant before 1848; the latter two emerged shortly after the 1848 Revolution, and shaped Galician politics until 1918. These orientations were not all mutually exclusive. Habsburg patriotism, for example, combined well with pro-Polish sympathies among Ruthenians before 1848, and with the national Ruthenian solution thereafter. Russophilism, on the other hand, began as a form of opposition to the pro-Austrian and pro-Polish stances.

The Revolution of 1848 marked a turning point in Polish and Ruthenian politics in Galicia. The pro-Polish movement lost many of its supporters. Ruthenians who had previously aligned themselves with the Polish nobility, such as the Safranowyches and the Nabutowyches, increasingly identified themselves as Ruthenians, foregrounding their non-Polishness. Between 1848 and 1918, Ruthenian political life was dominated by two political tendencies, one a nationally Ruthenian outlook that laid the basis for the Ukrainian political program in the twentieth century, the other Russophilic, endorsing closer ties with Russia. Each tendency self-defined and flourished via competition with the other.

Ruthenian Populists regarded Ruthenians as a distinct national group, different from both the Poles and the Russians. First emerging after the Revolution of 1848, and by the 1860s forming a major force in Galician political life, the Populists increasingly came to endorse the unification of the Ruthenians divided between the Russian Empire and the Habsburg Monarchy; by the end of the century, some advocated the formation of an independent Ukrainian state.

Russophilism also matured after 1848 as an alternative to the hitherto dominant pro-Polish and loyal Habsburg strains of Ruthenian political-intellectual culture. Few in this camp denied Ruthenian distinctiveness, but they generally believed that Ruthenians alone would be unable to withstand Polish influences in Galicia. The Russophiles advocated closer ties with Russia, and even the integration of Galicia's Ruthenians into the Greater Russian nation.[56] Despite close ties to elements in the Russian Empire, Russophilism was an authentically Galician affair; St. Petersburg supported the movement, but did not create it.[57] By the 1890s, the Russophiles were losing ground in Galicia, albeit remaining a significant and active force through 1918. By the turn of the twentieth century, Ruthenian populists gradually adopted the name of Ukrainians, and some advocated the unification of Ukrainian territory from the Austrian and Russian partitions.

In refusing to marry Safranowych, Precliczek's daughter Milcia shocks her father with the allegation that Safranowych is "a Muscovite outsider, a St. Georgian [a Russophile], and a spy for the [Russian] police."[58] Precliczek's choice of a fiancé for her had been based on the calculation that Ruthenians were trustworthy, more loyal to Vienna than Poles would ever be; but a German-speaking Austrian Czech might have realized that Ruthenians, too, were not a monolithic group, that some might have presented an even greater political danger than many of the Poles whom he had automatically excluded from the list of his potential sons-in-law.

This disappointment with Ruthenians leads Precliczek to redefine his nationality once more. "I am in fact a Galician," he declares on yet another occasion.[59] The broad category of "Galician" seems to pose no danger, including the Polish, Ruthenian, German, and Czech elements of the region under a single umbrella. This purported Galicianness, however, does not last long, for, "disappointed with Galician utilitarianism and unhappy with his own choice of nationality," he soon revives his Slavic roots, but mixes up places and nationalities: "I am in fact a Bohemian, Václaw Precliček from Jung-Bunzlau; Long live the Slavs!"[60] Even here, Precliczek rejects the concept of clear-cut nationality, preferring regional allegiances instead; forced to remain in Galicia by family circumstances, toward the end of his life he prefers to be a "Slav" from Bohemia.

Long after his departure from Lemberg, Sacher-Masoch remained true to his Galicianness and Ruthenianness. He was not oblivious to political divisions among Ruthenians, but easily crossed the boundaries between different camps. In 1861, he attempted to correspond with two prominent members of the Ruthenian intelligentsia in Galicia, Spyrydon Lytvynowych and Mykhailo Kuzems'kyi.[61] Both were important members of the Greek Catholic Church and the Ruthenian political establishment. Lytvynowych, an archbishop and later metropolitan, was one of the most prominent members of the Ruthenian Populist camp; as metropolitan, he held a permanent seat in the Galician Diet (revived after the Napoleonic Wars) and the Austrian parliament. Kuzems'kyi served as vice president of the Ruthenian National Council during the 1848 Revolution. Despite not himself being a Russophile, he enjoyed a good reputation among adherents of this outlook for his staunch opposition to Polish domination of the province. Sacher-Masoch seems to have been particularly impressed with Kuzems'kyi: years after the 1848 Revolution, the writer gave that name to a major protagonist in his masochistic novel.[62]

Tensions between Russophiles and Populists might not have mattered much to Sacher-Masoch. He was known for his sympathy with Pan-Slavism, but never specified what role his especially beloved Ruthenians would play in this broader framework.[63] He clearly grasped the extent of the Polish-Ruthenian conflict in Galicia. "Both [my] father and grandfather were good to Ruthenians," Sacher-Masoch commented in his correspondence, ascribing some degree of Ruthenophilia to his ancestors[64]—a reference that could not be neutral in the context of an ethnically heterogeneous Galicia and, in the late nineteenth century, one roiled by various nationalisms.

Sacher-Masoch's memoirs have survived, as have the different political disagreements surrounding his personality. The twentieth century marked a new phase in the author's reception. As Ruthenians turned into Ukrainians, their ethnic perception of Sacher-Masoch became less nuanced; his earlier endorsement of Pan-Slavism and his courtship with the Russophiles have been virtually forgotten. The memoirs of his sexual experiments have lived on as well, remaining hardly less controversial in the twenty-first century than when Krafft-Ebing first introduced the term "masochism." But above all, in the region he considered nearest and dearest, Sacher-Masoch is remembered as Galicia's native son, an Austrian writer who decided to become a Ruthenian.[65]

The Paradoxes of Modernization

Sacher-Masoch never received a response from Lytvynowych (who died in 1869);[66] and for the world reading public at large, his Ruthenian enterprise remains unknown, put in the shade by the far more glaring sexual aspects of his writing. But Sacher-Masoch's ethnic revelations in his numerous autobiographical writings are as important to the history of national identity in Central Europe as are other elements of his work to the history of European modernism and psychology. His Ruthenian claims present Austria's policies in Galicia in a new light. His grandfather Johann von Sacher brought with him to the new Austrian province the idea of uniformity; an archetypical Austrian without clear-cut national identification, he was meant to create more citizens in his own image, and to suppress any and all expressions of nationality. A century later, his famous grandson observed the emergence of several rival forms of nationalism in this grandson's native Galicia.

As a Germanophone Austrian writer, Sacher-Masoch had no restrictive nationality. The late nineteenth century, however, brought new ideological challenges, with the claims of modern nationalism transforming Habsburg politics. While the empire adjusted to new realities, imperial subjects were pressed to reconsider and reinvent their own identities. Sacher-Masoch might perhaps have preferred to remain what he had always been—simply a subject of the Habsburg Monarchy, and a member of its German-speaking literary establishment; but his cosmopolitan "Austrianness" came under increasing scrutiny in the 1860s. Pushed to declare his one true allegiance, Sacher-Masoch faced a variety of options, and was as creative with his nationality as with his sexuality.

In Jan Lam's novel, too, Wacław Precliczek approaches his nationality creatively. Over the years, he defines himself as a true Czech, German, Ruthenian, Slav, Bohemian, and Galician. Just like Sacher-Masoch, he remains ever committed to the Habsburg dynasty, and this loyalty is more important than his numerous nationalities. Both Sacher-Masoch and Precliczek, however, faced difficulties identifying themselves with the nonnational German aspect of the Habsburg Monarchy alone. In a Galicia increasingly divided along ethnic lines, each was forced to declare a single nationality.

Sacher-Masoch's and Precliczek's choices were products of a specific cultural and political climate in the monarchy. Sacher-Masoch's sexual and physiological experiments would have been less resonant just decades earlier; his literary success can be ascribed in part to the culture of Viennese modernity and its growing interest in eros and the unconscious.[67] His Ruthenian claims were even more historically contingent. Exotic and creative as he was, even Sacher-Masoch would probably have found it an insurmountable challenge to declare himself a Ruthenian only a century earlier, when Ruthenians had no elite nor institutional representation. Indeed, the Ruthenian choice would be hard to imagine even during the 1850s, when Sacher-Masoch was devoting sentimental stories, in German, to Galicia as his Polish fatherland.[68] But as Galicia and Galicia's Ruthenians acquired a new status, Sacher-Masoch changed his views as well. The entirely different status acquired by this national group in the nineteenth century, and Sacher-Masoch's claims of belonging to it, were products of the Austrian modernization of Galicia during the late eighteenth and nineteenth centuries.

Vienna's support of Ruthenians became an undisputed fact in the historiography of Galicia. On either side of the ethnic divide, Polish and Ruthenian historians, or alternatively, historians of Galician Poles and Ruthenians, tend to attribute some degree of intentionality to Austrian efforts: if Ruthenians benefited from Austrian modernization, and Poles suffered a loss in status as a result of it, then this must have been exactly the Austrians' goal. Such teleological projections present a view of Austria's program in Galicia that is incomplete, if not outright incorrect. The remarkable rise of Ruthenian status and political consciousness posed a danger not only to the Poles of Galicia, but to the Austrian authorities as well. Poles advocated the rebuilding of an independent Poland, of which Galicia would form a part; but in the second half of the nineteenth century, Ruthenians advocated various solutions to their political problems, of which the Russian option posed no less a threat to the Habsburg Monarchy than that of an independent Poland. The victory of Russophilism could spell Vienna's defeat at the hands of St. Petersburg in a war (virtual or otherwise) over territory, citizens, and loyalty.

Austrian policymakers were not completely oblivious to these self-inflicted dangers. Even before 1848, Austrian support for the Ruthenians was never unconditional, and imperial policies would thereafter be ever more restrictive. But the long-term effects of earlier policies were not easily reversible. Few Poles and even fewer Ruthenians fulfilled Vienna's hopes of adopting Austrianness, while members of the imperial ruling class in Galicia came to identify themselves either as Poles or even Ruthenians.

SEVEN

Administering the Jews

While Poles were becoming Austrians, Austrians were becoming Poles, and Ruthenians could not decide who to become, one group in Galicia seemed to remain unaffected by reciprocal assimilations. Comprising some 10 percent of the overall population, Galician Jews outnumbered their coreligionists living in all other Habsburg provinces combined. Carrying out statistical surveys of Jews was challenging, and estimates of the Jewish population in Galicia and other imperial territories vary greatly. It is, however, safe to state that during the 1770s to 1780s, the Jews of Galicia made up some two-thirds of the Jewish population of the entire monarchy.[1]

Taking possession of this new province, of course, did not mark Austria's first encounter with Jews. But in the eighteenth century, after numerous expulsions and restrictions, most Jews in the Habsburg Monarchy were confined to the lands of the Bohemian crown: Bohemia, Moravia, and Silesia. Though important socially and economically, the Jewish minority in Habsburg Italy was relatively small. Austrian officials feared that the number of Jews in the new province could further increase in subsequent years, and that, in migrating to other provinces, they could affect the overall demographic and social situation in the monarchy; the rate of demographic growth, moreover, was higher among Jews than it was among Christians.[2] Also worrisome to the imperial authorities was Jewish immigration: there being no functional border control, the Jews of partitioned Poland moved easily between various regions thereof, and could settle in Galicia. Most of these newcomers, and those already living in the province, were poorer than Jews elsewhere in the monarchy. This large Jewish minority required, in Vienna's view, new institutions of control.

The remarkable Jewish presence in Galicia caught the attention of Austrian officials from the very beginning of the imperial project in the region. In the early 1770s, Governor Pergen expressed frustration with the glaring presence of Jews in Lemberg and beyond. In the 1780s, Governor Brigido supervised Austrian reforms affecting the Jewish inhabitants of Galicia. While subjected to imperial innovations, these Jews also experienced a modernization of their own, one not imposed from outside.[3] Jews underwent their own Enlightenment, the Haskalah, which arrived in Galicia from Berlin via the Habsburg German territories. Similarly to the Ruthenians, some Jews eventually became known for their loyalty to Vienna. Neighbors to Polish landowners, Ruthenian peasants, and Austrian officials, Jews became an important factor of Vienna's domestic and international politics.

During the 1770s, Austrian officials did not conceal the fact that they meant to approach their "Galician Jewish question" through force of law. But radical policy intentions did not always lead to similarly dramatic consequences. Despite persistent attempts to control population size, Jewish demographic growth was greater in Habsburg Galicia than it had been under Polish-Lithuanian rule.[4] Even in the face of residency and movement restrictions, moreover, Jews from Galicia formed a visible presence in various provinces of the empire, and eventually in Vienna as well. Jewish autonomy persisted into the nineteenth century. The Austrian administration, at the same time, came to heavily rely on traditional Jewish institutions and the men—rabbis, elders, and community leaders—who headed them.[5]

The story of Jewish-Austrian relations in Galicia is thus much more than that of either Austrian oppression or Jewish resilience.[6] It is also a story of reciprocal adjustments and the complex coexistence of Austrian modernity and Jewish tradition. The survival of Jewish institutions highlights some important aspects of imperial mechanisms that were not confined to Jews alone. In turn, our understanding of the persistence of Jewish tradition requires a nuanced analysis of the routine of administration as an intermediary stage between policy designs and their results.

Between Poland and Austria

Galicia's Jewish population was part of the heritage of the Polish-Lithuanian Commonwealth. Before its disintegration in 1795, Poland-Lithuania was home to the largest Jewish population in Europe. Under Polish rule, Jews maintained rights of extensive self-government within their traditional kehillot, self-administered communities organized on a regional basis.[7] The kehilla was governed by the kahal, the community's member-elected leadership. All Jewish communities sent their representatives to the Council of Four Lands. This institution functioned as a Jewish parliament; it oversaw Jewish administrative and financial matters, coordinated the collection of taxes among Poland's Jews, and paid a lump sum of Jewish taxes to the Polish Diet.[8] Though imperfect, such organs of self-administration allowed the Jews of Poland to preserve their traditions and a degree of Jewish autonomy otherwise unknown in Europe.

Administrative reforms affecting Galician Jews began in 1776 with the establishment of the Jewish Directorium (*Jüdische Direktion*), a commission forming part of the Austrian civil administration in Lemberg. The twelve members of the Directorium—six German-speaking Austrian officials and six representatives of the local Jewry—became responsible for the governance of Jews in Galicia.[9] They supervised the election and internal functioning of community kahals, the keeping of statistics on Jewish communities, and the introduction of Austrian taxes. In its functions, the new institution somewhat resembled the Council of Four Lands;[10] but the Directorium was essentially a symbol of change, designed to eliminate the remnants of Jewish tradition.

The kahals, then, were not abolished, but placed under the jurisdiction of this new institution in Lemberg. "All Jews," announced an Austrian decree, "are to be united in one general entity, insofar as only uniform supervision can secure collective well-being."[11] Kahals were divided into four categories by size and tax liability. Each kahal was represented by an elder, who reported to the Directorium. Community leaders were required to appear regularly at their respective district administrations. All decisions concerning Jewish socio-political life, then, were to be coordinated with the Austrian civil authorities.

The innovation of the Directorium reflected Vienna's intentions as well as its early difficulties. In theory, Galician Jews should have fallen under the authority of German-speaking Austrian officials, just like other, Christian subjects. But the administration of Jewish communities remained inaccessible to Austrian bureaucrats; communal records were kept in Polish and Yiddish, which most Austrian officials found incomprehensible. The self-administration that survived from the Polish-Lithuanian period afforded a degree of autonomy, and the imperial authorities feared that Jewish leaders and rabbis, left to their own devices, might manipulate censuses so as to avoid Austrian taxes. The Directorium was thus meant to overcome these administrative obstacles and facilitate Austrian efforts. It became a mediator between the Austrian civil authorities and Jewish communal administration, combining members and coordinating efforts of each. Jewish elders administered their communities as they had done in the past, but after 1776, integrated into the new structures of civil administration, they kept statistics, carried out censuses, and collected new, Austrian taxes.[12]

With institutions transformed, the status of Jewish administrators—elders and rabbis—underwent change as well. Established in 1776 along with the Jewish Directorium was yet another new administrative office: the chief rabbi of Galicia, modeled on similar posts existing in other provinces.[13] Jews in each region that included a chief rabbinate nominated candidates for the position, but the final selection required the authorization of the Austrian civil authorities. No such office had existed in Poland-Lithuania; the position of rabbi had typically been passed down from father to son. The appointment of rabbis had required confirmation of the civil authorities, but in the Polish-Lithuanian Commonwealth, this did not necessarily imply any major infringement on Jewish autonomy, but rather reflected a mutually accepted symbiosis between Jewish and Polish-Lithuanian authorities.[14]

In 1776, forty-eight Galician Jewish electors took part in the preliminary selection of their chief rabbi. Two of the candidates under consideration, Ezekiel Landau and Leib Bernstein, traced their roots to Galicia, each having moved away and held positions elsewhere in Europe: Landau served as chief rabbi of Prague, and Bernstein held a rabbinic office in Berlin. In 1776, Maria Theresa personally favored Landau because of his earlier support of the Habsburg dynasty during the Seven Years' War. But although he was elected, Landau declined, and Leib Bernstein traveled from Berlin to Lemberg as the first chief rabbi of Galicia.[15]

The transition could not have been an easy one. Coming from Berlin to Lemberg implied a radical change of lifestyle and an encounter with an entirely different political and cultural tradition. Berlin at the time was a center of the Haskalah movement, home to such prominent Jewish intellectuals as Moses Mendelssohn, who advocated ending Jewish isolation and integrating Jews into broader European society. Such goals would require a shift of languages: Mendelssohn preferred German to Yiddish as one means toward breaking the social and cultural barriers that had long separated Jews from their Gentile neighbors.

While Berlin was a center of Jewish progressive thought, Lemberg was one of the capitals of Jewish tradition, a stronghold of Jewish conservatism. The differences between Berlin and Lemberg would have a profound impact on the Galician chief rabbinate of Bernstein, who, despite being a native of Poland, was treated upon his homecoming to Lemberg in 1776 as an outsider. Further complicating his activities was that, functionally, he represented the Jews of Galicia, but was bound by his obligations to the Austrian administration. In time he would become a twofold villain: accused by other Jews of being an imperial collaborator and lackey, and reprimanded by his Austrian superiors for foot-dragging.

Discontent with Bernstein was fueled not only by ideological but also by practical considerations. Before taking office in Berlin and Lemberg, Bernstein had held a rabbinate in Polish Zbaraż and later Brody, where he had made a considerable income as a merchant, during the 1760s ranking among the most prosperous residents of the town. Soon after Bernstein was appointed chief rabbi, several prominent Jews from Galicia filed a complaint to Vienna requesting a review of Bernstein's previous activities there. By sending their report to Vienna, the authors hoped to avoid the involvement of the Gubernium; local officials in Galicia were known to support Bernstein, unlike their colleagues in Vienna, who were more likely to take charges against him seriously. But Bernstein came through the review unscathed. Vienna forwarded the request to Lemberg, where the Gubernium conducted its own investigation, finding no fault with Bernstein's actions, and instead sentencing his accusers to two weeks in prison (later commuted to financial compensation).[16]

Bernstein remained in Galicia beyond the 1770s, and was soon involved in new reforms. In 1780, Joseph II became sole ruler, opening a new chapter in the history of Galician Jews. Whereas Maria Theresa had sought to combine Jewish practices from the previous period with new Austrian institutions, her son meant to eliminate Polish-Lithuanian holdovers entirely, and proceeded unilaterally with the creation of a German-speaking administration governing Christian and Jewish subjects alike.

Most of the reforms were eventually adjusted and reversed. One decision, however, has impacted the history of modern Europe virtually to the present day. In 1781, as part of his most important and long-lasting reform, Joseph introduced the Edict of Toleration, which equalized the status of the various religious confessions in the monarchy.[17] Described by historians as one of the first practical results of the Austrian Enlightenment, this edict was one of only two pieces of Josephinian legislation to go unrescinded by Joseph II himself and unreversed by his successors.[18]

This legislation had been prepared well ahead of its announcement. On 13 May 1781, the emperor submitted for the Court Chancellery's consideration the first draft of the edict. In a preamble to the document, Joseph II explained his intention to make the Jewish inhabitants of imperial lands into valuable citizens: they were to receive the right to send their children to German-language state-sponsored schools for Jewish pupils, as well as access to professional offices; they would be allowed to attend universities, and would be treated as equal before the law. Some Jewish residency restrictions were lifted. Jews were also encouraged to integrate into German-language imperial culture.[19]

Provisions of the legislation were discussed with members of the provincial administrations, and adjustments were made accordingly. As with many other reforms, the proposed Edict of Toleration raised questions among Joseph II's bureaucrats. In this case: How would the new policies affect the social and demographic status of the Jews in the monarchy? Would they not lead to the further growth, typically undesired among

Austrian administrators, of the Jewish population in the cities?[20] Joseph II incorporated some of the concerns voiced by the bureaucracy. Thus, the new legislation imposed a cap on the number of Jews in Vienna, and restricted Jewish migration among the provinces.[21] Jews were required to use German rather than Hebrew or Yiddish in education, but they were allowed to enter universities. They were expected to abandon their traditional apparel, but were given the right to engage in many professions hitherto barred to them. Equal rights also implied equal obligations; like all other inhabitants of the empire, Jews were subject to military conscription, the provision that raised the most criticism among Jews themselves, as it prohibited them from observing traditional religious practices.

The Edict of Toleration was widely discussed in Europe; Jewish progressive thinkers both in and outside the monarchy considered it the most remarkable achievement of the modern state. The legislation was received with much acclaim in Berlin: Mendelssohn's circle regarded it as a major step in Jewish political advancement. For the first time, a European government had lifted many of the ancient restrictions concerning Jews. To be sure, Mendelssohn criticized specific provisions, such as mandatory military conscription; but such reservations aside, reform-minded and pro-integration Jews came to see Joseph II as one of their allies.

The reception of Joseph II's toleration policies inside the monarchy was mixed. Restrictions inscribed into the edict were as important as the numerous privileges, leaving Jews themselves not entirely content with the innovation. Despite criticism, Joseph II proceeded with the planned reform. The Edict of Toleration was first introduced in Austria's German-speaking lands and Bohemia; other provinces soon followed suit, and by 1783, it had become the law of the land for all imperial regions except Galicia.

The specific provincial version of the Edict of Toleration for Galicia took many years to prepare, a delay that underscored the differences between this former part of Poland-Lithuania and other Habsburg regions. New policies required institutional change, which in turn required statistical information, a commodity Austrian officials found extremely difficult to procure. The final goal was the introduction of the same Germanophone Austrian administration existing in other provinces. But even as the aims were clear, their implementation was always problematic. What role, if any, would Jewish rabbis and administrators play within the new system? Rabbis, after all, had become essential to the governance of Galicia's Jews: their inclusion in administration had been authorized by Vienna, and excluding them would involve a major reversal of Austrian policies.

Austrian officials imitated some tactics of their Polish-Lithuanian predecessors in exploiting, toward their own ends, internal conflicts within Jewish communities. Tensions within the kehillot worsened as a result of the 1770s reforms; complaints and denunciations against Jewish elders and rabbis by other community members flooded Austrian institutions after 1776. Such documents, many of them anonymous, often described kehillot as rife with corruption.

In 1782, the Galician Gubernium formed a commission to review the Austrian Jewish administration in Galicia. Its final report highlighted widespread corruption among Jewish kahal elders: some wealthy kehillot members, Jacob Aron of Brody, for example, had managed to avoid Austrian taxation. At the same time, a number of poor Jews had been forced by their kahals to make payments that were not only excessive, but had never been authorized by the Austrian authorities in the first place.[22] Kahal elders were also accused of supplying false statistics.[23] The problematic nature of the involvement of elders and rabbis in imperial administration of the province's Jews was summed up by Austrian officials in a Galician Gubernium report thus: "One of the most important proofs attesting to the oppression of Galician Jews is that these Jews are often forced by their kahal elders to pay excessive fees and taxes."[24] There would be no better justification for administrative overhaul than indications that some Jews were using Austrian institutions to oppress their coreligionists.

In 1785, the Jewish Directorium was liquidated; now all Jews were subject to the exclusive jurisdiction of the Austrian civil authorities, which ruled out, by law and in practice, any Jewish involvement.[25] This administrative reform of 1785 thus brought an end to the decade-long practice of combined Austrian-Jewish administration in Galicia. The 1785 decree also imposed further limitations on Jewish marriage, migration, and residency rights, introduced new taxes, and limited the right to practice professions and trades.[26] Jews were forbidden by law to live in the countryside (although, as will be discussed below, exceptions were made), and barred from some of their hitherto primary economic activities. They no longer had the right to sell alcohol or run taverns in Galician villages, nor to rent land there.

Vienna's reorganization of the institution of the rabbinate in Galicia was carried out in a similar manner. Complaints regarding Bernstein's corruption started coming in to the Gubernium immediately after his appointment in 1777.[27] Vienna took action only in 1784, yet again using anonymous denunciations as a pretext for administrative change. The timing of the decision concerning Bernstein was meticulously chosen. In 1785, a decree from Vienna described the institution of rabbi as dangerous; it was said that holders of this office perpetuated the isolation of Jewish communities and hindered the access of Jewish youth to wider society.[28] That same year, the office of chief rabbi of Galicia was liquidated.

Though abolished in Galicia, the chief rabbinates of other provinces remained; Rabbi Landau, who had earlier declined to come to Galicia, held this post in Prague during the 1780s. Landau defended Jewish tradition against what he saw as the encroachments of modernity, but toward the end of his life, he cooperated with the Austrian authorities, endorsing the Edict of Toleration, use of the German language, and the creation of state-sponsored German-language schools for Jewish children.[29] Vienna's reforms regarding the Jews of Bohemia in the 1770s and 1780s were an example of cooperation between the most traditional members of the Jewish communities — rabbis — and the Austrian authorities, with their program of radical transformations.[30]

Institutional and individual cooperation, or rather the failure thereof, was not the only distinction between Galicia and other provinces. Most administrative reforms were introduced in Galicia later than elsewhere in the monarchy. Some measures were designed specifically for Galicia, and never contemplated for any other region. Through the years, Galicia retained its distinct status within the monarchy. Despite the most radical reforms, Galicia's Jews maintained an unprecedented degree of self-administration and hewed to traditions inherited from the Polish period.

In 1789, Galicia finally received its variant of the Edict of Toleration, different from decrees introduced years earlier in other provinces.[31] The original edict had specifically promoted Jewish integration; the Galician legislation of 1789 only recommended it. Jews of the former Poland-Lithuania retained a number of traditional rights and privileges held over from that polity.[32] Forbidden to buy real estate from Gentiles, Jews were allowed to sell and buy property among themselves.[33] They were required to attend state-sponsored German-language Jewish schools, and only those completing mandatory schooling were allowed to marry. Each of the provisions was thus contingent upon the others. The edict was as much about control as it was about rights.

Joseph II died in 1790 and his successor, Emperor Leopold II (1790–92), endorsed a more conservative line. The Edict of Toleration remained intact, but other changes and institutions were subject to scrutiny. Jewish communities were granted the right to resume their traditional kehilla governance, and the chief rabbinate was reestablished (though it remained vacant for long periods after 1792). Some of the residency restrictions, rescinded by Joseph II, were reenforced after 1790. Yet across different regimes and chronological divides, patterns of relationships between the Austrian authorities and Galician Jews remained unchanged: norms and restrictions were designed in response to concrete situations; disagreement between different branches of the Austrian bureaucracy left loopholes for manipulation; as a result, exceptions to the rules or open defiance of legislation became routine.

Negotiation

All these reforms shed light on Austrian intentions regarding the Jews of the former Poland-Lithuania. But plans alone do not explain why and how Jewish tradition proved so resistant to Austrian modernization. The key to the question of why Austrian schemes fell short lay in the reality of Jewish-Austrian coexistence, or even cooperation, in Galicia.

Beginning in the 1770s, Vienna's Jewish plans revealed serious frictions within the Austrian bureaucracy, and there was a great divide separating officials in the imperial capital from locally employed Austrians in offices across Galicia. The reaction of Austrian bureaucrats toward legislation regarding

Jews was in keeping with the usual pattern, namely, of Austrian officials on the periphery criticizing aspects of the projects emerging from the center. In 1784, the head of the Austrian administration in the Sambor district opposed the removal of Jews from the countryside; a great number of Jews—who made up some 30–40 percent of the district's total population—resided on the land (a state of affairs unheard of elsewhere in Europe).[34] The head of the Sambor administration argued that without Jews, the regional economy would suffer substantial setbacks. Of eighteen heads of regional offices in Galicia expressing an opinion on the proposal to prohibit the renting of land by Jews from Polish landowners, only eight supported the measure, the other ten preferring to leave the status of Jews on the land unchanged.[35] Brody, a small but economically important Jewish town on the Russo-Austrian border, deserves particular attention. The head of the Złoczower district, whose jurisdiction included Brody, stressed the danger of new residency and trade restrictions, which could adversely affect, he emphasized, the economy of the region in general.[36] Forcible military conscription of Jews, moreover, led them to flee to the neighboring town of Radziwiłow in the Russian Empire (just over the border from Austrian Brody). Such policy-induced out-migration would damage the local economy, in which Jews played a major role.[37]

For their part, Jews petitioned the local Austrian authorities in Galicia, requesting either the rescinding of new laws or, more often, the review of specific cases. In 1791, Jakob Landau and Mayer Schöner requested a review of recent legislation restricting the right of Jews to reside on the land and sell alcohol (both imposed as part of the 1785 reforms).[38] They cited the basic premises of Joseph II's 1789 promulgation of Galicia's toleration decree, as well as the original 1781 edict's equalization of the status of Jews and Christians in the monarchy. "With Jews removed from the land, there will no longer be a middleman between land-workers and merchants. . . . The removal of Jews from the land implies a violation of the provision that secured equal treatment for Jewish and Christian subjects."[39] As a Gubernium official summed up the petitioners' warnings regarding the Jewish immiseration that would follow the new restrictions: "Mayer Schöner of Buchach, in the name of Galician Jewry, appeals the decision to remove the Jews from the land and forbid them to keep taverns, insofar as [these decisions] would deprive thousands of families of their income and food provisions, and during this winter they would not be able to find any other sources of income."[40]

The Gubernium dismissed the accusations as unfounded. In one report, Austrian officials insisted that Galician peasants had supported the removal of Jews from the countryside.[41] The Gubernium also responded to Jewish appeals by citing instances of the damage Jews had allegedly done to the local economy and social relations. "The more harm the Jews cause by residing on the land, the more opportunities they discover to settle there permanently, and to escape Austrian supervision. . . . There is no other way to limit this harm than to travel through each of the localities in order to detect Jewish residents there and make proper statistics of Jewish families."[42] Austrian civil authorities were thus required to file general reviews of Jewish residents four times a year—a policy with no precedent in Austrian treatment of Poles or Ruthenians.

Yet some cases of landownership were indeed open to negotiation. In 1804, Anita Sawa of Bukowina (at the time under the jurisdiction of the Galician Gubernium) was accused by local officials of illegally residing on the land, and forced to pay a penalty of three hundred gulden. Sawa appealed to the Gubernium, claiming that the bureaucrats had misinterpreted Austrian legislation; she won her case and retained her residency rights.[43] In 1807, the president of the Galician Gubernium, Wacław Urmeny, reported to the Court Chancellery in Vienna that Jews still owned taverns in the Galician countryside, despite the recent prohibition.[44] In 1808, Spuk Brunnstein managed to buy a parcel of land in the Zaleszczyky district in Galicia, even though Jews were legally prohibited from purchasing such property.[45]

One noteworthy case concerned the production and trade of church apparel for the Ruthenian clergy. The issue became particularly charged, and interesting for historians, because it involved several different parties, and with them, different socio-ethnic Galician groups: Austrians, Jews, and Ruthenians. In September 1807, the Gubernium considered a case involving Jewish merchants in the Stryj district engaged in the production and trade of apparel for Greek Catholic Church dignitaries. "The Stryj district administration brings to the attention [of the Gubernium] that the Jew Aron Bobek, who is involved in the trade of church apparel, was detained in Zamość. . . . This activity is not allowed because . . . the production and trade of religious goods by Jews has been met with much anger on the part of believers."[46]

In deciding the case, the Gubernium barred Jews from dealing in church apparel for Greek Catholic Ruthenians. Austrian officials justified their decision by claiming that Jewish involvement in such matters could result in the indignation of local Greek Catholics.[47] But the Greek Catholic Bishop Angelowych intervened on behalf of the defendants, arguing in a letter (December 1807) to the Gubernium administration that removing Jews from this traditional profession would create difficulties for the Greek Catholic clergy and believers, who had long relied on Jews for these specific services. The Galician Gubernium soon reversed its earlier decision and allowed Jews to engage in commerce with Christians.[48] Thus, even when unable to reverse legislation, local authorities sometimes managed to creatively negotiate individual cases.[49]

In May 1809, a teacher at a German-language Jewish school in the town of Buchach (himself most likely not Jewish), writing under the pseudonym "Deutschmeister," filed a report to the Gubernium highlighting the failure of Austrian reforms in Galicia, and claiming that Galician Jews collectively defied Austrian legislation. "Deutschmeister" was especially troubled by the constant growth of the Galician Jewish population, despite the numerous restrictions designed to counter this.[50] As the Galician Gubernium's write-up put it: "The private teacher from a German-Jewish school in Buchach, Deutschmeister, [claims] that statistics on Jews are unreliable, because many secret marriages are not being taken account of in these statistics."[51]

Restrictions on marriage, residency, and migration formed the core of Austrian legislation regarding Jews. In 1786, only those Jews who had completed two years of Austrian German-language state-sponsored schooling were allowed to marry.[52] By law, rabbis could be penalized for officiating at unsanctioned marriages, and Jewish elders were required to denounce clergymen who defied these regulations.[53] The children of unofficially married couples were prohibited from inheriting their fathers' property. But most of these restrictions seem to have had only limited effects.

Austrian officials long admitted serious discrepancies between the number of marriage certificates issued to Jews by Austrian district administrations and the number of Jews who completed the mandatory education requirements and were thus statutorily qualified for such permission.[54] Debates on marriage restrictions had begun in the 1770s and continued well into the nineteenth century. In 1809, for example, one Anton Helzel came up with the proposal, eventually incorporated into official policy, "that no Jewish man under the age of thirty and no Jewish woman under the age of twenty-four should be allowed to get married."[55] But "Deutschmeister"'s report highlighted a different side of the problem. It was Austrian officials who issued the overwhelming number of false certificates—most couples receiving these without ever having attended the German-language Jewish schools—thus undermining the basic premise of Austrian legislation. Austrian bureaucrats, "Deutschmeister" believed, created a niche for manipulation that was widely exploited by various people throughout Galicia.

Vienna's inability to control Galician Jews, indeed, affected other regions of the monarchy. Since 1670, when most Jews were expelled from Vienna, the dynasty had guarded its right to severely limit the number of Jews in the imperial capital to only the most prosperous families.[56] The Jewish population of Vienna, nevertheless, gradually increased, in part because of the unstoppable immigration of Jews from other provinces, mainly Bohemia and Hungary. These rising numbers also included Jews of the former Poland-Lithuania, who often relocated in a multistep process via other Habsburg provinces.[57] In the early nineteenth century, a cohort of Jews from the former Poland-Lithuania graduated from the medical faculty of the University of Vienna and entered the Viennese middle class—an achievement that should have been impossible, given recent Austrian legislation.[58] These Jews, of course, made use of the new opportunities that presented themselves after Galicia became part of the Habsburg Monarchy.

Jewish Enlightenment

"Deutschmeister," who had accused his fellow Austrian functionaries of malfeasance, was himself a product of the Enlightenment and the reforms in Galicia during the 1770s–80s. Like most bureaucrats serving in the province, "Deutschmeister" was not a native there; he had arrived sometime after 1787, taking a position in one of the recently established schools. Leaving aside the lamentable fact that this particular individual had come to the province ostensibly to improve it via education, but was submitting complaints regarding its to him alarming number of Jews, such teachers of German came to provide a new type of learning for Jewish children. This education system was one of the most potent symbols of the Austrian Enlightenment, and one of the tangible products, especially, of Joseph II's toleration policies. Even before the introduction of the Edict of Toleration in Galicia, the new schools had enforced Jewish integration by providing a general type of nonreligious education in the German language.

Responsible for the new German-Jewish schooling project in the province was Herz Homberg, an iconic figure of the Jewish Enlightenment and Austrian Jewish reform in Galicia. Born in 1747 in Lieben (near Prague), Homberg had lived in Prague, Pressburg, Görz, Trieste, Vienna, Hamburg, and Berlin before coming to Lemberg. In Pressburg and Hamburg, Homberg received a traditional Talmud-based Jewish education. He later studied German literature in those cities as well as Berlin.[59] After leaving Bohemia, Homberg gradually shifted from a traditional to a more modern view of Jewish society. Between 1772 and 1782, he resided in Berlin, where he became a close associate of Moses Mendelssohn, supervised the education of his son Joseph. During the 1770s, he fell under the influence of the Enlightenment, Jewish and otherwise, reading works of the French philosophes, most notably Rousseau, and eventually endorsing the path of Jewish integration.[60]

In 1782, in a life-changing move, Homberg decided to leave Berlin. One reason for abandoning Berlin was prosaic: nearing his mid-thirties, he planned to start a family, and intended to exchange Mendelssohn's household in Berlin for the vibrant life of Vienna.[61]

Joseph II's toleration policies opened new professional opportunities for men like Homberg, who could hope to make careers of their own. Homberg accepted a position in the philosophy faculty at the University of Prague and expected a permanent appointment. When Vienna balked at appointing a Jew to a full professorship at the university, Homberg faced a serious professional crisis. Semi-employed, he finally gave up on his academic career and became a bureaucrat. Between 1782 and 1787, he spent time in Trieste as an official responsible for the introduction of German-language state-sponsored schools for local Jews.[62] In 1787, when Joseph II initiated a major reform of the education of Jews in Galicia, Homberg was invited to administer the establishment of new schools.[63]

The move from Trieste to Lemberg was, again, not accidental. Trieste was the center of the Jewish Haskalah in the Habsburg Monarchy, the most important stronghold of the maskilim; it also resembled non-Habsburg German cities, in that the major initiative for the creation of German-language schools for Jewish children in both cases came from maskilim, not state bureaucrats.[64] Homberg was the first (unbaptized) Jew to be appointed to supervise parts of Joseph II's reforms.[65]

Despite arriving by way of Italian Trieste, in Galicia Homberg represented the reform-oriented tradition of the Germanophone Jews of Central Europe. German-speaking Europe was the key territory of the Jewish Enlightenment, and contacts with this part of the world were crucial for Galicia. The Jewish Enlightenment in Galicia was mediated through intellectual and political contacts with Berlin, and even more, through German-speaking cities of the Habsburg Monarchy, Vienna and Prague. The Haskalah in general, as David Sorkin has explained, "lacked the division between lay and religious enlighteners" that existed elsewhere.[66] In Galicia, similarly, the boundary between the state-supported project of (Austrian) Enlightenment and the Haskalah was more fluid than elsewhere in the Habsburg Monarchy;[67] indeed, the Jewish Enlightenment in Galicia is hardly imaginable without the Austrian Enlightenment.

Several Enlightenments, then, crossed paths on Austria's eastern periphery. Austrian officials brought their own version of the Enlightenment, largely shaped in Vienna. The Jewish Enlightenment also arrived in Galicia from German-speaking Europe and via Vienna.[68] The goals that Emperor Joseph II and Moses Mendelssohn set for themselves were different. The former wished to educate Galician Jews so that they might be molded into loyal German-speaking citizens and placed under the control of Austrian administration, while the latter sought to lift Jews from their social isolation and backwardness. These divergent aims notwithstanding, the two endorsed similar means: the German language and Austrian-German schools were essential to both projects.

Cooperation between Austrian authorities and Jewish maskilim in Galicia, however, proved problematic. For one thing, Austrian bureaucrats moving to Galicia brought with them a number of prejudices; Vienna's policies were marked by the widespread perception of Galician Jews as economically and culturally backward, hence harmful.[69] German-Jewish schools were thus designed to improve manners and the economy all at once. But the attempted reform, again, revealed the numerous shortcomings of Austrian planning. Resources were meager, and funds were often improperly allocated. Because Homberg was responsible for the creation of the new schools, he soon became, somewhat like Chief Rabbi Bernstein before him, a double villain: to traditional Galician Jews, he was the Austrian government's enforcer; but to Vienna, he was an ineffective implementer of reforms.

Coming to Lemberg in 1787, Homberg proceeded, despite difficulties, with the program decided upon. Within a year, he had managed to establish 107 new German-Jewish schools in Galicia and had installed about 150 teachers.[70] In a report to the Galician Gubernium from 1790, Homberg mentioned thirty-seven children who had been educated in the new schools and were prepared to work as teachers.[71] But founding these schools was one thing; operating them was something else. Through the years, attendance remained problematic, with many parents boycotting. The qualifications of teachers and the quality of instruction, likewise, were questionable. Teachers and parents complained about each other, which Vienna encouraged; denunciations (anonymous and signed) of teachers by parents, and by colleagues as well, were published and displayed at synagogues.[72] An Austrian inspection in 1797 noted corruption, low-quality teaching, and inadequate administration.

Decisive to the entire enterprise was the relative cooperation of local Jews, whose reaction to the school initiative was often ambivalent, but not necessarily negative. In 1784, Rabbi Jakovke Landau welcomed the founding of a German-Jewish school in the town of Brody.[73] Exceptional in its large Jewish population (over 70 percent of the total), Brody otherwise exemplified the general trend: because most of its Jewish inhabitants were involved in commerce, many appreciated the new possibilities afforded by German-language schools, for practical reasons. Other, less commercially oriented communities outside of Brody similarly supported the new schools. Major opposition to the new educational system came not from rabbis but rather from many Jewish parents, who were determined to hold fast to tradition and refused to send their children to German-language institutions.

Their shortcomings aside, these schools did grant Jews entrée to social practices otherwise barred to them. The right to marry, technically contingent upon completing a course of education, was one important example. But the schools also provided opportunities for professional development. In 1801, Aron Sternfelt of Drohobych petitioned the Galician Gubernium for the right to run a business in Lemberg, attaching to his application "proof of his command of the German language, a certificate attesting to his ability to conduct business in German, and copies of his commercial books, kept in German."[74]

Vienna's initiative in creating German-language schools for Jewish children eventually raised concerns among bureaucrats in Galicia. Beginning in 1788, the Galician Gubernium filed petitions to Vienna requesting that such schools be closed, and that Jewish pupils be sent instead to the regular German-language educational institutions originally designed for Christian children. These requests were partly justified by financial considerations. All schools, Jewish and Christian, faced financial difficulties. Gubernium functionaries regularly noted a contrast between the huge financial investments being made in Jewish education and the catastrophic condition of corresponding non-Jewish institutions.[75] Jewish schools may have fared better economically than their non-Jewish counterparts because they were covered by new taxes imposed upon Jewish families: every fifth gulden of Jewish household income went toward the new schools.[76] Taxes were increased on Galicia's Christian population as well, but never so radically, and no specific amount was earmarked for educational reform.

Such an initiative, if approved, would mean, among other things, the end of Homberg's educational activities in Galicia. Acting to defend the German-Jewish schools, Homberg found support in Vienna. The two different views on Jewish schools—one represented by Homberg, the other held by Gubernium officials in Lemberg—resulted in a new confrontation between central authorities and provincial administrators. In 1788, the conflict was resolved in Homberg's favor, and the Jewish schools survived.

In the meantime, Homberg himself seemed increasingly restless in Galicia. Having been elevated to the rank of midlevel Austrian bureaucrat, he now reflected all the discontent mounting among such professionals. He had moved to Lemberg with his family and received a rather generous salary, almost three times the pay he had earned in Trieste.[77] But, by all accounts enthusiastic at the beginning of his mission, in time Homberg became more withdrawn. In 1799, he quit Galicia for Vienna, where he remained until 1802.[78]

Homberg returned to see the gradual decline of the German-Jewish schools, followed by their official dissolution in 1806—explainable in part by the general reversal of policies after the death of Joseph II. It was Emperor Francis II (1792–1835) who decided to close the German-Jewish schools. The decision to restore traditional Jewish schooling with rabbis rather than Austrian-German teachers was also a response to the wartime exigencies of the Napoleonic era. Many in Vienna regarded schools as carriers of Enlightenment ideas in a period when the Enlightenment had become associated with revolution and war. Rumors circulated in Vienna and Galicia that some teachers expressed pro-Napoleonic sympathies. While such teachers caught the interest of the Austrian police, many Jewish parents had continued to refuse to send their children to the German-language schools. The former, political consideration was the major cause, and the latter boycott perhaps more of a pretext, but both contributed to the official disfavor, decline, and ultimate closure of the schools in Galicia.[79]

German-language Jewish schools remained intact in other provinces, most notably in Bohemia and Trieste. The reason for Vienna's different attitude toward these institutions in different regions is not entirely clear. Dirk Sadowski, author of a major new work on Herz Homberg, attributes the disparity to the different numbers of and hence varying degrees of social "danger" represented by Jews across the Habsburg Empire. Jews in Bohemia, he argues, were less numerous and posed less of a threat; tensions surrounding German-Jewish schools in that kingdom were never as severe as in Galicia. In Austria's Italian territories, the project of German-language Jewish education proved successful.[80] In Galicia, however, the institutional structures of traditional kehillot, with their emphasis on top-down compliance, presented better instruments of security and loyalty inculcation than the new schools created under Joseph II.[81]

Despite the brevity of their existence in Galicia, the schools left behind an important legacy. Hundreds of students received a type of education otherwise unavailable, and could be expected to have a different view of Jewish society than their parents. Homegrown Galician maskilim, at least some of whom must have been educated in Homberg's schools, played an important role in the province beginning in the 1810s.[82] The German-Jewish schools formed an important aspect of the Austrian Enlightenment in Galicia; but the specifically Jewish Enlightenment truly took root largely due to the impact of these schools on Galician Jews.

The Haskalah reached its peak in Galicia years after Homberg's departure, when Jewish maskilim, many raised and educated in Galicia, actively sought the support of the Austrian imperial authorities.[83] In 1813, following in Homberg's footsteps, Isaak Perl organized the first German-language school for Jewish children in the Galician town of Tarnopol. Two years later, a similar school appeared in Brody, and 1830 saw the founding of one in Kraków as well (when the city did not belong to the Habsburg Monarchy).[84] In 1827, Meier Halevi Letteris, a Hebrew-language poet and maskil who had studied at the University of Lemberg, commemorated the death of an Austrian official with a lyric composed in German.[85] The following year, Governor Lobkowitz met a delegation of maskilim and endorsed the founding of the Society for the Dissemination of Useful Industry and Employment among the Jews of Galicia.[86] In 1829, Marek Bernstein, a Jew from Brody, wrote to Lobkowitz requesting that a school for Jewish artisans be established; the governor reacted favorably to the proposal, and invited Bernstein to his office in Lemberg. Actually opening the school was a matter of some years, but at least the current imperial administration of Galicia seemed rather open to Austrian-Jewish cooperation.[87]

In the 1840s, the Lemberg kahal included many Jews with doctoral degrees from Austrian universities, including Emanuel Blumenfeld, Oswald Menkes, Adam Barach-Rappaport, and Izak Aron Rosenstein. In 1842, the Lemberg kahal requested of the Gubernium that ten scholarships be granted to Jewish artisans. Two years later, a Jewish orphanage was founded in Lemberg, supervised by the kahal in cooperation with the Austrian civil authorities. During the 1840s, various kahals across Galicia petitioned for the removal of professional restrictions, and achieved some successes in this area. Austrian officials and Jewish maskilim had finally found common ground.

Tensions among Jews themselves, however, soon turned volatile. In the first half of the nineteenth century, Galicia became a battleground of two competing ideologies—the Haskalah and Hasidism. Whereas the Haskalah originally arrived in Galicia from the west, Hasidism came from the east, first emerging in Volhynia, a part of Poland annexed in 1795 by the Russian Empire. A mystic teaching that encouraged individual, unmediated contact with God, Hasidism questioned the traditional authority of Jewish communities and administrators. Long popular in the Russian parts of partitioned Poland, Hasidism came to prominence in Galicia only in the early nineteenth century.

Hasidism symbolized everything that the Haskalah sought to combat: mysticism, tradition, and social isolation; Joseph Levin, one of Galicia's leading maskilim, regarded it as a graver threat to Jewish life than Gentile authorities.[88] The Austrians found Hasidism distasteful as well, but for different reasons: Hasidic communities operated similarly to secret societies, and were difficult to control. For their part, adherents of Hasidism looked upon both Austrian officials and the maskilim as a major danger to Jewish culture and tradition.

It was some time before the Austrian government clarified its position regarding Hasidism. In 1814, the president of the Supreme Imperial Police and Censorship Office categorized the Hasidim as freemasons.[89] Hasidic books thus fell under the ban of censorship, and private religious assemblies were forbidden. But even then, limitations were more or less a formality, and prohibitions were not strictly enforced.[90] In 1829, Governor Lobkowitz expressed rather tolerant views of Galician Hasidism, citing the report of a censor in Lemberg whose competence was Hebrew-language publications; according to this write-up, most Hasidim were loyal Habsburg subjects.[91] In 1838, the Austrian government acknowledged the dangers of Hasidism, but still issued no new restrictions against it.[92]

While Galician Hasidism was to some extent aided by Austrian toleration or noninterference, Galician maskilim benefited even more from cooperation. The maskilim generally approved of Austrian rule; the Hasidim considered it harmful. Neither suffered from open political persecution on the part of the government, but each launched bitter attacks against the other, and each side appealed to Austrians for help in resolving conflicts that were essentially intra-Jewish.[93] While some kahals petitioned for the further removal of restrictions and expansion of civil rights, others concentrated instead on the revival of ancient practices.

One sign of progressives being in the ascendant was the rise of Rabbi Abraham Kohn, who oversaw the founding of the first reformist temple in the Galician capital in 1840, and was appointed chief rabbi of the district of Lemberg in 1847. A supporter of Jewish German-language integration, he gave sermons in German, eliciting protests from tradition-minded Jews, who petitioned the Gubernium to rescind his appointment as chief rabbi. When the Austrians refused, some traditionalists took matters into their own hands; in September 1848, a traditional Jew poisoned Rabbi Kohn and his son. The news of one Jew murdered by another caused a sensation in Galicia. Obviously, Galician Jewry was not monolithic; internal divisions were sometimes stronger and harder to resolve than concurrent conflicts between Jews and Gentile civil authorities.

Austrian policies toward Jews during the years preceding the 1848 Revolution were marked by a certain ambivalence. The Gubernium introduced a number of new residency restrictions in Lemberg in 1846–47, charging the kahal with supervising their implementation; a number of

Jews were to be expelled from the city, in effect, by their own religious leaders. When kahal members refused to carry out the orders, a new conflict erupted between Jewish elders and the Austrian authorities.[94] A series of Austrian concessions followed almost immediately. The Gubernium planned the opening of a Galician diet for the spring of 1848, and several Jews from Lemberg were invited to join its sessions. When the revolution broke out, some Jews sided with the Poles and supported Polish demands.[95]

During the second half of the nineteenth century, Jews became active political players in Galicia. They sent deputies to the local diet and the Austrian parliament,[96] and formed various political alliances. As Galician politics and social life became more complex over time, Jewish involvement in it evolved as well. The Austrian reforms in education, politics, and culture produced some important results. A growing number of Jews descended from inhabitants of the former Poland-Lithuania spoke German as their native language; some assimilated fully, defining themselves as Austrians or even Germans. But the option of Polish identification became increasingly appealing in the second half of the nineteenth century. In the Revolution of 1848, Jewish representatives were included in the Polish delegation to the emperor; after 1848, many accepted Polish culture and the Polish language as their native tongue. Assimilation into Ruthenian culture was more rare, but hardly unheard of.[97] All of these cultural identity choices were, in a way, products of the Enlightenment.

The Modernizing Empire and Traditional Jews

The annexation of Galicia, William McCagg argued, shaped Habsburg Jewish policy across the monarchy in the 1780s.[98] Some privileges introduced in the Edict of Toleration were accompanied by numerous restrictions by which Vienna sought to control the masses of Jewish subjects in its new province. But the formerly Polish-Lithuanian Jews defied new Austrian legislation, the many restrictions imposed on them often producing only a limited impact. Traditional Galician Jews succeeded where a modernizing empire failed.

Austrian officials oversaw changes in Jewish administration and the establishment of Jewish schools, supported the Jewish Enlightenment in a limited way from the point of view of what was useful to Vienna, and halted the spread of Hasidism. Some of the reforms pertaining to Jews were common to all provinces of the monarchy, while others were designed specifically for Galicia; still others arose in response to particular Galician realities, and were later introduced in other provinces.[99] There is no doubt that the Habsburg rulers intended to reorganize their new Jewish subjects on a new Austrian model, the better to meet the monarchy's financial and political needs; to this end they imitated some aspects of Jewish administration from other provinces, for example establishing a chief rabbinate in Galicia; and they also reformed governance by bringing in Austrian officials to supervise Jewish political and economic matters. New taxes supplied the empire with revenue, and new schools provided German-language education to Jewish children. But these practices also revealed a crucial retreat from the earlier ideal of uniformly Austrian administration. Traditional and allegedly backward Galician Jews proved to be a most serious obstacle to the modern bureaucracy of a reforming monarchy.

Jews' increased political participation changed their status both within Galicia and in the monarchy at large, but it hardly influenced the broader perception of Polish Jews empire-wide. The stereotype of backward *Ostjuden* moving into different Habsburg regions from Galicia, survived through 1918. The lifting of restrictions, however, did open new opportunities that were difficult to ignore. Access to new schools and professions almost inevitably stimulated integration, and eventually assimilation. In the second half of the nineteenth century, Galicia's Jews had a variety of options to choose from; while many held fast to Jewish tradition and religion, many others were eager to follow the socio-professional example of their Christian neighbors. None of this would have been possible had the Austrian designs of the eighteenth century, intended to curtail Jewish population growth and migration, been executed as originally planned.

EIGHT

Bureaucracy and Revolutions
1846–1848

In the period of 1846–48, Galicia underwent changes arguably more dramatic than at any other time before or after. A Polish national uprising in the province in 1846 very quickly turned into a bloodbath. Polish patriots, mostly nobles or aristocrats, had prepared a new revolution in an effort to overthrow Austrian rule. This time, the uprising was planned for Western Galicia and Kraków, then a free city under the protectorate of the three major powers; fearful that Uniate Ruthenian peasants in Eastern Galicia might find the Polish cause unappealing, the revolutionaries decided to target western regions of the province, where Polish Roman Catholics were in the majority. Organizers of the revolt had expected that Polish peasants would support the national cause, joining a struggle against the Austrian authorities. These calculations proved wrong. When the revolution was still in its initial stage, peasants took up arms against nobles and landowners. Thus at the midpoint of the nineteenth century, in the center of Europe, an ostensible struggle for national independence turned instead into bloody social warfare and intra-ethnic massacres.

In 1846, the peasants' massacre of landlords brought Galicia to the front pages of European periodicals and the tribunes of its legislatures. In Paris, French parliamentarians discussed Habsburg policies in the province; in Berlin, Prussian journalists described Austria's oppression of its Polish subjects.[1] The peasant revolt raised many questions among observers across Europe, but especially, closest to home, among Poles themselves. From the standpoint of Polish elites and subsequent historians, peasants seemed to have little in the way of organizational capacity, or even motive, to carry out a large-scale uprising. Austrians had reason to fear a Polish national revolution; perhaps, some thought, they had stirred up peasant unrest as a counterforce against aristocratic Polish independence-seekers.

Politicians, intellectuals, and journalists in Berlin, Paris, St. Petersburg, and Warsaw explored Austria's role in the massacre. Did Austrian bureaucrats instigate peasant revolt? Did they pay farmers to kill their Polish landlords? How did the failed revolution, and the massacre that followed, reflect Austria's standing in Galicia and Vienna's long-term policies toward its Polish subjects? The events of 1846 remain to the present day one of the most difficult moments in the Polish historical imagination, and the question of Austrian responsibility is debated as hotly now as it was in the mid-nineteenth century.[2]

The controversy surrounding the 1846 revolt reveals important nuances in the scholarship of Eastern Europe, the Habsburg Monarchy, and its provinces. First of all, Eastern Europe has become associated, to some extent, with violence; it is symbolic that the revolt of 1846 was one of the few events in the province's political history to draw the attention of scholars and intellectuals dealing not only with Galicia or even Eastern Europe, but with Europe at large. Secondly, the conventional image of a foreign bureaucracy in confrontation with national elites shaped the long-term perception of 1846.[3] Both arguments—that of Austrian responsibility for the violence, and denial of that responsibility—are contingent upon a particular understanding of the bureaucracy as a coherent, single-minded body, with each of its members acting in unison.

Today, the 1846 uprising is rarely remembered outside of Poland; it was overshadowed by the major revolution that exploded two years after its suppression. This better-known upheaval started in Palermo and Paris in early 1848; in February, it reached Vienna, spreading to other Habsburg provinces within weeks, and hit Galicia in March 1848. If the 1846 revolt was exclusively Polish, the Revolution of 1848 was decidedly European. Austrians, Poles, Ruthenians, and Jews all became involved, albeit to various degrees. Each emerged from the revolution with a new status scarcely imaginable before 1848.

The revolution witnessed a remarkable realignment of different political forces in Galicia. For the first time in the history of Austrian Galicia, or of Rus' Czerwona and Małopolska, three groups competed for political authority in the region. For many years following the annexation of Galicia in 1772, Polish elites conceived of themselves as objects or victims of Austrian politics, just as, for centuries in the Polish-Lithuanian Commonwealth, Ruthenians had done with regard to Polish rule. Austrian and Polish dominance in these periods had always been relative. Since the 1780s, Vienna had increasingly relied on local Polish elites in Galicia. Ruthenian elites had eventually benefited from Austria's church and educational reforms. Between 1772 and 1848, with the exception of the 1809 interlude, the Austrians remained firmly in control. Much of this changed in 1848, after which no single political group would hold an exclusively dominant or exclusively dominated status. In 1848, Austrian political choices were contingent upon Polish and sometimes Ruthenian initiatives, and were often shaped in response to these.

In the revolution-beset monarchy of 1848, Galicia presented an important exception. The events of 1846 were more important for the province than the revolution that followed.[4] The former in a way determined the course of the latter: the year 1848, though not without disturbances, was less dramatic in Galicia than in other regions of the monarchy. Violence was not nearly as widespread in Galicia in 1848 as it had been two years prior. Some major reforms in the province were drafted in response to 1846, rather than to the monarchy-wide revolution. The year 1848 is mainly important as a symbolic divide, a turning point revealing certain long-term changes that had hitherto only barely manifested themselves.

Between 1830 and 1846

Prior to 1846, nothing seemed to predict impending catastrophe. A new set of officials came to the province after 1831 in a major change of civil and police administration meant to head off revolutionary outbreaks of the sort that had taken place in Russian Poland in 1830–31. In 1832, August Lobkowitz was replaced as governor by Ferdinand d'Este, whose arrival in the province from Milan marked a new chapter in the history of Austrian Galicia. If Lobkowitz had been somewhat exotic because of his Polish claims, d'Este stood out from other bureaucrats because of his previous professional path. He had made his career in the military, fighting with the Austrians against the Napoleonic armies in Italy. D'Este was the first and only Habsburg official to head Galicia without any experience in civil administration before his appointment to the governorship. His tenure would combine military, police, and civil functions in a manner quite unusual in the history of Austrian administration during peacetime—one, indeed, more typical for Russian imperial rather than Habsburg territories.[5] Only once before had Galicia been governed by an Austrian military officer: in 1774 when, after Governor Pergen's dismissal, General Andreas Hadik von Futak temporarily took over the administration. But Hadik's involvement was brief, and before 1830 the combination of military and civil authority was rather uncommon. The year 1831 had created a new precedent, allowing the mix of military and civilian administration to return.

During late 1831 and 1832, Austrian police and civil officials reported that political stability had been restored to Galicia. Polish aristocrats and Austrian bureaucrats at the time enjoyed each other's company at public events in Lemberg as they had often done in the past. Social life returned to normal, and politics gave little cause for concern.[6] This normalcy was, of course, somewhat deceptive; Polish activists who survived the events of 1831 soon allied in various conspiracies and began preparing a new revolution.

The events of 1846 in a way stemmed from those of 1831. Governor Lobkowitz did not save the Polish revolution, but he helped rescue a number of its organizers, who kept true to their aims even after the devastating defeat. Within months, conspirators began plotting another uprising, this time to be staged in Galicia. On 31 December 1831, the Polish National Committee was founded in Paris under the leadership of Joachim Lelewel. In 1836, Józef Dwernicki and Jan Ledóchowski led efforts to establish the Confederation of the Polish People, based in Tarnów in Galicia.[7] Another conspiratorial network, the Society of the Polish People, operated in the Russian and Austrian parts of former Poland. The Polish Democratic Society, originally founded in

1832, opened branches in Galicia in 1837. Its members, who included Adam Gurowski, Jan Nepomucen Janowski, Tadeusz Krępowiecki, Ignacy Romuald Płużański, and Franciszek Wiesiołowski, planned the restoration of Poland to its pre-1772 boundaries.[8]

While Polish conspirators debated the political order of a future Polish state, Austrian police agents infiltrated their conspiracies and observed the political ferment in Galicia. During the 1830s, Austrian officers occasionally attended meetings of Polish secret societies and danced at gala balls held by Polish aristocrats, gaining familiarity not only with programs of social entertainment, but also with the details of Polish political projects.[9] Practically every day, one agent noted, Polish nobles gathered for some sort of entertainment. Józef Baworowski regularly hosted different festivities. Wincenty Krosnowski, Countess Ponińska, and the ladies Olszewska and Szeptyczka also opened their houses for celebrations. Polish salons were never empty, hosting crowds of nobles interspersed with bureaucrats and undercover police agents.[10] In February 1833, an unusually large number of Polish nobles from the different partitions arrived in Lemberg. Austrian police agents expressed no doubt as to the purpose of the visit and the subsequent meetings that were held.

"[Austrian] bureaucrats and officers only rarely appear in Polish salons," one Austrian police agent noted in a report.[11] Either he or some of his colleagues attended Polish salons and conspiratorial meetings; Austrian police reports sometimes contained such great detail that they could only have been filed by an eyewitness. But many other Austrians avoided Polish circles, mainly due to the social and financial gaps separating the masses of Austrian civil servants, living on their official incomes, from Polish aristocrats, many of whom had been independently wealthy for generations.

By 1831, and even more so by 1846, at least some German-speaking Austrian bureaucrats would have felt themselves to be under dual pressure: on the one hand, from their superiors in the higher administration, handing down the central policies of the monarchy; and on the other, from family members who had become increasingly ethnically assimilated in the previous decades. Wincenty Pol, son of an Austrian German bureaucrat and sympathizer with Polish conspirators, certainly experienced the double pressure of a competing Polishness and Germanness;[12] and in Jan Lam's novel *Capowice High Society*, Wacław Precliczek experiences this dilemma quite starkly. As an Austrian official during the 1830s and the 1840s, Precliczek combats Polish conspiracies during his work hours; but in his leisure, at home, he is pressured by his Polish wife to help Polish revolutionaries instead. Domestic influence proves to have a greater impact on Precliczek than professional duties. Inspired by his wife, he helps rescue Polish rebels by creating a new hideout in the attic of the building that serves as the office of the local Austrian administration.[13]

The Galician police chief Leopold von Sacher-Masoch senior made stifling rebellion his highest priority. His agents infiltrated numerous Polish conspiracies, but he demanded more, insisting that a large-scale program of prevention was necessary to defuse these plots before they exploded into open revolution. Of all the Austrian officials in Lemberg and Vienna, it was Sacher-Masoch who advocated arguably the most radical solution to the Polish problem.

In the early 1830s, the Austrian police captured some Polish conspirators, both residents of Galicia and outsiders from other areas of the former Poland-Lithuania. But even then, punishment was applied with great caution. Chancellor Metternich believed that the main threat to the monarchy emanated not from Galicians but rather from Polish border-crossers. He also feared that large-scale suppression might further alienate Austrian Poles.[14] He advocated selective prosecution; even when arrested, most Poles of Galician descent were released from prison shortly afterward. An 1833 decree discouraged collective arrests. In the summer of 1835, several prominent Galicians who had been arrested earlier were released.[15] A new series of arrests followed in 1837–38, with equally mixed results. In 1839, most of the incarcerated Galicians were again freed.[16] The Austrian police succeeded in weakening many of the existing Polish conspiracies, but did not break them entirely. Even after still another round of repressive measures in 1841–42, some of the most important members of the conspiratorial organizations remained free and active.

Revolution in Preparation

Activists spared Austrian police persecution during the 1830s included Polish Democratic Society members Ludwik Gorzkowski, Jan Tyssowski, and Edward Dembowski,[17] who became leading figures in the preparation of a new uprising. They developed a bold plan that would use a public gala ball organized by Governor d'Este himself as the launch pad for a Polish revolution.

Edward Dembowski and Franciszek Wiesiołowski arrived in Lemberg in December 1845, their mission being to distribute instructions in preparation for the revolt. Polish women, who so often hosted various celebrations in salons, were expected to play a key part in the initial stage of the revolution. The plan called for the women to distract the Austrian officers by dancing with them, at which point activists would disarm them and launch the uprising right then and there, at the governor's residence. This scheme required the presence in Galicia of many political activists, but by that December, still too few had arrived in the province. Fearing defeat, the organizers decided to postpone the beginning of the revolution.[18] But they did not cancel their plans entirely; the center of the planned uprising was moved to Western Galicia, to the region of Tarnów and to Kraków, which after 1815 had the status of a free city under the protectorate of Austria, Prussia, and Russia. In some respects, Tarnów was more suited to an uprising than Lemberg, since most peasants there were ethnic Poles. Franciszek Wiesiołowski, who carried out propaganda work in Tarnów, expected that peasants would take part in a Polish national revolution.

On 18 February 1846, revolution broke out in the countryside surrounding Tarnów; that same night, Polish landlords faced the consequences of its organizers' false expectations. A would-be struggle for national independence soon turned into a class-war bloodbath, with peasants mobilizing their own forces and taking up arms against aristocratic revolutionaries. Polish nobles faced a shocking disaster, suddenly having to defend themselves not against Austrian officers, but rather farmers of their own ethnicity. The catastrophe forced the organizers to revise their initial plans and call off revolutionary moves elsewhere. But news of the peasant uprising in Tarnów traveled to neighboring regions, and there too peasants resorted to violence. Within days, peasant revolts spread over Western Galicia, to Sanok, Bochnia, Wieliczka, Jaslo, Podgorce, and Rzeszów—all fairly homogeneous Polish areas, with some percentage of Jews but practically no Ruthenians.[19]

Peasant rebels seemed to show no mercy. Polish noble landowners were often killed on the spot, even before they had a chance to realize what was happening. Karol Cotarski and Michał Groszynski, landowners from Olesno and Bolesław respectively, Baron Konopka, the priests Morgenstern and Ciesłowski, and many others fell victim in the first days following the announcement of the national revolution on 18 February. Approximately 450 nobles who had planned to participate in the revolution perished as a result of peasant violence in the environs of Tarnów alone. Some two hundred nobles were buried during the first three days of the peasant revolt.[20] Only seventeen landowners from around Tarnów managed to escape to the city, rescuing themselves from inevitable assaults.[21] Houses and granaries went up in flames. The killings subsided after February, but the spring months March and April witnessed other kinds of violence. Even in the fall of 1846, peasants were still burning landowners' property and destroying harvests. Spreading unevenly, the uprising did not cover all of Galicia. Lemberg was full of news and rumors about the events taking place in the western parts of the province, but the capital experienced nothing more than general anxiety.[22] The countryside east of Lemberg, where Ruthenians formed a majority, also remained remarkably calm.

The uprising was eventually brought under control by the Austrian army.[23] By 4 March, Austrian officials noted the gradual return of order in the problematic districts of Wadowice and Bochnia; two days later, Austrian troops arrived from Hungary, and officials reported on the return of order in Galicia.[24] Some instances of peasant violence were recorded through the end of the summer, but casualties were rarer than in the earlier months.

Tarnów symbolized all the aspects of the failed revolution: suspicions of secret transfers of money and collusion between Austrian and peasant leaders, and a delayed response by the imperial authorities. Official incitement behind the peasant revolt was suspected in other regions as well; some Polish contemporaries and subsequent historians alleged, for instance, that

Carl Bernd, head of the Austrian regional administration in Bochnia, had paid peasants for each of the murdered landowners. In Wieliczka, local officials were also thought to have distributed cash among farmer-rebels.[25]

When the violence subsided, the Austrians published lists of those involved in organizing the would-be Polish revolution, including several hundred nobles from Galicia and elsewhere who had survived and were later prosecuted by the Austrian authorities.[26] Trials of Polish revolutionaries accused of staging anti-Habsburg revolts continued through 1848. This time, Chancellor Metternich showed no leniency; some of the noblemen who had survived the peasant violence were executed by the Austrian authorities, while many others ended up in prison. Enraged by the very attempt to stage an anti-Austrian revolution, however abortive it proved in reality, Metternich believed that Polish landowners had fallen victim to their own miscalculations. On 3 March 1846, he expressed his view of the uprising in a letter to Count Apponyi: in effect entering a war without any army, Polish independence-seekers had overestimated the power of national appeal; any revolution that involved the nobility but excluded peasants would be doomed.[27] They sought to build "democracy without the people,"[28] and failed.

Austrian Involvement

Few Poles, in 1846 and the years that followed, would accept Metternich's explanation. The memories of the massacres have haunted Polish intellectuals and historians to the present day. The belief has persisted that Austrian bureaucrats knew about the revolution in advance, took countermeasures, and incited peasants to take up arms against their landlords, and paid a "reward" for each aristocrat killed. Peasants alone, the argument goes, lacked the resources and organizational capacity to stage such a massive revolt, whereas Austrian bureaucrats had this capacity, and moreover had strong motives to do so. There is no direct evidence to support or refute these claims. The century-and-a-half-long debate is based largely on such indirect considerations as the presumption of Austrian hatred of Poles, or the belief that Polish peasants would not stage a revolt on their own, that the violence must have been financially incentivized by Austrian bureaucrats.

The fact that the Austrians indeed knew of the revolutionary plans ahead of time is no longer in doubt. In December 1845, Governor d'Este traveled to Wadowice in the western part of Galicia to greet the Russian emperor. During the meeting, the two discussed Polish political conspiracies in the province.[29] By then, administrative personnel had supplied the governor with numerous reports on rebel conspiracies. While d'Este conferred with the Russian emperor, the governor's right hand in the Gubernium, Baron Franz Krieg, compiled evidence on the forthcoming rebellion; and in December, Laddäus Lederer, head of the Austrian district administration in Rzeszow, reported that a Polish uprising was imminent.[30] Governor d'Este, however, refused to acknowledge that these threats meant outright revolution.[31] He was also reluctant to enforce any preventive measures, and opposed political repressions or the establishment of military rule in Galicia.[32] D'Este seems to have believed that peasants would remain loyal to Vienna.

While civil officials debated the possibility of a revolution, Police Chief Leopold von Sacher-Masoch senior advocated immediate measures toward heading it off. In his report to Joseph Sedlnitzky, the Austrian Empire's chief of police, Sacher-Masoch advised closing the University of Lemberg, establishing a punishment commission, and expanding the police in Galician towns—all of this before February 1846.[33] Sedlnitzky endorsed Sacher-Masoch's approach; writing to Governor d'Este, he advised setting up closer cooperation between the civil, military, and police administrations in the province. But the governor would hear none of it; from his point of view, Sacher-Masoch's initiatives were disproportionally harsh and untimely.

D'Este was one of a broad cohort of Austrian civil officials who acknowledged the existence of revolutionary ferment but refrained from harsh preventive measures which, in their view, could further antagonize the Poles and make revolt even more likely. For his part, Johann Georg von Ostermann, whose sons were suspected of involvement in the 1830–31 revolution, had remained in Galicia as an Austrian civil servant; in May 1846, when reports about the uprising and violence started coming in, Ostermann refused to take them seriously, believing that the accounts must be exaggerated.[34]

Of such officials, one came to play a particularly important role. Joseph Breinl von Wallernstein headed the local administration of the Tarnów region, and witnessed the outbreak of the nobles' independence struggle and the peasants' violent backlash against it. As an Austrian official responsible for maintaining order in his region, Breinl attracted the attention both of his Austrian superiors and of various Polish participants in these events. Shortly after 1846, his behavior during the revolt became the subject of heated debate.

One of Breinl's colleagues, Moritz von Sala, who in 1846 worked in the Galician Gubernium, in 1867 published a memoir of the uprising, accompanied by a detailed analysis of events and individual motives. Confusion surrounding the Polish revolt, Sala explained, had begun even before its outbreak. In early February 1846, as Sala informed his readers, Breinl wrote to Vienna describing how conspirators were preparing a new Polish revolution in Galicia.[35] Franciszek Wiesiołowski was at the time carrying out political propaganda in Tarnów and environs. On 15 February, Breinl received a response from Vienna in which he was instructed to immediately arrest Wiesiołowski.[36] After this directive, the correspondence between Breinl and his superiors took an unusual turn. Instead of following the instructions, Breinl wrote back explaining that Wiesiołowski's propaganda would have no effect. "How," he wondered, "do these Polish nobles plan to carry out a revolution without peasant support?" If the peasants turned against them, he continued, a bloodbath would ensue.[37] Polish nobles believed that peasants would join them in a national revolution; Breinl suspected the opposite.[38] Both proved wrong, albeit in different ways. Breinl refused to arrest Wiesiołowski, and Polish nobles indeed undertook a rebellion in Galicia; but his supposition that peasants would turn against aristocratic independence-seekers proved correct, and the would-be revolution ended in disaster.

Breinl's reluctance to arrest Wiesiołowski gave rise to questions about his motives. Even more confusing were subsequent events in the Tarnów region, where peasant bands were particularly well organized under the leadership of Jakub Szela. An "official assassin," as described by the Polish aristocrat Aleksander Wielopolski, Szela was suspected of cooperating with the Austrian authorities.[39] Despite being illiterate, Szela became a charismatic leader who managed to rally many other peasants to his cause. Long before 1846, he had coordinated farmers' lawsuits against landowners. Since the 1780s, Austrians had encouraged peasants to file complaints against their landlords in the courts. Most of these cases resulted in failure, as judges typically rejected peasant complaints against nobles. But, increasingly popular among peasants, Szela could easily mobilize large crowds for struggle of a different sort. In 1846, he managed to channel the age-old discontent into the streets, in the form of armed revolt. Suspicions later arose that Szela received assistance from the Tarnów commissar Joseph Breinl.

Breinl and Szela were both, in a way, products of Austria's policies in Galicia.[40] In the 1780s, as part of his agricultural reform, Joseph II had introduced a new Austrian office in the Galician countryside, the so-called *Mandatarien*—German-speaking officials working within the framework of Austrian regional administrations to supervise relations between landowners and peasants. Though theoretically neutral mediators, these Austrian officials served to defend the interests of farmers against their landlords. They monitored the implementation of new Austrian land regulations, ensuring that landlords would not demand from their peasants more work or higher dues than allowed by the decrees on these matters. Even more important, the *Mandatarien* assisted peasants in filing complaints against their landlords to local courts. Since the 1780s, Vienna had encouraged cooperation between its officials and peasants in Galicia; thus both Breinl and Szela acted within a framework created by Austrian officials.

Of course, Vienna's promotion of an alignment between officials and farmers in no way means that it encouraged violence as a method of redress of peasants' complaints. The claim that Habsburg bureaucrats were responsible for the killings hinges on the presumption that while Austrian officials would unconditionally suppress any national uprising, many might, under certain circumstances, support a peasant revolt as the lesser of two evils; but such a thesis finds no support in historical evidence. For Austrian officialdom, the events of 1846 in Galicia revived memories of earlier bloody jacqueries, most notably the one in Bohemia in 1775. Peasant movements always produced chaos, and as such were dangerous to the state. In 1846, the Austrian authorities were concerned about not only individual deaths, but also the destruction of property wrought by the uprising.

To accuse the Austrian bureaucracy as an entity, then, would be to fall into a trap of misinterpretation. Even if some bureaucrats were willing to cooperate with the peasants, many others would have found a peasant uprising as horrifying as a revolt for national independence. Disagreements within the Austrian bureaucracy were the norm, and each crisis made such tensions worse. The events of 1846, as Hans-Christian Maner has explained, revealed serious miscommunication between Vienna and Lemberg.[41] Some praised the loyalty of the peasants, while others found their violence more alarming than anything undertaken by aristocrats hoping to revive a Polish homeland. No one within the upper administration seems to have endorsed the backlash against the nobles unconditionally.

Galician Gubernium Vice President Baron Franz Krieg, never particularly sympathetic toward Polish noble landowners, admitted in a note to Vienna of 23 February that the support of Polish peasants had been invaluable during the revolution; without it, Krieg remarked, the Austrian authorities would have been faced with a very difficult situation in Galicia. Even so, he defined peasant violence as dangerous to the monarchy. Evincing no special concern for the fate of individual nobles, Krieg had reason to believe that uncontrolled violence would adversely affect the Habsburgs' standing in Galicia.[42]

Krieg's role in suppressing the peasant uprising can hardly be overstated; in the Gubernium he championed the harshest policies, sharing the view of a colleague from a different department, Police Chief Sacher-Masoch. Like many of his fellow officials in Galicia, Krieg had begun his career in the military and transferred to civil administration after being appointed to the province. Among Polish elites, Krieg quickly gained the reputation of a Polonophobe; but his status in Galicia, as well as his treatment of the Poles there, was perhaps a bit more complicated than the negative image many attached to him. Krieg had one foot in elite Polish society: his wife, Dorota Wadowska, was a Pole. At least one of his colleagues, the Tarnów administration head Breinl, described Krieg as sympathetic toward Poles.[43] All such bureaucrats had personal motives that inevitably influenced their understanding of politics.

In the spring of 1846, Prince Lazansky, then vice president of the Galician Gubernium, traveled across the province to assess the situation. Why had the peasant revolt turned violent in some districts and not in others? Lazansky found his answer in the various responses provided by local Austrian authorities. Unlike Krieg, Lazansky had no interest in crediting any peasant involvement in suppressing the nobles' revolt, as such mass actions posed serious dangers reaching well beyond Galicia.[44] The vice president's writings reveal much confusion as to what was happening and why.

On 25 February, Lazansky praised Breinl's response to the attempted rebellion.[45] Within days, in early March 1846, Lazansky questioned his own initial assessment and, perhaps first among Habsburg officials, raised the question of Austrian responsibility. Lazansky believed that different patterns of violence could not be attributed to peasants alone. Regional officials across Galicia responded differently to the uprising, thus causing variations in peasant actions. Some Austrian officials suppressed peasant violence at its inception, while others did nothing to stop it.[46] Many officials, Lazansky contended, showed remarkable inefficiency during the uprising.[47]

After peasant violence was brought under control, Vienna initiated a major review of the Austrian administration in Galicia. Many senior Gubernium staff members—including d'Este, Krieg, and Lazansky—were dismissed for their inadequate response to the revolt; while these individuals lost their positions because they had failed to prevent the nobles' independence bid, some of their colleagues were fired for their excessive punishment of its organizers. The head of the Galician police, Leopold von Sacher-Masoch, who had fiercely suppressed the revolt,[48] was fired as well; his response to Polish landowners involved in plotting a national revolution was deemed unnecessarily harsh.

The 1846 Polish uprising reveals important nuances of the Austrian administration. Metternich, Sedlnitzky, and Kolowrat in Vienna, and d'Este, Lazansky, and Krieg in Lemberg knew about the conspiratorial networks of Polish patriots, but were probably not familiar with the exact plans of lower-ranking Austrian bureaucrats in various Galician districts.

Between Vienna, Lemberg, and Tarnów, mismatched expectations and uncoordinated actions resulted in tragedy.

1848

A new cohort of officials began making their way into Galicia. In the spring of 1846, Rudolph Stadion replaced d'Este as governor, and on 6 July 1847, Philipp Kraus replaced Krieg as vice president of the Galician Gubernium.[49] With a new administration installed in Lemberg, Austrian policies were expected to take a new turn as well. Stadion perceived his new assignment in civilizational terms, conveying this in a letter to his sister Juža: "The fate of Galicia and the monarchy depends upon this mission no less than it depends upon military actions in the field."[50] Stadion offered his services toward the pacification of the province.

But the new governor was transferred to Vienna within months of his appointment, and replaced by none other than his own brother, Franz Stadion. Nepotism had been frowned upon by Joseph II during the 1770s and 1780s; over the years, for instance, several decrees forbade succession from father to son. To be sure, different members of many families served in the Austrian administration concurrently, but direct succession was uncommon. Brothers often held posts in different provinces—the Brigidos, spread between the Littoral and Galicia, being a prominent example. Sons followed in their fathers' footsteps by entering the administration, but they rarely held exactly the same positions. The Stadion family was one such dynasty that both confirmed and defied the rules of meritocratic succession: members of the family held posts across the monarchy, and brother succeeded brother as governor of Galicia.

On 27 April 1847, Franz Stadion became the new governor.[51] He traveled to Galicia from the Adriatic, yet another example of rotations that brought Austrian officials from the Italian coastlines across the entire monarchy to Galicia. Arriving in Lemberg shortly after the suppression of the 1846 revolt, Stadion barely escaped what could have become the most awkward episode in his career. The memories of the failed uprising were still fresh in the minds of Poles. Austrian punitive measures also continued through 1848, and death sentences were common. One execution coincided with what was to be the date of Stadion's arrival in Lemberg. Instead of suspending the execution, he diverted his route, traveled around Galicia, and arrived in Lemberg only days later.[52]

This unpleasant coincidence had no impact on either Stadion's work or his reputation among Galicians. He was one of the few Austrian officials whose appointment was welcomed and anticipated by Polish inhabitants of the province; he was also one of the few to have previously worked there. Born in Vienna in 1806, Stadion started his career in Galicia, first coming to Lemberg in 1828 and appointed in April 1829 to a low-ranking position in the province's Stanisław district.[53] Before moving to Tyrol in 1832, Stadion had bought parcels of land in Galicia. In 1841, he was appointed governor of the Austrian Littoral. In 1847, Count Kolowrat, head of the Austrian-Bohemian Chancellery, personally supported Stadion's appointment as governor of Galicia, as part of the effort to stabilize the province after the recent uprising.[54]

Shortly after his arrival, Stadion filed a report describing the overall situation in the province. He commented favorably on the return of stability to Galicia after 1846, but found the Austrian administration here to be in a disastrous state.[55] When the new governor took office, Poles flooded him with complaints about the misconduct of the previous administration,[56] which Stadion seems to have taken seriously. He ordered the establishment of a commission to investigate the functioning of the different branches of administration.[57] Stadion professed to favor governance by compromise, not by force; an effective Austrian administration could only be created by consensus with Polish elites.

Having arrived in Galicia shortly after the suppression of an uprising, Stadion soon faced the outbreak of full-blown revolution. Just over a year after the Polish revolt had been put down, new turmoil transformed imperial politics and society. Revolution originally broke out in the Bourbon Kingdom of Sicily in January 1848. Anxious that the turbulence might spread, Vienna imposed martial law in its Italian territories. But it was the revolutionary outburst in Paris, not Palermo, that eventually triggered subsequent disturbances across the Habsburg Monarchy. On 3 March, to the jubilation of throngs in Vienna, Metternich resigned, signaling a new era in the history of the monarchy; the following day, the Austrian government promised a constitution, and on 25 April, the Pillersdorf Constitution was introduced. The first Austrian parliament met in Vienna in July 1848. It transferred to the small Bohemian town of Kremsier in the fall, holding sessions even during the most radical phase of the revolution.[58]

Designed to ease revolutionary tensions, the constitution had little effect in this regard. Given the anticipation of great change, there was dissatisfaction all around with the limited nature of reforms; Czechs were unhappy with the centralist idea written into the constitution, and Poles were unhappy with their unchanged status within the monarchy. Fears circulated in Vienna, meanwhile, that the Habsburgs were on the verge of losing Hungary.

Events in Galicia never turned as violent, or as dangerous to Vienna, as they did in Hungary. In part the relative calm was explainable by the aftermath of 1846—months of repression, trials, and punishments had had a strong impact on Polish activists—but also reflected long-term developments in Galicia. Over the years, the populations of German- and Polish-speaking elites had increasingly overlapped, via mixed marriages and also through shared involvement in Austrian administration. Polish nobles and Austrian bureaucrats, then, did not always occupy diametrically opposed positions.

Franz or Franciszek Smolka was a key figure of the Polish revolution in Galicia in 1848. His father, Wincenty Smolka, traced his roots to Silesia and had arrived in Galicia in the late eighteenth century as an Austrian officer. Wincenty married a Polish woman and settled in Galicia permanently. His son grew up speaking German, but as a young man engaged with Polish friends and classmates at the University of Lemberg.[59] In the 1840s, Smolka got involved in Polish political conspiracies and quickly became a leader of the Polish independence movement, in 1848 standing at the forefront of Polish political mobilization in Galicia.

News of the revolution in Vienna reached Lemberg in March 1848; on 15 and 18 March, demonstrations took place in Kraków and Lemberg respectively. Polish activists ordered the creation of a national guard and prepared for large-scale political action; on 19 March, a program of reforms on behalf of all Galicia's inhabitants was presented to the governor. Its authors, Florian Ziemiałkowski and Franciszek Smolka, demanded autonomy for Galicia within the monarchy, the expansion of the Polish language in education and administration, and amnesty for political prisoners. In early April, without waiting for the governor's response, they submitted their program to the emperor. On 14 April, the Polish National Council was formed, with Smolka and Ziemiałkowksi at its head.[60]

The Polish plan of a united political representation, however, suffered a serious blow just weeks after the council's foundation. Ruthenians soon produced their own distinct political program, with the conservative politician Mykhailo Kuzems'kyi drafting a series of petitions that were presented to the governor on 19 April. This Ruthenian project constituted a model of Habsburg patriotism; it requested certain cultural and national concessions and anticipated the division of Galicia into two provinces, Western Galicia with its capital in Kraków, which would be predominantly Polish, and Eastern Galicia, administered from Lemberg/Lwów, which would be mainly Ruthenian.[61] On 2 May 1848, Ruthenian activists gathered in Lemberg to form their separate political representation, the Ruthenian National Council (*Rus'ka Rada*), with the involvement of several Austrian officials of Ruthenian descent: Iakym Khomyns'kyi, a secretary of the Gubernium, Kyrylo Vinkov'kyi, and Kerechyns'kyi, a physician employed in the municipal administration of Lemberg.[62] Most Ruthenian demands were granted, probably at the personal insistence of Governor Stadion.[63]

In May 1848, Ivan Vahylewych, a Ruthenian writer and prominent representative of the Ruthenian cultural revival of the 1830s, organized an institution that became known as the *Rus'kyi Sobor*. Frustrated with Ruthenian conservatism, as manifested especially in the social composition of the Ruthenian National Council, which the Greek Catholic clergy dominated, Vahylewych and his colleagues supported Ruthenian endeavors in culture, but advocated a political alliance with the Poles.[64]

Three separate political institutions thus emerged in Lemberg in the spring of 1848. One was culturally and politically Polish; another was culturally and politically Ruthenian; the third was culturally Ruthenian, but politically Polish-oriented. These different and competing political groups could counter or neutralize one another even without Vienna's military or political intervention. For that matter, most Ruthenians declared their unconditional support for Vienna.

The political mobilization of Ruthenians was perhaps the most surprising outcome of the 1848 Revolution in Galicia. For centuries, Ruthenian nobles, with some notable exceptions, had acted in tandem with Polish nobles. Well into the 1830s, the emerging Ruthenian intelligentsia preferred the well-developed Polish language over the nascent Ruthenian. Along with their Polish friends and acquaintances, Ruthenian students at the University of Lemberg supported the 1830 Polish revolution in the Russian Empire.[65] Vienna had long tried to stem consistently strong Polish political aspirations through an equally consistent support of the Ruthenian minority in Galicia. In light of these frequent Polish-Ruthenian alignments, and Ruthenians' preferences for Polish culture, Austrian efforts might have seemed futile; but in 1848, this long-term support paid valuable political dividends.

Governor Stadion advised that Ruthenian patriotism should be instrumentalized; thus the Polish political movement would be weakened, and Polish claims on Galicia would be contested.[66] His decisions were based on his broader views of the monarchy and Galicia's place within it: to him, the Polish-Ruthenian conflict in Galicia was reflective of a heterogeneous empire in which different ethnicities were often bound to share a single administrative space. Stadion emphasized that the Habsburg dynasty's hold on Galicia was particularly tenuous; Slavs formed an overwhelming majority of the population, and the German minority was marginal. If Vienna failed to secure its position in Galicia, the province would almost inevitably become a prey of Russia.[67] Despite strong influences from the great power to the east, Ruthenians of Galicia expressed their willingness to remain part of the Habsburg Monarchy, and not to toy with ideas of annexation to the empire of the tsars.[68]

It is unclear whether Stadion initiated the establishment of the Ruthenian National Council or only granted his support after it had been created. By endorsing this institution, he opened himself to the accusations of enraged Polish revolutionaries, who considered the burgeoning Ruthenian political movement to be an Austrian plot.[69] In January 1849, Florian Ziemiałkowski discussed the political situation in Galicia during a speech in the Austrian parliament. Incensed by the Austrian response to the revolution, Ziemiałkowski claimed that Stadion had invented the distinction between Ruthenians and Poles as part of an effort to undermine Polish Galicia.[70] Ziemiałkowski did not deny cultural differences between Poles and Ruthenians, or that the language of the latter was not exactly the same as Polish; but like many of his contemporaries, he considered these differences to be reversible. He rightly noted that some Ruthenian-speaking Galicians considered themselves Poles. Ziemiałkowski contended that without Austrian intervention, Ruthenians would not have adopted the politically active stance they had taken at the outbreak of the 1848 Revolution.

Ziemiałkowski's statements elicited retorts from Ruthenians as well as other politicians across the monarchy. Metropolitan Jakymowych, head of the Ruthenian Greek Catholic Church and a deputy in the Austrian parliament, protested Ziemiałkowski's remarks. Also critical was František Palacký, a prominent figure in the Czech national revival, who noted that, contrary to such dismissive claims, Galician Ruthenians were part of a larger Ruthenian population consisting of ten million people across the borders of the Habsburg and Russian empires.[71] Ziemiałkowski's contentions thus produced the exact opposite of what he had likely hoped; for the first time, the Ruthenian question became an issue of parliamentary debate in a constitutional monarchy.[72]

Ziemiałkowski, in any case, had presented a rather distorted vision of the Austrian bureaucracy in Galicia. Ruthenians benefited from Austrian support, true enough; but their consolidation as a political force during 1848 can hardly be attributed to Austrian initiative alone. In 1848, Polish patriots omitted Ruthenians entirely from their political program, thus laying claim to all of Galicia for themselves and effectively ignoring the other major Slavic presence there.[73] In response, the Ruthenian political program in 1848 was pro-Habsburg, but mainly anti-Polish.[74]

Stadion's support for Ruthenians was never unconditional. In spite of endorsing many Ruthenian demands, the governor left a major one unfilled, namely the division of Galicia into an eastern and a western province. The status of Galicia within the monarchy was not merely an administrative matter, but also a highly charged political issue, the meaning of which fluctuated with circumstances. In 1772 and 1795, Vienna had annexed two territories, Eastern and Western Galicia respectively, and between 1795 and 1803, these two regions existed as separate provinces.[75] They were united into a single province, with its capital in Lemberg, in 1803. The Austrians lost most of Western Galicia to Russia as a result of the Napoleonic Wars, which also created the precedent of a quasi-independent Polish region between the different partitions. Kraków, a free city under the combined protectorate of the three partitioning powers, created numerous temptations for Polish revolutionaries, and quickly became a thorn in the Russians' side. After the defeat of the Polish uprising of 1831, the Russian authorities expected Kraków to be annexed to Galicia under Austrian control; but, still a free city, in 1846 it became one of the centers of the planned (and failed) national revolution. Concerned that this precedent could repeat itself in the future, and that events in Kraków would directly bear on the political situation in Russia's Polish territories, Russian officials pressured their Austrian counterparts to annex Kraków into the Habsburg Monarchy, a step that was officially taken on 11 November 1846.[76] The city's annexation revived debates about the administrative organization of Galicia. As the monarchy's largest province, it was difficult to govern from a single center in Lemberg. Chancellor Metternich and his colleagues attributed Austria's failure to prevent the 1846 revolt to inefficient administration, an inability to control large expanses of land. In February 1847, Metternich authorized the division of Galicia into two provinces.[77]

Mere months later, however, Stadion advised calling off this move, and keeping Galicia intact as a single province.[78] His view was based upon his estimation of the Ruthenian political movement as potentially even more dangerous than the Polish one. If granted a separate province, the governor maintained, the Ruthenians might succumb to Russian propaganda, and might one day wish to join the Russian Empire.[79] Stadion well understood the nuances of Galicia's geopolitical gravitation between Vienna, Warsaw, and St. Petersburg. Just as Poles could be drawn to Warsaw, Ruthenians could find themselves politically attracted to St. Petersburg. A pro-Russian turn in Ruthenian politics could have devastating consequences for Vienna; so it would be best from Austria's point of view if, within one province, Ruthenians and Poles could balance each other's separatist proclivities.

Ruthenian and Polish politics took a new turn after 1848, but the most visible results of the 1848 revolutions were in the domain of social rather than ethnic relations. In 1848, Vienna completed the emancipation of the peasants, abolishing all dues and payment requirements to landlords across the monarchy. It is fitting that of all the Austrian provinces, Galicia was the first to witness the emancipation, a testament to Stadion's initiatives; the mechanisms of the process reveal important nuances of imperial administration between Lemberg and Vienna.

Peasant emancipation was one theoretical aspect of the 1846 uprising that came to fruition during 1848: in 1846, aristocratic Polish patriots had promised land and freedom in an effort to draw Polish peasants to the national cause, but had not been believed.[80] After the suppression of the 1846 revolt, Austrian officials also debated the position of peasants in relation to their landlords; in 1847, the Austrian government reduced the obligations of the former in Galicia to the level established in Bohemia.[81] The events of 1848 brought new urgency to the land question. Polish leaders hoped to use the momentum to announce the liberation of the peasants, and expected to gain their support with the promise of new social rights. The date of the announcement was set for Easter Sunday, 25 April 1848.

News of these plans leaked to the Austrians, reaching Governor Stadion on 15 April.[82] He immediately sent an urgent message to Vienna, but time was not on his side; it would take days, if not weeks, to deliver the post to the imperial capital and back to Lemberg. Stadion was, however, determined to proceed with the planned reform: the initiative for peasant emancipation, he believed, must come from Austrian officials rather than Polish landowners. On 17 April, acting unilaterally, Stadion announced the abolishment of all peasant dues and payments in Galicia, effective 15 May.[83] In mid-April, meanwhile, the Austrian government debated plans for peasant emancipation throughout the monarchy; by the end of the month, a consensus seems to have been reached on the need to proceed with the reforms. Even then, many could not agree on the mechanisms and timing of the measure.[84] Stadion, then, had effectively emancipated peasants in Galicia without authorization from above.

The peasant reform reflected the new political realities in Galicia. Polish landowners were enraged, believing, perhaps with good reason, that the Austrians had stolen their initiative from them. Perceiving themselves as victims of Austrian foul play, these Poles, however, failed to notice the key shift in Habsburg policies in Galicia. The year 1848 was hardly a period of triumphs for Vienna. The peasant reform signaled Austrian weakness, not strength: the emancipation had been enacted in Galicia as a response to a Polish initiative.

In the summer of 1848, the revolution in Galicia turned violent. Vienna's consistent refusal to make concessions to Polish activists resulted in an outbreak of hostilities. Since April 1848, Poles had demanded official recognition of the Polish national guard. The Austrians refused and ordered the guards to disarm voluntarily. The constitution and parliament had created new opportunities for political debate, but the full autonomy anticipated by Poles was nowhere in sight, and in the summer of 1848, barricades were erected in the center of Lemberg. When Poles refused to disarm and dismantle the barricades, the Austrians resorted to force, opening fire on 1 November, and causing a number of important buildings to be engulfed in flames. This episode signaled the beginning of the end of the revolution in Galicia.[85]

By late November, the barricades were dismantled. Revolutionary tensions eased with time. Some of the initiatives that first emerged during 1848 would take root. Social and economic initiatives generated important long-term results as well. As is typical of revolutions, 1848 produced many paradoxes. The monarchy survived as a uniform state, but the numerous reform initiatives paved the way, albeit indirectly, for the Austro-Hungarian compromise of 1867. The years 1848–49 saw the issuance of three different constitutions in Vienna. None was implemented in full; but constitutional ideals took hold, and were never completely eradicated, a state of affairs hardly feasible before the revolution. And while Poles did not receive autonomy, and Ruthenians failed to secure the division of the province into two, each group emerged from the revolution in a stronger position than before. Peasant conditions improved only gradually, but in the long run, 1848 marked a radical turn in social relations in the countryside.

The Austrian officials who governed Galicia through 1848 parted ways thereafter. The wheel of group rotations, which had become such an important part of administrative routine, would turn once more. Appointed Austria's minister of the interior, Franz Stadion left Galicia for Vienna in July 1848.[86] In Vienna, Stadion led a cohort of ministers who had worked under him in the past. Leo Thun, for instance, had arrived in Galicia when Rudolph Stadion took office, and served under both Stadion brothers, eventually moving to Bohemia in the summer of 1848 and then on to Vienna. As a minister in the 1850s, he became a leading authority in the field of education reform.[87]

While Austrians were moving away from Galicia, Poles became ever more prominent in its administration. Rotations remained an essential aspect of professional careers, but they took new forms after 1848. Despite failing to achieve autonomy, Poles secured important successes in the revolution, and their presence in the administration would no longer be contested. The old Austrian dream of making Galicia a purely German province was decidedly dead. Ruthenians profited from the revolution, meanwhile, even more than Poles; for the first time in history, the former were acting as a political entity on par with the latter.

At the same time, the Revolution of 1848 revealed the resilience of Austrian political structures. Requests for autonomy were common across the monarchy, but outright irredentist demands were rather rare even among radicals. The events of 1848 in Galicia, in particular, say more about Austria's long-term successes than its failures. Even if Stadion had, as some Poles claimed, made use of Ruthenian aspirations, he had done so masterfully, and certainly not all by himself. The ability to channel this political force required long-term efforts, in which many of Stadion's colleagues had participated in the past. Though caught unawares by the revolution, the Austrian bureaucracy was, in a way, well positioned to face the tasks accompanying radical political upheavals. Many bureaucrats were bound by their loyalty to the Habsburg sovereigns and by their collective identification with the monarchy, which they represented. The year 1848 opened a new era in the history of the Austrian Empire, but it also revealed continuities between the eighteenth and nineteenth centuries. Like many of his fellow officials, Franz Stadion was a product of the Josephinian era, whose lasting consequence was a cohort of German-speaking, supranational bureaucrats who brought the idea of unity to Austria's provinces.

CONCLUSION

1848, 1867, and Beyond

The year 1848 was a turning point in the history of the Habsburg Monarchy. The revolution brought an end to any illusions that ethnic differences could be effaced by an ostensibly neutral Austrian German bureaucracy, and after 1848, the national question would dominate Habsburg politics. In the upheaval's immediate aftermath, however, political changes wrought by the revolution appeared reversible, and nationalism had not yet reached its extremes.

In 1849, Emperor Francis Joseph rescinded his government's constitutional experiments and dissolved parliament. Ten years of neo-absolutism followed, but absolutism never recovered in full. The year 1860 saw another great change in the history of the monarchy: The October Diploma (1860) and the February Patent (1862) marked the return of regional parliamentary assemblies and a bicameral parliament. Provincial diets met for sessions in 1860; their deputies selected representatives to the imperial parliament. No free parliamentary elections took place during the 1860s, but provincial elites secured the right to participate in the decision-making process, on both the local and the imperial levels.

Almost twenty years after the revolution, in 1866, Austria lost another major war to Prussia. In 1867, the Habsburg Monarchy concluded a historic compromise with the Kingdom of Hungary, creating Austria-Hungary, a state consisting of two equal polities. Between 1867 and 1918, Austria and Hungary were governed separately from one another, sharing only a common army and foreign ministry. The two territories of the monarchy—Cisleithania under Vienna and Transleithania under Budapest—followed two different historical trajectories, with Vienna, due to its policies vis-à-vis national minorities, gradually gaining a better reputation for toleration and leniency than Budapest.

Clearly, 1867 was by no means simply a consequence of 1848. It was a compromise in an era of postrevolutionary experiments, of great significance for Vienna, the provinces, and above all, Hungary. When Hungarians celebrated their victory, political elites of other parts of the monarchy—most notably, the Czechs of Bohemia and the Poles of Galicia—anticipated that their regions, too, would soon be granted a Hungary-like autonomous status. These hopes remained alive for some years after 1867, but no other territory would be allowed to enter into federation with Vienna as an equal member. Still, though their expectations did not materialize in full, after 1867 Poles did secure a limited autonomy. Their language became dominant in administration and education, and Polish officials eventually gained a hold over the administration.

The year 1867, in turn, brought an end to the authentically Austrian period in the history of Habsburg Galicia. Bureaucrats would no longer rotate through Trieste, Amsterdam, or Laibach en route to Vienna and thence to Galicia. Public space in the province would become both less diverse and more contested. Before 1867, many Austrian bureaucrats there, their backgrounds as diverse as possible, were European almost by design, but after 1867, the vast majority of Galician officials were Polish. Nationalism became integral to imperial administration.

Even after Germanophone Austrian bureaucrats vacated their offices in Galicia, they left behind a very important legacy. Galicia was no longer the same region of Poland the Austrians had annexed in 1772. Its façade had undergone quite dramatic changes. New government buildings, schools, theaters, and amphitheaters, as well as parks and alleys, proliferated across the province, and above all in its capital—which, now that it was under Polish control, we may once more call Lwów. The most important changes, however, were well hidden behind new architectural façades. During their almost century-long rule, the Austrians had transformed old patterns of coexistence in Galicia, enforcing new types of relations among Poles, Ruthenians, and Jews.

By supporting Ruthenians against Poles, Vienna had secured loyal allies and made the return of exclusively Polish dominance in the province impossible. The long-standing policy of playing one ethnicity against the other had at least twofold implications for Vienna. On the one hand, it ensured a degree of lasting control since, just as before 1848, Polish-Ruthenian tensions, or internal conflicts within these respective groups, could require intervention from the imperial capital. When acting on behalf of Ruthenians, as Habsburg officials did on some occasions after 1848, Vienna blocked Polish initiatives and thus prevented Galician Poles' monopolization of administration and policy.

But new dangers stemming from Ruthenian initiatives, on the other hand, became increasingly harder to overlook. While benefiting from Austrian support, Ruthenians learned political organizing by imitating Polish models. Despite never making national demands as radical as those of Poles, Ruthenians, too, participated in the progressive transformation of Galician society along national lines. When unable to make clear national choices, constantly vacillating among Polish, Ruthenian/Ukrainian, and Russian options, they posed serious dilemmas for Vienna. Ruthenian nationalism was not invented by Vienna, just as Russophilism was not forced upon Galicia by St. Petersburg. Both were products of borderland politics, not without Vienna's involvement.

In 1848, Johann Georg von Ostermann, head of the Sanok administration, reappraised his life, career, and position in Galicia. In October of that year, dismayed at recent developments in Galicia, especially the rebellion and massacres of 1846, he asked for transfer from the province. He described his feeling of helplessness and personal failure: "The more than seventeen years during which I, as an Austrian citizen, did my best to fulfill my professional obligations under existing circumstances did not bring the anticipated results. The recent situation, which is connected to national developments, does not permit a non-local German to anticipate a satisfying future."[1] Ostermann hoped, during a requested leave of absence, to find a position for himself elsewhere in the monarchy. But this effort proved unsuccessful, and still in 1848, he returned to Stanisławów, where his family resided.

Men like Ostermann, who identified with a German-speaking dynasty and a monarchy in which ethnic difference was theoretically immaterial, experienced a shock to their worldview in the wake of 1848. In 1867, when Polish elites secured autonomy for Galicia, many Germanophone Austrian officials had to choose between retirement or relocation, and for many of these, the year 1867 proved a time of personal crisis. Some were in the midst of their careers—too old for new venues and appointments, but too young for retirement. Most importantly, by 1867, many of them had put down roots in Galicia, built families, homes, and a lifestyle they could not easily change. Ostermann, for example, by 1867 had an extended family—several children and grandchildren, whose whole lives had been spent in Galicia and who had no desire to move anywhere else. Ostermann protested his enforced early retirement, but to no avail. His position was reassigned to Polish-speaking officials.[2]

Under the pressure of new circumstances, Ostermann made some surprising choices. In 1866, he started writing his memoirs, but chose a rather unconventional venue for publication, sending his texts to the Galician periodical *Slovo* (*The Word*), at the time a major organ of the Russophile movement. The decision to choose a Ruthenian over a Polish publication must have been determined by Ostermann's overall disappointment with Polish elites and the way they had treated their Austrian colleagues between 1848 and 1867. But the choice of a Russophile periodical, as opposed to a Ruthenian Populist one, was also symbolic.

By this time, some of Ostermann's children and grandchildren were becoming increasingly involved in the Ruthenian movement. His children, it seems, were more content than he was with the Galician reality. His son and grandson married Ruthenians. Other younger members of the family took the Polish path instead, but their families were just as enmeshed in the new Galicia, divided as it was along Polish-Ruthenian lines.

Like the real-life Ostermann, the fictional Wacław Precliczek of Jan Lam's *Capowice High Society* is fired in 1867. He too suffers a major life

CONCLUSION 1848, 1867, AND BEYOND

crisis, being forced to retire too early in his career, but too late for a new professional path. His family moves to the provincial capital, where his Polish-speaking wife and daughter feel at home. But having never managed to learn the Polish language, Precliczek can communicate with Poles, and for that matter with Ruthenians, only with great difficulty.

Some other Austrians, however, planned their departure from Galicia with great care. Before leaving Lwów in the summer of 1848, Governor Franz Stadion groomed a successor. It had become clear that he would soon transfer to Vienna, and equally obvious that the officials replacing his administration would be chosen from a different cohort, with the involvement of Poles.

Unwilling to leave the selection of the next governor to chance, Stadion supported Agenor Count Gołuchowski, a one-time mayor of Lwów, councillor of the Galician Gubernium, and most recently the Gubernium's vice president.[3] A native of Galicia, Gołuchowski had received a law degree from the University of Lwów.[4] He had entered the administration as an unpaid official and was promoted in 1846 on the recommendation of Baron Krieg, then the vice president of the Gubernium. When Krieg lost his position the same year, Gołuchowski stayed, and was soon promoted yet again, in April 1848, becoming vice president of the Gubernium.[5] Within months he was first in line as a candidate for the position of governor.

Gołuchowski's rapid progress through the administration in 1847–48 generated a great deal of envy among colleagues. As rumor had it, he had gained favor by his policy suggestions during 1848, allegedly "betraying" his people by, despite himself being an Austrian official of Polish descent, advising Stadion to support Ruthenian political initiatives as a counterweight to the Poles. News leaked to the public that it was Gołuchowski—and not Stadion—who had encouraged the foundation of the Ruthenian National Council in May 1848.[6] The Austrians had reason to value Gołuchowski for his nationality-neutral approach to Galician politics, but some fellow Poles accused him of trading the Polish cause for Austrian favors.[7] In 1848, Stadion's support did not suffice for Gołuchowski to rise to the very top of the Galician administration. Under Polish pressure, Vienna conceded to the appointment of a different Polish politician as the new governor.[8]

Fig. Concl.1: Count Agenor Gołuchowski. Portrait by Antoine Maurin, 1846. Polish National Library, Digital Collection Polona.

In July 1848, Wacław Zaleski became the first person of Polish descent to serve as governor of Galicia. Like Gołuchowski, Zaleski was well known in the province; a native, he had previously been active in its cultural and intellectual life before switching to politics. In the 1830s, for instance, he had shown an interest, especially characteristic of the age of Romanticism, in Polish and Ruthenian folk songs, a collection of which he compiled and published. Zaleski was attuned to the great variety of Galicia's cultural life; but like many of his contemporaries, he believed Ruthenianness to be part of a broader Polish culture, and that the Ruthenian language was a variant of Polish.[9]

Over the years, Zaleski's politics would radicalize along national lines. In early 1848, before becoming governor, he had worked in Vienna as a *Referent* for Polish affairs in the Ministry of the Interior.[10] In June 1848, he supported Stadion's decision to halt the planned division of Galicia into two provinces.[11] From July 1848 on, he exploited his position as governor to gain further concessions for Poles. His most important decision was to attempt the adoption of Polish as the mandatory language of education in place of German.

Such initiatives were too radical to gain the endorsement of Zaleski's Austrian colleagues in Vienna, and in the fall of 1848, relations between Poles and Austrians seemed to reach their crisis point. During a meeting of the Ministerial Council in January 1849, a decision was reached by vote to remove Zaleski from Galicia, with one Austrian minister summing up the concern that "Zaleski has many valuable qualities, but he has demonstrated increasingly pro-Polish views."[12] With Zaleski's dismissal imminent, Stadion, now minister of the interior, stepped in to push once again for the appointment of Gołuchowski, whom he recommended as a neutral politician enjoying the support of Ruthenians.[13] In February 1849, Agenor Gołuchowski replaced Zaleski as governor, a compromise candidate satisfying the requirements of Poles and Austrians alike.[14]

Gołuchowski would go on to hold three nonconsecutive tenures as governor of Galicia, in 1849–59, 1866–68, and 1871–75. In 1859, he became the first person of Polish descent to serve as the Habsburg Monarchy's minister of the interior.[15] One of the empire's most successful Polish statesmen ever, Gołuchowski remained long torn between his Polishness and his Austrianness. At the time of his first gubernatorial appointment, many of his own national group considered him to be, at the very least, lacking in Polish patriotism.[16] He had taken no part in the revolutions of 1846 and 1848, and had originally been promoted on the recommendation of the anti-Polish administrator Baron Krieg. While in office, he seemed to prioritize Vienna's initiatives over Polish national interests.

His politics, however, became increasingly nationality-oriented over time. Within the new Galicia, where Poles secured greater control over the administration, Gołuchowski supported the Polish claim for exclusive dominance of the province. This required the suppression of the Ruthenian movement, which Gołuchowski had promoted, if only indirectly, in 1848. Thus in the 1850s, he sought to correct what had been, from the pro-Polish standpoint, his previous mistakes.

Irreversibly damaging to Gołuchowski's reputation among Galician Ruthenians would be his proposed language reform of 1859, in which he advised replacing the Cyrillic alphabet with the Latin one in Ruthenian textbooks, starting with primary schools. The literacy of Ruthenian children would thus have to come in the same alphabet used in Polish, rather than in the Cyrillic in which Ruthenians had written for centuries. Logically enough, Gołuchowski assumed that the change of alphabet would help eliminate differences between the Polish and Ruthenian languages, and that it could help promote Polonization.[17] In correspondence with colleagues in Vienna, he justified his language initiatives with reference to the political situation in Galicia, arguing that Ruthenians bore an excessive sympathy for Russia (which of course utilized Cyrillic as well, Ruthenian and Russian being East Slavic languages as opposed to the West Slavic Polish); the change in alphabet, then, could help reduce Russophilism.[18]

The language reform provoked virulent criticism from Ruthenians, providing a rare opportunity for an alliance of otherwise competing political groups, the Populists and the Russophiles. For that matter, reception of the measure in Vienna was mixed.[19] Not all Ruthenians, as Gołuchowski's colleagues knew, were Russophiles; many identified as Populists and remained committed to the Habsburg dynasty. The radical transition from Cyrillic to Latin could gravely undermine this commitment, causing more political harm than benefit. Count Johann Rechberg, prime minister of the empire, opposed Gołuchowski's initiatives, thereby further solidifying Ruthenian support for the Austrians.[20]

Though important for the province, the alphabet battles of 1859 played a rather marginal role in the overall political situation in the monarchy. That same year, the empire suffered a defeat in Lombardy at the hands of combined French-Italian forces; as a result, Vienna lost most of its Italian territories except Venice to what would soon form a unified Italy. The neo-absolutism adopted in 1849 seemed to have backfired, and Emperor Francis

Joseph revised his policies, inaugurating a renewed era of constitutional experimentation.

In 1859, the emperor dismissed a number of senior officials and ministers. On 21 May of that year, Agenor Gołuchowski became the new minister of the interior. His appointment revealed the victory of the federalist camp over the centralists. A conservative politician, Gołuchowski defended the integrity of the monarchy, but advocated its reorganization on the federal principle; like his mentor Franz Stadion, he supported a constitutional order and regional parliamentary representations in the provinces. Gołuchowski's endorsement of parliamentary rule resulted in a decree ordering the reopening of local diets and the imperial parliament. On 15 May 1860, the first session of the revived Galician Diet opened in Lwów.[21] That same year, an Austrian parliament met in session for the first time in over a decade.

But Gołuchowski's premature dismissal just a year later, in December 1860, revealed a sudden reversal of political priorities and the return of centralism.[22] Though his tenure in Vienna was rather brief, his reform initiatives had long-term consequences for the entire monarchy. The imperial parliament and provincial assemblies remained in being, with some interruptions, through 1918, and the parliamentary principle was never fully reversed. The year 1860 also paved the way for the federalization that would be enacted in 1867.

Between 1859 and 1866

The composition and functioning of the bureaucracy changed along with the political turn, with the rotation of bureaucrats in and out of Galicia, in particular, taking a new form. In the past, many officials had moved from Vienna and other regions to Galicia to represent the Austrian government there; after their service in the province, most ended up somewhere else, but few would rise to the top of Vienna's political establishment. This pattern was broken in 1848. Now the reverse rotation—from Lwów to Vienna—became increasingly common. The two Stadions paved the way of promotion via Galicia for several of their former subordinates; for instance, Philipp Kraus, who had served as vice president of Galicia Gubernium in 1847, became minister of finance in April 1848, and Leo Thun, who had come from Trieste to Lwów with Stadion, eventually moved on to Vienna as minister of education.[23]

In 1861, Alexander Count Mensdorff-Pouilly was appointed the new governor of Galicia. One of the most illustrious personalities ever employed in the administration of the province, Mensdorff hailed from a well-known family with important political networks across the monarchy. His father, Emanuel Pouilly, originally from French Lorraine, was a former head of the Austrian War Council; through this parentage, Alexander Mensdorff secured access to members of Austria's political establishment, right up to the Habsburg family and Prime Minister Felix Schwarzenberg. Before arriving in Galicia, Mensdorff had a career in the military, seeing combat in 1848 in Italy and Olmütz; in 1852, he was a commissar in Holstein, and in 1853 was appointed Austria's ambassador to St. Petersburg.

Prior to 1861, Mensdorff had never worked in Austria's civil administration. Such a fusion of military and civilian authority had taken place only twice before in Galicia: briefly in 1774, and once again in 1831, following the suppression of the Polish revolution in Warsaw; nor had either of the men involved, Hadik and d'Este, fully justified the expectations placed upon them. But in the early 1860s the political exigencies of Galicia yet again called for new means of control.

Since 1860, Poles in the Russian Empire had been preparing for a new revolution, and news of these plans leaked to the Austrian and Russian authorities. Given the time he had spent in his diplomatic capacity in Russia, Mensdorff seemed especially well equipped to deal with the new revolutionary dangers in the Polish borderland. In 1861, he moved from St. Petersburg to Lwów, where he was to enforce security on Austria's eastern periphery. Learning from its previous mistakes, Vienna now took prevention seriously.

In January 1863, a new revolution indeed broke out in Warsaw, causing a great deal of confusion in Vienna; as in 1830, Austrian officials took long to clarify their official position. This latest upheaval revived debates on Austria's involvement in the Polish question. For his part, Johann Rechberg, at the time Austria's foreign minister, expressed regret concerning Vienna's participation in the Polish partitions; the territories that Austria had thereby gained on its eastern periphery, he believed, had been more trouble to the monarchy over the years than they were worth. Rechberg now harked back to an Austrian-Polish solution previously promoted by a number of Polish aristocrats, and supported among Austrian officials, most recently by August Lobkowitz in 1831; according to this idea, Poland should be restored, in federal unity with Austria under Habsburg rule. Rechberg's initiatives were unprecedented: for the first time in Galicia's history, an Austrian minister endorsed the reestablishment of a Polish state.[24] Precisely because of their novelty and radicalism, Rechberg's ideas found no support among his fellow ministers. Any radical Polish solution could lead to a confrontation with Russia, which the Austrians sought to avoid.

Before Habsburg officials managed to clarify their position regarding the Polish revolution, Polish independence-seekers in Russia, having organized an unprecedentedly formidable army, scored important successes in the field. Approximately 200,000 volunteers fought on the Polish side and captured a number of provincial towns. By April 1863, however, St. Petersburg dispatched 270,000 soldiers to Warsaw, and by July of that year, this force swelled to 340,000.[25] Even without international assistance, the Poles resisted the Russian army for sixteen long months. However, as in 1830, ultimate victory could only have been achieved with outside support.[26] During the months of uncertainty, the Austrian authorities in Galicia remained in suspense, with Mensdorff instructed to maintain political stability in his province, and decrees issued from Vienna forbidding the involvement of Austrian subjects in the revolution taking place over the border. On 2 February 1863, Mensdorff ordered Austrian frontier guards to forbid passage of any kind into Russia.[27] In February 1864, he introduced martial law. With such restrictions in place, the political situation in Galicia remained relatively calm.

When the Polish uprising was finally suppressed in the spring of 1864, a new era opened in the history of the partitioned Polish territories. As earlier, Polish political life continued to shift away from Russian Poland and toward Austrian Galicia. But the 1860s was a different political epoch from the time of Lobkowitz; the failure of several consecutive revolutions, in 1830–31,

CONCLUSION 1848, 1867, AND BEYOND

1846, and 1863, affected Poles' political allegiances across the partitions. Even in 1863, some Poles in Galicia rejected a radical military solution, and remained committed to Vienna.[28] Polish loyalties under the partitions, as Piotr Wandycz has noted, were never static, but rather contingent upon specific historical and political circumstances.[29]

The failure of the Warsaw revolution, of course, disappointed Poles across all borders; many began to accept the inevitability of imperial dominion over their traditional territories. But the implications of foreign rule varied depending on the particular partition of one's residence. Among the three dividing powers, Austria seemed to offer the richest opportunities for Polish political life. True, Galicia ranked as the most economically backward of all the Polish partitions; but the Habsburg system afforded possibilities of political participation of the kind that were unknown in the other partitions. Over the course of the nineteenth century, Poles generally came to accept Austria as the lesser evil (or the least of three of them).

After 1864, more Poles than ever before supported cooperation with Vienna; many saw the future of Poland as inextricably linked with Austria. Polish conservatives in Kraków included a number of prominent politicians and intellectuals who maintained that the earlier Polish political system had been dysfunctional and believed that Austria offered the best possible conditions for Polish cultural and political life. Thus the demise of the 1863 Polish revolution, in a way, yielded important dividends for Vienna's imperial project.

Also reaping the benefits of the events of 1863 was Governor Mensdorff, whose work in Galicia opened new career opportunities for him in Vienna. The twentieth-century Polish historian Henryk Wereszycki would describe Mensdorff as a mediocre personality, "both a bad general and a bad civil official,"[30] but the governor's Austrian contemporaries must have had a different opinion of him. Senior officials in Vienna praised Mensdorff's activity in Galicia for precisely the same reason that Wereszycki would later condemn it: on his watch, the impact of the Polish revolution on the province had been minimal, and Austrian officials managed to keep local politics under control. Mensdorff was richly rewarded for his work in Galicia, in 1864 replacing Rechberg as foreign minister.[31]

CONCLUSION 1848, 1867, AND BEYOND

Mensdorff's service in this post, however, soon turned to disaster; in particular, growing tensions between the Austrian and Prussian monarchies escalated during his tenure. At the core of the problem was the Austro-Prussian struggle for dominance in the German Federation. In 1864–66, questions surrounding the northern German region of Schleswig-Holstein triggered the decisive confrontation. A combined Austro-Prussian force seized Schleswig-Holstein from Denmark in 1864 and annexed it to the German Federation; Prussia was to be responsible for the administration of Schleswig, while Austria took control of Holstein. In 1866, Prussia used a dispute over Holstein as a pretext for military intervention against the Austrian Empire. Prussia's victory over the Habsburgs in this conflict altered the course of Central European history: most German-speaking territories eventually united under Berlin in the German Empire, while Austrian elites, with Vienna's international standing weakened, were forced to introduce sweeping domestic changes culminating in the Austro-Hungarian Compromise.

In light of these dramatic international developments, the political situation in Galicia might have appeared of marginal significance, but it was precisely in 1866 that Mensdorff again intervened in the province's politics. In February of that year, Austrian ministers were selecting a new governor for Galicia; Freiherr von Paumgarten, who had taken office after Mensdorff, had come under attack for his inefficiency.[32] Two candidates, Adam Potocki and Agenor Gołuchowski, were considered for the position. Both were Poles, and well known in Galicia and Vienna.[33] Mensdorff was the only minister to vote against both candidates and oppose the appointment of a Pole as governor of Galicia.[34] His colleagues had little objection to appointing a Pole to the office, so long as that individual had demonstrated loyalty to Vienna. Potocki enjoyed support among Galician Poles, but his political allegiances were not entirely clear, raising suspicions among Austrians. Gołuchowski, whom some Poles looked upon with mistrust, had a solid reputation for Habsburg loyalty, and was once again selected as governor.

The Gołuchowski of 1866 was not the same individual with the same political outlook as the Gołuchowski of 1849, or for that matter of 1859. In the early 1860s, he had managed to antagonize both the Ruthenians and

Jews of Galicia, even as these groups were particularly known for their support for Vienna;³⁵ but in 1865, he changed his policies yet again, supporting the limited use of the Ruthenian language in the provincial diet. He also advocated lifting anti-Jewish restrictions, for instance, the prohibition against Jews purchasing land in the Galician countryside.

Around the same time of Gołuchowski's return to administering Galicia, a change of government was taking place in Vienna itself. In 1865, Richard Belcredi replaced Anton Schmerling as prime minister. The new imperial government favored a parliamentary system over centralist rule. Galician Poles took advantage of the opportunity to press for further concessions; that same year, the Polish politician Antoni Helcel filed a memorandum to Vienna, requesting extended autonomy for Galicia, which he asserted could lead to cooperation and reciprocal benefit.³⁶ Governor Gołuchowski also became a major proponent of Galician autonomy, advocating investing the Galician Diet with actual political authority and the creation of such separate central institutions as a Galician Court Chancellery.³⁷

After 1867, Gołuchowski became a prominent advocate of the further federalization of the monarchy, with Galicia to be included as the third equal member. Gołuchowski's ideas seem to have received some support in Vienna; Foreign Minister Count von Beust agreed, for instance, that granting extensive autonomy to Galicia could secure long-term Polish loyalty to the Habsburgs.³⁸ But a new status for Galicia and more federalization would mean the almost inevitable need to include Bohemia as yet another equal member. The early agreement with Hungary had been a hard-to-reach compromise for the Austrians, and few officials had any eagerness for further federalization. Minister of Justice Ritter von Komers supported the expansion of the jurisdiction of the Galician Diet requested by Gołuchowski, but opposed granting Galicia a distinct status within the monarchy.³⁹

When Polish elites secured autonomy for Galicia in the wake of the Austro-Hungarian Compromise in 1867, by Austrian decree, German ceased to be the mandatory language of administration and education. Most German schools were liquidated; between 1867 and 1918, Galicia had only two German-language high schools, one in Lwów and the other in Brody. In 1869, Polish was declared the official language of the Galician administration.

This hard-won autonomy, however, satisfied no one. Poles believed they had received too little, while Ruthenians feared that Poles had gained too much. Polish politicians secured extensive rights in the areas of provincial administration and education, but this was hardly the same thing as political and economic independence from Vienna. Meanwhile, with Polish replacing German, Polish-speaking bureaucrats assuming formerly Austrian offices, and the imperial administration generally nationalized by Polish elites, another group was left disconsolate: many Austrian bureaucrats who had served in Galicia before 1867 moved away, not always of their own volition. As early as 1849, Gołuchowski had purged such Austrian officials as were particularly loathed by Polish landowners.[40] In 1866, Gołuchowski initiated another major overhaul of the administration, dismissing several top-level Gubernium officials who were reluctant to cooperate with the new Polish authorities. Gubernium councillors and heads of district administrations, including Alexander Summer, Karl Wohlfart, and Heinrich Hehn, were fired, all replaced by Polish colleagues of Gołuchowski who had earlier held office in other provinces of the monarchy.[41]

It had been common for Poles to lament the centralist—Austrian—administration before 1848; but now Poles sought to monopolize authority in the new post-1867 administration, and it was the Ruthenians' turn to complain about Polish hegemony. Both Austrian and Polish domination were, of course, relative; just as the Austrian administration had never been exclusively German, neither would the Polish administration ever be exclusively Polish. Before 1867, Polish elites had infiltrated Austrian structures and, oftentimes with the assistance of Austrian bureaucrats themselves, had hindered the implementation of Vienna's policies.

But personnel rotations were not always determined by ethnic considerations alone. Gołuchowski, for example, was highly critical of some Poles involved in the new governance of Galicia; in a fit of anger, he once described the provincial diet led by his fellow Pole Leon Sapieha as "an asylum for morally impaired noblemen."[42] At least some of Galicia's new Polish managers were as incompetent as their German-speaking predecessors in the eighteenth century and after; a change of ethnicity in the administration was no guarantee of its quality.

CONCLUSION 1848, 1867, AND BEYOND

More important changes concerned the structure of socio-political life in the province. Before 1848, the political scene of Galicia resembled a triangle within which the Austrians occupied the most important corner. But this geometry changed with the realignment of political forces after 1867. The Austrian element in Galician politics became increasingly weak. Poles came to occupy a dominant position, with Ruthenians their main competitors. Galician Jews entered politics as well; though a relatively small minority, they sometimes shaped electoral alliances and parliamentary coalitions. The twentieth century would see an explosion of anti-Jewish mass violence in this region, but in the nineteenth century, Jewish-Polish and Jewish-Ruthenian electoral groupings supplied many candidates to the Galician Diet and the Austrian parliament.

Poles, Ruthenians, and Jews were all divided in their identities and allegiances. Galicia, as Harald Binder has illustrated, presented a model of three dualisms: Poles were divided between Austria-supporting conservatives who endorsed status quo and democrats who favored the expansion of Galician autonomy and democratic reforms; Ruthenians were divided between Russophiles and, on the other hand, Populists who endorsed the unity of Ruthenians/Ukrainians across the Austro-Russian imperial divide. The Jews were perhaps the most divided of all, split amongst Orthodox, Hasidim, and assimilated Jews, who chose to become Germans, Poles, or even Ruthenians.[43] Vienna no longer controlled political life in the province to the same extent it had before 1848, but the political scene of nineteenth-century Galicia was very much a product of earlier Austrian efforts here. Galicia was an Austrian achievement.

A number of Austrian and Polish officials involved in the administration of Galicia between 1848 and 1867 left an important mark on the history of the monarchy. A bureaucratic family pattern, by which sons followed in their fathers' footsteps, became common. Thun, Zaleski, Gołuchowski, Potocki, and Mensdorff-Pouilly were all familiar names in the monarchy's political establishment right up till 1918. Filip and Wacław Zaleski, son and grandson of the first Polish governor of Galicia, both held positions in the imperial administration, the former serving also as a governor of Galicia, the latter as a minister for Galician affairs in Vienna.[44] After 1867, Alfred Potocki became the empire's minister of agriculture and later its first prime minister of Polish descent.[45] Agenor Gołuchowski the younger, son of the province's second Polish governor, became Austria's foreign minister and minister for Galicia.[46] Mensdorff's son had a diplomatic career, and would take part in ministerial decisions regarding the annexation of Bosnia in 1908.[47] In the 1890s, Leo Thun's son served as governor of Bohemia.[48] All these men were products of the Austrian modernization, and sons of the new Galicia.

How is it, Polish historian Władysław Łoziński asked in 1901, that after years of Austrian-German rule, Polish society managed to galvanize itself into achieving a dominant political position within a multiethnic state without renouncing its own national aspirations?[49] A prolific historian, Łoziński analyzed various aspects of Galician history during the early years of Austrian rule. Like many of his Polish colleagues, he treated this subject mainly in terms of Austrian oppression and Polish deprivation; the Habsburg yoke, he explained, was alleviated in 1848 and still more in 1867, when Poles replaced German-speaking Austrians in administration.

But then how was it, one may further ask, that Poles took over Austrian institutions with such remarkable ease, as described by Łoziński? If Austrian Germans had formerly held such exclusive control over the administration of Galicia, denying Polish access to important offices and depriving Polish elites of administrative experience, how could these Poles have integrated so easily into administrative institutions? Łoziński attributed this success to the Poles' resilience in the face of subjugation by a foreign state. But Polish fortitude was only one aspect of Austrian-Polish coexistence. Long before 1848, Poles had occupied important positions in the Austrian administration; both before and after that year, some advocated cooperation with Vienna. Austrian rule over Galicia was never unilateral, nor was it entirely oppressive.

The year 1848 brought the long chapter of the Austrian Enlightenment to a close. To be sure, Enlightenment ideas had come under critical scrutiny as early as the 1780s. Joseph II's successors Leopold II and Francis II both rejected and abandoned the ideas of the Enlightenment with its focus on perfectibility and equality. Yet practical measures built upon the premises of the Enlightenment were never fully eradicated. New social and administrative hierarchies—however imperfect—persisted well beyond the 1790s. So did the professional bureaucracy that was another product of the Enlightenment. As R. J. W. Evans emphasizes, many of the bureaucrats who coordinated the Habsburg government's actions during 1848 were products of the Austrian Enlightenment.[50] In their patriotism, loyalty, and dedication to the cause of the empire, they embodied the ideal model of imperial officials as envisioned by Emperor Joseph II in the 1780s. It was partly because of these bureaucrats that the empire survived the Revolution of 1848 intact.

The year 1848 also revealed the hollowness of dreams dating back to the Enlightenment. Galicia stood as a major example of frustrated expectations. It never became a model province of the monarchy, remaining a symbol of backwardness instead. Its economy not only did not improve, it worsened. The region never became Austrian-German, but rather a Polish-Ruthenian-Jewish battleground. Instead of moving closer to Central Europe, Galicia seemed to slide ever eastward. This nationality-preoccupied Galicia, however, was built upon imperial institutions created by the Austrians. The bureaucracy and administration persisted, through numerous changes of political regimes, even to the present day. Along the way this bureaucracy only faintly resembled the ideal institution conceived by Enlightenment-minded Habsburg rulers in the eighteenth century; it took on a life of its own, but it never disappeared entirely.

The Austrian bureaucracy reveals its long-term success through its numerous failures. Inefficiency, corruption, and the dubious qualifications of many bureaucrats were always intractable problems, never fully resolved. The image of the unqualified, lazy, and inefficient Austrian bureaucrat was expressed in various literary and historical accounts. But this seemingly disastrous bureaucracy achieved some major successes. While centrifugal tendencies never disappeared, the monarchy did survive for many years, despite nationalism, wars, and numerous domestic and international conflicts. Its demise in 1918 could be blamed on an inefficient bureaucracy and Vienna's failure to enact effective central governance. But the same bureaucracy, it should be remembered, helped keep the empire intact through many tumultuous decades.

Modern nationalism was another product of the empire. Vienna did not, of course, invent ethnic-cultural difference, but its policies and its bureaucracy created the many opportunities Polish and later Ruthenian elites availed themselves of to identify ever more insistently along national lines. Austrian absolutism had been conceived as enforcing a uniformly Germanophone Austrian society of loyal subjects, but stimulated ethnic and cultural diversity instead. Austrian-German bureaucrats, having arrived in Galicia from across the entire monarchy and beyond were supposed to replicate citizens in their own image: loyal, German-speaking, and supranational. But many of these chose other trajectories, and decided to become Poles or Ruthenians instead.

This local absorption especially reveals the contradictoriness of Austrian efforts in Galicia. While integration and assimilation were always reciprocal and multidirectional, in the long run they favored Polishness over Germanophone Austrianness. Such preferences were most dangerous when they impacted political loyalties: descendants of mixed German-Polish families could grow up to become Polish patriots. While some fathers held positions in the Austrian administration, their sons fought for the Polish cause, for the revival of the Polish state.

Answering the questions of how and why local bureaucrats helped promote nationalism against Vienna's intentions requires a careful analysis of Austrian policies and their implementation in the *longue durée*, from the eighteenth century through the nineteenth. Some intentions never materialized because many of the bureaucrats dispatched to carry them out were unqualified to perform professional administrative work. Other policies were flawed from the beginning, marred by an unconcealed Austrian bias concerning Galicia; not all such stereotypes were baseless, but they sometimes caused more harm to those harboring them than to those to whom they were applied.

The Josephinian ideal of flawless bureaucrats bound by unquestioning loyalty to Vienna misfired once applied to reality. Some officials who wound up in Galicia proved underqualified, corrupt, or both. Many found new diversions in the province, for instance spending time in resorts rather than offices; or, what was of greater cultural-political import, they learned Polish and forgot German, and made a new home for themselves in Galicia. These bureaucrats also redesigned their relations with the central authorities in Vienna. In the period of high centralism and absolutism, subaltern bureaucrats in the provinces were only meant to implement reforms, wielding no independent authority; Emperor Joseph II believed that a bureaucrat's main task was to demonstrate total compliance, to follow whatever instructions came from Vienna. But few of the Galician governors matched this expectation. As heads of the administration, they came to play an ever more important role in the province, defining the course of reforms and sometimes overruling central legislation.

This unwarranted intervention of officials into policymaking produced much tension between different branches of administration, and between the individuals employed in them. The process of negotiation often resulted in provincial bureaucrats' outright negation of core reforms, well before these reforms would be reversed by the central authorities in Vienna. Even when not directly questioning the basis of directives they were meant to implement, local bureaucrats opened new policy and political niches by finding gaps in central legislation and helping various actors negotiate exceptions to imperial decrees. Even when intended reforms were carried out, their outcomes only faintly resembled initial expectations. The key hindrance to centralization, then, came not from local aristocratic elites, but rather from Austria's own bureaucrats, conceived even as they originally had been as pillars of this same absolutism.

In Austrian Galicia, politics, culture, and economics were closely intertwined; early on, it became common knowledge that many of the province's Polish nobles were better off financially than most bureaucrats employed there. Local high society strongly appealed to Austrian officials, who, while not lacking titles, could hardly compete in rank and status with illustrious Polish aristocrats. To be sure, not all Poles had noble status, and relatively few of those that did were affluent. But those few soon came to exert a rather strong influence on the Austrian bureaucracy. As gaps between officials in Vienna and Lemberg were widening, socializing between bureaucrats and nobles in Galicia was becoming increasingly common, and these growing contacts helped bridge the divide originally separating the two groups in 1772.

CONCLUSION 1848, 1867, AND BEYOND

These two processes of provincial bureaucrats' struggle for autonomy from Vienna, and of their establishing closer ties with local elites were not directly causally linked, but took place concurrently, with consequences for Galicia and the monarchy. Even when still denied access to top positions in the administration, Polish nobles found various methods of influencing Austrian politics, for example, by forging professional and personal ties with individual Austrian bureaucrats. In the nineteenth century, the aristocratic appeal gained an increasingly national coloration. Most Austrian bureaucrats moved away from Galicia after it gained autonomy in 1867. Some, however, stayed, and their children eventually contributed to the building of nationality-oriented Galicias, whether Polish or Ruthenian/Ukrainian.

Neither Poles nor their Ruthenian and Jewish neighbors ever resigned themselves to the status of passive observers as subjects of imperial politics. All, in different ways, shaped Vienna's decisions concerning Galicia, exerting definite influences upon Austrian bureaucrats. Each group's sociopolitical life would one way or another build upon the province's Austrian experience. Galicians' encounter with modernity was invariably an imperial (or multi-imperial) one, and all in some way benefited from Austrian modernization.

A Galicia divided on national lines also revealed the contradictory legacy bequeathed by Austrian bureaucrats. On the one hand, these officials had made nationalism possible, but on the other, they prevented its radicalization. Even in the new, post-1867 Galicia, nationalisms never reached the extremes they would attain elsewhere. In the nineteenth century, most Ruthenians, and a growing number of Poles (especially after 1863) accepted Austrian rule and advocated cooperation with Vienna. Polish conservatives believed Polish needs would be served better by Austrian than by Russian or Prussian rule. Ruthenians were even more pro-Vienna, and Austrians reciprocated this friendship. Neither did Galician Jews have cause to be entirely antagonistic to the Austrian authorities; Jewish residence restrictions in the Habsburg Monarchy were milder than in Russia, and educational and professional opportunities greater.

Russian and Austrian rule created much ground for comparison, in which Vienna has often been seen in a more favorable light. In the Polish and Ukrainian historical imagination, the Habsburg Monarchy secured a place as the most lenient and tolerant of the three partitioning powers. Some of the reforms initially eliciting much discontent from contemporaries have received more positive resonance among historians; Austrian achievements in education, for instance, are impossible to ignore. The experience of parliamentarism and party struggles in local diets and the Austrian parliament, moreover, proved crucial to both Poles and Ukrainians in the twentieth century.

Despite five decades of Soviet rule in Eastern Galicia and Polish Communist rule in Western Galicia—now parts of Ukraine and Poland, respectively—their Austrian heritage proved impossible to erase. If Austria has not entirely lost interest in its former imperial domains, the reciprocal interest of Galicians in their former Habsburg sovereigns is perhaps even stronger. Contemporary politics of course plays no little role in shaping historical imagination, but in hindsight, Ukrainian narratives of history look upon the Austrian years quite fondly, as a salutary period in national formation. None of this would have been achieved without the bureaucracy. Corrupt and unqualified as it was in the short term, the Austrian bureaucracy proved, in the long run, an instrument of modernity.

NOTES

Introduction

1. Franco Venturi, *Utopia and Reform in the Enlightenment* (Cambridge: Cambridge University Press, 1971), 2.
2. Franz J. Szabo, *Kaunitz and Enlightened Absolutism 1753–1780* (Cambridge: Cambridge University Press, 1994), 6.
3. Derek Beales, "Was Joseph an Enlightened Despot?" in Ritchie Robertson and Edward Timms, eds., *The Austrian Enlightenment and Its Aftermath* (Edinburgh: Edinburgh University Press, 1991), 3; R. J. W. Evans, "Culture and Authority in Central Europe," in *Austria, Hungary, and the Habsburgs: Essays on Central Europe, c. 1693–1867* (Oxford: Oxford University Press, 2006), 59.
4. For precise geographical definitions see Stanisław Grodziski, *Historia ustroju społeczno-politycznego Galicji 1772–1848* (Wrocław: Zakład Narodowy im. Ossolińskich, 1971), 26.
5. On the general statistics see Rudolf A. Mark, *Galizien unter österreichischer Herrschaft: Verwaltung—Kirche—Bevölkerung* (Marburg: Herder-Institut, 1994), 2.
6. Larry Wolff, *Inventing Eastern Europe: The Map of Civilization on the Mind of the Enlightenment* (Stanford: Stanford University Press, 1994).
7. In 1833, during a trip to Lemberg on his way to Czernowitz, Metternich noted that the "Orient starts to show here." "Metternich à sa femme, 21 October, 1833," in *Memoirs of Prince Metternich*, ed. Prince Richard Metternich, trans. Mrs. Alexander Napier, vol. 4 (London: R. Bentley, 1881), 20.
8. Derek Beales, *Joseph II*, 2 vols. (Cambridge: Cambridge University Press, 1987–2009), 2:349.
9. Heinrich Börnstein, *Fünfundsiebzig Jahre in der Alten und Neuen Welt: Memoiren eines Unbedeutenden*, vol. 1 (Leipzig: Verlag von Otto Wigand, 1881), 36.

10. On links between Lemberg and Trieste, see Eva Faber, "Beziehungen—Gemeinsamkeiten—Besonderheiten: Das österreichische Küstenland und Galizien in der 70er und 80er Jahren des 18 Jahrhunderts," in Walter Leitsch et al., *Polen und Österreich im 18. Jahrhundert* (Warsaw: Semper, 2000), 53–79. The recently published diaries of Ludwig Zinzendorf, who was governor of Trieste during the 1780s, also well reveal important connections between Trieste and Lemberg. See Grete Klingenstein et al., *Europäische Aufklärung zwischen Wien und Triest: Die Tagebücher des Gouverneurs Karl Graf Zinzendorf 1776–1782*, 4 vols. (Vienna: Böhlau, 2009).

11. See for example, on the Netherlands, Renate Zedinger, *Die Verwaltung der Österreichischen Niederlande in Wien (1714–1795): Studien zu den Zentralisierungstendenzen des Wiener Hofes im Staatswerdungsprozess der Habsburgermonarchie* (Vienna: Böhlau, 2000); on Lombardy: Brigitte Mazohl-Wallnig, *Österreichischer Verwaltungsstaat und administrative Eliten im Königreich Lombardo-Venetien 1815–1859* (Mainz: Philipp von Zabern, 1993); on Trieste: Ugo Cova, *L'amministrazione austriaca a Trieste agli inizi dell'800* (Milan: Giuffre, 1971).

12. Karl Megner, *Beamte: Wirtschafts- und sozialgeschichtliche Aspekte des k.k. Beamtentums* (Vienna: Verlag der Österreichischen Akademie der Wissenschaften, 1986); Waltraud Heindl, *Gehorsame Rebellen: Bürokratie und Beamte in Österreich 1780 bis 1848* (Vienna: Böhlau, 1990).

13. P. G. M. Dickson, "Monarchy and Bureaucracy in Late Eighteenth-Century Austria," *English Historical Review* 110, no. 436 (April 1995): 356; Szabo, *Kaunitz and Enlightened Absolutism*, 6.

14. The stereotype of a permanent conflict between the imperial administration and local elites is well reflected in the works on different Habsburg provinces. See, for example, on Hungary: Eva Balazs, *Hungary and the Habsburgs 1765–1800: An Experiment in Enlightened Absolutism*, trans. Tim Wilkinson (Budapest: Central European University Press, 1997); on the Netherlands: Zedinger, *Die Verwaltung der Österreichischen Niederlande in Wien*; on Trieste: Giorgio Negrelli, *Comune e Impero negli storici della Trieste asburgica* (Varese: Giuffrè, 1968). One notable exception that stresses reciprocal acceptance and cooperation between center and periphery is David Laven, *Venice and Venetia under the Habsburgs 1815–1835* (Oxford: Oxford University Press, 2002).

15. Horst Glassl, *Das österreichische Einrichtungswerk in Galizien (1772–1790)* (Wiesbaden: In Kommission bei Otto Harrasowitz, 1975).

16. Grodziski, *Historia ustroju społeczno-politycznego Galicji*.

17. See Christoph Augustynowicz and Andreas Kappeler, "Einleitung," in Christoph Augustynowicz and Andreas Kappeler, eds., *Die galizische Grenze 1772–1867: Kommunikation oder Isolation?* (Berlin: LIT Verlag, 2007), 1; Hans-Christian Maner, "Zentrum und Grenzregionen in der Habsburgermonarchie im 18. und

19. Jahrhundert: Eine Einführung," in Hans-Christian Maner, ed., *Grenzregionen der Habsburgermonarchie im 18. und 19. Jahrhundert: Ihre Bedeutung und Funktion aus der Perspektive Wiens* (Münster: LIT Verlag, 2005), 10.
18. R. J. W. Evans, "Nationality in East-Central Europe: Perception and Definition before 1848," in *Austria, Hungary and the Habsburgs*, 101.
19. Larry Wolff, *The Idea of Galicia: History and Fantasy in Habsburg Political Culture* (Stanford: Stanford University Press, 2010), 4.
20. Isabel Röskau-Rydel, *Niemiecko-austriackie rodziny urzędnicze w Galicji 1772–1918: Kariery zawodowe — środowisko — akulturacja i asymilacja* (Kraków: Wydawnictwo Naukowe Uniwersytetu Pedagogicznego, 2011).
21. On the "non-Austrian bureaucracy," see Henryk Wereszycki, "Dzieje Galicji jako problem historyczny," in *Niewygasła przeszłość* (Kraków: Znak, 1987), 180–83.
22. Piotr S. Wandycz, "The Poles in the Habsburg Monarchy," in Andrei S. Markovits and Frank Sysyn, eds., *Nationbuilding and the Politics of Nationalism: Essays on Austrian Galicia* (Cambridge: Harvard Ukrainian Research Institute, 1982), 68.
23. The Administrative Archive in Vienna contains the most valuable collection of sources, but most of them are heavily damaged by fire and have been described by historians as unusable. This book is built upon thousands of those documents that have been in part preserved.

Chapter 1. Bureaucratic Enlightenment and Galicia

1. Robert Musil, *Der Mann ohne Eigenschaften*, 20th ed., ed. Adolf Frisé (Reinbeck bei Hamburg: Rowohlt, 1987), 18, 32–33. Translation from German is mine.
2. On Musil and his *The Man Without Qualities*, see David S. Luft, *Robert Musil and the Crisis of European Culture, 1880–1942* (Berkeley: University of California Press, 1980).
3. See Stefan Zweig, *The World of Yesterday* (various editions).
4. On the Habsburg myth in Austrian literature see Claudio Magris, *Der habsburgische Mythos in der modernen österreichischen Literatur* (Salzburg: O. Müller, 1966).
5. On the Austrian Empire as *Beamtenstaat* par excellence see Eva Kreisky, "Zur Genesis der politischen und sozialen Funktion der Bürokratie," in Heinz Fischer, ed., *Das politische System Österreichs* (Vienna: Europaverlag, 1974), 181–233; *Das Beamtentum in Österreich. Eine sozialpolitische Schrift* (Vienna: Druck und Verlag von Friedr. Förster und Brüder, 1861).
6. Habsburg rulers were also crowned as kings of Bohemia. The union of the (Holy Roman) imperial and Bohemian crowns was established in 1526, after the coronation of Ferdinand I (1503–64). See Robert A. Kann, *A History of the Habsburg Empire, 1526–1918* (Berkeley: University of California Press, 1974), 33.

7. Elective in principle, the title of Roman Emperor remained inherited by members of the Habsburg dynasty. A good brief definition of the Holy Roman Empire is in Christopher Clark, *Iron Kingdom: The Rise and Downfall of Prussia, 1600–1947* (Cambridge: The Belknap Press of Harvard University Press, 2006), 4–5.
8. On the foundation of districts in the monarchy, see Christian D'Elvert, *Zur österreichischen Verwaltungs-Geschichte, mit besonderer Rücksicht auf die böhmischen Länder* (Vienna: H. Geyer, 1970), 352. A more recent analysis: Waltraud Heindl, *Gehorsame Rebellen: Bürokratie und Beamte in Österreich 1780 bis 1848* (Vienna: Böhlau, 1990), 73.
9. The dedication: Johann Heinrich Gottlob von Justi, *Staatswirthschaft oder Systematische Abhandlung aller oeconomischen und cameral-wissenschaften*, vol. 1 (Leipzig, 1755), 10.
10. On differences between cameralism and *Polizeiwissenschaft* see Justi's "Vorrede" in Johann Heinrich Gottlob von Justi, *Grundsätze der Polizeiwissenschaft in einem vernünftigen, auf den Endzweck der Polizei gegruendeten Zusammenhange*, 2d ed. (Göttingen: In Verlag der Witwe Bandenkoeff, 1759).
11. Justi, *Grundsätze der Polizeiwissenschaft*, 6.
12. Michael Holzmann, *Materialien zu einer Sonnenfels-Biographie*, ed. Hugo Gold (Brünn: Jüdischer Buch- und Kunstverlag, 1931), 198.
13. On Sonnenfels' role in the reform of censorship see Franz J. Szabo, *Kaunitz and Enlightened Absolutism 1753–1780* (Cambridge: Cambridge University Press, 1994), 187.
14. This is one of the overarching themes in his introduction: Joseph von Sonnenfels, *Grundsätze der Polizey, Handlung, und Finanz: Zu dem Leitfaden des politischen Studiums*, vol. 1 (Vienna: bei J. Edlen von Kurzbek, 1786), 1–5.
15. Albion W. Small, for example, in his 1909 study, describes cameralism as a "lost chapter in the history of social sciences." See Albion W. Small, *The Cameralists: The Pioneers of German Social Polity* (1909; Kitchener: Batoche Books, 2001) 3. On Justi as the most important German cameralist, see ibid., 19. Despite receiving some attention from scholars in the twentieth century, this intellectual trend remains in the shadow of the Enlightenment. It is all too easy to forget that in German-speaking Europe, cameralism was a key aspect of the Enlightenment, the latter scarcely understandable without the former.
16. Derek Beales, "Was Joseph II an Enlightened Despot?" in Ritchie Robertson and Edward Timms, eds., *The Austrian Enlightenment and Its Aftermath* (Edinburgh: Edinburgh University Press, 1991), 3.
17. Ritchie Robertson, "Joseph Rohrer and the Bureaucratic Enlightenment," in Robertson and Timms, *The Austrian Enlightenment and Its Aftermath*, 22.
18. R. J. W. Evans, "Preface," in *Austria, Hungary and the Habsburgs: Essays on Central Europe, c. 1693–1867* (Oxford: Oxford University Press, 2006), viii.
19. Joseph von Sonnenfels, "Der Mann ohne Vorurtheil," in Joseph von Sonnenfels, *Gesammelte Schriften*, vol. 1 (Vienna: Baumeister, 1783), 126–397.

20. Part of the translation is cited after Derek Beales, "Was Joseph II an Enlightened Despot?" 12–13. The document is most commonly referred to as Joseph II's *Hirtenbrief*, 1783. See *Eine Probe der weisen Regierung Josephs des Zweyten in einem Handbillet an seine Chefs und sämtliche geistliche und weltliche Obrigkeiten* (Vienna, 1784). The other, slightly different edition is "Josephs Erinnerungen an seine Staatsbeamte am Schlusse des Jahres 1783," in Johann George Megerle von Mühlfeld, *Handbuch für alle kaiserlich-königliche, ständische und städtische Beamte*, vol. 2 (Vienna: bey Johann Georg Ritter von Mössle, 1809), 6–11. It was republished in the twentieth century by Friedrich Walter in his collection of documents on Austrian administration as "Grundsätze für jeden Diener des Staates ('Hirtenbrief' 1783)" in *Die österreichische Zentralverwaltung, pt. 2: Von der Vereinigung der österreichischen und böhmischen Hofkanzlei bis zur Einrichtung der Ministerialverfassung (1749–1848), vol. 4: Die Zeit Josephs II und Leopolds II (1780–1792). Aktenstücke*, ed. Friedrich Walter (Vienna: Adolf Holzhausens Nachfolger, 1950), 123–32.
21. This argument is developed in Friedrich Walter, *Die Geschichte der österreichischen Zentralverwaltung in der Zeit Franz II (I) und Ferdinands I 1792–1848* (Vienna: Holzhausen, 1956), 124–25.
22. Walter, "Grundsätze," 124.
23. See, for example, Karl Vocelka, "Enlightenment in the Habsburg Monarchy: History of a Belated and Short-Lived Phenomenon," in Ole Peter and Roy Porter, eds., *Toleration in Europe* (Cambridge: Cambridge University Press, 2000), 196–212; Robertson and Timms, *The Austrian Enlightenment and Its Aftermath*. On the political and intellectual phenomenon of Josephinism see Ferdinand Maas, *Der Josephinismus: Quellen zu seiner Geschichte in Österreich: Amtliche Dokumente aus dem Wiener Haus-, Hof- und Staatsarchiv*, vol. 1 (Vienna: Herold Verlag, 1951).
24. "§6. Hofentschliessung vom 23. Jänner 1778," in Megerle von Mühlfeld, *Handbuch für alle kaiserlich-königliche, ständische und städtische Beamte, deren Witwen und Waissen*, vol. 2 (Vienna: bey Johann Georg Ritter von Mössle, 1809), 9. Official requirements from all incoming bureaucrats are discussed in Heindl, *Gehorsame Rebellen*, 135.
25. "Hofentschliessung vom 19. Juni 1765," "Hofentschliessung vom 28. März 1776," in Mühlfeld, *Handbuch*, 61; "Hofkanzlei vom 1 Hornung 1804," in J. F., *Handbuch der Gesetze, Verordnungen und Vorschriften für k.k. österreichische Staatsbeamte* (Vienna: Wilhelm Braumüller, 1857), 3.
26. Derek Beales, *Joseph II*, 2 vols. (Cambridge: Cambridge University Press, 1987–2009), 2:93. See also Ernst Wangermann, *From Joseph II to the Jacobin Trials: Government Policy and Public Opinion in the Habsburg Dominions in the Period of the French Revolution* (Oxford: Oxford University Press, 1959), 5–16.
27. For a general overview of these publications, see Ludwig Neulinger, "Die Beamten im Spiegel der josephinischen Broschüren," *Biblos* 29 (1980): 175–83.

28. These three works were published anonymously, but all are attributed to Joseph Richter: *Die Regierung des Hanswurstes: Eine Komödie aus dem vorigen Jahrhundert* (Salzburg, 1786); *Das Handbillet des Hanswurstes: Eine Beilage zur Regierung des Hanswurstes* (Salzburg, 1786); *Der Tod des Hanswurstes: Die letzte Beylage zur Regierung des Hanswurstes* (Salzburg, 1787).
29. Richter, *Die Regierung des Hanswurstes*, 7.
30. [Joseph Richter], *Warum wird Kaiser Joseph von seinem Volk nicht geliebt?* (Vienna: Wucherer, 1787).
31. Walter, *Die österreichische Zentralverwaltung*, 124.
32. Sangilla von Freundsperg, *Die Hofräthe in ****: Ein altes Manuscriptsfragment* (Vienna: in Linharts Buchbindergewölbe am Kohlmarkte beym Baylerthore, 1782), 1, 7, 10 (on the privilege of birth), 24 (on marrying well), 40.
33. *Fragment eines Gespräches über das Verhältniss des Staates mit seinen Beamten* (Sieghartstein: in der Mossfleckischen Buchhandlung, 1783), 3, 6.
34. Ibid., 29.
35. Ibid., 34.
36. *Schicksale eines Praktikanten von 55 Jahren: Als eine Warnung für die Herrn Studenten* (Vienna: bey Sebastian Karti, 1781), 30.
37. Ibid.
38. Musil, *Der Mann ohne Eigenschaften*, 375.
39. Heindl, *Gehorsame Rebellen*, 25.
40. The Habsburgs borrowed the idea of qualification tables from Prussia. See Walter L. Don, "The Prussian Bureaucracy in the Eighteenth Century," pt. 2, *Political Science Quarterly* 47, no. 1 (1932): 75–94.
41. On the Black Lists see Heindl, *Gehorsame Rebellen*, 27.
42. Waltraud Heindl has argued that the qualification tables demonstrated the state's hold on its bureaucracy. Another historian, Walter Don, claimed that state officials became the slaves of the state. Heindl, *Gehorsame Rebellen*, 27; Don, "The Prussian Bureaucracy in the Eighteenth Century," 94.
43. Vienna skipped the second partition in 1793.
44. Larry Wolff, "Inventing Galicia: Messianic Josephinism and the Recasting of Partitioned Poland," *Slavic Review* 63, no. 4 (Winter 2004): 820.
45. Edith Rosenstrauch-Königsberg, "Galizien nach der ersten Teilung Polens—eine Stätte der Begegnung," in *Zirkel und Zentren: Aufsätze zur Aufklärung in Österreich am Ende des 18 Jahrhunderts*, ed. Gunnar Hering, introd. Ernst Wangermann (Vienna: Deuticke, 1992), 245.
46. Szabo, *Kaunitz and Enlightened Absolutism*, 66.
47. A detailed analysis of this: Larry Wolff, *The Vatican and Poland in the Age of the Partitions: Diplomatic and Cultural Encounters in the Warsaw Nunciature* (Boulder: East European Monographs, 1988), 9–14.
48. Wolff, *The Vatican and Poland in the Age of the Partitions*, 3.

49. Hans-Jürgen Bömelburg, "Aufgeklärte Beamte gegen barock-katholischen Adelseliten: Ein Vergleich der österreichischen und preußischen Verwaltungspraxis in Galizien und Westpreußen (1772–1806)," in Walter Leitsch and Stanislaw Tarkowski, eds., *Polen und Österreich im 18. Jahrhundert* (Warsaw: Semper, 2000), 23–24.
50. Ignaz Beidtel, *Geschichte der österreichischen Staatsverwaltung 1740–1848*, vol. 1 (Innsbruck: Verlag der Wagnerischen Universitäts-Buchhandlung, 1896), 160.
51. Stanisław Grodziski, *Historia ustroju społeczno politycznego Galicji, 1772–1848* (Wrocław: Zakład Narodowy im. Ossolińskich, 1971), 27.
52. P. G. M. Dickson, *Finance and Government under Maria Theresia 1740–1780*, 2 vols. (Oxford: Oxford University Press, 1987), 1:286.
53. On similarities between Hungary and Galicia see ibid., 54–56, 103–104. On the option of uniting Hungary and Galicia, ibid., 286.
54. *Wienerisches Diarium von Staats-, vermischten, und gelehrten Neuigkeiten*, Nro 103 (Mittwoch den 23 Christmonat 1772).
55. Grodziski, *Historia ustroju społeczno politycznego Galicji*, 154.
56. A detailed chronological account of administrative reorganization of Galicia: ÖStA, AVA, HK III A 3, 309a: Hofkommission in galizischen Angelegenheiten, 1792–1793: Galizische Hof-deputation u. Hofkanzley Errichtung und Aufhebung.
57. Rudolf A. Mark, *Galizien unter Österreichischer Herrschaft: Verwaltung—Kirche—Bevölkerung* (Marburg: Herder-Institut, 1994), 6.
58. Wolff, "Inventing Galicia," 821.
59. HHStA, StK, Vorträge, 113: Maria Theresa to Kaunitz, 2 September 1773.
60. On Poland's paradoxical political development see Hubert Orlowski, *"Polnische Wirtschaft": Zum deutschen Polendiskurs der Neuzeit* (Wiesbaden: Harrassowitz, 1996), 97–101.
61. Jerzy Michalski, ed., *Historia sejmu polskiego*, vol. 1: *Do schyłku szlacheckiej rzeczypospolitej* (Warsaw: Państwowe Wydawnictwo Naukowe, 1984), 151.
62. Teresa Zielińska, *Magnateria polska epoki saskiej: Funkcje urzędów i królewszczyzn w procesie przeobrażeń warstwy społecznej* (Warsaw: Zakład Narodowy imienia Ossolińskich, Wydawnictwo Polskiej Akademii Nauk, 1977), 46.
63. On the myth of Polish nobility, see Daniel Beauvois, *Pouvoir russe et noblesse polonaise en Ukraine 1793–1830* (Paris: CNRS Editions, 2003), 24–49.
64. Gershon David Hundert, *Jews in Poland-Lithuania in the Eighteenth Century: A Genealogy of Modernity* (Berkeley: University of California Press, 2004), 3.
65. Vadym Adadurov, "L'viv u napoleonivsku epokhu," *L'viv: Misto, suspil'stvo, kul'tura* 3 (1999): 209.
66. Joseph to Maria Theresia, Lemberg, 1 August 1773, in Alfred Ritter von Arneth, ed., *Maria Theresia und Joseph II: Ihre Korrespondenz samt Briefen Joseph's an seinen Bruder Leopold*, 2 vols. (Vienna: Druck und Verlag von Carl Gerold's Sohn, 1868), 2:13.

67. Franz Kratter, "Sechster Brief: Philosophische Fakultät," in *Briefe über den itzigen Zustand von Galizien: Ein Beitrag zur Statistik und Menschenkenntnis*, pt. 1 (1786; Berlin: Helmut Scherer Verlag, 1990), 49.
68. For information on Kratter see Stanisław Schnür-Pepłowski, *Galiciana, 1772–1812* (Lwów, 1896), 15–21.
69. Edith Rosenstrauch-Königsberg, "Ratchkys Reise nach Galizien im Auftrag Kaiser Joseph II," in *Zirkel und Zentren*, 117.
70. ÖStA, AVA, HK II A 6, 229: Neue Provinzen. Staatsverwaltung, Galizien bis 1776.
71. Jerzy Lukowski, *The Partitions of Poland 1772, 1793, 1795* (London: Longman, 1999), 83.
72. Karin Friedrich, *The Other Prussia: Royal Prussia, Poland and Liberty, 1569–1772* (Cambridge: Cambridge University Press, 2000), 48.
73. Horst Glassl, *Das Österreichische Einrichtungswerk in Galizien (1772–1790)* (Wiesbaden: In Kommission bei Otto Harrasowitz, 1975), 51.
74. Roman Rybarski, *Skarbowość Polski w dobie rozbiorów* (Kraków: Nakładem Polskiej Akademii Umiejętności, 1937), 9.
75. A concise recent overview of the intellectual tradition of the Polish Enlightenment is Richard Butterwick, "What Is Enlightenment (Oświecenie)? Some Polish Answers," *Central Europe* 3, no. 1 (May 2005): 19–37.
76. Henryk Hinz and Adam Sikora, eds., *Polska myśl filozoficzna: Oświecenie, Romantyzm* (Warsaw: Państwowe Wydawnictwo Naukowe, 1964), 17–47. On the Polish Enlightenment see also Zdzisław Libera, *Od Sejmu Czteroletniego do Napoleona* (Warsaw: Wydawnictwo Instytutu Badań Literackich PAN, 2004).
77. On Kołłątai and the Educational Commission see Jerzy Lukowski, *Liberty's Folly: The Polish-Lithuanian Commonwealth in the Eighteenth Century, 1697–1795* (London: Routledge, 1991), 218–28; Andrzej Walicki, *Poland Between East and West*, 12–13. On the commission and a new education curriculum see also Butterwick, "What Is Enlightenment (Oświecenie)?" 24–25.
78. On the religious aspects of the Polish Enlightenment see Lukowski, *Liberty's Folly*, 232.

Chapter 2. Civilizers at Work

1. HHStA, StK, Vorträge, 113: Maria Theresa to Kaunitz, 2 September 1773.
2. In 1776, only two Polish officials were allowed to take up positions in the Galician Gubernium: Hans-Christian Maner, *Galizien: Eine Grenzregion im Kalkül der Donaumonarchie im 18. und 19. Jahrhundert* (Munich: IKGS Verlag, 2007), 44.
3. On the continuities of the Austrian bureaucracy between the 1780s and 1848, see R. J. W. Evans, "Josephinism, 'Austrianness,' and the Revolution of 1848," in *The Austrian Enlightenment and Its Aftermath* (Edinburgh: Edinburgh University Press, 1991), 145–60.

4. A detailed biography is Paul P. Bernard, *From the Enlightenment to the Police State: The Public Life of Johann Anton Pergen* (Urbana: Illinois University Press, 1991), 4.
5. Bernard, *From the Enlightenment to the Police State*, 55. On the Kaunitz-Pergen cooperation, see also Franz J. Szabo, *Kaunitz and Enlightened Absolutism, 1753–1780* (Cambridge: Cambridge University Press, 1994), 193.
6. On Pergen's involvement in educational reform, see Joseph Alexander Freiherr von Helfert, *Die Gründung der Österreichischen Volksschule durch Maria Theresia* (Prague: Friedrich Tempthy, 1860), 191–94.
7. For a detailed outline of his program, see ibid., 191–94. James Van Horn Melton, *Absolutism and the Eighteenth-Century Origins of Compulsory Schooling in Prussia and Austria* (Cambridge: Cambridge University Press, 1988), 204.
8. For a detailed discussion of the "German episode" see Helfert, *Die Gründung der Österreichischen Volksschule*, 190–251.
9. Bronisław Pawłowski, *Zajęcie Lwowa 1772 przez Austryę* (Lwów: Nakładem Towarzystwa Miłośników Przeszłości Lwowa, 1911), 55.
10. Franz Szabo, for example, found reason "to believe that this appointment was something equal to a promotion." See Franz J. Szabo, "Austrian First Impressions of Ethnic Relations in Galicia: The Case of Governor Anton von Pergen," in *Polin: Studies in Polish Jewry* 12 (1999): 50.
11. Horst Glassl, *Das österreichische Einrichtungswerk in Galizien (1772–1790)* (Wiesbaden: In Kommission bei Otto Harrasowitz, 1975), 35.
12. On the annexation and administration of the Banat, see Josef Kallbrunner, *Das kaiserliche Banat: Einrichtung und Entwicklung des Banats bis 1739* (Munich: Verlag des Südostdeutschen Kulturwerks, 1958).
13. Pawłowski, *Zajęcie Lwowa*, 53–60.
14. Members of the so-called Confederation of Bar, who between 1768 and 1772 staged a rebellion against the Polish king Stanisław August because of his reliance on Russia, thereby constituting, for the governor, an example of aristocratic fractiousness.
15. ÖStA, AVA, HK, II A 6 (Gal)—1776, 229, August 1772: Pro Nota des Grafen von Pergen.
16. HHStA, StK, Vorträge 111: 1773 (I-V): Februar Copia des Grafen Pergens Berichts addo Lemberg den 25. Januar 1773.
17. On Tadeusz Dzieduszycki, see Kazimierz Karolczak, *Dzieduszyccy: Dzieje rodu. Linia poturzycko-zarecka* (Kraków: Wydawnictwo Naukowe Akademii Pedagogicznej, 2001), 39. On Polish loyalty toward the Habsburg court, see Stanisław Grodziski, "Schyłek stanu szlacheckiego na ziemiach polskich," in Janina Leskiewiczowa, ed., *Społeczenstwo polskie XVIII i XIX wieku* (Warsaw: Państwowe Wydawnictwo Naukowe, 1987), 98.
18. Szabo, "Austrian First Impressions of Ethnic Relations in Galicia," 53.
19. ÖStA, AVA, HK, II, A, 6, 229: Pro Nota, Pergen, 30 August 1772.

20. On the shortage of proper buildings, see Wacław Tokarz, *Galicya w początkach ery józefińskiej w świetle ankiety urzędowej z roku 1783* (Kraków: Akademia Umiejętności, 1909), 337.
21. ÖStA, AVA, HK, II A 6 (Gal)–1776, 229, May 1776.
22. ÖStA, AVA, HK, II A 6, 229, (Gal)—1776: Sätze und Anfragen des Grafen von Pergen, September 1772. Władysław Łoziński, *Galiciana: Kilka obrazków z pierwszych lat historyi galicyjskiej* (Lwów: Nakładem Karola Wilda, 1872), 6.
23. Bernard, *From the Enlightenment to the Police State*, 97.
24. HHStA, StK, Vorträge, 110. 1772 (VIII–XII): Kaunitz to Maria Theresa, 11 November 1772.
25. On gaps in the historiography of the central Austrian bureaucracy, see P. G. M. Dickson, "Monarchy and Bureaucracy in Late Eighteenth Century Austria," *English Historical Review* 110, no. 436 (April 1995): 326–67.
26. Ibid., 356.
27. Karl Megner, *Beamte: Wirtschafts- und sozialgeschichtliche Aspekte des k.k. Beamtentums* (Vienna: Verlag der Österreichischen Akademie der Wissenschaften, 1986), 30.
28. On the shortage of officials: HHStA, HR, 5: Journal von der Reiße S. Majest. In Galizien samt Beilagen 1773, vol. 2, p. 8; Pergen's report of April 1773: ÖStA, AVA, HK III A 4, 321, Gubern, Nd. Regierung Galizien—1783, April 1773: Vortrag ex April 1773.
29. Pawłowski, *Zajęcie Lwowa*, 55.
30. HHStA, StK, Vorträge, 110: Kaunitz to Maria Theresa, 11 November 1772.
31. ÖStA, AVA, HK III A 4, 321, Gubern, Nd. Regierung Galizien—1783: Vortrag ex April 1773. TsDIAUL, f. 146, op. 4, spr. 120: Besondere Akten, Gubernator Pergen, Chlennyi spysok sluzhbovciv hubernatorstva (z anketnymy danymy).
32. HHStA, HR, 5: Journal von der Reiße S. Majest. In Galizien samt Beilagen 1773, vol. 2, p. 8, 34. On the shortage of bureaucrats see also Glassl, *Das österreichische Einrichtungswerk in Galizien (1772–1790)*, 88.
33. ÖStA, AVA, HK, III A 4, 321: Gubern, Nd. Regierung Galizien—1783, ex April 1773.
34. Svjatoslav Pacholkiv, "Das Werden einer Grenze: Galizien 1772–1867," in Waltraud Heindl and Edith Saurer, eds., *Grenze und Staat: Passwesen, Staatsbürgerschaft, Heimatrecht und Fremdengesetzgebung in der österreichischen Monarchie, 1750–1867* (Vienna: Böhlau, 2000), 535; Rudolf A. Mark, *Galizien unter österreichischer Herrschaft: Verwaltung-Kirche-Bevölkerung* (Marburg: Herder-Institut, 1994), 2. On shortages of bureaucrats see also Glassl, *Das österreichische Einrichtungswerk in Galizien*, 88.
35. Bernard, *From the Enlightenment to the Police State*, 67–75, 93–111.
36. On language requirements and preferences for Bohemia: HHStA, StK, Vorträge, 113: Kaunitz to Joseph II, 2 September 1773.

37. HHStA, StK, Vorträge 113, 1773 (IX–XII), 2. September 1773: Elaborat zur Beantwortung der von S.M. dem Kaiser aufgestellten 154 Fragenpunkte.
38. Characteristics of individual officials: TsDIAUL, f. 146, op. 4, spr. 20, Besondere Akten, Gubernator Pergen, Chlennyi spysok sluzhbovtsiv hubernatorstva (z anketnymy danymy). The most detailed documentation on Kaunitz's selection, his correspondence with Pergen, the transportation of bureaucrats from Bohemia, Silesia, and Hungary to Galicia, financial expenditures, and the first arrangements in Galicia is TsDIAUL, f. 146, op. 1, spr. 123, Perepyska pro pryznachennia i zvil'nennia sluzhbovtsiv, 1772–1773.
39. ÖStA, HK, Vorträge, 113, 1773 (IX–XII): Vortrag des Fürsten Kaunitz, 2. September 1773.
40. A complete list of the Gubernium personnel in 1773 is TsDIAUL, f. 146, op. 4, spr. 120. On the appointment of Gubernium personnel in April–May 1773 see ÖStA, HK, III A 4, 321 Gubern. Nd Regierung, Galizien, –1783: Vortrag 15. April 1773. TsDIAUL, Besondere Akten, Gubernator Pergen. Chlennyi spysok sluzhbovtsiv hubernatorstva (z anketnymy danymy), pp. 1–2.
41. TsDIAUL, f. 146, op. 4, spr. 120, Besondere Akten, Gubernator Pergen. Chlennyi spysok sluzhbovtsiv gubernatorstva (z anketnymy danymy).
42. Tokarz, *Galicya w początkach ery józefińskiej*, 20.
43. HHStA, StK, Vorträge, 113: Vortrag des Fürsten Kaunitz, 2. September 1773.
44. ÖStA, AVA, HK, II A 6 (Gal)—1776, 229: Pergen an Kaunitz, 5 Februar 1773; Alfred Ritter von Arneth, *Geschichte Maria Theresia's*, vol. 10 (Vienna: Wilhelm Braumüller, 1879), 86.
45. Glassl, *Das österreichische Einrichtungswerk in Galizien*, 95; HHStA, StK, Polen III: Faszikel 13, Innere Verwaltung 1772–1803: Systematisierung der galizischen Regierung, 228.
46. ÖStA, AVA, HK IV M I, 1319: Polizeibehörden Galizien, 1773; HHStA, SK, Vorträge, 113: Vortrag des Fürsten Kaunitz, 2. September 1772. Paul Bernard argues that "Pergen bluntly ignored Maria Theresa's wish that a majority of the members of his administration be drawn from a pool of names recommended to him by the court." See Bernard, *From the Enlightenment to the Police State*, 98. This seems to be an overstatement. It took about a year for Kaunitz to produce a list. By that time, Pergen had already filled some posts. Kaunitz, himself aware of the difficulties, endorsed the governor's actions.
47. HHStA, StK, Polen III Fasz. 13: Innere Verwaltung 1772–1803 Polen, Fasz. 71: Pergen, Lemberg, September 1773, pp. 23–26.
48. HHStA, Polen III, Fasz. 13: Innere Verwaltung 1772–1803: Nachricht von der bey dem Gouvernement in Galizien beobachtenden Untätigkeit, p. 16.
49. HHStA, Polen III, Fasz. 13: Innere Verwaltung 1772–1803: Nachricht von der bey den Gouvernement in Galizien beobachtenden Untätigkeit, p. 20.

50. HHStA, Polen III, Fasz. 13: Innere Verwaltung 1772–1803: Nachricht von der bey den Gouvernement in Galizien beobachtenden Untätigkeit, p. 18.
51. Paul Bernard describes the growing opposition and conspiracies against Pergen at the Galician Gubernium. See Bernard, *From the Enlightenment to the Police State*, 108–11.
52. HHStA, Polen III, 1773, Innere Verwaltung 1772–1803. Fasz. 13: Nachricht von der bey den Gouvernement in Galizien beobachtenden Untätigkeit.
53. HHStA, StK, Polen III 14. Innere Verwaltung 1772–1803. Polen, Fasz. 71. Pergen to Maria Theresa, Leopol, October–November 1773, pp. 24–25.
54. HHStA, HR, 5, Joseph's II assessment of Pergen in 1773: Journal von der Reiße S. Majest. in Galizien samt Beilagen 1773, vol. 2, pp. 7–8.
55. The Galician Court Chancellery was disbanded in 1777, created again in 1797, and liquidated again in 1802. See ÖStA, AVA, HK III A 3, 309a: Galizische Hofdeputation u. Hofkanzlei Errichtung und Aufhebung, Hofkommission in galizischen Angelegenheiten, 1792–1793.
56. On Auersperg's appointment: ÖStA, AVA, HK, III A 4, 321: Maria Theresa to Graf Wrbna, Ex majo 1774.
57. Barbara Lasocka, *Teatr Lwowski w latach 1800–1842* (Warsaw: Państwowy Instytut Wydawniczy, 1967), 19. On the lack of achievements in Galicia during Auersperg's governorship see Arneth, *Geschichte Maria Theresia's*, 10:95. On Joseph II's disappointment with Auersperg see also Glassl, *Das österreichische Einrichtungswerk in Galizien*, 87.
58. On parallels between the Austrian Littoral and Galicia, see Eva Faber, "Beziehungen—Gemeinsamkeiten—Besonderheiten: Das österreichische Küstenland und Galizien in der 70er und 80er Jahren des 18 Jahrhunderts," in Walter Leitsch et al., eds., *Polen und Österreich im 18. Jahrhundert* (Warsaw: Semper, 2000), 53–79.
59. ÖStA, AVA, HK, III A 4, 321 Gubern. Nd Regierung, Galizien, –1783, 36 ex November 1776: Status des Kaiserlich Königlichen Provinzial u. Cameral Personalis.
60. Brigido was alternatively described as Kommissär, Regierungspräsident, and most often as Gouverneur. For the sake of clarity and convenience, I will only use the term Governor here.
61. Governors and other top administrative personnel usually resided in allocated housing in the center of Lemberg.
62. The Gubernium published annual reports, which listed all the employed personnel, their current and previous positions, and their salaries. See ÖStA, AVA, HK, III A 4, 321: Nd. Regierung, Galizien—1783, 36 ex November 1776: Status des Kaiserlich. Königl. Provinzial u. Cameral Personalis Kais. Königl. Landes Gubernium.

63. Vienna kept various records of its officials. One of the best sources on the composition of the Austrian bureaucracy is the so-called *Conduitlisten*, the qualification tables that recorded every bureaucrat beneath the rank of minister. On the *Conduitlisten*, see above, p. 33.
64. On the Brigidos see Grete Klingenstein et al., *Europäische Aufklärung zwischen Wien und Triest: Die Tagebücher des Gouverneurs Karl Graf Zinzendorf 1776–1782*, 4 vols. (Vienna: Böhlau, 2009), 4:75. Also Archivio di Stato di Trieste. Giudizio Civico e provinciale in Trieste. Atti civili busta 86, fedecommesso Brigido.
65. On Pompeius von Brigido as governor of Trieste, see Ugo Cova, *L'amministrazione austriaca a Trieste agli inizi dell'800* (Milan: Giuffrè, 1971), 9; HHStA, KA, KFA, 86 [alt 79], Brigido 1792. On Johann Wenzel von Brigido see Johann Svoboda, *Die Theresianische Militär-Akademie zu Wiener-Neustadt und Ihre Zöglinge von der Gründung der Anstalt bis auf unsere Tage*, vol. 1 (Vienna: Seidel, 1873), 3.
66. Salzburg at the time did not belong to the Habsburg Monarchy but formed a semi-independent bishopric. In the late eighteenth century it hosted one of the best universities in German-speaking Europe. See David Sorkin, *The Religious Enlightenment: Protestants, Jews and Catholics from London to Vienna* (Princeton: Princeton University Press, 2008), 221.
67. See Joseph Hans Irmen, ed., *Die Protokolle der Wiener Freimaurerloge "Zur wahren Eintracht" (1781–1785)* (Frankfurt am Main: Peter Lang, 1994), 322; Hermann Schüttler, *Die Mitglieder des Illuminatenordens 1776–1787/93* (Munich: Ars Una, 1991), 30.
68. HHStA, KA, KFA, 86 [alt 79]: Brigido aus Galizien 1792; Arneth, *Geschichte Maria Theresia's*, 10:97.
69. Charles Ingrao, *The Habsburg Monarchy 1618–1815*, 2d ed. (Cambridge: Cambridge University Press, 2000), 203.
70. Brigido was bilingual in German and Italian. He corresponded in German with his mother and in Italian with his brothers. HHStA, Kaiser Franz Akten alt 165: Präsentation von verschiedenen Hofstellen, Wien, 24 Febr. 1759.
71. Maria Theresa's endorsement of Brigido: Klingenstein et al., *Europäische Aufklärung zwischen Wien und Triest*, 11 January 1778, 2:116.
72. Arneth, *Geschichte Maria Theresia's*, 10:98.
73. Klingenstein et al., *Europäische Aufklärung zwischen Wien und Triest*, 2:116.
74. Ibid., 30 December 1777, 90.
75. See Derek Beales, *Joseph II*, 2 vols. (Cambridge: Cambridge University Press, 1987–2009), 2:48.
76. Klingenstein et al., *Europäische Aufklärung zwischen Wien und Triest*, 31 July 1777, 2:22.
77. On Joseph II's disappointment with Galicia's administration, see Glassl, *Das österreichische Einrichtungswerk in Galizien*, 88.

78. HHStA, FA, HR, 11, Alt 11/3: Joseph II Bericht aus Galizien, 1780, 9.
79. HHStA, FA, HR, 11, Alt 11/3: Joseph II Bericht aus Galizien, 1780, 10.
80. On the complaints and denunciations: ÖStA, AVA, HK III A 4, 401: k.k. Kreisämter Dalm, Gal.—1786: Joseph Graf von Brigido über die Denunciation eines Joseph Branda.
81. Łoziński, *Galiciana*, 37.
82. Tokarz, *Galicya w początkach ery józefińskiej*, 60.
83. On Guinigi and Strosseldo see Władysław Łoziński, "Pierwsi urzędnicy niemieccy," 48–50.
84. Tokarz, *Galicya w początkach ery józefińskiej*, 93.
85. Ibid., 44.
86. Klingenstein et al., *Europäische Aufklärung zwischen Wien und Triest*, 23 January 1779, 3:353.
87. HHStA, FA, HR, 11, Alt 11/3: Joseph II Bericht aus Galizien, 1780, 9.
88. Klingenstein et al., *Europäische Aufklärung zwischen Wien und Triest*, 30 December 1777, 2:90.
89. ÖStA, AVA, HK II A 6, 231. Gal. 1777–1783: Nota 1 ex September 1780.
90. Beales, *Joseph II*, 1:365.
91. ÖStA, AVA, HK, III A 5, 402: Brigido, Die Mangel und die dagegen einzuleitende Abhilfe.
92. Tokarz, *Galicya w początkach ery józefińskiej*, 56. On the financial situation in Lemberg see Janina Bielecka, *Kontrakty lwowskie w latach 1768–1775* (Poznań: Nakładem Poznańskiego Towarzystwa Przyjaciół Nauk, 1948).
93. On rents in Lemberg see Joseph Rohrer, *Bemerkungen auf einer Reise von der türkischen Grenze über die Bukowina durch Ost- und Westgalizien, Schlesien und Mähren nach Wien* (Berlin: Scherer, 1989), 156.
94. Tokarz, *Galicya w początkach ery józefińskiej*, 56–57.
95. ÖStA, AVA, HK, III. A. 5, 402 A: k.k. Kreisämter, Galizien 1787–März 1808.
96. ÖStA, AVA, HK, III A 4, 321, Gubern. Nd Regierung, Galizien—1783, Maio 1774: Für die polnische Aktenliquidierung.
97. On Brigido's vision of the Habsburg Monarchy and Galicia's role within it: HHStA, KA, KFA, 10 [alt 11], Galizische Angelegenheiten, 1792: Vorschlag des Gouv. Grafen Brigido über das Begehren der Galizischen Stände.
98. ÖStA, AVA, HK, II A 6, 231, Gal. 1777–1783: Nota, 1 ex September 1780.
99. TsDIAUL, f. 146, op. 1, spr. 233, Besondere Akten. Korolivskyi komisar graf Brigido.
100. ÖStA, AVA, HK III A 5, 401: k.k. Kreisämter, Dalm. Gal.—1786: Bericht über die Denunciation eines Joseph Branda.
101. ÖStA, AVA, HK, III A 4, 321, Gubern. Nd. Regierung, Galizien–1783: Extractus Protocoli Der Kaiser. Königl. Oberste Justiz Stelle von 24. Dezember 1782.
102. "1788, Kreisschreiben über die Nachholung der mangelnden Berufsstudien, für wirklich Angestellte, und nicht Angestellte," in *Kontynuacya Wyrókow y Rozkazów*

Powszechnych w Galicyi y Lodomeryi Królestwach (Leopoli: Typis Antonii Piller Sacr. Caes. Reg. Apost. Majest. Generalis. Typogr., [1773]), 95.
103. ÖStA, AVA, HK, III B 1, 423: Vorschriften für Beamte—1799, 46 ex Juni 1787 (an Galicien).
104. Tokarz, *Galicya w początkach ery józefińskiej*, 74.
105. ÖStA, AVA, HK, II A 6, 232: Margelik, Galizien Betreffend Ausarbeitung.
106. Jan Fellerer, *Mehrsprachigkeit im galizischen Verwaltungswesen (1772–1914): Eine historisch-soziolinguistische Studie zum Polnischen und Ruthenischen (Ukrainischen)* (Cologne: Böhlau, 2005), 43; Tokarz, *Galicya w początkach ery józefińskiej*, 62.
107. Tokarz, *Galicya w początkach ery józefińskiej*, 5.
108. On the preferences for local languages see Fellerer, *Mehrsprachigkeit*, 43.
109. Beales, *Joseph II*, 1:365.
110. Roman Rozdolski, *Stosunki poddańcze w dawnej Galicji*, vol. 1 (Warsaw: Państwowe Wydawnictwo Naukowe, 1962), 25.
111. See Roman Rozdolski, *Die Große Steuer- und Agrarreform Josefs II* (Warsaw: Państwowe Wydawnictwo Naukowe, 1961), 9–10. On the landowners' payment in Poland see Lukowski, *Liberty's Folly: The Polish-Lithuanian Commonwealth in the Eighteenth Century, 1697–1795* (London: Routledge, 1991), 9. During the 1780s, Austrian officials still debated the mechanisms of tax collection. At the center of the debates was the question of how to calculate the tax—whether it should be based on the value of land or on the income that land potentially produced. Each of the numbers would be difficult to calculate precisely. In either case, Austrian officials would have to rely on the landlords who were obliged to submit their own good faith estimates of the land's value and its approximate income.
112. Scholars have long explained that the reforms of the Austrian Enlightenment were driven primarily by pragmatic and often simply fiscal considerations. See for example P. G. M. Dickson, *Finance and Government under Maria Theresa 1740–1780*, 2 vols. (Oxford: Oxford University Press, 1987), 1:15.
113. Rozdolski, *Die Große Steuer- und Agrarreform Josefs II*, 20.
114. Archiwum Państwowe w Krakowie, Teki Barwieńskiego, Einteilung der Materien über die H. Gubernialrathe: Brigido Akten nr. 101, 3. Januar 1784.
115. Rozdolski, *Stosunki poddancze*, 123–24.
116. Władysław Łoziński, "Anonim," in *Galiciana*, 111–17.
117. HHStA, Kabinettsarchiv, Kaiser Franz Akten, 10 [alt 11]: Galizische Angelegenheiten, 1792: Rapport des gub. Rath. Lezzeny über die galizischen Sachen.
118. On the founding of new schools: ÖStA, AVA, HK, II A 3, 26, 877, Mai 1774: Continuatio Protocolli in Galizischen Einrichtungssachen, Add. 16. und 18. Aprilis 1774.
119. Mieczysław Adamczyk, *Szkoły obce w edukacji Galicjan* (Warsaw: Oficyna Wydawnicza Rytm, 2003), 59.

120. On the Germanization of education in Galicia under Joseph II see Stefan Ignacy Możdżeń, *Historia wychowania, 1795–1918* (Kielce: Wydawnictwo Stachurski, 2000), 180; Stanisław Michalski, ed., *Dzieje szkolnictwa i oświaty na wsi polskiej*, vol. 1. (Warsaw: Ludowa Spółdzielnia Wydawnicza, 1982), 249.
121. ÖStA, AVA, HK, II A 6, 232: Margelik, Galizien Betreffend Ausarbeitung.
122. On school creation and poor attendance see ÖStA, AVA, HK, II A 6, 232: Margelik, Galizien Betreffend Ausarbeitung.
123. ÖstA, AVA, HK, II A 6, 231: Ad 108 ex Dezember 1783.
124. The Gubernium's arrangements for the establishment of schools and preparation for the opening of the university: ÖStA, AVA, HK, II A 6, 230, 159 ex Juli 1783: Brigidos Handbillet. Brigido's participation in the opening of the university: Ludwik Finkel, *Historia Uniwersytetu Lwowskiego* (Lwów: Nakładem Senatu Akademickiego C.K. Uniwersytetu Lwowskiego, 1894), 56.
125. Stanisław Pepłowski, *Teatr Polski we Lwowie (1780–1881)* (Lwów: Skład Główny w Księgarni Gubrynowicza i Schmidta, 1859), 41.
126. Brigido's report: TsDIAUL, f. 146, op. 1, spr. 154, An Seine Maje. Des galizischen Königr. Kommissar Grafen von Brigido gehorsamste Anzeige Januar 1784, 1–34.
127. On translations and reinterpretations see Fellerer, *Mehrsprachigkeit*, 71.
128. Tokarz, *Galicya w początkach ery józefińskiej*, 117.
129. Beales, *Joseph II*, 2:248.
130. TsDIAUL, f. 146, op. 1, spr, 136. Besondere Akten: Doklad gubernatora Brigido, 1793, p. 2.
131. Łoziński, "Anonim," 111–17.
132. Roger Bauer, *Die Welt als Reich Gottes: Grundlage und Wandlungen einer österreichischen Lebensform* (Vienna: Europa Verlag, 1974), 38.
133. ÖStA, AVA, HK, III A 3, 309a: Bericht, 11.V.1793.
134. On Brigido's last year in Lemberg, the denunciation, and his retirement see ÖStA, AVA, HK, 325, 3 A 4, Gal: Aus der Präsidialkanzlei, April 1794.
135. Bernard, *From the Enlightenment to the Police State*, 115–58.
136. ÖStA, AVA, HK, III A 3, 309a: Bericht, 11.V.1793.
137. On Joseph II and Enlightenment despotism see Derek Beales, "Was Joseph II an Enlightened Despot?" in Ritchie Robertson and Edward Timms, eds., *The Austrian Enlightenment and Its Aftermath* (Edinburgh: Edinburgh University Press, 1991), 1–21.

Chapter 3. The Napoleonic Test

1. Brigido's report from 1790: "Bericht des Grafen Brigido, Januar 1790," in Paul von Mitrofanov, *Joseph II: Seine politische und kulturelle Tätigkeit*, trans. V. von Demelič, vol. 1 (Vienna: C. W. Stern, 1910), 226. Brigido's report from 1793: TSDIAUL, f. 146, op. 1, spr. 136, Besondere Akten: Doklad gubernatora Brigido, 1793, p. 2.

2. Ernst Wangermann, *From Joseph II to the Jacobin Trials: Government Policy and Public Opinion in the Habsburg Dominions in the Period of the French Revolution* (Oxford: Oxford University Press, 1959), 118–20.
3. The literature on the Jacobin conspiracies in the Habsburg Monarchy focuses almost exclusively on Austria and Hungary. See, for example, Stephan Tull, *Die politischen Zielvorstellungen der Wiener Freimaurer und Wiener Jakobiner im 18. Jahrhundert* (Frankfurt am Main: Peter Lang, 1993).
4. Kaziemirz Bartoszewicz, *Dzieje Galicyi: Jej stan przed Wojna i "Wyodrobnienie"* (Warsaw: Nakładem Gebethnera i Wolffa, 1917), 27.
5. The most comprehensive analysis of the annexation and integration of Western Galicia is Tadeusz Mencel, *Galicja Zachodnia 1795–1809: Studium z dziejów ziem polskich zaboru austriackiego po III rozbiorze* (Lublin: Wydawnictwo Lubelskie, 1976).
6. Karl A. Roider, *Baron Thugut and Austria's Response to the French Revolution* (Princeton: Princeton University Press, 1987), 27.
7. On the Poles' attitudes towards France during the Napoleonic wars see Marceli Handelsman, *Napoléon et la Pologne*, trans. Henri Grégoire, vol. 1 (Brussels: Maurice Lamertin, 1925), 3; Christopher A. Blackburn, *Napoleon and the Szlachta* (Boulder: East European Monographs, 1998); Henri Perreyve, *La Pologne (1772–1865)* (Paris: E. Dentu Libraire, 1865), xiii–xvii.
8. Marceli Handelsman, *Francja-Polska 1795–1845: Studia nad dziejami myśli politycznej. Rozwój narodowości nowoczesnej*, vol. 2 (Warsaw: Nakładem Gebethnera i Wolffa, 1926), 22.
9. Marceli Handelsman, *Napoleon et la Pologne, 1806–1807, d'après les documents des Archives nationales et les archives du Ministère des affaires étrangères* (Paris: Félix Alcan, 1909), 108.
10. On the role of Jews: HHStA, Polen III 13, Innere Verwaltung 1772–1803: Considérations sur la Pologne Autrichienne relativement à ses frontières et aux moiens de defender ce Pais par des forteresses, pp. 372–91.
11. On the meetings: AMAE, CP, Pologne, vol. 331, juillet–septembre 1812. Ambassadeur Pradt, Résident Aubernon mission à Lemberg, 5 mai 1812. Aubernon report no. 4, p. 159.
12. AMAE, CP, Pologne, vol. 331, juillet–septembre 1812, 19 juillet 1812, no. 34, p. 30.
13. Report on Aubernon's secret mission to Brody: AMAE, CP, Pologne, 1812, vol. 331, Lettre d'Aubernon, Lemberg, 28 septembre 1812, p. 678.
14. Marceli Handelsman, *Rezydenci napoleońscy w Warszawie 1807–1813* (Kraków: Akademia Umiejętności, 1915), 6.
15. HHStA, SK, Vorträge, 181, 1809: I–IV: Graf Wurmser über die neue Französische Manipulationen in Galizien, Februar 1809; HHStA, KA, KFA, 86 [Alt]: Berichte von Wurmser, 1807; HHStA, SK, Korrespondenz mit Galizischem Gubernium, Polizei Berichte, 1783–1813, 1.

16. Vadym Adadurov, "L'viv u napoleonivsku epokhu," in *L'viv: Misto, suspil'stvo, kul'tura*, vol. 3, Spetsial'nyi vypusk Visnyka L'vivs'koho universytetu, Seriia istorychna (L'viv: L'vivskyi derzhavnyi universytet imeni Ivana Franka, 1999), 217.
17. Emil Kipa, "Wywiad austriacki w sprawach polskich w przedniu wojny 1809 roku," in *Studia i skice historyczne* (Wrocław: Zakład Narodowy im. Ossolińskich, 1959), 94–95.
18. Vadym Adadurov, "Francuz'ko-avstriiski vzaiemyny kintsia 1806 roku v svitli lystuvannia komanduiuchogo 'neitralnym kordonom v Polshchi' polkovnyka Adama Al'berta Naipperga," *Visnyk L'vivskogo Universytetu: Seria istorychna* 33 (1998): 242–44.
19. Vadym Adadurov, "Napoleon i Halychyna: Vstanovlennia frantsuzkoho tymchasovoho protektoratu v 1809 rotsi," *Visnyk L'vivskoho Universytetu: Seria istorychna* 34 (1999): 449–50.
20. On the Austrian plans to attack the Duchy of Warsaw from Galicia, see Marian Zgórniak, "Galizien in den Kriegsplänen Österreichs und Österreich-Ungarns," *Studia Austro-Polonica* 5 (1996): 295–307. See also *Rys historyczny kampanii odbytej w roku 1809 w Księstwie Warszawskiem pod dowództwem księcia Józefa Poniatowskiego* (Kraków: Nakładem Księgarni J. K. Żupańskiego & K. J. Heumanna, 1889), 37.
21. AMAE, CP, vol. 326, Pologne 1809–1810, 17 avril 1809, p. 57.
22. AMAE, CP, vol. 326, Pologne 1809–1810, p. 55: M-r Serra, Résident, Pulawy le 21 mars.
23. Barbara Grochulska, *Księstwo Warszawskie* (Warsaw: Wiedza Powszechna, 1966), 151.
24. Bronisław Pawłowski, *Warszawa w r. 1809* (Toruń: Nakładem Towarzystwa Naukowego w Toruniu, 1948), 58.
25. Bronisław Pawłowski, *Wojna polsko-austriacka 1809* (Warsaw: Oficyna Wydawnicza Volumen, Dom Wydawniczy Bellona, 1999), 221–22.
26. AMAE, CP, Pologne, vol. 326, Pologne 1809–1810: M-r Serra, Varsovie 18 mai 1809, p. 76.
27. Adadurov, "L'viv u napoleonivsku epokhu," 224.
28. Ibid., 225.
29. On financial hardships in Lemberg in 1809 see Józef Białyna Chołodecki, *Lwów po kongresie wiedeńskim (1815–1823)* (Lwów: Z drukarni i litografii Piller-Neumanna we Lwowie, 1930), 3.
30. Pawłowski, *Wojna polsko-austriacka 1809*, 187–88.
31. Adadurov, "L'viv u napoleonivsku epokhu," 225.
32. Isabel Röskau-Rydel, ed., *Deutsche Geschichte im Osten Europas: Galizien, Bukowina, Moldau* (Berlin: Siedler Verlag, 1999), 42.
33. "Herzogtum Warschau," *Wiener Zeitung*, no. 76, 8 July 1809.

34. Adadurov, "L'viv u napoleonivsku epokhu," 224.
35. HHStA, SK, Polen, III, 39: Galizien-Dietrichstein, 1809, IX–XII.
36. Marian Kukiel, *Dzieje oręża polskiego w epoce napoleońskiej* (Poznań: Nakładem Zdzisława Rzepeckiego i Ski, 1912), 163.
37. Adadurov, "L'viv u napoleonivsku epokhu," 225.
38. Kukiel, *Dzieje oręża polskiego*, 184.
39. Pawłowski, *Wojna polsko-austriacka 1809*, 197.
40. AMAE, CP, Pologne, vol. 326, Pologne 1809–1810, pp. 81–82: Bellefrois à Serra, Tykocin, 26 mai 1809.
41. AMAE, CP, Pologne, vol. 326, Pologne 1809–1810, p. 106: Sokolow à Poniatowski, 24 juin 1809.
42. Pawłowski, *Wojna polsko-austriacka 1809*, 366.
43. AMAE, CP, Pologne, vol. 326, Pologne 1809–1810, p. 96: Serra, Varsovie, le 19 Juin 1809.
44. AMAE, CP, Pologne, Vol. 326, Pologne 1809–1810, p. 103: Au Quartier général d'Ulanow, 21 juin, 1809.
45. Pawłowski, *Wojna polsko-austriacka 1809*, 366.
46. Ibid., 198.
47. Eberhard Mayerhoffer von Vedropolje, *Österreichs Krieg mit Napoleon I 1809* (Vienna: Seidel & Sohn, 1904), 4.
48. For more on this see Adadurov, "L'viv u napoleonivsku epokhu," 226.
49. HHStA, Polen III, 38: Dietrichstein, De retour à Cracau.
50. The Russo-Austrian negotiations concerning the transfer of administration back to the Austrian authorities lasted until October 1809. HHStA, SK, Polen III, 40: Nota des galizischen Landesgouverneurs, Grafen von Wurmser über die Angelegenheiten in Galizien, 16. September 1809.
51. Adadurov, "L'viv u napoleonivsku epokhu," 227.
52. HHStA, Polen III, 38, Galizien Dietrichstein 1809, V–IX: Dietrichstein Bericht, 11. Juni 1809.
53. Alexander Fredro, the famous poet of Polish Romanticism, noted Jewish support for the Poles. Adadurov, "L'viv u napoleonivsku epokhu," 222.
54. Ibid., 221.
55. HHStA, Polen III, 38: Dietrichstein, 20. Mai 1809.
56. HHStA, KA, KFA, 50, Galizien 1806–1810: Verzeichniss jener Galizischen Güterbesitzer und Insassen, welche sich durch Anhauptlichkeit an den Staat, Beförderung der Landeskultur, und Unterstützung der durchmarschierten russ.-kais. Herrn in einem vorteilhaften Licht gezeigt haben.
57. HHStA, KA, KFA, 50: Galizien 1806–1810: Gegenwärtiger Oberste Kanzler Graf v. Ugarto von galizischem Gouverneur vorgelegte Verzeichniss.
58. HHStA, Polen III, 38: Krakau den 5. Juni 1809, Dietrichstein, III Epoque, De retour à Cracau.

59. ÖStA, AVA, HK, III A 4 339: Galizien May 1810–1811: Nota an galizischen Landesgouverneur Grafen von Wurmser.
60. TsDIAUL, f. 147, op. 1. spr. 657, Besondere Akten, Graf Wurmser, 1809, p. 13.
61. HHStA, SK, Polen II 40: Galizien, Dietrichstein 1809, September 1809: Copia des Schreiben des Fürsten von Dietrichstein an den Hofrat von Baum vom 13. September 1809.
62. HHStA, SK, Polen II 40: Galizien, Dietrichstein 1809, September 1809: Copia des Schreiben des Fürsten von Dietrichstein an den Hofrat von Baum vom 13. September 1809.
63. HHStA, KA, KFA, 50, Galizien 1806–1810: Sur la Système de l'Organisation de la Régie du Royaume de Galicie.
64. ÖStA, HK III A 4, 339: Galizien Mai 1810–April 1811: Nota des Grafen Wurmser, November 1809.
65. On Goëss see also Barbara Lasocka, *Teatr Lwowski w latach 1800–1842* (Warsaw: Państwowy Instytut Wydawniczy, 1967), 49.
66. Wacław Mejbaum, "Rządy austriackie w Galicji pomiędzy wojna w roku 1809 a 1812," *Biblioteka Warszawska* 4 (1910): 28.
67. On Aubernon's meeting with Goëss: AMAE, CP, Pologne, vol. 331, juillet–septembre 1812: 5 août 1812, Aubernon report no. 4, p. 159; Ambassadeur Pradt. Résident Aubernon, Aubernon mission à Lemberg: Aubernon's report: Joint à la dépêche septembre 1812, no. 70, p. 676.
68. On this episode see Larry Wolff, *The Idea of Galicia: History and Fantasy in Habsburg Political Culture* (Stanford: Stanford University Press, 2010), 66–71.
69. AMAE, CP, Pologne, vol. 331, juillet–septembre, 1812, Ambassadeur Pradt. Résident Aubernon. Aubernon mission à Lemberg: Aubernon, Joint à la dépêche septembre 1812, no. 70, p. 679.
70. On Goëss's memorandum and his concept of the *echte Galizianer* see Hans-Christian Maner, *Grenzregionen der Habsburgermonarchie im 18. und 19. Jahrhundert: Ihre Bedeutung und Funktion aus der Perspektive Wiens* (Münster: LIT Verlag, 2005), 62; Kazimierz Bartoszewicz, *Dzieje Galicyi: Jej stan przed wojną i "wyodrębnienie"* (Warsaw: Nakład Gebethnera i Wolffa, 1917), 29. See also Wolff, *The Idea of Galicia*, 80.
71. On Goëss's role see Bronisław Łoziński, "Z historyi Stanów Galicyjskich II," in Bronisław Łoziński, *Szkice z historyi Galicyi w XIX wieku*, Z przedmową i pod kierunkim prof. dr. Wacława Tokarza (Lwów: Nakładem Geberthnera w Warszawie; Gubrynowicza i Syna we Lwowie, 1913), 20–24.
72. Mejbaum, "Rządy austriackie w Galicji pomiędzy wojna w roku 1809 a 1812," 28.
73. ÖStA, Polizeihofstelle, 1810, 1239: Graf Goëss, 25. Aug. 1810.

Chapter 4. Between Vienna, St. Petersburg, and Warsaw

1. Rita Krueger, *Czech, German, and Noble: Status and National Identity in Habsburg Bohemia* (New York: Oxford University Press, 2009), 25–27; Robert Joseph Kerner, *Bohemia in the Eighteenth Century: A Study in Political, Economic, and Social History with Special Reference to the Reign of Leopold II, 1790–1792* (1932; Orono: Academic International, 1969), 3–13.
2. On the role of German Bohemian elites in Vienna see Manfred Fleischer, *Die politische Rolle der Deutschen aus den böhmischen Ländern in Wien 1804–1918: Studien zur Migration und zum Wirken politisch-administrativer Eliten* (Frankfurt am Main: Peter Lang, 1999). On the ten most important aristocratic families in Bohemia see Krueger, *Czech, German, and Noble*, 30. On the most prominent members of the Lobkowitz family between the sixteenth and the nineteenth centuries: Philipp Schlesinger, *Erinnerung an August Longin Fürsten von Lobkowitz* (Vienna, 1842), 8–11.
3. Stanislav Kasík et al., *Lobkowiczové: Dějiny a genealogie rodu* (České Budějovice: Veduta, 2002), 176–78.
4. Constant von Wurzbach, *Biographisches Lexikon des Kaiserthums Oesterreich*, vol. 15 (1866; Bad Feilnbach: Schmidt Periodicals, 2001), 337; Patrick de Gmeline, *Histoire des princes de Lobkowicz* (Paris: Berger-Levrault, 1977), 206–8.
5. Lobkowitz's appointments: ÖStA, AVA, HK, III A 4, Gal, 1823–Wien, 23. März 1825: Budweiser Kreishauptmann Fürsten August v. Lobkowitz Ernennung zum Vizepräsidenten des galizischen Landesguberniums; HHStA, StK, Index, 1826, p. 597: Lobkowitz Fürst August, Dessen Ernennung zum Gouverneur in Galizien.
6. Anon., *Austria and the Austrians*, vol. 2 (London, 1837), 35.
7. HHStA, STK, Index, 1828: Nota an den Hofkriegsrath 28. Nov. 1828.
8. For Constantine's biography and his functions in the Kingdom of Poland see Evgenii Karnovich, *Tsesarevich Konstantin Pavlovich* (St. Petersburg: Izdanie Suvorina, 1899).
9. Piotr Wandycz, *The Lands of Partitioned Poland 1795–1918* (Seattle: University of Washington Press, 1974), 65, 74.
10. "Metternich à Neuman, Vienna, 1 janvier 1826," in *Memoirs of Prince Metternich, 1773–1815*, ed. Prince Richard Metternich, trans. Mrs. Alexander Napier, vol. 4 (1880; New York: H. Fertig, 1970), 269.
11. TsDIAUL, f. 146, op. 1, spr. 1179, pp. 6–7: Lobkowitz an Landesgouverneur Taafe. Lemberg, 17. Dezember 1825.
12. TsDIAUL, f. 146, op. 1, spr. 1181, pp. 6–7: Metternich an Fürsten Lobkowitz. Wien, 29. Jänner 1826.
13. Bortnowski, *Powstanie listopadowe w oczach Rosjan* (Warsaw, 1964), 18.

14. An interesting discussion of Russia's policies toward the Polish nobles during this period is Daniel Beauvois, *Pouvoir russe et noblesse polonaise en Ukraine 1793–1830* (Paris: CNRS Edition, 2003), 68–69.
15. Sixty percent of all the military promotions in the Russian Empire in the period between 1826 and 1831 were in Polish units. Władysław Zajewski, "Wokół genezy powstania listopadowego w 150 rocznicę nocy 29.XI.1830 roku," in Jerzy Skworonek and Maria Żmigrodzka, ed., *Powstanie listopadowe 1830–1831. Geneza— uwarunkowania—bilans—porównania* (Wrocław: Zakład Narodowy im. Ossolińskich, 1983), 12.
16. Wandycz, *The Lands of Partitioned Poland*, 72; Hans-Christian Maner, *Galizien: Eine Grenzregion im Kalkül der Donaumonarchie im 18. und 19. Jahrhundert* (Munich: LIT Verlag, 2007), 71; Stefan Kiniewicz, *Historia Polski, 1795–1918* (Warsaw: Państwowe Wydawnictwo Naukowe, 1969), 116.
17. TsDIAUL, f. 146, op. 1, spr. 1186, pp. 1–2: Lobkowitz an Taafe, Lemberg, 30. Februar, 1823, p. 1. Similar reports: TsDIAUL, f. 146, op. 1, spr. 1186, pp. 8–9: An das k.k. Landesgubernium. Czernowitz, 8. Oktober 1823; TsDIAUL, f. 146, op. 1, spr. 1186, p. 11: Lobkowitz an Taafe, Tarnopol, 2. Oktober 1823.
18. TsDIAUL, f. 146, op. 1, spr. 192, pp. 6–9: Lobkowitz an Grafen Saurau, 4. Oktober 1823 (quotation, p. 6).
19. Gernot Seide, *Regierungspolitik und öffentliche Meinung im Kaisertum Österreich anläßlich der polnischen Novemberrevolution (1830–1831)* (Wiesbaden: Harrassowitz, 1971), 91.
20. The library was constructed by and named after Józef Maxymilian Ossoliński, a prominent Polish aristocrat in Galicia. On Lobkowitz's support of the Ossolineum foundation: Markiian Prokopovych, *Habsburg Lemberg: Architecture, Public Space, and Politics in the Galician Capital, 1772–1914* (West Lafayette: Purdue University Press, 2009), 136.
21. Reports from Russia: HHStA, Russland III, 84: 1828–1829, Varia: Admiral Mordwinoff: Mordwinoff an Kaiser Nicolas. Lemberg, 14. Dezember 1828.
22. HHStA, Konsulate, Warschau, VI, 1826–1828: Lorenz, Warschau, 14. Dezember 1826.
23. HHStA, StK Konsulate, Warschau 1826–1828: Lorenz, Warschau, 14. Dezember 1826.
24. Józef Dutkiewicz, *Austria wobec powstania listopadowego* (Kraków: Gebethner & Wolff, 1933), 24; Józef Białyna Chołodecki, *Lwów w czasie powstania listopadowego* (Lwów: Nakładem Towarzystwa Miłośników Przeszłości Lwowa, 1930), 14.
25. HHStA, MKA, 1829, 18, N. 489/1829: Angabe des Fürsten Ludwig Jablonowsky dtto 18. März 1829.
26. In his comprehensive biography of Adam Czartoryski, historian Adam Zawadski refers to "the provocative overtures made to Austria's Polish subjects by Prince Lobkowitz, the governor of Galicia," but he gives no further details. See W. H.

Zawadski, *A Man of Honor: Adam Czartoryski as a Statesman of Russia and Poland 1795–1831* (Oxford: Oxford University Press, 1993), 297.
27. Seide, *Regierungspolitik und öffentliche Meinung im Kaisertum Österreich*, 18.
28. ÖStA, AVA, HK, Praes., 60, N 302/829: Bericht des Galizischen Landespräsidenten mit Nachrichten aus Russland.
29. See, for example, an Austrian report on the political conspiracies in Russian Poland, and Austria's neutrality: HHStA, StK, Notenwechsel mit der Hofkanzlei, 44, 1826: An den Obersten Kanzler (Gr. V. Saurau) Wien, 22. Februar 1826.
30. HHStA, StK, AS, 3, N. 311: Lobkowitz an Metternich, Lemberg, Februar 1830.
31. HHStA, StK, AS, 3, N. 311: Lobkowitz an Metternich, Lemberg, Februar 1830.
32. HHStA, StK, AS, 3, N. 312: Metternich an Lobkowitz, Wien, 28. Februar 1830.
33. HHStA, StK, AS, 3, N. 312: Metternich an Lobkowitz, Wien, 28. Februar 1830.
34. On Polish reliance upon Austria see Isabel Röskau-Rydel, *Kultur an der Peripherie des Habsburger Reiches: Die Geschichte des Bildungswesens und der kulturellen Einrichtungen in Lemberg von 1772 bis 1848* (Wiesbaden: Harrassowitz, 1993), 49.
35. A century after the suppression of the revolution, the interwar Polish historian Józef Feldman still considered Vienna friendly toward the Polish cause. See Józef Feldman, *Sprawa polska w roku 1848* (Kraków: Nakładem Polskiej Akademii Umiejętności, 1933), 246–47.
36. BCK, 5308, p. 111: Czartoryski à Lobkowitz, (date and signature destroyed).
37. HHStA, StK, Provinzen Galizien, 2: Fürst Lobkowitz, Über die polnische Revolution. Lemberg, 13. Dezember 1830.
38. HHStA, StK, Provinzen, Galizien, 2: Fürst Lobkowitz, Über die polnische Revolution. Lemberg, 13. Dezember 1830.
39. HHStA, StK, Provinzen Galizien, 2: Fürst Lobkowitz, Über die polnische Revolution. Lemberg, 13. Dezember 1830.
40. Lists of Polish subjects who moved to Warsaw: TsDIAUL, f. 146, op. 4, spr. 1777.
41. HHStA, MKA, 454, N. 1419/831: Brief des Hrn. Grafen Zaluski aus Zasicnica bei Przemysl, 28. April 1831. Über die Stimmung des Volkes in Galizien.
42. In Hugo Lane's estimates, some 177 students, around 10 percent of the entire student body, took part in the uprising. Lane draws his figures from the works of early twentieth-century Polish historians. See Hugo Lane, "The Galician Nobility and the Border with the Congress Kingdom Before and During the November Uprising," in Christoph Augustynowicz and Andreas Kappeler, eds., *Die galizische Grenze 1772–1867: Kommunikation oder Isolation?* (Berlin: LIT Verlag, 2007), 158.
43. All the reports are filed in TsDIAUL, f. 146, op. 4, spr. 314, 315.
44. A detailed account of this episode is in Isabel Röskau-Rydel, *Niemiecko-austriackie rodziny urzędnicze w Galicji 1772–1918: Kariery zawodowe—środowisko— akulturacja i asymilacja* (Kraków: Wydawnictwo Naukowe Uniwersytetu Pedagogicznego, 2011), 253–54.
45. Ibid., 253.

46. Dutkiewicz, *Austria wobec powstania listopadowego*, 24.
47. HHStA, STK, AS, 3, 312: Metternich an Lobkowitz. Wien, 28. Februar 1830. See also Seide, *Regierungspolitik und öffentliche Meinung im Kaisertum Österreich*, p. 32.
48. HHStA, Konferenzakten, 18, N. 95/831. Dienstschreiben des Gouverneurs von Galizien Fürsten von Lobkowitz 6. Januar 1831.
49. BPP, 346/7: Lobkowitz to Czartoryski, Kopel, 18 avril 1831, 1, 3.
50. On the spread of cholera and Austrian cordoning measures see HHStA, KA, 18: 54–184/1831. Bericht des obersten v. Lebzettein an den Hofkriegsrath-Präsidenten, Add. Lemberg 6. Januar 1831. The *Gazeta Lwowska* and the *Lemberger Zeitung* also published regular reports about both the spread of disease and the Austrian cordoning measures. On border control during the revolution see Svjatoslav Pacholkiv, "Enstehung, Überwachung und Überschreitung der galizischen Grenze 1772–1867," in Augustynowicz and Kappeler, *Die Galizische Grenze*, pp. 181–83.
51. The *Gazeta Lwowska* and the *Lemberger Zeitung* published regular reports from Poland and also numerous announcements of travel restrictions issued by the Austrian government. For examples see "Inländische Nachrichten," *Lemberger Zeitung*, 5 January 1831; "Wiadomości krajowe: Okólnik," *Gazeta Lwowska*, 5 January 1831.
52. HHStA, MKA, 56, N. 1977/831: Vortrag des Präsidenten der Polizeistellen vom 14. August 1831.
53. BCK, 5303/4, p. 297: Czartoryski à M. le Prince Lobkowitz, 5 mai 1831, p. 297.
54. BCK, 5303/4, p. 300: Czartoryski à Lobkowitz, 7 mai 1831.
55. BCK, 5303/4, p. 299: Czartoryski à Lobkowitz, 7 mai 1831.
56. BCK, 5302, p. 251: Czartoryski à Lobkowitz, undated.
57. For a detailed analysis of negotiations concerning Polish refugees and their status in the Habsburg Monarchy see Bronisław Pawłowski, "Przyczynki do polityki austriackiej w czasie powstania polskiego w r. 1831," *Kwartalnik Historyczny* 23 (1909): 161–69, 25 (1911): 197–227.
58. Wurzbach, *Biographisches Lexikon des Kaiserthums Oesterreich*, 15:338.
59. Pawłowski, "Przyczynki do polityki austriackiej w czasie powstania polskiego w r. 1831," p. 198.
60. BPP 346/7, p. 3: Lobkowitz to Czartoryski, Kopel, 18 avril 1831.
61. BCK 5308, p. 283: Czartoryski to Lobkowitz, undated.
62. Dutkiewicz, *Austria wobec powstania listopadowego*, 82.
63. HHStA, STK, Provinzen Galizien, 2: Lobkowitz an Metternich, Lemberg, 2. Dezember 1831.
64. Gmeline, *Histoire des princes de Lobkowicz*, 208.
65. BCK, 5302, p. 246: Czartoryski to Lobkowitz, 29 lipca 1831.
66. "Journal de la Princess Mélanie (1832), 21 août," in *Memoirs of Prince Metternich*, trans. Mrs. Alexander Napier, ed. Prince Richard Metternich, vol. 5. (1880; New York: H. Fertig, 1970), 247.

67. Wurzbach, *Biographisches Lexicon des Kaiserthums Oesterreich*, 15:338.
68. On the *Informationsbüro* see Fritz Reinöhl, "Die österreichischen Informationsbüros des Vormärz, ihre Akten und Protokolle," *Archivalische Zeitschrift* 5 (1938): 261–88.
69. HHStA, IB, 6, pp. 418–33: Berichte des Polizeidirektors Lemberg, Januar 1833.

Chapter 5. Austrian Bureaucracy and Polish Aristocracy

1. ÖStA, AVA, HK III A 4, 339: Nota an galizischen Landesgouverneur Grafen von Wurmser, Oktober/November 1809.
2. Władysław Łoziński, "Pierwsi urzędnicy niemieccy," in *Galiciana: Kilka obrazków z pierwszych lat historyi galicyjskiej* (Lwów: Nakładem Karola Wilda, 1872), 70.
3. Piotr S. Wandycz, "The Poles in the Habsburg Monarchy," in Andrei S. Markovits and Frank Sysyn, eds., *Nationbuilding and the Politics of Nationalism: Essays on Austrian Galicia* (Cambridge: Harvard Ukrainian Research Institute, 1982), 68.
4. Numbers vary greatly because of imprecise statistics and different calculations. According to the Austrian military conscription of 1786, there were more than 36,000 adult noblemen in Galicia. See Krzysztof Ślusarek, *Drobna szlachta w Galicji 1772–1848* (Kraków: Księgarnia Akademicka, 1994), 35. For a detailed analysis of various numbers and statistics see also Emanuel Rostworowski, "Ilu było w Rzeczypospolitej obywateli szlachty?" *Kwartalnik Historyczny* 94, no 3 (1987): 1–28.
5. The statistics of Polish nobles in Galicia are as imprecise as the calculations of Polish nobles in Poland-Lithuania itself. It is plausible to assume, following Krzystof Ślusarek's calculations, that somewhere between 30,000 and 37,000 nobles resided in Galicia during the early years of Austrian rule. See Ślusarek, *Drobna szlachta*, 32–41. Horst Glassl calculated 38,168 nobles in Galicia in 1777 and 29,911 in 1780. See Glassl, *Das österreichische Einrichtungswerk in Galizien (1772–1790)* (Wiesbaden: In Kommission bei Otto Harrasowitz, 1975), 15. The earlier conscriptions of 1777 and 1786 recorded some thirty to forty thousand titled nobles in Galicia, which fell within the 3 percent margin.
6. Ślusarek, *Drobna szlachta*, 35.
7. Ibid., 5.
8. For a detailed analysis see Jerzy Jedlicki, *Klejnot i bariery społeczne: Przeobrażenia szlachectwa polskiego w schyłkowym okresie feudalizmu* (Warsaw: Państwowe Wydawnictwo naukowe, 1968), 84.
9. On the venality of offices, see Teresa Zielińska, *Magnateria polska epoki saskiej: Funkcje urzędów i królewszczyzn w procesie przeobrażeń warstwy społecznej* (Wrocław: Zakład Narodowy im. Ossolińskich, 1977), 30.
10. Ibid., 10.

11. Most titles were inherited, but some could be acquired by distinctive military or civil service. See Peter Frank-Döfering, ed., *Adelslexikon des österreichischen Kaisertums 1804–1918* (Vienna: Herder, 1989), 628–31.
12. This regulation was made into law by legislation of 1775 and 1782. See Tadeusz Mencel, "Magnateria polska w Galicji w polityce władz austriackich w latach 1795–1809," in Janina Leskiewiczowa, ed., *Ziemiaństwo polskie 1795–1945* (Warsaw: Państwowe Wydawnictwo Naukowe, 1985), 38; Ślusarek, *Drobna szlachta*, 83.
13. Rostworowski, "Ilu było w Rzeczypospolitej obywateli szlachty?" 4; Ślusarek, *Drobna szlachta*, 41. On the Hungarian nobility, see P. G. M. Dickson, *Finance and Government under Maria Theresia 1740–1780*, 2 vols. (Oxford: Oxford University Press, 1987), 1:55.
14. See Roman Marcinek and Krzysztof Ślusarek, *Materiały do genealogii szlachty galicyjskiej* (Kraków: Towarzystwo Wydawnicze "Historia Iagellonica,"1996).
15. Irena Rychlikowa, "Studia nad ziemiaństwem Galicji: Rzecz o marnotrawstwie badawczego trudu," *Przegląd Historyczny* 77, no. 3 (1986): 557.
16. The complete list: the Czartoryski, Giedroyć, Jabłonowski, Korwin-Krasińska, Lubomirski, Ossolin-Ossoliński, Poniatowski, Poniński, Radziwiłł, Sanguszko, Sapieha, and Sułkowski families. See Sławomir Górzyński, *Arystokracja polska w Galicji: Studium heraldyczno-genealogiczne* (Warszawa: Dig, 2009), 27. The Ossoliński family is one exception to this general rule. Jerzy Ossoliński received a princely title in Poland-Lithuania in 1764. While such titles were usually extended to the entire family, Jerzy Ossoliński received his *ab persona*, without the right of inheritance. His descendants bore the title of count.
17. Holders of the most important administrative offices in Poland were concurrently granted seats in the Polish Senate. See Zielińska, *Magnateria polska epoki saskiej*, 10–74.
18. Tadeusz Mencel cites forty-four princes who received their titles around 1800. See Mencel, "Magnateria polska," 29–44.
19. For a detailed description see Sławomir Górzyński, *Arystokracja polska w Galicji. Studium heraldyczno-genealogiczne* (Warsaw: DiG, 2009), 24–72.
20. Very good examples of Austrian policies and their effects, expressed in numbers, are found in Irena Rychlikowa, "Galicyjski odłam narodu szlacheckiego w latach 1772–1815," *Kwartalnik Historyczny* 2 (1988): 83–119, and Rychlikowa, "Studia nad ziemiaństwem Galicji," 535–57.
21. A recent overview of the argument regarding the continuities of Austrian and Polish policies is Sławomir Górzyński, "Arystokracja polska w Galicji," in Tadeusz Epsztein et al., eds., *O polskich elitach raz jeszcze: Studia ofiarowana Profesor Janinie Leskiewiczowej z okazji dziewięćdziesiątych wrodzin* (Warsaw: DiG, 2009), 69–76.
22. Daniel Beauvois, *Pouvoir russe et noblesse polonaise en Ukraine 1793–1830* (Paris: CNRS Edition, 2003), 43. For a detailed discussion see the chapter "Pospólstwo ludzi wolnych" in Jedlicki, *Klejnot i bariery społeczne*, 134–82.

23. Ślusarek, *Drobna szlachta*, 119.
24. Ibid., 121.
25. The best available analysis of the Russian policies toward the Polish nobles is Beauvois, *Pouvoir russe et noblesse polonaise en Ukraine*.
26. On cooperation between the Austrian authorities and Polish aristocrats, see Mencel, "Magnateria polska," 27–84; Sławomir Górzyński, *Nobilitacje w Galicji w latach 1772–1918* (Warsaw: DiG, 1997), 12.
27. Stanisław Grodziski, "Parlamentaryzm na ziemiach polskich w epoce porozbiorowej," in Bardach et al., *Dzieje Sejmu Polskiego*, 122.
28. HHStA, StK, Polen III: Privatangelegenheiten, Grenzziehung, der [Z]ipser-Städte mit Polen, 1760–1805, Mai 1775, Pro Memoria, pp. 140–43. On the Dzieduszyckis see Kazimierz Karolczak, *Dzieduszyccy: Dzieje rodu. Linia poturzycko-zarzecka* (Kraków: Wydawnictwo Naukowe Akademii Pedagogicznej, 2001).
29. HHStA, Polen III: Privatangelegenheiten, Grenzziehung, der [Z]ipser-Städte mit Polen, 1760–1805, 1749–69, Privatangelegenheiten 1760–1805, pp. 143–52.
30. P. G. M. Dickson explains Empress Maria Theresa's decision to convene the Galician Diet as part of an effort to foster the loyalty of Polish nobles; *Finance and Government under Maria Theresia*, 1:287. On the 1782 meeting see Glassl, *Das österreichische Einrichtungswerk in Galizien (1772–1790)*, 100. On the Galician diet see also Franciszek Jaworski, *Nobilitacya miasta Lwowa* (Lwów: Nakładem Towarzystwa Miłośników Przeszłości Lwowa, 1909), 40.
31. Robert Joseph Kerner, *Bohemia in the Eighteenth Century: A Study in Political, Economic, and Social History with Special Reference to the Reign of Leopold II, 1790–1792* (1932; Orono: Academic International, 1969), 28.
32. Rita Krueger, *Czech, German, and Noble: Status and National Identity in Habsburg Bohemia* (New York: Oxford University Press, 2009), 76.
33. Ibid.
34. HHStA, Polen III: Privatangelegenheiten, Grenzziehung, der [Z]ipser-Städte mit Polen, 1760–1805, 1749–69, Privatangelegenheiten 1760–1805, 143–52.
35. HHStA, Polen III: Privatangelegenheiten, Grenzziehung, der [Z]ipser-Städte mit Polen, 1760–1805, 1749–69, Privatangelegenheiten 1760–1805, 143–52.
36. Joseph Kortum, *Magna Charta von Galizien oder Untersuchung der Beschwerden des Galizischen Adels polnischer Nation über die österreichische Regierung* (Jassy, 1790).
37. HHStA, KA, KFA, 133 Alt: Galizisch-Ständische Gegenstände 1791.
38. Stanisław Grodziski, *Historia ustroju społeczno politycznego Galicji, 1772–1848* (Wrocław: Zakład Narodowy im. Ossolińskich, 1971), 157.
39. Stanisław Grodziski, "Uwagi o elicie społecznej Galicji 1772–1848," in Janina Leszkiewiczowa, ed., *Społeczeństwo polskie XVIII i XIX wieku: Studia o grupach elitarnych*, vol. 7 (Warsaw: Państwowe Wydawnictwo Naukowe, 1982), 153.
40. Mencel, "Magnateria polska," 51.

41. Grodziski, *Historia ustroju społeczno politycznego Galicji*, 158.
42. A detailed analysis is Hans-Jürgen Bömelburg, "Aufgeklärte Beamte gegen barock-katholischen Adelseliten: Ein Vergleich der österreichischen und preußischen Verwaltungspraxis in Galizien und Westpreussen (1772–1806)," in Walter Leitsch and Stanisław Tarkowski, eds., *Polen und Österreich im 18. Jahrhundert* (Warsaw: Semper, 2000), 19–40.
43. Józef Białynia Chołodecki, *Lwów w czasie powstania listopadowego* (Lwów: Nakładem Towarzystwa Miłośników Przeszłości Lwowa, 1930), 14.
44. On the so-called "mixed subjects" and their properties in different partitions see ÖStA, AVA, Polen III: Fasz. 13: Innere Verwaltung 1772–1803, pp. 266–72.
45. Mencel, "Magnateria polska," 51.
46. Stanisław Grodziski, "Poddani mieszani (sujets mixtes) na ziemiach polskich w latach 1772–1815," in Stanisław Grodziski, *Studia galicyjskie: Rozprawy i przyczynki do historii ustroju Galicji*, ed. Grzegorz Nieć (Kraków: Księgarnia Akademicka, 2007), 69.
47. The so-called mixed subjects, Polish aristocrats who owned land in different states, faced particularly difficult choices. At the turn of the century, they were forced to decide on their permanent place of residence, and thus abandon or sell their properties elsewhere. Józef Dzieduszycki, who owned property in Russia and Austria, eventually settled in Galicia. See Karolczak, *Dzieduszyccy*, 61.
48. Roman Taborski, *Polace w Wiedniu* (Wrocław: Zakład Narodowy imienia Ossolińskich, 1992), 31.
49. Michał Pawlikowski, *Pamiętniki Waleryana Dzieduszyckiego* (Warsaw: Drukarnia Polska, 1939), 5.
50. Taborski, *Polace w Wiedniu*, 31.
51. Mencel, "Magnateria polska," 52.
52. Taborski, *Polace w Wiedniu*, 31.
53. See for example Count Margelik's report on the personnel of Galician districts in 1783. ÖStA, AVA, HK, II A 6, 232: ex December 1783 (II. Teil): Galizien Betreffend, Ausarbeitung.
54. TsDIAUL, f. 575, op. 1, spr. 33. Einführung einer Stiftung für hierländige Adelsleute, p. 5.
55. Łoziński, "Homagium," in *Galiciana*, 25–31.
56. Paul P. Bernard, *From the Enlightenment to the Police State: The Public Life of Johann Anton Pergen* (Urbana: Illinois University Press, 1991), 111.
57. Stanisław hr. Wodzicki, *Wspomnienia z przeszłości od roku 1768 do roku 1840* (Kraków: Drukarnia Leona Paszkowskiego, 1874), 171.
58. Joseph Rohrer, *Bemerkungen auf einer Reise von der türkischen Grenze über die Bukowina durch Ost- und Westgalizien, Schlesien und Mähren nach Wien* (Vienna: Pichler, 1804), 153.
59. On theater life, see Barbara Lasocka, *Teatr lwowski w latach 1800–1842* (Warsaw: Państwowy Instytut Wydawniczy, 1967). On wandering theaters specifically, p. 11.

60. The episode is described in Jerzy Got, *Na wyspie Guaxary: Wojciech Bogusławski i teatr lwowski 1789–1799* (Kraków: Wydawnictwo literackie, 1971), 15.
61. On the theater in the Jablonowski Garden, see ibid., 18; Lasocka, *Teatr lwowski*, 19.
62. On summer and winter theaters, see Viktor Proskuriakov and Yurii Yamash, *L'vivski teatry: Chas i arkhitektura* (L'viv: Tsentr Ievropy, 1997), 16–17.
63. Stanisław Schnür-Pepłowski, *Obrazy z przeszłości Galicyi i Krakowa (1772–1858)* (Lwów: Nakładem Księgarni Gubrynowicza i Schmidta, 1896), 39.
64. Got, *Na wyspie Guaxary*, 89.
65. Larry Wolff, *The Idea of Galicia: History and Fantasy in Habsburg Political Culture* (Stanford: Stanford University Press, 2010), 55–56.
66. Lasocka, *Teatr lwowski*, 74.
67. Schnür-Pepłowski, *Obrazy z przeszłości Galicyi i Krakowa*, 38–39.
68. On these activities, see Leopold von Sacher-Masoch, *Polnische Revolutionen: Erinnerungen aus Galizien* (Prague: F. A. Gredner, 1863), 3.
69. Austrian officials were concerned, and rightly so, that carnivals could become hotbeds of Polish political activity, and that Polish revolutionaries from both Galicia and other areas of Poland, could attend and make their plans without fear of being recognized. Got, *Na wyspie Guaxary*, 66–68.
70. Schnür-Pepłowski, *Obrazy z przeszłości Galicyi i Krakowa*, 37.
71. Got, *Na wyspie Guaxary*, 66.
72. Ibid., 131.
73. Rohrer, *Bemerkungen auf einer Reise*, 15.
74. Isabel Röskau-Rydel, *Kultur an der Peripherie des Habsburger Reiches: Die Geschichte des Bildungswesens und der kulturellen Einrichtungen in Lemberg von 1772 bis 1848* (Wiesbaden: Harrasowitz, 1993), 47.
75. Sacher-Masoch, *Polnische Revolutionen*, 2.
76. Ibid., 3.
77. Rohrer, *Bemerkungen auf einer Reise*, 152.
78. On the use of French in salons in Lemberg/Lwów, see Isabel Röskau-Rydel, *Niemiecko-austriackie rodziny urzędnicze w Galicji 1772–1918: Kariery zawodowe — środowisko — akulturacja i asymilacja* (Kraków: Wydawnictwo Naukowe Uniwersytetu Pedagogicznego, 2011), 292.
79. Janina Bielecka, *Kontrakty lwowskie w latach 1768–1775 (wpływ pierwszego rozbioru Polski, 1772 r., na kontrakty lwowskie)* (Poznań: Nakładem Poznańskiego Towarzystwa Przyjaciół Nauk, 1948), 32.
80. HHStA, KA, KFA, 86: Berichte von Wurmser, 1804.
81. Röskau-Rydel, *Niemiecko-austriackie rodziny urzędnicze w Galicji*, 294.
82. Maurycy Dzieduszycki, *Życiorys Wincentego Pola* (Warsaw, 1936), iii.
83. Röskau-Rydel, *Niemiecko-austriackie rodziny urzędnicze w Galicji*, 301.
84. Ibid., 303.
85. Ibid., 217–18; Irena Homola-Skąpska, *Józef Dietl i jego Kraków* (Kraków: Wydawnictwo Literackie, 1993), 8–14.

86. Röskau-Rydel, *Niemiecko-austriackie rodziny urzędnicze w Galicji*, 101.
87. They did not do so, but the allegations survived into the twentieth century. See, for example, Arnon Gill, *Die Polnische Revolution 1846: Zwischen nationalem Befreiungskampf des Landadels und antifeudaler Bauernerhebung* (Munich: Oldenbourg, 1974), 209.
88. Röskau-Rydel, *Niemiecko-austriackie rodziny urzędnicze w Galicji*, 150.
89. Zygmunt Kaczkowski, *Mój pamiętnik z lat 1833–1843* (Lwów, 1899), 32.
90. One such example is Stanisław Szczepanowski, *Nędza Galicyi w cyfrach i program energicznego rozwoju gospodarstwa krajowego* (Lwów: Gubrynowicz i Schmidt, 1888).
91. Galicia was one of few regions in the monarchy that was almost untouched by industrialization. Other regions with a similar economy were in southern Hungary and the Austrian Alpine territories. See Ferdinand Tremel, "Der Binnenhandel und seine Organisation: Der Fremdenverkehr," in Alois Brusatti, ed., *Die Habsburgermonarchie 1848–1918*, vol. 1: *Die wirtschaftliche Entwicklung* (Vienna: Österreichische Akademie der Wissenschaften, 1973), 381.
92. Alison Frank, *The Oil Empire: Visions of Prosperity in Austrian Galicia* (Cambridge: Harvard University Press, 2005), 29.
93. See the reports of the Austrian police: HHStA, IB, 6, pp. 418–33: Stimmungs- und Administrations-Bericht der Lemberger Polizei-Direktion für den Monat Januar 1833.

Chapter 6. Literature, Politics, and Galician Ruthenians

1. Sacher-Masoch's Jewish stories are explored from both literary and historical perspectives in David Biale, "Masochism and Philosemitism: The Strange Case of Leopold von Sacher-Masoch," *Journal of Contemporary History* 17 (1982): 305–23.
2. Larry Wolf, "Introduction" in Leopold von Sacher-Masoch, *Venus in Furs*, trans. Joachim Neugroschel (New York: Penguin Books, 2000), xiii.
3. Bernard Michel, *Sacher-Masoch (1836–1895)* (Paris: Editions Robert Laffont, 1989), 11.
4. On Sacher-Masoch's nationality claims, see his *Polnische Revolutionen: Erinnerungen aus Galizien* (Prague: F. A. Credner, 1863), vi.
5. Sacher-Masoch's exotic personality has long attracted much attention from scholars. Most recently, Larry Wolff has explored Sacher-Masoch as a prism through which to analyze the history of Galicia and "especially for understanding what Galicia meant conceptually to Galicians of the 1830s and 1840s." See the chapter "The Galician Childhood of Sacher-Masoch: From Folk Songs to Massacres" in Larry Wolff, *The Idea of Galicia: History and Fantasy in Habsburg Political Culture* (Stanford: Stanford University Press, 2010), 111–57. See also Biale, "Masochism and Philosemitism."

6. On Johann von Sacher's birth date, see Hanns Jäger-Sunstenau, "Zweifacher Waffenwechsel im 19. Jahrhundert: Khoß-Sterneg, Sacher-Masoch," *Adler* 17–18, no. 7 (1996): 280. For Don Mathias Sacher see Hulda Edle von Sacher-Masoch, "Erinnerungen an Sacher-Masoch," in Michael Farin, ed., *Leopold von Sacher-Masoch: Materialien zu Leben und Werk* (Bonn: Bouvier Verlag, 1987), 5.
7. This story is recounted by Alexander von Sacher-Masoch, "Sacher-Masoch: Aus seinem Leben" (1928), in Leopold von Sacher-Masoch, *Der Judenraphael: Geschichten aus Galizien*, ed. Adolf Opel (Vienna: Böhlau, 1989), 5.
8. The story of the Sachers' nobilitation is as confusing as the history of the family itself. Their genealogy is based upon several autobiographical accounts; the several accounts of their nobilitation are each based upon individual—and biased— sources, composed by different members of the family between the sixteenth and the nineteenth centuries.
9. Hofrath von Sacher-Masoch, "Memoiren eines österreichischen Polizeidirektors," *Auf der Höhe: Internationale Revue* 2 (1882): 104.
10. Hulda Edle von Sacher-Masoch, "Erinnerungen an Sacher-Masoch," 10; Alexander von Sacher-Masoch, "Sacher-Masoch: Aus seinem Leben," 6.
11. Hulda Edle von Sacher-Masoch, "Erinnerungen an Sacher-Masoch," 6.
12. TSDIAUL, f. 146, op. 4, spr. 2119, p. 3.
13. Jäger-Sunstenau, "Zweifacher Waffenwechsel im 19. Jahrhundert," 281.
14. On these doctors and their characteristics: ÖStA, AVA, HK, II A 6 (Gal)—1776, 229, December 1772.
15. "Hr. Franz Masoch, der Arzneikunde Doktor, Prof. des medizinisch-theoretischen Unterrichts für Wundärzte, Mitglied der Wiener Fakultät, woh. Am Krakauer Thor Pro. 97," *Schematismus für die Königreiche Ostgalizien und Lodomerien, samt einem Schreibkalender und Namensregister für das Jahr 1801* (Lemberg: Joseph Piller, 1801), 90.
16. Leopold von Sacher-Masoch, *Jewish Life: Tales from Nineteenth-Century Europe* (Riverside: Ariadne Press, 2002), 206. See also the memoirs of Leopold von Sacher-Masoch's grandson, Alexander Sacher-Masoch, "Sacher-Masoch: Aus seinem Leben," 5–12.
17. Jäger-Sunstenau, "Zweifacher Waffenwechsel im 19. Jahrhundert," 281.
18. Constant von Wurzbach, *Biographisches Lexikon des Kaiserthums Oesterreich*, vol. 28 (Vienna: K.k. Staatsdruckerei, 1874), 12.
19. Alexander von Sacher-Masoch, "Sacher-Masoch: Aus seinem Leben," 9.
20. Serhii Plokhy, *Unmaking Imperial Russia: Mykhailo Hrushevsky and the Writing of Ukrainian History* (Toronto: University of Toronto Press, 2005), 28.
21. Oliver Bruck, "Die Gartenlaube für Österreich: Vom Scheitern des Projektes einer österreichischen Zeitschrift nach Königgrätz," in Klaus Amann et al., *Literarisches Leben in Österreich 1848–1890* (Vienna: Böhlau, 2000), 357.

22. [Leopold von Sacher-Masoch], *Eine Galizische Geschichte 1846* (Schaffhausen: Verlag der Friedr. Hurterschen Buchhandlung, 1858), vii.
23. For a textual analysis of these categories, see Vitaly Chernetsky, "Nationalizing Sacher-Masoch: A Curious Case of Cultural Reception in Russia and Ukraine," *Comparative Literature Studies* 45, no. 4 (2008): 476.
24. Wurzbach, *Biographisches Lexikon*, 28:25.
25. Jan Lam, *Wielki świat Capowic* (Kraków: Universitas, 2002), 52, 77, 77, 58.
26. Ibid., 78, 78 (emphasis in the original), 91.
27. On the rise and decline of some of these families see Aleksander Jabłonowski, *Historya Rusi Południowej do upadku Rzeczypospolitej Polskiej* (Kraków: Akademia umiejętności, nakładem Funduszu Nestora Bucewicza, 1912), 182, 322.
28. Ibid., 320.
29. ÖStA, AVA, HK, II A 6 (Gal)—1776, 229: Liberum Exercitium Religionis, September 1772.
30. Franz J. Szabo, *Kaunitz and Enlightened Absolutism 1753–1780* (Cambridge: Cambridge University Press, 1994), 235–36.
31. Anton Korczok, *Die Griechisch-Katholische Kirche in Galizien* (Leipzig: Teubner, 1921), 29.
32. See Jan Mikrut, *Bischöfe aus Galizien berichten an Kaiser Franz I: Ein Beitrag zur Geschichte der katholischen Kirche in der Habsburgmonarchie* (Vienna: Wiener Dom-Verlag, 1995), esp. pp. 114–15.
33. Wacław Tokarz, *Galicya w początkach ery józefińskiej w świetle ankiety urzędowej z roku 1783* (Kraków: Akademia Umiejętności, 1909), 380.
34. Ibid., 384.
35. John-Paul Himka, "German-Ukrainian Relationships," in John-Paul Himka and Hans-Joachim Torke, eds., *German-Ukrainian Relationships in Historical Perspective* (Edmonton: Canadian Institute of Ukrainian Studies, 1994), 31.
36. Vadym Adadurov, "L'viv v napoleonivs'sku epokhu," in *L'viv: Misto, suspil'stvo, kul'tura*, vol. 3, Spetsial'nyi vypusk Visnyka L'vivs'koho universytetu, Seriia istorychna (L'viv: L'vivskyi derzhavnyi universytet imeni Ivana Franka, 1999), 217.
37. ÖStA, AVA, HK, III A 4, 337, April 1805: Geistliche Referenten in publico ecclesiastico.
38. ÖStA, AVA HK, III A 4: Gubern. Nd. Regierung, p. 339, 1813.
39. Jan Fellerer, *Mehrsprachigkeit im galizischen Verwaltungswesen (1772–1914): Eine historisch-soziolinguistische Studie zum Polnischen und Ruthenischen (Ukrainischen)* (Cologne: Böhlau, 2005), 107; Anna Veronika Wendland, *Die Russophilen in Galizien: Ukrainische Konservative zwischen Österreich und Russland 1848–1915* (Vienna: Verlag der Österreichischen Akademie der Wissenschaften, 2001), 33.
40. Andrew Wilson, *The Ukrainians: Unexpected Nation* (New Haven: Yale University Press, 2000), 102. See also Wendland, *Die Russophilen in Galizien*, 33–36.

41. On Ruthenian assimilation into high Polish culture and "gente Rutheni natione Poloni" more specifically, see John-Paul Himka, "The Construction of Nationality in Galician Rus': Icarian Flights in Almost All Directions," in Ronald Grigor Suny and Michael D. Kennedy, eds., *Intellectuals and the Articulation of the Nation* (Ann Arbor: University of Michigan Press, 2002), 111–16.
42. Fellerer, *Mehrsprachigkeit*, 43.
43. Jan Lewicki, *Ruch Rusinów w Galicji w pierwszej połowie wieku panowania Austrji (1772–1820)* (Lwów: Nakładem autora, 1879), 7.
44. On the effects of the Austrian reforms upon the Ruthenians see also Paul R. Magocsi, *The Roots of Ukrainian Nationalism: Galicia as Ukraine's Piedmont* (Toronto: Toronto University Press, 2002), esp. p. 15.
45. Röskau-Rydel, *Niemiecko-austriackie rodziny*, 264–65.
46. Ibid., 265.
47. Ibid., 269.
48. Lisbeth Exner, *Leopold von Sacher-Masoch* (Hamburg: Rowolt, 2003), 16; on Handscha's influence upon Sacher-Masoch see also Joseph Kehrin, "Dr. Leopold Ritter von Sacher-Masoch" (1871), in Farin, *Leopold von Sacher-Masoch*, 11.
49. Wolff, *The Idea of Galicia*, 176–77.
50. Lisbeth Exner, "Szenen meines Lebens." Sacher-Masoch autobiographischen Schriften, in *Leopold von Sacher-Masoch*, ed. Ingrid Spörk and Alexandra Strohmaier (Graz: Literaturverlag Droschl, 2002), 285.
51. Hofrath von Sacher-Masoch, "Memoiren eines österreichischen Polizeidirektors," *Auf der Höhe: Internationale Revue* 2 (1882): 104–23.
52. Spain became part of the Habsburg lands in 1516, eventually under a separate branch of the dynasty, but when that branch died out the Austrian Habsburgs were unable to make good their claim to inherit that part of the Spanish Habsburg territories in the War of the Spanish Succession, 1701–14.
53. On Sacher-Masoch's "exotic cultivation of a Ruthenian identity," see Wolff, *The Idea of Galicia*, 116.
54. Jäger-Sunstenau, "Zweifacher Waffenwechsel im 19. Jahrhundert," 281.
55. Plokhy, *Unmaking Imperial Russia*, 28. On Sacher-Masoch and his Ruthenian connections see Ostap Sereda, "Leopold von Zacher-Masoch i ukraïns'kyi natsionalnyi rukh u Halychyni u 60-kh rokach XIX st.," in *Prosfonyna: Istorychni ta filologichni rozvidky, prysviacheni 60-richiu akademika Yaroslava Isaiewytcha*, Ukraina: Kulturna spadshchyna, natsional'na svidomist', derzavnist', vol. 5 (L'viv: Instytut ukrainoznavstva im. Krypiakewycha NANU, 1998), 561–69.
56. A general overview of the divisions in the Ruthenian camp is Ostap Sereda, "'Whom Shall We Be?' Public Debates over the National Identity of Galician Ruthenians in the 1860s," *Jahrbücher für Geschichte Osteuropas* 49, no. 2 (2001): 200–212.
57. Wendland, *Die Russophilen in Galizien*, 52.

58. Lam, *Wielki świat Capowic*, 134.
59. Ibid., 157.
60. Ibid., 160.
61. On Kuzems'kyi see Wendland, *Die Russophilen in Galizien*, 103; John-Paul Himka, *Religion and Nationality in Western Ukraine: The Greek Catholic Church and the Ruthenian National Movement in Galicia 1867–1900* (Montreal: McGill Queen's University Press 1999), 36.
62. Wolff, *The Idea of Galicia*, 115.
63. Leopold von Sacher-Masoch, *Ecrits autobiographiques et autres textes*, trans. and introd. Michel-Francois Demet (Paris: Editions Léo Scheer, 2004), 19.
64. Sereda, "Leopold von Zacher-Masoch," 565.
65. On the perception of Sacher-Masoch in contemporary Ukraine (prior to 2008) see Chernetsky, "Nationalizing Sacher-Masoch," 471–76. On the debates surrounding Sacher-Masoch in contemporary L'viv see Ostap Sereda, "Mazokhiada," zaxid.net.
66. Plokhy, *Unmaking Imperial Russia*, 28.
67. An excellent analysis of the culture and politics of Viennese modernity is Carl Schorske, *Fin-de-siècle Vienna: Politics and Culture* (New York: Knopf, 1980).
68. Sacher-Masoch, *Eine Galizische Geschichte*, vii.

Chapter 7. Administering the Jews

1. There are no precise statistics of the Jewish population of Galicia. Scholars estimate between 215,000 and 250,000 Jews in Galicia out of 357,000 for the entire monarchy for the year 1785. See William O. McCagg, Jr., *A History of Habsburg Jews, 1670–1918* (Bloomington: Indiana University Press, 1989), 27; Wolfgang Häusler, "Toleranz, Emanzipation und Antisemitismus: Das österreichische Judentum des bürgerlichen Zeitalters (1782–1918)," in Anna Drabek et al., *Das österreichische Judentum* (Vienna: Jugend und Volk, 1974), 85.
2. Jósef Buzek, *Wpływ polityki żydowskiej rządu austriackiego w latach 1772–1788 na wzrost zaludnienia żydowskiego Galicyi* (Kraków: Czcionkami Drukarni Uniwersytetu Jagiellońskiego, 1903), 95.
3. Gershon Hundert, *Jews in Poland-Lithuania in the Eighteenth Century: A Genealogy of Modernity* (Berkeley: University of California Press, 2004), esp. 1–9.
4. For a detailed discussion of the Jewish demographic developments in Galicia see Buzek, *Wpływ polityki żydowskiej*, 91–127. See also Teresa Andlauer, *Die jüdische Bevölkerung im Modernisierungsprozess Galiziens (1867–1914)* (Frankfurt am Main: Peter Lang, 2001), 35.
5. In referring to community leaders and elders, I use on the terms found in Austrian-Jewish documents from the time: *Kahalvorsteher, Älteste*.
6. On forceful Germanization and anti-Semitism during the first decades of Austrian rule, see Joshua Shanes, *Diaspora Nationalism and Jewish Identity in Habsburg*

Galicia (Cambridge: Cambridge University Press, 2012), 20–29. On Jewish resilience, see Nancy Sinkoff, *Out of the Shtetl: Making Jews Modern in the Polish Borderlands* (Providence: Brown Judaic Studies, 2004), 1.

7. On different definitions of Jewish community and Jewish communal administration see Anatol Leszyński, "The Terminology of the Bodies of Jewish Self-Government," in Anthony Polonsky et al., *The Jews in Old Poland 1000–1795* (London: I. B. Tauris, 1993), 119–32. The kahal originally only meant the elders of Jewish communities, but eventually came to define communities at large.
8. On the Council of Four Lands, its competencies and major functions, see S. Ettinger, "The Council of Four Lands," in *Old Poland 1000–1795*, 93–110.
9. Majer Bałaban, *Dzieje żydów w Galicyi i Rzeczypospolitej Krakowskiej 1772–1868* (Lwów: Nakł. Księgarni Polskiej B. Połonieckiego, 1916), 21–23.
10. On the political, economic and social functions of the kahal after 1776 see Wolfgang Häusler, *Das galizische Judentum in der Habsburgermonarchie: Im Lichte der zeitgenössischen Publizistik und Reiseliteratur 1772–1848* (Vienna: Verlag für Geschichte und Politik, 1979), 15–17.
11. ÖStA, AVA, HK, IV T 1, 1520, Duldung der Juden Galizien bis 1784: Allgemeine Ordnung für die gesammte Judenschatft des Königreichs Galizien und Lodomerien 1776.
12. On the Jewish census during the 1770s and 1780s, see ÖStA, AVA, HK, IV T 1, 521: Duldung der Juden, Galizien 1785–1796, April 1785; ÖStA, AVA, HK, IV T 1, 521: Bei der Instruktion zur Beschreibung und Einrichtung der Judengemeinden.
13. On the chief rabbi of Galicia see N. M. Gelber, "Aryeh Leib Bernstein: Chief Rabbi of Galicia," *Jewish Quarterly Review*, n.s. 14, no. 3 (1924): 303–27.
14. Adam Teller, "Laicyzacja wczesnonowożytnego społeczeństwa żydowskiego: Rozwój rabinatu w polsce w XVI wieku," *Kwartalnik Historyczny* 110, no. 3 (2003): 23.
15. Gelber, "Aryeh Leib Bernstein," 317–24.
16. On Bernstein's work in Poland and the conflict in Galicia, see Börris Kuzmany, *Brody: Eine galizische Grenzstadt im langen 19. Jahrhundert* (Vienna: Böhlau, 2011), 127.
17. The Edict of Toleration was actually a series of decrees, issued between 1781 and 1789.
18. David Vital, *A People Apart: The Jews in Europe, 1789–1939* (New York: Oxford University Press, 1999), 32.
19. Häusler, "Toleranz, Emanzipation und Antisemitismus," 84–86.
20. See "Toleranzpatent, Staatsgutachten, Toleranzpatententwurf der HK," in A. F. Pribram, ed., *Urkunden und Akten zur Geschichte der Juden in Wien*, vol. 1: 1526–1847 *(1849)* (Vienna: Wilhelm Braumüller, 1918), 440–94.
21. "Toleranzpatent für Niederösterreich, 2. Januar 1782," ibid., 494.

22. ÖStA, AVA, HK, IV T 4, 1541. Schuldenwesen der Juden, 1782–1800: Untersuchung, ca 1800.
23. ÖStA, AVA, HK, IV T 10, 1554, V, 1784: Eine Instruktion für die Judenrevisoren.
24. ÖStA, AVA, HK, IV T 11, 1563, Mai 1794.
25. ÖStA, VA, Hofkanzlei, IV T 1, 521: Galizien, Die Sitzung vom 19. Mai 1785. The original legislation was published in various Austrian collections in the eighteenth and nineteenth centuries. See, for instance, Michael Stöger, *Darstellung der gesetzlichen Verfassung der galizischen Judenschaft* (Lemberg: Rubin und Millikowski, 1833), 3–6.
26. Häusler, "Toleranz, Emanzipation und Antisemitismus," 84.
27. Gelber, "Aryeh Leib Bernstein," 318.
28. ÖStA, AVA, HK, IV T 10, 1554: Vorsteher jüdischer Gemeinden, Böhm, Gal,—1804, 1800.
29. On Landau between tradition and modernity see Sharon Flatto, *The Kabbalistic Culture of Eighteenth Century Prague: Ezekiel Landau (the "Noda Biyehudah") and His Contemporaries* (Oxford: Littman Library of Jewish Civilization, 2010). On his cooperation with the Austrians, in particular, see p. 50. More generally see Ruth Kestenberg-Gladstein, "The Jews between Czechs and Germans in the Historic Lands, 1848–1918," in *The Jews of Czechoslovakia: Historical Studies and Surveys*, vol. 1 (Philadelphia: Jewish Publication Society of America, 1968), 41–45; Eli Lederhendler, *The Road to Modern Jewish Politics: Political Tradition and Political Reconstruction in the Jewish Community of Tsarist Russia* (New York: Oxford University Press, 1989), 64.
30. Kestenberg-Gladstein, "The Jews between Czechs and Germans," 41–47.
31. Häusler, "Toleranz, Emanzipation und Antisemitismus," 83.
32. Josef Karniel, *Die Toleranzpolitik Kaiser Josephs II* (Gerlinger: Bleicher Verlag, 1985); Friedrich Walter, *Die Geschichte der österreichischen Zentralverwaltung in der Zeit Franz II (I) und Ferdinands I 1792–1848* (Vienna: Adolf Holzhausen Verlag, 1956), 441–46.
33. Karniel, *Die Toleranzpolitik Kaiser Josephs II*, 445.
34. On the numbers see Bałaban, *Dzieje żydów*, 32.
35. Wacław Tokarz, *Galicya w początkach ery józefińskiej w świetle ankiety urzędowej z roku 1783* (Kraków: Akademia Umiejętności, 1909), 357, 368.
36. ÖStA, AVA, HK II A 6, 231: Ad 108 ex Dezember 1783.
37. ÖStA, AVA, HK III A. 5, 402, 1789.
38. ÖStA, AVA, HK IV T 11, 1562, ex Dez. 1791: An das Galizische Landesgubernium, Wien den 9. Dezember 1791.
39. ÖStA, AVA, HK, IV T 11, 1562 Gal. Steuren der Juden, 1785–1792: ex Dez. 1791, p. 159.
40. ÖStA, AVA, HK IV T 11, 1562 Gal. Steuren der Juden, 1785–1792: 22 ex April 1791, p. 154.

41. ÖStA, AVA, HK IV T 11, 1562: An das Galizische Landesgubernium, Wien den 9. Dezember 1791.
42. ÖStA, AVA, HK, IV T 10, 1554: Vorsteher der jüdischen Gemeinde, Boehm, Gal—1804. 1784: Eine Instruction für die Juden Revisoren.
43. ÖStA, AVA, HK IV T 2, 1530: August 1804.
44. ÖStA, AVA, HK IV T 2, 1530: Galiz. Landespräsident Bericht, ex April 1808.
45. ÖStA, AVA, HK IV T 2, 1530: Galiz. Landespräsident Bericht, ex April 1808.
46. ÖStA, AVA, HK IV T 2, 1530: Handel, Besitz der Juden Gal. 1801–1815, 198 ex Sept. 1807, p. 399.
47. ÖStA, AVA, HK, IV T 2, 1530: Über ein Antrag des Stryjer Kreisamtes, ex Sept. 1807.
48. ÖStA, VA, Hofkanzlei IV T 2, 1530: Metropolit Angelowicz über den von Juden getriebenen Handel mit Apparaten des gr. Kath. Clerus, 10, Dezember 1807.
49. Sawa's case: ÖStA, AVA, HK IV T 2, 1530, August 1804.
50. Demographic regulations formed the core of the Austrian reforms in Galicia during the 1770s and 1780s. After 1787, Vienna made marriage regulations contingent upon educational requirements. For the original legislation see "Schulbesuch als Bedinung der Heiratsbewilligung, April 15–8. Aug. 1785," in Pribram, *Urkunden und Akten zur Geschichte der Juden in Wien*, 1:576–77.
51. ÖStA, AVA, HK, IV T 8, 1548: Ehen der Juden, Galizien, 31 ex mai 1809, p. 172.
52. ÖStA, AVA, HK, IV T 8, 1548: An den k.k. Hofkriegsrath 1786.
53. Tokarz, *Galicya w początkach ery józefińskiej*, 364.
54. ÖStA, AVA, HK, IV T 8, 1548: Dekret des Galizische Guberniums, Wien, 2. November 1804.
55. ÖStA, AVA, HK, IV T 8, 1548: Ehen der Juden, Galizien. 31 ex mai 1809, ex febr 1809, p. 145.
56. William O. McCagg, *A History of Habsburg Jews, 1670–1918* (Bloomington: Indiana University Press, 1989), 1.
57. Ibid., 47–51.
58. Jerzy Holzer, "Enlightenment, Assimilation, and Modern Identity: The Jewish Elite in Galicia," *Polin* 12 (1999): 79–85.
59. A good recent analysis of Homberg is Dirk Sadowski, *Haskalah und Lebenswelt: Herz Homberg und die jüdischen Schulen in Galizien 1782–1806* (Göttingen: Vandenhoeck & Ruprecht, 2010). On Homberg's early development, see pp. 48–49. A brief biography of Herz Homberg is Helmut Teufel, "Ein Schüler Mendelssohns—Herz Homberg als jüdischer Propagandist der Josephinischen Aufklärung," in Gerhard Ammerer and Hanns Haas, eds., *Ambivalenzen der Aufklärung: Festschrift für Ernst Wangermann* (Vienna: Verlag für Geschichte und Politik, 1997), 187–204. For a comprehensive, if somewhat dated analysis of Homberg's work in Galicia, see Majer Bałaban, "Homberg in Galizien: Historische Studie," *Jahrbuch für jüdische Geschichte* 19 (1916): 189–221.

60. Sadowski, *Haskalah und Lebenswelt*, 49–52.
61. Ibid., 59.
62. Jonathan Frankel, "Assimilation and the Jews in Nineteenth-Century Europe: Towards a New Historiography?" in Jonathan Frankel and Steve J. Zipperstein, eds., *Assimilation and Community: The Jews in Nineteenth-Century Europe* (Cambridge: Harvard University Press, 1992), 20.
63. Bałaban, "Homberg in Galizien," 200.
64. Sadowski, *Haskalah und Lebenswelt*, 75.
65. Ibid., 122.
66. David Sorkin, *The Religious Enlightenment: Protestants, Jews and Catholics from London to Vienna* (Princeton: Princeton University Press, 2008), 175.
67. On the convergence of the Jewish Haskalah and the Austrian Catholic Enlightenment, see ibid., 197, 213.
68. On Galicia's acceptance of the Enlightenment, see Frankel, "Assimilation and the Jews," 1–37; Israel Bartal, "'The Heavenly City of Germany' and Absolutism à la Mode d'Autriche: The Rise of the Haskalah in Galicia," in Jacob Katz, ed., *Toward Modernity: The European Jewish Model* (New Brunswick: Transaction Books, 1987), 33–42. On the struggle between the Haskalah and Hasidism and the role of Austrian authorities in this struggle, see Raphael Mahler, *Hasidism and the Jewish Enlightenment: Their Confrontation in Galicia and Poland in the First Half of the Nineteenth Century* (Philadelphia: Jewish Publication Society of America, 1985). Recently, Glenn Dynner has claimed that the Jewish Enlightenment in Eastern Europe was generally weak: "neither extensive emancipation nor acculturation prevailed in Eastern Europe during this period and one may doubt the potency of comparatively weak Jewish Enlightenment." Glenn Dynner, *Men of Silk: The Hasidic Conquest of Polish Jewish Society* (Oxford: Oxford University Press, 2006), 15.
69. Sadowski, *Haskalah und Lebenswelt*, 105.
70. Bałaban, "Homberg in Galizien," 201.
71. Dirk Sadowski, "Maskilishes Bildungsideal und josephinische Erziehungspolitik," *Leipziger Beiträge zur jüdischen Geschichte und Kultur* 1 (2003): 151.
72. Bałaban, "Homberg in Galizien," 206.
73. Sadowski, *Haskalah und Lebenswelt*, 114. There were several individuals named Landau who played an important role in Jewish life and reform during the 1780s, Jakovke Landau being one of them.
74. ÖStA, AVA, HK IV T 2, 1530: Handel, Besitz der Juden Gal. 1801–1815, Februar–Juli 1801.
75. Sadowski, *Haskalah und Lebenswelt*, 151.
76. Ibid., 110.
77. Ibid., 121.
78. Ibid., 377.
79. Bałaban, *Dzieje żydów*, 71.

80. Lois C. Dubin, *The Port Jews of Habsburg Trieste: Absolutist Politics and Enlightenment Culture* (Stanford: Stanford University Press, 1999), 111.
81. Sadowski, *Haskalah und Lebenswelt*, 377–81.
82. Bałaban, *Dzieje żydów*, 85.
83. Sinkoff, *Out of the Shtetl*, 95.
84. Michael Stanislawski, *A Murder in Lemberg: Politics, Religion, and Violence in Modern Jewish History* (Princeton: Princeton University Press, 2007), 17.
85. Ibid., 30, 32.
86. Ibid., 32.
87. Bałaban, *Dzieje żydów*, 103.
88. See Marcin Wodziński, *Haskalah and Hasidism in the Kingdom of Poland: A History of Conflict* (Portland: Littman Library of Jewish Civilization, 2005), 26.
89. Mahler, *Hasidism and the Jewish Enlightenment*, 70.
90. For a detailed description of Austrian policies toward Hasids, see ibid., 71–85.
91. Ibid., 93.
92. Larry Wolff, *The Idea of Galicia: History and Fantasy in Habsburg Political Culture* (Stanford: Stanford University Press, 2010), 125.
93. Bałaban, *Dzieje żydów*, 101. In the first half of the nineteenth century, Jews of Galicia were deeply divided among different denominations and movements: the traditionalists, the maskilim, the Hasidim, as well as different groups of "modernists." Michael Stanisławski, *A Murder in Lemberg*, 29–30.
94. Bałaban, *Dzieje żydów*, 137–44.
95. On Polish-Jewish friendship during the revolution, see Rachel Manekin, "Taking It to the Streets: Polish-Jewish Print Discourse in 1848 Lemberg," *Jahrbuch des Simon-Dubnow Instituts* 7 (2008): 215–27. An interesting early analysis of different political and intellectual trends among Galician Jews was published in 1892 by a Polish-Jewish historian from Galicia, Wilhelm Feldman: *Asymiliatorzy, syjoniści i Polacy: Z powodu przełomu w stosunkach żydowskich w Galicyi* (Kraków, 1893)
96. The second half of the nineteenth century is a separate period in the history of formerly Polish Jews under the partition. It has been addressed in great detail in the literature.
97. Jewish assimilation during the nineteenth century is also a separate field of historiography. Examples of recent research are Joshua Shanes, "Neither Germans nor Poles: Jewish Nationalism in Galicia before Herzl, 1883–1897," *Austrian History Yearbook* 34 (2003): 191–213; Tomasz Gąsowski, *Między gettem a światem: Dylematy ideowe żydów galicyjskich na przełomie XIX i XX wieku* (Kraków: Instytut Historii, 1996).
98. McCagg, *A History of Habsburg Jews*, 15.
99. William McCagg argues that Joseph II's Jewish reforms were shaped in response to the shocking reality of Galician Jews. Thus, the annexation of Galicia must have triggered Jewish reforms across the entire monarchy. Ibid.

NOTES TO PAGES 206–211

Chapter 8. Bureaucracy and Revolutions

1. For detailed discussion see Alan Sked, "Austria and the 'Galician Massacres' of 1846," in Lothar Höbelt and Thomas Gotte, eds., *A Living Anachronism? European Diplomacy and the Habsburg Monarchy. Festschrift für Francis Roy Bridge zum 70. Geburtstag* (Vienna: Böhlau, 2010), 49–118.
2. A good overview of the different historiographies of 1846 is Thomas W. Simons, Jr., "The Peasant Revolt in Galicia: Recent Polish Historiography," *Slavic Review* 30, no. 4 (December 1971): 795–817.
3. This perception is strong in Polish national historiography. See for example, Stefan Kiniewicz, ed., *Rok 1848 w Polsce: Wybór źródel* (Wrocław: Zakład Narodowy im. Ossolińskich, 1948); Irena Koberdowa, *Polska wiosna ludów* (Warsaw: Wizda Powszechna, 1967); Marian Stolarczyk, *Działalność Lwowskiej Centralnej Rady Narodowej: W świetle źródeł centralnej rady narodowej* (Rzeszów: WSP, 1994). A similar perception in the research on 1846: Grodziski, "Rok 1846 w Galicji: Przyczyny i konsekwencje," in *Studia Galicyjskie: Rozprawy i przyczynki do historii ustroju Galicji*, ed. Grzegorz Nieć (Kraków: Księgarnia Akademicka, 2007).
4. For this argument see Larry Wolff, *The Idea of Galicia: History and Fantasy in Habsburg Political Culture* (Stanford: Stanford University Press, 2010), 160.
5. Constant von Wurzbach, *Biographisches Lexikon des Kaiserthums Oesterreich*, vol. 4 (Vienna: K.k. Staatsdruckerei, 1858), 86–87. In Russia, governors typically combined military and civil authority in one person. Their military functions were often more important than their role in civil administration.
6. See Austrian police reports from January 1833: HHStA, IB, 6: Stimmungs- und Administrations-Bericht der Lemberger Polizei-Direktion für den Monat Januar 1833, pp. 418–33.
7. On different phases in the development of Polish conspiracies, see Arnon Gill, *Die polnische Revolution 1846: Zwischen nationalem Befreiungskampf des Landadels und antifeudaler Bauernerhebung* (Munich: Oldenbourg, 1974), 107.
8. On these groups, see Stefan Kieniewicz, *Konspiracje galicyjskie, 1831–1845* (Warsaw: Książka i Wiedza, 1950), esp. 139–70.
9. HHStA, IB, 6: Stimmungs- und Administrations-Bericht der Lemberger Polizei-Direktion für den Monat März 1833, pp. 359–78.
10. HHStA, IB, 6: Stimmungs- und Administrations-Bericht der Lemberger Polizei-Direktion für den Monat Januar 1833, p. 418.
11. HHStA, IB, 6: Stimmungs- und Administrations-Bericht der Lemberger Polizei-Direktion für den Monat Januar 1833, p. 419.
12. See above, pp. 148–50.
13. Isabel Röskau-Rydel, *Niemiecko-austriackie rodziny urzędnicze w Galicji 1772–1918: Kariery zawodowe—środowisko—akulturacja i asymilacja* (Kraków: Wydawnictwo Naukowe Uniwersytetu Pedagogicznego, 2011), 296, 301.

14. Kieniewicz, *Konspiracje galicyjskie*, 199.
15. Ibid.
16. Ibid., 160–69.
17. On the Polish Democratic Society see Bronisław Baczko, *Poglądy społeczno-polityczne i filozoficzne Towarzystwa Demokratycznego Polskiego* (Warsaw: Książka i Wiedza, 1955).
18. Moritz Freiherr v. Sala, *Geschichte des polnischen Aufstandes vom Jahre 1846* (Vienna: Im Verlag von Carl Gerold's Sohn, 1867), 164–66.
19. HHStA, StK, Provinzen, Galizien, 4: Bericht des Vizepräsidenten Grafen Lazansky an Staats u. Konferenz-Minister Grafen Kolowrat, Tarnow, 25. Februar 1846, Abschrift eines Schreibens des Kreis-Polizei Direktors Kroch an Residenten von Lichmann aus Teschen, 26. Februar 1846.
20. "Correspondence: Ignacy Strzelbicki (mandatariusz kameralny z Brzostka). List II, Kołaczyce, 17 marca 1846," in Józef Sieradzki and Czesław Wycech, eds., *Rok 1846 w Galicji: Materiały źródłowe* (Warsaw: Państwowe Wydawnictwo Naukowe, 1958), 235.
21. Ibid.
22. HHStA, StK, Provinzen, Galizien, 4: Bericht des Kreishauptmannes Breinl an den k.k. Hofkanzlei-Präsident, add. Tarnow 5. März 1846.
23. HHStA, StK, Provinzen, Galizien, 4: S-kön. Hoheit Ferdinand von Grafen Hardegg, Lemberg 23. Februar 1846.
24. HHStA, StK, Provinzen, Galizien, 4: Bericht des Rzeszower Kreisvorstehers an das galizische Landespräsidium, add. 4. März 1846, Schreiben des mährisch-schlesischen Gouverneurs an den Herren Präsidenten der Obersten Polizei-Hofstelle, Grafen von Sedlnitzky, add. Brünn, 6. März 1846.
25. HHStA, StK, Provinzen, Galizien, Varia Generalia de 1846, 4: Bericht des Vizepräsidenten Grafen Lazansky an den Galizischen Generalgouverneur, add. Sandec 7. März 1846.
26. HHStA, StK, Provinzen, Galizien, 4.
27. "Metternich an Apponyi in Paris, 7 März 46," in Richard Metternich-Rinneburg, ed., *Aus Metternich's nachgelassenen Papieren*, vol. 5, pt. 2: *1816–1848* (Vienna: Wilhelm Braumüller, 1883), 194, 196–204.
28. Metternich quoted in Alan Sked, *The Decline and Fall of the Habsburg Empire 1815–1918* (London: Longman, 1989), 64. Sked describes Metternich as having personally paid specific attention to the Galician events of 1846.
28. Sala, *Geschichte des polnischen Aufstandes vom Jahre 1846*, 126.
30. Ibid., 129.
31. Michal Chvojka, *Josef Graf Sedlnitzky als Präsident der Polizei- und Zensurhofstelle in Wien (1817–1848): Ein Beitrag zur Geschichte der Staatspolizei in der Habsburgermonarchie* (Frankfurt am Main: Peter Lang, 2010), 317.

32. See Sala, *Geschichte des polnischen Aufstandes vom Jahre 1846*, 132–37; Austrian police reports from the 1830s contain all the details about Polish conspiracies: HHStA, Informationsbüro, 6: Berichte des Polizeidirektors Lemberg.
33. Chvojka, *Josef Graf Sedlnitzky als Präsident der Polizei- und Zensurhofstelle in Wien*, 322.
34. Röskau-Rydel, *Niemiecko-austriackie rodziny*, 259.
35. Sala, *Geschichte des polnischen Aufstandes vom Jahre 1846*, 183.
36. Czesław Wycech, *Powstanie chłopów w roku 1846: Jakub Szela* (Warsaw: Ludowa Społdzielnia Wydawnicza, 1955), 112.
37. Sala, *Geschichte des polnischen Aufstandes vom Jahre 1846*, 192.
38. See Leopold von Sacher-Masoch, *Polnische Revolutionen: Erinnerungen aus Galizien* (Prague: F. A. Gredner, 1863), 5.
39. Wolff, *The Idea of Galicia*, 179.
40. On this long-term perspective, see the interesting study by Stanisław Grodziski, "Rok 1846 w Galicji: Przyczyny i konsekwencje," 211–19.
41. Hans-Christian Maner, *Galizien: Eine Grenzregion im Kalkül der Donaumonarchie im 18. und 19. Jahrhundert* (Munich: LIT Verlag, 2007), 82.
42. HHStA, StK, Provinzen Galizien, 4: Gubernial-Präsident Freih. v. Krieg an Gr. Inzaghi, Lemberg 23. Februar 1846.
43. Röskau-Rydel, *Niemiecko-austriackie rodziny*, 152.
44. HHStA, StK, Provinzen Galizien, 4: Bericht des Vizepräsidenten Grafen Lazansky an Staats- u. Konferenz-minister Grafen Kolowrat, Tarnow, 25. Februar 1846.
45. HHStA, StK, Provinzen, Galizien, 4: Bericht des Vizepräsidenten Grafen Lazansky an den galizischen Generalgouverneur, Tarnow 25. Februar 1846.
46. HHStA, StK, Provinzen Galizien, 4: Bericht des Vizepräsidenten Grafen Lazansky an Galizischen Generalgouverneur, add, Sandec 7. März 1846.
47. On loyal peasants see HHStA, StK, Provinzen Galizien, 4: Bericht des Rzeszower Kreisvorstehers an das galizische Landesgubernium, add. 4. März 1846.
48. On Sacher-Masoch's support of the Habsburgs during 1846, see Wolff, *The Idea of Galicia*, 159.
49. Hans Schlitter, *Aus Österreichs Vormärz*, vol. 1: *Galizien und Krakau* (Zurich: Amalthea Verlag, 1920), 60.
50. Cited from S. Frankfurter, *Graf Leo Thun-Hohenstein, Franz Exner und Hermann Bonitz: Beiträge zur Geschichte der österreichischen Unterrichtsreform* (Vienna: Alfred Hölder, 1893), 28.
51. On Stadion's career in Galicia as well as other offices across the Habsburg Monarchy see Rudolph Mattausch, "Franz Graf Stadion (1806–1853)," *Neue österreichische Biographie ab 1815* (Vienna: Amalthea Verlag, 1956–), 14:62–73.
52. This episode is described in detail in Juliusz Starkel, *Rok 1848* (Lwów: Nakładem Księgarni Gybynowicza i Schmidta, 1899), 68.
53. Rudolf Hirsch, *Franz Graf Stadion* (Vienna: Verlag von Eduard Hügel, 1861), 21–22.

54. Schlitter, *Aus Österreichs Vormärz*, 44.
55. Ibid., 55.
56. Hirsch, *Franz Graf Stadion*, 55.
57. Ibid., 51.
58. A. J. P. Taylor described this first Austrian parliament, convened in July 1848, as the only full Reichstag in the history of the Austrian monarchy, and a "double compromise": "the liberals accepted the empire, the empire accepted liberalism." A. J. P. Taylor, *The Habsburg Monarchy 1809–1918* (London: Hamish Hamilton, 1957), 70.
59. Röskau-Rydel, *Niemiecko-austriackie rodziny*, 105.
60. Stefan Kieniewicz and Franciszka Ramotowska, eds., *Protokoły posiedzeń Rady Narodowej Centralnej we Lwowie (14.IV–29.X.1848)* (Warsaw: DiG, 1996), iv–vi.
61. See "Petition des ruthenischen Volkes in Galizien, welche durch die Hände Sr. Exzellenz des Herrn Gouverneurs von Galizien Franz Graf Stadion Seiner Majestät unterbreitet worden ist. Lemberg 19. April 48," in Rudolf Wagner, ed., *Die Revolutionsjahre 1848/49 im Königreich Galizien-Lodomerien (einschließlich Bukowina): Dokumente aus österreichischer Zeit* (Munich: Verlag "Der Südostdeutsche," 1983), 26–28. A detailed description of Ruthenian mobilization and Ruthenian demands is Oleh Turii, "Ukrains'ka 'Vesna narodiv,'" Oleh Turii, ed., in *Holovna Rus'ka Rada 1848–1851: Protokoly zasidan' i knyga korespondentsii*, (uporiadnyky Uliana Kryshtalovych, Ivan Svarnyk) (L'viv: Instytut istorii tserkvy, 2002), ix–xxxii.
62. Jan Kozik, *The Ukrainian National Movement in Galicia: 1815–1849* (Edmonton: Canadian Institute of Ukrainian Studies, 1986), 179.
63. A concise description of Ruthenian politics during the 1848 revolution is in Paul R. Magocsi, *The Roots of Ukrainian Nationalism: Galicia as Ukraine's Piedmont* (Toronto: Toronto University Press, 2002), 67–72. See also Turii, "Ukrainska 'Vesna narodiv,'" xii.
64. On the Rus'kyi Sobor and Vahylevych see Peter Brock, "Vahylevych and the Ukrainian National Identity," in Andrei Markovits and Frank Sysyn, eds., *Nationbuilding and the Politics of Nationalism: Essays on Austrian Galicia* (Cambridge: Harvard Ukrainian Research Institute, 1982), 111–48.
65. Hugo Lane, "The Galician Nobility and the Border with the Congress Kingdom after the November Uprising," in Christoph Augustynowicz and Andreas Kappeler, eds., *Die galizische Grenze 1772–1867: Kommunikation oder Isolation?* (Berlin: LIT Verlag, 2007), 157–69.
66. "Nr. 30. Ministerrat, Wien, 7. Mai 1848," PÖM, Abt. 1: Thomas Kletečka, ed., *Die Ministerien des Revolutionsjahres 1848* (Vienna: Verlag der Österreichischen Akademie der Wissenschaften, 1996), 171.
67. "Nr. 23. Ministerrat, Wien, 30. April 1848," ibid., 127–35.
68. "Nr. 30. Ministerrat, Wien, 7. Mai 1848," ibid., 170–78.

69. On Stadion's role in the foundation of the Ruthenian Council see ibid., xxv. On Stadion's support of the Ruthenians see also "Nr. 33. Ministerrat, Wien, 10. Mai 1848," ibid., 191–98.
70. "Reichstag von Kremsier, Sitzung 22.1.1849," in Wagner, *Die Revolutionsjahre 1848/49 im Königreich Galizien-Lodomerien*, 21. Ziemiałkowski's statements and his claims that Vienna invented the Ruthenians made their way into the historiography. One of the earliest mentions is in Mattausch, "Franz Graf Stadion," 69.
71. "Reichstag von Kremsier, Sitzung 23.1.1849," in Wagner, *Die Revolutionsjahre 1848/49 im Königreich Galizien-Lodomerien*, 24.
72. See Ziemałkowski's response to his opponents, ibid.
73. Turii, "Ukrains'ka 'Vesna narodiv,'" xi.
74. See, for example, Anna Veronika Wendland, *Die Russophilen in Galizien: Ukrainische Konservative zwischen Österreich und Russland 1848–1915* (Vienna: Verlag der Österreichischen Akademie der Wissenschaften, 2001), 40.
75. The most comprehensive analysis of the annexation and integration of Western Galicia is Tadeusz Mencel, *Galicja Zachodnia 1795–1809: Studium z dziejow ziem polskich zaboru austriackiego po III rozbiorze* (Lublin: Wydawnictwo Lubelskie, 1976). On the organization of the West Galician Gubernium see ÖStA, VA, HK, IIIA 4, 325: ex Februar 1796. Materials from the work of the West Galician *Einrichtungskommission*: ÖStA, HK III A 4, 326 Gubern. Nd Regierung, Galizien Mai 1796–1797.
76. Schlitter, *Aus Österreichischs Vormärz*, 1:63.
77. Mattausch, "Franz Graf Stadion," 68.
78. "Petition des ruthenischen Volkes in Galizien. Lemberg 19. April 48," in Wagner, *Die Revolutionsjahre 1848/49 im Königreich Galizien-Lodomerien*, 26–28; for a detailed description of Ruthenian mobilization and demands, see Turii, "Ukrains'ka 'Vesna narodiv.'"
79. See Austrian ministerial debates about Russia's threatening influences on Galicia: "Nr. 23. Ministerrat, Wien, 30. April 1848," PÖM, Abt. 1, 127–35; "Sitzung 19. Mai 1859–2/3. März 1860; Ministerkonferenz, 8.12.1859," PÖM, Abt. 4: Stefan Malfèr, ed., *Das Ministerium Rechberg*, vol. 1 (Vienna: Verlag der Österreichischen Akademie der Wissenschaften, 2003), 283.
80. Detailed analysis of Polish emancipation plans in Stefan Kieniewicz, *Pomiedzy Stadionem a Goslarem: Sprawa włościańska w Galicji w 1848 r.* (Wrocław: Zakład Narodowy im. Ossolińskich, 1980).
81. C. A. McCartney, *The Habsburg Empire 1790–1918* (London: Weidenfeld and Nicolson, 1968), 310.
82. For details of the Polish program see Bronisław Łoziński, *Agenor Gołuchowski w pierwszym okresie rządów swoich (1846–1859)* (Lwów: Nakładem Ksiegarni H. Altenberga, 1901), 19.

83. Wagner, *Die Revolutionsjahre 1848/49 im Königreich Galizien-Lodomerien*, 11.
84. "Nr. 20. Ministerrat Wien, 26. April 1848," *PÖM*, Abt. 1, 107.
85. For a detailed description see Starkel, *Rok 1848*, 316–20.
86. Hirsch, *Franz Graf Stadion*, 22.
87. F.I.S., *Gr. Agenor Golukhovskii i galitskaia Rus' v 1848–1859* (L'vov: Izdanie O. A. Markova, 1901), 6.

Conclusion

1. Isabel Röskau-Rydel, *Niemiecko-austriackie rodziny urzędnicze w Galicji 1772–1918: Kariery zawodowe — środowisko — akulturacja i asymilacja* (Kraków: Wydawnictwo Naukowe Uniwersytetu Pedagogicznego, 2011), 261.
2. Ibid., 266.
3. On Gołuchowski's promotion to the position of vice president of the Galician Gubernium: "Nr. 9. Ministerrat, Wien, 10. April 1848," *PÖM*, Abt. 1: Thomas Kletečka, ed., *Die Ministerien des Revolutionsjahres 1848* (Vienna: Verlag der Österreichischen Akademie der Wissenschaften, 1996), 51–54.
4. F.I.S., *Gr. Agenor Golukhovskii i galitskaia Rus' v 1848–1859* (L'vov: Izdanie O. A. Markova, 1901), 50.
5. Ibid., 51.
6. Bronisław Łoziński, *Agenor hrabia Gołuchowski w pierwszym okresie rządów swoich (1846–1859)* (Lwów: Nakładem Księgarni H. Altenberga, 1901), 130; Juliusz Starkel, *Rok 1848* (Lwów: Nakładem Księgarni Gybynowicza i Schmidta, 1899), 225.
7. Łoziński, *Agenor hrabia Gołuchowski*, 60; Stanisław Pijaj, *Między polskim patriotyzmem a habsburskim lojalizmem: Polacy wobec przemian ustrojowych monarchii Habsburskiej* (Kraków: Historia Iagellonica, 2004), 16.
8. F.I.S., *Gr. Agenor Golukhovskii i galitskaia Rus'*, 8.
9. A recent analysis of Zaleski's publication is Larry Wolff, *The Idea of Galicia: History and Fantasy in Habsburg Political Culture* (Stanford: Stanford University Press, 2010), 117. On Zaleski's approach to the Ruthenians, see ibid., p. 119.
10. On Załeski and his politics in Vienna, see C. A. McCartney, *The Habsburg Empire 1790–1918* (London: Weidenfeld and Nicolson, 1968), 404.
11. "Nr. 68. Ministerrat Wien, 11. Juni 1848," *PÖM*, Abt. 1, 408.
12. "Nr. 14. Ministerrat, Kremsier, 8. Jänner 1849," *PÖM*, Abt. 2: Thomas Kletečka, ed., *Das Ministerium Schwarzenberg*, vol. 1: *5. Dezember 1848–7. Jänner 1850* (Vienna: Verlag der Österreichischen Akademie der Wissenschaften, 2002), 88.
13. Debates about the next governor and Stadion's characterization of Gołuchowski: "Nr. 15. Ministerrat, Olmütz, 12. Jänner 1849," ibid., 94.
14. Ibid.
15. See Michał Bobrzyński, *Z moich pamietników* (Wrocław: Zakład Narodowy im. Ossolińskich, 1957), 1, 7.

16. Röskau-Rydel, *Niemiecko-austriackie rodziny*, 107.
17. On Gołuchowski's initiative and its retraction: "Nr. 27. Ministerrat, Wien, 14. März 1861—Protokoll II, KZ. 879-MCZ. 798," *PÖM*, Abt. 5: Horst Brettner-Messler, ed., *Die Ministerien Erzherzog Rainer und Mensdorff*, vol. 1: 7. *Februar 1861–30. April 1861* (Vienna: Verlag der Österreichischen Akademie der Wissenschaften, 1977), 155. On the alphabet battles see also Ann Sirka, *The Nationality Question in Austrian Education: The Case of Ukrainians in Galicia, 1867–1914* (Frankfurt am Main: Peter Lang, 1980), 51.
18. See the introduction to Stefan Kieniewicz, ed., *Galicja w dobie autonomicznej (1850–1914): Wybór tekstów* (Wrocław: Wydawnictwo Zakładu Narodowego im. Ossolińskich, 1952), x.
19. On the Ruthenian protests: "Ministerkonferenz, Wien, 11. Juni 1859, KZ.2319-MCZ.132," in *PÖM*, Abt. 4: Stefan Malfèr, ed., *Das Ministerium Rechberg*, vol. 1: *19. Mai 1859–2./3. März 1860* (Vienna: Verlag der Österreichischen Akademie der Wissenschaften, 2003), 43–44.
20. Ibid.
21. Bobrzyński, *Z moich pamietników*, 7. On the Galician Diet see Stanisław Grodziski, *Sejm Krajowy galicyjski 1861–1914* (Warsaw: Wydawnictwo Sejmowe, 1993); on its functions, ibid., 84–85.
22. For a detailed discussion see Franciszek Ksawery d'Abancourt, *Era konstytucyjna austro-węgierskiej monarchii od 1848 do 1881* (Kraków: Privately published, 1881), 28–29. Also Kieniewicz, *Galicja w dobie autonomicznej*, xii.
23. F.I.S., *Gr. Agenor Golukhovskii i galitskaia Rus'*, 6.
24. A detailed analysis of international diplomacy surrounding the Polish uprising of 1863 is Richard B. Elrod, "Austria and the Polish Insurrection of 1863: Documents from the Austrian State Archive," *International History Review* 8, no. 3 (1986): 416–37. For the debates about a possible restoration of Poland see ibid., 424.
25. See Edward Walewander, *Die österreichische Presse und der polnische Januaraufstand* (Frankfurt am Main: Peter Lang, 1991), 31.
26. On the importance of international assistance, see Henryk Wereszycki, *Austria a powstanie styczniowe* (Lwów: Wydawnictwo Zakładu Narodowego im. Ossolińskich, 1930); Wereszycki, *Austria a powstanie styczniowe*, 87.
27. Ibid., 75.
28. On projects of Polish-Austrian cooperation during the 1860s see Pijaj, *Między polskim patriotyzmem a habsburskim lojalizmem*, 29; Kazimierz Olszański, *Prasa galicyjska wobec powstania styczniowego* (Wrocław: Zakład Narodowy im. Ossolińskich, 1975), 23.
29. Piotr Wandycz, "The Poles in the Habsburg Monarchy," in Andrei Markovits and Frank Sysyn, eds., *Nationbuilding and the Politics of Nationalism: Essays on Austrian Galicia* (Cambridge: Harvard Ukrainian Research Institute, 1982), 68–93.
30. Wereszycki, *Austria a powstanie styczniowe*, 58.

31. A detailed description of Mensdorff-Pouilly's family background and career is Helmut Rumpler, "Mensdorff-Pouilly, Alexander, Graf von," in *Allgemeine Deutsche Biographie und Neue Deutsche Biographie*, vol. 17 (Berlin: Duncker & Humblot, 1994), 87–88.
32. "Nr. 107. Ministerrat, Prag, 29. Oktober 1866, KA. 3903-MRZ. 107," *PÖM*, Abt. 6: Horst Brettner-Messler, ed., *Das Ministerium Belcredi*, vol. 2: 8. April 1866–6. Februar 1867 (Vienna: Verlag der Österreichschen Akademie der Wissenschaften), 290–91.
33. For discussion of candidates and Gołuchowski's nomination, see "Nr. 89. Ministerrat, Wien, 21. Juli 1866, KZ. 2127-MRZ.89," ibid., 171–73.
34. Ibid., 172.
35. See "Nr. 107. Ministerrat, Prag, 29. Oktober 1866, KA. 3903-MRZ. 107," ibid., 291.
36. A detailed analysis of Helcel's memorandum is in Pijaj, *Między polskim patriotyzmem a habsburskim lojalizmem*, 29–33.
37. For a detailed analysis of Gołuchowski's memorandum, see ibid., 84.
38. "Promemoria des Grafen Gołuchowski wegen einer künftigen Sonderstellung Galiziens," Nr. 126. Ministerrat, Wien, 6. Februar 1867, *PÖM*, Abt. 6, 2:409–10.
39. Ibid.
40. Łoziński, *Agenor hrabia Gołuchowski*, 118.
41. Pijaj, *Między polskim patriotyzmem a habsburskim lojalizmem*, 77.
42. Röskau-Rydel, *Niemiecko-austriackie rodziny*, 152.
43. On the "three dualisms" see Harald Binder, *Galizien in Wien: Parteien, Wahlen, Fraktionen und Abgeordnete im Übergang zur Massenpolitik* (Vienna: Verlag der Österreichischen Akademie der Wissenschaften, 2005), 34.
44. Leon Biliński, *Wspomnienia i Dokumenty, 1846–1919*, vol. 1 (Warsaw: Nakładem Ksiegarni F. Hoesicka, 1924), 205.
45. Dorota Litwin-Lewandowska, *O Polska Rację Stanu w Austrii. Polacy w życiu politycznym Austrii w okresie monarchii dualistycznej (1867–1918)* (Lublin: Wydawnictwo Uniwestytetu Marii Curie-Skłodowskiej, 2008), 124.
46. On Gołuchowski junior, see Czesław Partacz, *Od Badeniego do Potockiego: Stosunki polsko-ukraińskie w Galicji w latach 1888–1908* (Toruń: Wydawnictwo Adam Marszałek, 1997), 60.
47. Biliński, *Wspomnienia*, 7.
48. Waldemar Łazuga, *"Rządy polskie" w Austrii: Gabinet Kazimierza hr. Badeniego 1895–1897* (Poznań: Wydawnictwo Naukowe UAM, 1991), 114.
49. Łoziński, *Agenor hrabia Gołuchowski*, 4.
50. R. J. W. Evans, "Josephinism, 'Austrianness,' and the Revolution of 1848," in Ritchie Robertson and Edward Timms, eds., *The Austrian Enlightenment and Its Aftermath* (Edinburgh: Edinburgh University Press, 1991), 146.

INDEX

Absolutism, 8, 9, 27, 28, 63, 77, 82, 135, 231, 249, 250
Adriatic, 62, 63, 99, 220
Alexander I, 88, 91, 93, 109, 110, 111, 125
Amsterdam, 232
Angelowych, 166, 168, 169, 194
Apponyi, Anton von, 64, 214
Armenians, 5, 42, 53
Aron, Jacob, 189
Assimilation, 9, 249; Austrian-Polish, 8, 13, 14, 15, 148, 152, 173; Austrian-Polish-Ruthenian, 204; Austrian-Ruthenian, 15, 171, 172; Polish-Ruthenian, 173
Aubernon, 89–90, 99–100
Auersperg, family, 24, 62, 65
Auersperg, Heinrich von, 62–65, 66–68, 135, 142–43; governor of Galicia, 67; opening of the Galician diet, 135; salary, 68; support of theaters, 142, 143
Auersperg, Madame, 65
Aufklärung. *See* Enlightenment
Augustynowicz, 53
Austria, 2, 3, 6, 21, 87, 92, 94, 114, 115, 118, 231, 243. *See also* Austrian Empire
Austria-Hungary, 21, 231
Austrian Empire, 7, 12, 14, 16, 21, 22, 84, 88, 89, 100, 103, 106, 112, 118, 225, 230, 243. *See also* Austria
Austrian War Council, 240
Austrian-Polish War, 84, 86, 88

Austro-Hungarian Compromise, 2, 228, 243, 244
Austro-Turkish wars, 51
Autonomy, Galicia, 3, 11, 244

Backwardness, Galicia, 3, 4, 43, 47, 55, 68, 127, 154, 242, 248
Balkans, 113
Banat, 46, 51, 62, 64, 65, 161
Banat of Temesvár, 10, 64
Barach-Rappaport, Adam, 202
Barbareum, 168
Bauer, Roger, 80
Baum, Baron, 89
Baworowski, Józef, 210
Beales, Derek, 4, 9, 27, 70, 77
Beck, Anton von, 59
Belcredi, Richard, 244
Belgium, 23
Bellefrois, 94
Bel'sk, 5
Berger, count, 32
Berlin, 7, 44, 106, 163, 183, 185, 186, 188, 196, 197, 206, 207, 243
Bernd, Carl, 214
Bernstein, Leib, 185–87, 190, 198, 202, 287, 288
Bernstein, Marek, 201
Bess, Karl von, 59
Beust, von, 244

INDEX

Bielawski, Antoni, 139
Binder, Harald, 246
Black Lists, 33
Blekynski, 97
Blumenfeld, Emanuel, 202
Bobek, Aron, 194
Bobowski, Józef, 139
Bochnia, 35, 213, 214
Bogusławski, Wojciech, 143
Bohemia, 3, 6, 7, 10, 11, 15, 21, 23, 37, 46, 57, 59, 64, 70, 73, 107, 109, 112, 137, 140, 158, 160, 165, 166, 177, 182, 190, 195, 196, 200, 201, 222, 227, 229, 232, 244, 247, 255; annexation to the Habsburg Monarchy, 21; bureaucrats from, 49; Edict of Toleration, 188; model for Galicia, 37; nobility, 160; peasant uprising, *1775*, 217
Bolesław, 213
Böll, Franz, 59
Borderlands: Austrian-Ottoman, 52; Austrian-Russian, 2, 10, 52, 87, 88, 112, 123, 125, 192; Bohemia, 10; Galician, 2, 5, 10, 87; Habsburg, 10; Italian, 10, 48; Polish-Ukrainian, 2; politics of, 233
Bosnia, 247
Bourbons, 221
Bratkowski, Leo (Lev), 59, 81
Breinl, Joseph von Wallerntein, 216–19, 293
Brigido: brothers, 64; family, 64, 65, 220; Madame, 65; soial networks, 65
Brigido, Hieronim von, 64
Brigido, Joseph Karl von, 6, 14, 46–48, 59, 62, 64, 65, 73, 76–81, 83, 84, 109, 112, 137, 138, 141, 142, 144, 183, 265, 266, 268; on Heinrich von Auersperg, 67; career before Galicia, 64; on church reform, 77; dismissal from Galicia, 80; education, 64; on Enlightenment, 78; meeting with Joseph II, 71; on peasant reform, 73; policies of bureaucracy, 69; report from Galicia, 1780, 68; on school reform, 76
Brigido, Pompeius von, 59, 64
Brody, 89, 90, 153, 186, 189, 192, 199, 201, 244; Austrian-Russian borderland, 63, 110; Napoleonic Wars, 89; economy and commerce, 63, 192; espionage, 89; Jewish population, 89
Brünn, 136
Brunnstein, Spuk, 193
Brzezany, 97
Buchach, 192, 194
Budapest, 232
Budweis, 109
Bujakowski, Ignacy von, 59, 80–81
Bukowina, 193
Bulla, Joseph, 143
Byobzanski, Ludwik, 114, 115

Cameralism, 25–27
Capua, 46, 64
Carinthia, 99
Carniola, 62, 64
Catherine the Great, 133
Catholic Church, 35, 51. *See also* Roman Catholic Church; Roman Catholicism
Catholicism, 42, 44. *See also* Catholic Church; Roman Catholic Church
Catholicism, Eastern, 23
Central Europe, 16, 20, 100, 163, 179, 243, 248
Centralization, 8, 24, 43, 63, 136, 250
Chamber of Commerce, 124
Charles, Archduke, 90
Charles V of Spain, 160, 162
Chłopicki, Józef, 116
Ciesłowski, 213
Cisleithania, 232
Clement IV, Pope, 35
Commercial Council of Carniola, 64
Conduitlisten, 33, 258
Confederation of Bar, 261
Confederation of the Polish People, 209
Congress of Vienna, 100, 109
Constantine, Prince, 109
Cotarski, Karol, 213
Council of Four Lands, 184, 287
Court Chancellery: Austrian, 66; Austrian-Bohemian, 23, 37, 39, 52, 71, 73, 79, 187, 193, 221; Galician, 39, 40, 62, 244; Hungarian, 23
Croatia, 23, 46

Czartoryska, Isabella, 144
Czartoryski, Adam, 97, 116, 119–23, 140
Czartoryski, Kazimierz, 140
Czernowitz, 253

Dalmatia, 99
D'Ellex, 80, 81
Dembowski, Edward, 212
Denmark, 243
D'Este, Ferdinand, 208, 209, 212, 215, 219, 220, 240
Deutschmeister, 194–96
Dickson, P. G. M., 12
Diderot, 27
Die Presse, 163
Diet: Bohemia, 137; Galicia, 76, 113, 133, 136, 137, 178, 239, 244; Galicia, 1775, 135; Galicia, 1776, 136; Galicia, 1817, 102, 104, 138; Poland, 135, 184
Dietl, family, 151
Dietl, Franz Joachim, 150
Dietl, Johann Georg, 150
Dietl, Józef, 150, 151, 152
Dietrichstein, 93, 95, 96, 97
Drohobych, 199
Duchy of Warsaw, 88, 90–92, 96, 98, 140
Dwernicki, Józef, 120, 209
Dzieduszycka, Salomea, 140
Dzieduszycki, family, 117, 140, 167
Dzieduszycki, Józef, 136, 139
Dzieduszycki, Tadeusz, 54, 140
Dzieduszycki, Walerian, 140

East-Central Europe, 11, 16, 17
Eastern Europe, 8, 13, 16, 17, 207
Eastern Galicia, 5, 17, 86, 87, 95, 96, 100, 128, 206, 223, 226, 252
East-Europeanism, 6
Economy, Galicia, 3, 4, 63, 68, 153
Edict of Toleration, 187, 188, 190, 191, 196, 204
Educational Commission, 44, 260
Eger, Hofrat, 73
Engerman, 95
Enlightenment, 4, 5, 6, 9, 23, 25, 26, 27, 29, 41, 47, 78, 79, 107, 196, 200, 204, 247;
anti-, 79; Austrian, 3, 6, 12, 20, 26, 27, 32, 44, 63, 82, 187, 196, 197, 201, 247, 248; European, 4; French, 16, 27; French influences, 4, 27, 29, 44; in Galicia, 45; German, 4; ideas of, 1, 4; Jewish, 183, 197, 201, 205, 290; Polish, 44; politics of, 4; products of, 6
Erfurt, 51
Evans, R. J. W., 4, 13, 248

Fabricius, family, 173
Fabricius, Johann Baptist, 171
Fabricius, Johanna Maria, 171–73
Fabricius, Pelagia, 172
February Patent, 231
Federalization, 239
Ferdinand, Archduke, 91, 92, 94, 97, 124
Ferdinand I, 21
Fitek, Franz, 59
France, 16, 27, 28, 29, 44, 79, 88, 91, 100
Francis II, 63, 80, 109, 119, 124, 132, 247
Francis Joseph, 231, 238
Frankfurt, 165
Frederick I, 35
Fredro, family, 167
Freemasons, 203
French Foreign Ministry, 90
French revolution, 79, 86, 87
French Revolutionary Wars, 14, 63, 83, 84, 86, 103
Freundsperg, Sangilla von, 31
Friedrich, Karin, 43

Galicia and Lodomeria, kingdom of, 16, 37
Galician Information Bureau, 125
Galician Personal Guard, 140
Gallenberg, Sigismund von, 67
Gartenlaube für Oesterreich, 164
Gazeta Lwowska, 117, 118, 120
German Empire, 243
German Federation, 243
German states, 3, 21, 25, 50, 163
Germanization, 3, 134
Germany, 44, 90
Ghent, 162
Glassl, Horst, 12, 13, 51

INDEX

Goëss, Peter von, 6, 89, 99–102, 138, 144, 145
Golitsyn, Sergei, 92, 97
Gołuchowski, Agenor, 235–38, 243–46; governor of Galicia, 237; mayor of Lwów, 235; minister of interior, 237, 239; reputation among Galician Poles, 243
Gołuchowski, Agenor, junior, 247
Gorchakov, 94
Görz, 196
Gorzkowski, Ludwik, 212
Graz, 46, 62, 64, 65, 162, 164
Great Britain, 87
Greek Catholic Church, 168, 169, 170, 172, 173, 174, 178, 194, 223, 225. *See also* Uniate Church, Catholicism, Eastern
Greek Catholic metropolitanate, 168
Grodziski, Stanisław, 12
Groszynski, Michał, 213
Gruet, Ignazius, 59
Gubernium: Banat, 64; foundation, 23; Galician, 40, 57, 58, 63, 64, 67, 69, 73, 74, 76, 77, 78, 80, 89, 97, 98, 109, 110, 111, 139, 142, 147, 161, 169, 186, 189, 192, 193, 194, 198, 199, 200, 202, 203, 204, 218, 219, 223, 235, 245; Inner Austrian, 64; West Galician, 40
Guinigi, Vinzent, 64, 67
Gurowski, Adam, 210

Habsburg hereditary territories, 37
Habsburg, Karolina Maria von, 145
Habsburg Monarchy, 1, 2, 3, 4, 5, 6, 8, 9, 12, 16, 20, 21, 22, 25, 26, 27, 28, 29, 34, 39, 44, 59, 69, 81, 82, 83, 86, 87, 88, 91, 95, 100, 105, 106, 113, 116, 118, 124, 125, 131, 133, 139, 149, 156, 158, 160, 161, 163, 164, 176, 179, 182, 195, 197, 201, 207, 221, 224, 231, 237, 251, 252; *1809*, 84, 88, 95; annexation of Galicia, 35, 54; annexation of Kraków, 226; borderlands, 10; Enlightenment, 25; French Revolutionary Wars, 83; historiography of, 13; in the Holy Roman Empire, 22; noble tites, 131; parititons of Poland, 34; treatment of Polish subjects, 114

Hadik, Andreas Futak von, 47, 62, 209, 240
Halych, 168
Hamburg, 196
Hamburger Zeitschrift Omnibus, 175
Handscha, 174
Hasidim, 203
Hasidism, 202, 203, 205
Haskalah, 183, 186, 197, 201, 202. *See also* Enlightenment: Jewish
Hauer, Franz von, 102, 138
Hehn, Heinrich, 245
Helcel, Antoni, 244
Helzel, Anton, 195
Hoffman, Żorża, 143
Holstein, 240, 243
Holy Roman Empire, 21, 22, 25, 49, 50, 129, 130, 131, 255
Homberg, Herz, 198, 200, 201, 290
Hordyński, 141
Hôtel de l'Europe, 9
Hôtel de Russie, 9
Hrushevs'kyi, Mykhailo, 175
Hundert, Gershon David, 42
Hungary, 5, 22, 23, 37, 39, 46, 51, 64, 67, 158, 195, 213, 231, 232, 244; 1848, 222; annexation to the Habsburg Monarchy, 21; autonomy, 232; French Revolutionary Wars, 83; kingdom of, 3, 21, 23, 37; model for Galicia, 37; social structure, 37

Illyria, 46
Istanbul, 7
Italy, 3, 6, 7, 10, 11, 21, 59, 63, 83, 136, 201, 209, 221, 238, 240

Jabłonowski, Ludwik, 113
Jabłonowski, Maciej, 144
Jakymowych, 225
Janowski, Jan Nepomucen, 210
Japhet in Search of His Nationality. *See* Lorm, Hieronimus
Jarosław, 37, 75
Jaslo, 213
Jesuits, 76
Jewish Directorium, 184, 185, 189

INDEX

Joseph II, 9, 22–23, 30, 28–31, 33, 34, 37, 39, 43, 49, 57, 61, 63, 66, 65–67, 71, 73, 74, 76, 77, 78, 79, 80, 132, 133, 136, 137, 140, 143, 168, 187, 188, 191, 192, 197, 198, 217, 247, 248, 250; on bureaucracy, 28–29, 31; church reform, 76; end of life, reform reversal, 78; inclusion of Polish nobles in Galician administration, 66; land and tax reforms in Galicia, 89–90; making of bureaucracy in Galicia, 51; pastoral letter, 28, 29, 134; peasant reform, 71; on Johann Anton von Pergen, 50; policy of bureaucracy, 33; reforms in Galicia, 71; school reform in Galicia, 75; travels, 28; trip to Galicia, 1773, 42; trip to Galicia, 1780, 66
Judaism, 23
Justi, Johann Heinrich von, 25, 26

Kaczkowski, Zygmunt, 152
Kakania, 18, 20, 21, 33. *See also* Musil, Robert
Kałusz, 151, 161
Kantakuzena, Princess, 141
Kanzlisten, 57
Karpinski, Franciszek, 140
Kaunitz, Wenzel Anton von, 35, 37, 39, 49, 50, 51, 58, 60, 62, 65, 80, 81, 83, 133, 162, 168, 258, 259, 263; education, 22; policy of bureaucracy, 49; selection of bureaucrats for Galicia, 51, 58, 59, 81
Kazimierz, 35
Kerechyns'kyi, 223
Kermenyi, Joseph, 84
Kiersky, 53
Kinsky, Maria Theresia, 139
Knopp, Joseph Ignaz, 57
Koczian, Hofrat, 57, 61
Kohlmanhuber, 80
Kohn, Abraham, 203
Kołłątai, Hugo, 44, 140, 260
Kolowrat, family, 24, 107
Kolowrat, Ludwig von, 71, 73, 79, 219, 221
Komers, Ritter von, 244
Komorowski, Peter, 97
König, Johann, 59

Königgrätz, 163, 164
Konopka, 213
Koranda, Joseph, 73
Kosciuszko uprising, 144
Kossakowska, Katarzyna, 67, 141
Krafft-Ebing, Richard, 178
Kraków, 2, 5, 16, 17, 35, 40, 86, 98, 100, 138, 139, 149, 150, 151, 206, 226, 242; annexation to the Austrian Empire, *1846*, 226; capital of Western Galicia, 223; free-city, *1815*, 212; university, 149
Kratter, Franz, 43
Kraus, Philipp, 220, 240
Kremsier parliament, 222
Krępowiecki, Tadeusz, 210
Kressel, Baron, 79
Krieg, Franz, 150, 166, 215, 218, 219, 220, 235, 237, 271, 294
Krosnowski, Wincenty, 210
Kuczera, Franz Hraubenthal von, 64
Kulczycka, Anna, 150
Kuzems'kyi, Mykhailo, 178, 223
Kyiv, 17
Kyiv guberniia, 114

Laibach, 46, 64, 232
Lam, Jan, 158, 165, 166, 171, 179, 211, 234
Lamm, Zenon Konrad, 165
Landau, Ezekiel, 185, 186, 190
Landau, Jakob, 192
Landau, Jakovke, 199
Lazansky, 219
Le Gaulois, 175
Lederer, Laddäus, 215
Ledóchowski, Jan, 209
Leipzig, 165, 175
Lemberg, 9, 10, 15, 37, 40, 42, 43, 48, 51, 52, 53, 55, 57, 60, 62, 63, 65, 67, 75, 76, 77, 89, 92, 93, 95, 102, 106, 110, 111, 113, 117, 135, 136, 139, 141, 143, 144, 145, 147, 148, 149, 151, 153, 157, 162, 169, 177, 184, 186, 197, 199, 200, 202, 204, 210, 211, 212, 213, 218, 220, 221, 223, 226, 227, 228, 250, 254; Bernardine Cathedral, 77; casino, 67; censorship office, 203; chaos in 1809, 92; cholera epidemics, 161; coffeehouse

Lemberg, (*continued*)
  culture, 141; coffee-houses, 128;
  Franciscan monastery, 143; Greek
  Catholic seminary, 168; Jabłonowski
  garden, 142; Jewish ghetto, 161; Jewish
  population, 183; kahal, 202, 203;
  Kontrakten, 143; Lewandowski coffee-
  house, 142; living costs, 68, 147;
  population of, 144; salons, 147; social
  life, 144; social life, 1831–32, 209;
  theater, 127, 142, 143; university, 76, 111,
  117, 161, 201, 215, 222; Voronovsky Palace,
  143. *See also* L'viv; Lwów
Lemberger Zeitung, 120
Leopold II, 63, 80, 132, 136, 137, 191, 247
Leopold-Orden, 161
Letteris, Meier Halevi, 201
Levin, Joseph, 202
Lewicki, Jan, 170
Lewyckyi, Petro, 172
Lezzeny, 74
Liberum veto, 41
Lieben, 196
Lippa, Joseph von, 59, 81
Lithuania, 111
Littoral, 48, 220, 221
Lobkowitz, August von, 6, 15, 106, 107, 108,
  109, 110, 111, 112, 113, 114, 115, 116, 117, 118,
  119, 120, 121, 122, 123, 124, 125, 126, 127,
  143, 152, 201, 203, 208, 209, 241; career
  before Galicia, 109; correspondence
  with Adam Czartoryski, 119; dismissal
  from Galicia, 123; meeting with Polish
  revolutionaries, 114; policies in Galicia,
  111; Polish claims, 112; support of Polis
  culture, 111
Lobkowitz, family, 24, 107
Lodomeria, 37
Lombardy, 21, 23, 102, 103, 238
London, 49
Longchamps, Eleonora, 149
Lorenz, 112
Lorm, Hieronimus, 163, 164
Lorraine, 7, 240
Lower Austria, 49, 81, 150
Łoziński, Władysław, 128, 247

Lubomirska, Elżbieta, 140
Lubomirski, family, 117, 167
Lubomirski, Henryk, 98
L'viv, 9, 16, 17. *See also* Lemberg; Lwów
Lwów, 16, 42, 76, 92, 166, 223, 232, 235, 239,
  240, 244. *See also* Lemberg; L'viv
Lwów, university, 235
Lytvynowych, Spyrydon, 178, 179

Magna Charta, 137
Mainz, 49
Malopolska, 5, 208
Mandatarien, 217
Maner, Hans-Christian, 218
Margelik, Jan Václav, 64, 70, 75, 76, 267
Maria Theresa, 6, 22, 23–25, 27, 28, 30, 35,
  37, 41, 49, 51, 60, 63, 65, 67, 132, 144,
  145, 185; annexation of Galicia, 35;
  centralization, 24; church reform in
  Galicia, 168; on Enlightenment, 27;
  general reforms, 22, 23; Jewish reforms,
  187; school reform in Galicia, 74
Maskilim, 44, 198, 201, 202, 203
Masoch, Charlotte von, 162
Masoch, family, 161
Masoch, Franz von, 161, 162
Masochism, 178
McCagg, William, 204
Megner, Karl, 57
Mehoffer, family, 152
Meller-Zakomel'skii, Nikolai, 94, 95
Mendelssohn, Moses, 186, 188, 196, 198
Menkes, Oswald, 202
Mensdorff-Pouilly, Alexander von, 6,
  240–43, 246, 247, 298
Messarosch, 67
Metternich, Klemens von, 105, 106, 110,
  115, 119, 123, 166, 211, 214, 219, 222, 226,
  253; correspondence with August
  Lobkowitz, 110; on international
  security, 105; Orient, 6; resignation,
  222; response to the Polish revolution,
  1830–31, 211
Metternich, Mélanie, 124
Mezzodi, Antonio, 142
Mierzwinski, Karol, 139

INDEX

Ministerial Council, 237
Model province, Galicia, 3, 4, 6, 20, 43, 49, 248
Modernity, 2, 252
Modernization, 13, 247
Montesquieu, 27
Moravia, 182
Morgenstern, 213
Musil, Robert, 18, 20, 21, 33
Myslynice, 67

Nabutowych, 166
Napoleon, 87, 88, 91–93, 96, 98, 99, 100, 103, 169, 200
Napoleonic Wars, 16, 87, 100, 102, 109, 133, 168, 178, 200, 226
Nationalism, 145, 167, 178, 179, 231, 232, 233, 248, 249, 251
Nationalisten, 70
Neo-absolutism, 231, 238
Netherlands, 3, 7, 21, 22, 64, 67, 79, 83
Nicholas I, 110, 115, 123
Niemczewicz, Ignaz, 97
Nobilitation, Galicia, 130, 131, 278
Nobility: Austria's German territories, 130; Bohemia, 160; Habsburg Monarchy, 129; hierarchies in Galicia, 130; Hungary, 37, 130; percentage in Galicia, 2; Polish, 8, 9, 37, 41, 42, 43, 53, 54, 66, 137, 250, 277, 278; Polish, hierarchies, 129; Polish, percentage in Galicia, 128; Polish complaints about Austrian administration, 67; Polish in different partitions, 139; Polish inclusion in the Austrian administration, 49, 69, 70

October Diploma, 231
Oechner, Baron, 120, 121
Olesno, 213
Olmütz, 240
Olszewska, 210
Orient, 253
Oriental Academy, 50
Orthodoxy, 23, 35, 42, 167
Ossolińeum, 101

Ossoliński, family, 140
Ossoliński, Józef Maksymilian, 137, 140
Ossoliński Library, 111
Ostermann, family, 117, 151, 172, 173
Ostermann, Georg Benjamin von, 117, 118, 171, 172
Ostermann, Georg Johann Wilhelm von, 172
Ostermann, Iwanna von, 172
Ostermann, Johann Georg von, 117, 151, 171, 215, 233, 234
Ostermann, Moritz Hugo von, 117
Oświęcim, principality, 5
Ottoman Empire, 7, 21, 51, 64, 110, 113

Pagnis, 60, 68
Palacký, František, 225
Palermo, 207, 221
Pan-Germanism, 163, 165
Pan-Slavism, 178
Paris, 16, 29, 79, 89, 90, 92, 93, 94, 121, 175, 206, 207, 221
Pergen, Johann Anton von, 6, 14, 46–48, 52, 53, 55–57, 59–62, 64, 81, 124, 141, 168, 209, 263; arrival in Galicia, 51; career before Galicia, 49–51; education reform, 50; first impressions of Galicia, 58–59; on Galician Jews, 183; on Polish nobility, 56, 60; reports from Galicia, 52; request for a transfer, 61
Perl, Isaak, 201
Piast family, 112
Piedmont, 10, 11, 92
Pillersdorf Constitution, 222
Płock, 93
Płużańki, Ignacy Romuald, 210
Podgorce, 213
Podolia, 5, 111
Pol, family, 149, 151
Pol, Wincenty, 148, 149, 150, 151, 152, 210
Poland, 6, 17, 28, 35, 41, 42, 43, 44, 45, 55, 83, 84, 87, 88, 96, 100, 103, 106, 107, 112, 114, 115, 118, 119, 122, 125, 135, 139, 144, 180, 202, 207, 209, 210, 232, 241, 252; eastern, 2; economy, 43; first partition, 5, 56; Jewish population, 184; kingdom

Poland (continued)
  of, 109, 110, 114, 115, 117, 120; maps of, 37; partitions of, 2, 20, 34, 35, 54, 86, 87, 106, 131, 139, 242; Prussian, 43; reforms, 44; revolutions, 2; Russian, 10, 114, 120, 125, 208, 241; towns, 43. *See also* Poland-Lithuania; Polish-Lithuanian Commonwealth
Poland-Lithuania, 3, 5, 8, 10, 41, 42, 43, 56, 128, 129, 130, 131, 132, 134, 135, 139, 140, 144, 167, 185, 188, 191, 195, 204; Jewish minority, 184; partitions of, 54, 132; reforms of nobility, 132. *See also* Poland; Polish-Lithuanian Commonwealth
Police, 162, 209
Police science, 25, 26, 27
Polish Democratic Society, 209, 212
Polish National Committee, 209
Polish National Council, 223
Polish national guard, 228
Polish-Lithuanian Commonwealth, 35, 41, 43, 53, 54, 131, 138, 141, 153, 183, 185, 208. *See also* Poland; Poland-Lithuania
Polizeiwissenschaft. *See* Police science
Poll, Franz Xaver, 149
Polonization, 238
Poniatowski, Andrzej, 139
Poniatowski, Józef, 84, 85, 91, 92, 94, 96, 97, 98, 140, 271, 278
Poniatowski, Stanisław August, 139, 144
Ponińska, 210
Populists, 176, 178, 234, 238, 246
Portugal, 6
Potocka, Countess, 144
Potocki, Adam, 243, 246
Potocki, Alfred, 140, 246
Potocki, Artur, 140
Potocki, family, 117, 140
Prague, 23, 107, 136, 158, 162, 185, 190, 196, 197
Precliczek, Wacław, 158, 159, 165, 166, 170, 171, 174, 177, 179, 180, 211, 234, 235
Pressburg, 196
Prosvita, 172
Protestantism, 23, 35, 51

Prussia, 7, 16, 21, 22, 25, 28, 34, 35, 50, 51, 53, 83, 86, 87, 88, 100, 106, 139, 144, 163, 206, 212, 231, 243
Przemyśl, 37, 53, 75

Radziwiłł, family, 144, 167
Radziwiłów, 192
Rechberg, Johann, 238, 240, 241, 242
Red Rus'. *See* Rus' Czerwona
Reischach, Judas, 66
Retschratner, Anna, 150
Revue Bleue, 175
Richter, Joseph, 30, 31
Riedel, Freidrich Justus, 51
Rohrer, Joseph, 147
Roman Catholic Church, 50, 53, 169. *See also* Roman Catholicism
Roman Catholicism, 168, 206. *See also* Roman Catholic Church
Romanovs, 111
Romanticism, 148, 149, 236
Rome, 42, 167
Rosenstein, Izak Aron, 202
Röskau-Rydel, Isabelle, 13
Roth, Joseph, 18
Rousseau, 27, 196
Rozhnetsky, General, 92
Rus' Czerwona, 5, 167, 208
Rus'kyi Sobor, 223
Russ' palatinate, 5
Russia, 34, 86, 87, 88, 89, 93, 96, 99, 100, 106, 109, 110, 111, 112, 113, 114, 115, 118, 119, 120, 121, 122, 123, 212, 224, 240, 241, 251, 261. *See also* Russian Empire
Russian Empire, 2, 7, 17, 34, 37, 63, 84, 86, 87, 88, 101, 106, 110, 112, 117, 122, 125, 133, 176, 177, 192, 202, 224, 225, 226, 240
Russophilism, 176, 177, 178, 180, 233, 234, 238, 246
Russo-Turkish War, 122
Ruthenia, 5
Ruthenian National Council, 178, 223, 224, 235
Rzeszów, 213

INDEX

Sacher, family, 160, 161, 165, 283
Sacher, Johann Nepomuk von, 161, 175
Sacher, Mathias, 160
Sacher, Thomas, 160
Sacher-Masoch, Leopold von, 157–59, 163–65, 167, 174, 177–80; academic career, 162; *Auf der Höhe*, 175; on the Austrian Empire, 164; autobiography, 175; *Choses vécues*, 175; *Don Juan of Kolomea*, 162; family history, 159, 160; masochism, 157, 178; memoirs, 175; on Pan-Slavism, 163; Ruthenian claims, 164, 175; Ruthenian nanny (*see* Handscha); *Venus in Furs*, 157, 158; writings, 158
Sacher-Masoch, Leopold von, senior, 145, 162, 174, 215, 218
Safranowych, family, 171
Safranowych, Johann von, 166, 170, 177
Sala, Moritz von, 216
Salaries, bureaucrats in Galicia, 58, 68
Salzburg, 64
Sambor, 128, 192
Sandomierz, palatinate, 5
Sanguszko, family, 117, 167
Sanguszko, Roman, 123
Sanok, 117, 151, 213, 233
Sapieha, Leon, 245
Sapieha, Paweł, 145
Sawa, Anita, 193
Saxony, 59, 87, 88
Scheiner, Franz, 57
Schleswig, 243
Schleswig-Holstein, 243
Schmerling, Anton, 244
Schönbrunn, peace treaty, 1809, 95
Schöner, Mayer, 192
Schwarzenberg, Anna Berta von, 107
Schwarzenberg, Felix, 240
Sedlnitzky, Joseph von, 106, 114, 118, 119, 215
Seeling, family, 152
Sejm, 41
Serra, 92, 94
Seven Years' War, 50, 186
Sicily, kingdom of, 221
Sierakowsky, 53
Silesia, 35, 53, 57, 59, 151, 182
Singer, Anton, 59
Skarbek, 141
Slovenia, 23, 62
Slovo, 234
Smolka, family, 151
Smolka, Franz (Franciszek), 151, 152, 222, 223
Smolka, Wincenty, 151, 222
Society for the Dissemination of Useful Industry and Employment, 201
Society of the Polish People, 209
Sonnenfels, Joseph von, 26, 27, 28, 29; on absolutism, 28; on patriotism, 28
Sorkin, David, 197
Spain, 21, 160, 175
St. Petersburg, 2, 7, 14, 15, 89, 91, 92, 93, 94, 103, 106, 110, 111, 112, 114, 115, 122, 133, 139, 177, 207, 226, 233, 240, 241
Stadion, brothers, 229, 239
Stadion, Franz von, 6, 220, 229, 230, 235, 237, 240
Stadion, Juža, 220
Stadion, Philip, 91
Stadion, Rudolph, 220, 229
Stadnicki, Jan, 145
Stanisławów, 165, 172, 234
State Chancellery, 23, 39, 50, 51, 62
State Council, 50, 51
State-building, 1, 3, 16, 26
Sternfelt, Aron, 199
Strasbourg, 59
Strassoldo, Rudolf von, 67
Stryj, 169, 193, 194
Styria, 99
Summer, Alexander, 245
Supreme Imperial Police, 203
Sweden, 87
Switzerland, 21
Szabo, Franz, 4, 12, 51
Szekely, Mailath, 84
Szela, Jakub, 216, 217, 294
Szeptyczka, 210
Szumlanski, 97
Szydlowski, Adam, 97

INDEX

Tabula rasa, Galician, 9, 40, 41, 47
Tarnopol, 101, 201
Tarnów, 75, 209, 212, 213, 216, 220
Tatishchev, Vasilii, 110, 114, 122
Taxation Commission, 65
Thanhauser, Karl, 59
Theiner, Johan, 59
Thun, Leo, 229, 240, 246, 247
Thürheim, Ludowika (Lulu), 144
Tilsit peace treaty, 91
Törrock, 57
Transleithania, 232
Transylvania, 23, 51, 66
Trautmansdorf, 80
Trembliński, 141
Trieste, 6, 10, 16, 23, 44, 46, 48, 59, 62, 63, 64, 65, 73, 99, 136, 142, 153, 196, 197, 200, 232, 240, 254
Turka, 70
Tuscany, 21, 136
Tychowicz, Ignat, 172
Tyrol, 221
Tyssowski, Jan, 212

Ugarto, Aloys von, 64, 97
Ukraine, 2, 17, 252
Uniate Church, 42, 53, 167. *See also* Greek Catholic Church
Union of Brest, 167
Urbino, Johann Georg, 64
Urmeny, Wacław, 193

Vahylewych, Ivan, 223
Vatican, 35, 42
Venetia, 21
Venice, 102, 238
Venturi, Franco, 4
Vienna, 2, 3, 4, 5, 6, 7, 8, 9, 10, 11, 12, 13, 14, 15, 16, 23, 24, 28, 29, 37, 39, 40, 41, 42, 43, 44, 45, 47, 48, 49, 50, 51, 52, 53, 55, 57, 58, 60, 61, 62, 65, 67, 68, 69, 70, 71, 73, 74, 76, 77, 78, 79, 82, 83, 86, 87, 89, 90, 93, 94, 95, 96, 97, 98, 99, 100, 101, 102, 103, 104, 105, 106, 107, 110, 111, 112, 113, 114, 115, 117, 118, 119, 120, 121, 122, 123, 124, 125, 126, 132, 133, 134, 135, 136, 137, 138, 139, 140, 145, 147, 150, 151, 153, 157, 163, 166, 167, 168, 170, 171, 175, 177, 180, 181, 183, 186, 188, 189, 190, 191, 193, 195, 196, 197, 198, 200, 204, 207, 208, 211, 215, 216, 217, 218, 219, 220, 222, 224, 226, 227, 228, 229, 232, 233, 235, 237, 238, 239, 240, 241, 242, 243, 244, 245, 246, 249, 250, 251
Vienna university, 150, 195
Vinkov'kyi, Kyrylo, 223
Volhynia, 5, 37, 111, 202

Wadowice, 213, 215
Wadowska, Dorota, 218
Wandycz, Piotr, 14, 111, 128, 242
War of the Spanish Succession, 79, 160
Warmia, 149
Warsaw, 15, 17, 59, 88, 92, 93, 95, 106, 114, 115, 121, 123, 132, 138, 144, 145, 147, 151, 207, 226, 240, 241; in 1809, 84, 91; annexation to Prussia, 1795, 139; Austrian embassy, 1830–31, 121; Austrian take-over, 1809, 91; capital of Poland-Lithuania, 53; revolution of 1863–64, 240, 242
Wasilewski, Tadeusz Chochlik, 139
Weber, Max, 20, 29
Weglinski, 97
Wellenberg, count, 32
Wereszycki, Henryk, 242
Western Galicia, 5, 17, 86, 87, 95, 96, 100, 101, 150, 206, 213, 223, 226, 252, 296
White Mountain, battle of, 107
Wieliczka, 35, 161, 213, 214
Wielopolski, Aleksander, 216
Wiesiołowski, Franciszek, 210, 212, 216
Wohlfart, Karl, 245
Wolff, Christian, 26
Wolff, Larry, 6, 13, 40, 100
Wołodkowicz, Henryk, 94
Wratislaw, Count von, 61
Wurmser, Christian von, 84, 95, 97, 98, 99, 147, 148
WWI, 2, 18
WWII, 17

INDEX

Zaleski, Filip, 246
Zaleski, Wacław, 236, 237, 246
Zaleski, Wacław, junior, 246
Zaleszczyky, 193
Zamość, 194
Zamoyski, Count, 93
Zator, principality, 5
Zbaraż, 186

Ziemiałkowski, Florian, 223, 225
Zinzendorf, family, 65, 141
Zinzendorf, Ludwig von, 65, 73, 141, 254, 265
Ziołecka, Joanna, 165
Złoczow, 192
Zoll, family, 152
Zweig, Stefan, 18